PACIFICA RADIO
THE RISE OF AN ALTERNATIVE NETWORK
UPDATED EDITION

In the series

AMERICAN SUBJECTS

Edited by Robert Dawidoff

Matthew Lasar

Pacifica Radio

The Rise of an Alternative Network

Updated Edition

Temple University Press
Philadelphia

To Vera Hopkins:

archivist, historian, true believer.

Temple University Press, Philadelphia 19122

First edition published 1999
Updated edition published 2000
Printed in the United States of America

♾ The paper used in this publication meets the requirements of the American National Standard for Information Sciences—Permanence of Paper for Printed Library Materials, ANSI Z39.48-1984

Library of Congress Cataloging-in-Publication Data

Lasar, Matthew, 1954–
Pacifica radio: the rise of an alternative network, updated edition / Matthew Lasar.
p. cm. — (American subjects)
Includes bibliographical references and index.
ISBN 1-56639-777-4
(pbk.: alk. paper)
1. Pacifica Radio. 2. Alternative radio broadcasting—United States. I. Title. II. Series.
HE8697.75.U6L37 1998
384.54′06′573—dc21 98-19096
CIP

Contents

SERIES FOREWORD

WHEN THE Muggletonian idealists who founded the Pacifica Foundation's experiment in listener-sponsored radio began broadcasting in California's Bay Area in 1949, they did not imagine that their initiative would eventually serve as a template for the cultural and ideological history of the American liberal left in the post-World War II period. Listener-supported radio was meant to re-engage the American citizen in the highest purposes of individual and civic freedom. Pacifica did not use the Jeffersonian term "free marketplace of ideas" but their humanist vision of communication, in effect, rescued the old Jeffersonian phrase from its history of compromise with the American marketplace and relocated it pointedly outside. KPFA was hardly the first American utopian experiment, but it was the first American virtual utopia (admittedly in airspace rather than cyberspace), an interactive community to replace the real world that afforded neither interaction nor community.

Lewis Hill and his associates were motivated by a shared pacifist conviction that could not have been less convenient in Cold War America. World War II had ironically devastated the American pacifist movement. The consensus that the war was a good war made the humanist pacifist opposition seem naïve at best and treasonous at worst. The ensuing Cold War was a battle of ideologies fought with the economic, military, political, and strategic weapons at the disposal of great powers. The freedom of thought Pacifica was founded to stimulate and educate foundered in a nation whose intellectual weapons of choice were foregone conclusion and ideological presupposition. The kind of public forum Pacifica envisioned was challenging at a time when the most important information was the kind one could keep secret and the most influential debate was with the spectre of an international enemy.

The result, as Matthew Lasar's history of the Pacifica network shows, is that a grab bag utopia of the air became one of the few American places which hosted contentious, candid and continuous airing of the very issues and points of view the official culture preferred to keep under wraps. Lasar's absorbing book transcribes the broadcast and institutional history of the Pacifica Foundation's attempt to establish listener supported radio into an illuminating cultural history of the American liberal left. Lewis Hill's ambition for Pacifica's first experiment, KPFA—to introduce Americans to the "wholeness" of the political problem facing the world from the pacifist humanist perspective—was lost in the struggle of liberal and left politics and culture to survive and understand Cold War America. As Lasar shows, KPFA and Pacifica became a forum for the American liberal left because of the Cold War and its short and long-term effects on the climate and context of American freedom.

Pacifica Radio: The Rise of an Alternative Network offers a compelling examination of recent American cultural history. KPFA became the American Hyde Park. The broadcasts and the fascinating, intense behind-the-scenes history of the station illustrate what happened to American liberal politics and culture as a result of the Cold War. Lasar's book helps us see why it was that American liberalism could not sustain its rhetorical commitment to the highest American ideals and the realities of American politics and world power. Lasar traces the cultural history of the liberal left through KPFA, then KPFK in Los Angeles and WBAI in New York City. Beat culture, identity culture, youth culture, shock culture, sex and obscenity, and political protest challenged the host culture of Pacifica. Their challenges on and off the air transformed it from a culturally genteel institution that fostered traditional cultural views, good politics, good music, good education, and good manners into a hot spot in which every kind of "good" was challenged. Pacifica made or encountered the connections between obscenity and the First Amendment, between the personal and the political, between pacifist conscientiousness and revolution, between civil and uncivil disobedience, before the rest of the nation did. It is a brilliantly conceived history because Pacifica was small enough and its participants articulate enough so that the human story of cultural change comes alive on the page.

Pacifica Radio is more than a revealing history of the American liberal left. It details the history of the American media and the reasons we have a pervasive rather than an independent media in the United States. It also illuminates the fascinating cultural history of San Francisco and the Bay Area. Lasar's account of the changing content and purpose of the station's broadcasts has independent interest. He shows how Pacifica became a site of cultural conflict and change that its founders neither foresaw nor really understood. The book thrills with the voices, antics, opinions, ideals, and visions of a vivid cast of American characters. Perhaps the most important thing about Lasar's book is its capturing of how the best laid plans of the highest minded people went so contentiously, unpredictably, and wonderfully astray. Pacifica's humanist vision of communication sponsored a particular sort of communication that not only transformed Pacifica but also influenced the nation.

In the end, Lasar leaves the reader ready to take up the disturbing questions the history of Pacifica raised and continues to raise. This is a book about what happens when people actually try to institute genuine dialogue, peaceful co-operation, and the breakdown of ideological and cultural boundaries to make such ideals the working basis of community. His book encourages us to begin thinking about what such enterprises require and whether we are willing and able to pay the price.

This exhaustively researched, clearly condensed, narratively exuberant, and intelligent book creates a perspective on the development of Cold War American liberal left culture. We have needed one to think through the history of a time that had everything but perspective. In "Dunes, " poet A. R. Ammons wrote what could be Lasar's epigraph: "Firm ground is not available ground."[1] It is the measure of his achievement that Matthew Lasar has given such a clear view of the ground that shifted under Pacifica and continues to shift under anybody who hopes to institutionalize the marginal, that is, to realize the ideal.

Robert Dawidoff

1. Ammons, A.R., *The Selected Poems.* Expanded Edition. New York: W.W. Norton Co., 1986.

Preface to the Updated Edition

Karl Marx once said that when history turns a corner, the intellectuals are the first to fall off the train. I lost my seat on July 13, 1999, when listener-supported KPFA-FM in Berkeley underwent a series of convulsions that received worldwide press coverage. That day local media activists intercepted an e-mail message indicating that members of the Pacifica Foundation's national board favored selling the station to "logical and qualified buyers" in order to capitalize the organization. Several hours later, Pacifica dispatched a corporate security firm to close the station. Over fifty KPFA staff and supporters were arrested for trespassing on the institution they had kept alive for decades. During the next three turbulent weeks, Pacifica spent almost $500,000 in its conflict with KPFA. The city of Berkeley became engulfed in marches, rallies, sit-ins and teach-ins over the issue. The battle peaked with a day-long demonstration of over 10,000 KPFA supporters, demanding the re-opening of the station and the resignation of the Pacifica board.

Pacifica Radio had just been published. It argues that in the 1950s and 60s, McCarthyism forced the Pacifica radio network to define itself less as an institution in search of humanist dialogue—the goal of its founders—and more as a defender of the right of the individual to speak. In the tortuous course of this transition, "alternative radio" was born, along with a difficult question: Could listener-sponsored radio live by dissent alone?

But watching KPFA's staff and supporters—many of them my friends—being led out of their building in handcuffs, I felt the need for a broader explanation of this awful scene. In the ensuing weeks of the conflict between Pacifica and the station's supporters, I looked for some analysis that reached beyond incidents or personalities for its conclusions. The result is the postscript of this updated edition.

The postscript herein, *A Crisis of Containment*, argues that the events of the summer of 1999 in Berkeley were rooted in two decades of government policy hostile to what by the 1970s had come to be called "community" radio and what I call local access broadcasting. These policies trapped an insurgent cultural movement inside tiny, inadequate spaces, creating generations of embittered managers who gradually lost faith in the possibility of democratic governance for non-commercial, listener-supported radio. Ultimately, this planned marginalization resulted in Pacifica governors who, judging by their actions, regarded legal accountability to their constituents as an impediment to the business of the organization. At KPFA-FM in Berkeley they collided with thousands of people who thought otherwise.

Although I served as a volunteer at KPFA in the 1980s, most of this book was written afterwards, in an atmosphere of relative distance from Pacifica radio's current affairs. The postscript was not. As soon as this book hit the stands Pacifica began taking actions that I regarded as dangerously out-of-sync with the democratic rhetoric heard articulated daily on the network's national and local programs. I said as much in many public statements. I have written the postscript in the first person so that the reader will not mistake me for a more detached scholarly observer. Indeed, I dedicate it to the KPFA community—its paid and unpaid staff, its subscribers and its supporters—who have endured far more than should be expected of a group of people who, in the end, simply want to broadcast and hear good things on the radio.

Preface to the First Edition

A CALL is being sounded throughout the United States. It echoes from our schools, spiritual institutions, houses of government, and newspapers. It is a plea for public dialogue and an acknowledgment of its absence in our time. Our magazines and talk shows offer a steady stream of authorities who worry that Americans do not congregate, volunteer, join, vote, or, most important, talk enough.[1] Our foundations donate generous sums to promote what they call "civic culture."[2] Recent books on American life, with chapter titles such as "Can We Talk?" or "Can We Be Brought Together?" call for greater communication between blacks and whites (or Jews), women and men, those who favor and those who oppose the legality of abortion, Republicans and Democrats, white women and women of color.[3] The World Wide Web—arguably the last technological panacea of the twentieth century—hosts numerous sites that help organize or instruct people in the art of discussion.[4]

Much of this admirable activity is motivated by civic pride, patriotism, or sociability. But the crusade for dialogue also seems to be fueled by fear, either vaguely sensed or explicitly experienced. Immigration, globalization, identity politics, the supposed breakdown of the family, the decline of our cities—all these phenomena have produced a generation of writers who think we had better start talking as soon as possible.

Since the 1960s our nation has experienced an "unraveling," according to one historian.[5] We are a "disunited" culture, bereft of singular purpose, thanks to the "cult of ethnicity." Another author pleads for a return to assimilationism—for us to be "Americans simply," above all else. "Let us celebrate that choice," argues Nathan Glazer, "and agree it would be better for America if more of us accepted that identity as our central one, as against ethnic and racial identities."[6]

Even those observers sympathetic to such sentiments detect more than a bit of ahistorical panic in all this. As sociologist Todd Gitlin observes, these anxious expressions presume the existence of a lost golden age when "an incontestable consensus reigned, and deserved to reign, about the virtue of Western civilization, the nature of merit and authority, the rules of reason, the proper constitution of canon and curriculum, the integrity of American history, the civility of men."[7] Once upon a time, "we" knew who "we" were. How do we get back home?

Given this pervasive sense of the present, it may surprise some to discover that back in the hypothetical good old days, people worried about the same problems we worry about today. In 1952, a group of psychologists gathered in Asilomar, California, to hear Lewis Hill's diagnosis of the condition of American society and culture. Hill, general manager of the country's first listener-supported FM radio station, expressed concern about a relatively new phenomenon—the widespread availability of privacy, or what he called "the Private Room." Consumerism and suburbanization had produced a generation of people able to define themselves largely by their capacity to keep others away. "In fact, the place of identity and consciousness in modern man is very much identified, perhaps inseparably, with the tile bathroom and the ninety-nine dollar bedroom suite that complement its psychic mirrors," Hill said. "It has a patch of yard in front and a garbage can in back; and a window no one can look in unless the owner raises the blind." Within private rooms Americans formulated those values "which in other times were assigned to a concept of the soul and to a community of labor, however unequal."[8]

Where in this new landscape lay the chance for the articulation of a "firm communal value system"? asked Hill.[9] And how did this new culture prepare the individual for what Hill metaphorically described as "the Man at the Door"—an intruder with a different point of view or a deadly "alien enemy." The door must be opened, he declared. Communication with the threat—whatever it might be—must be encouraged, not shunned. "If this is too much to hope for," Hill concluded, "someone will have to explain to us how we can do with less."[10]

This book tells the story of a small group of people who, possessed of an idealism almost incomprehensible in our time, thought that dialogue could save the world. *Pacifica Radio: the Rise of an Alternative Network* traces the early evolution of the Pacifica Foundation, the first nonprofit FM radio network in the United States, created by pacifists, explicitly to encourage communication and the breakdown of ideological barriers. The story begins with Lewis Hill, Pacifica's founder, and the creation of KPFA-FM in Berkeley in 1949; it follows the foundation's acquisition of two more signals—in Los Angeles and New York City—ending in 1964, a turning point in the network's history.

"The essence of history," writes historian Louis J. Halle, ". . . is the contrast between the immensity of its movement and the limitations of the individuals who, often with the greatest gallantry, put themselves at grips with it."[11] The Pacifica Foundation, created in 1946, had its ideological roots in a set of communitarian values drawn from Gandhian pacifism, anarchism, and cooperativism. The organization saw its primary mission as promoting "a pacific world" by encouraging creative exchange between people of diverse backgrounds and beliefs and, secondarily, as an advocate of free speech and individual rights. The original Pacificans hoped to attract a mass audience to their dialogue-oriented project.

The onset of McCarthyism, however, gradually forced the foundation to define itself primarily as a haven for unpopular ideas, and for the absolute right of individuals to speak such ideas. By 1949, the foundation had largely abandoned its efforts to attract a broad listenership. Instead, its first radio station, KPFA in Berkeley, served in the 1950s as a refuge for an educated audience deeply alienated from American politics and culture. By the late 1950s, a second generation of Pacificans adopted a more aggressive broadcasting style, openly challenging the actions of what the historian Daniel Yergin calls the "national security state."[12] The consequent conflicts with that state only intensified the foundation's need to emphasize the unpopular individual's right to "dissent" as its raison d'être, creating what would later be called "alternative radio" along with a crisis of meaning. What larger mission unified a world of dissenters, some of the network's participants began to ask. What higher purpose, if any, did free speech broadcasting serve besides the right of the individual to speak?

Pacifica Radio: the Rise of an Alternative Network celebrates this country's only independent noncommercial radio system and its daring, even heroic, contributions to our culture. Pacifica's story also illustrates how easily any attempt to promote public interaction can be disrupted. The Pacifica Foundation's early struggles reflect one of the characteristics of American society: a "self divided," in Richard Randall's words, continually forced to choose between the desire for community and individual autonomy, between dialogue and dissent.[13]

My scholarship, and the work of many others, has depended on the labor of the dedicated archivist Vera Elizabeth Somers Hopkins. "My mother was very peace minded," Hopkins once wrote. "Therefore, I have always been peace minded." Born and raised in the pacifist Church of the Brethren, Hopkins studied sociology during the 1930s at the Claremont

Graduate School. Her passionate advocacy of social justice inspired her master's thesis, a devastating critique of the *Los Angeles Times'* hostile coverage of Upton Sinclair's 1934 campaign for governor. As an undergraduate, Hopkins anticipated the Pacifica idea by more than a decade: "Survival of a democratic form of government is predicated upon a high degree of freedom for open discussion of the issues which face the electorate. . . . It assumes that the rules will be changed by means other than force through war or coercion of individuals."[14]

Following World War II, Hopkins and her husband, John, moved to Berkeley, where he opened an electrical repair shop, eventually manufacturing custom FM radios for KPFA listeners, and she began her forty-year career as an archivist for the Pacifica Foundation. In the last decade of her service, she wrote an invaluable history of KPFA. From the thousands of crucial documents relating to Pacifica history she had saved, she assembled her "Sampler from Pacifica Foundation."[15] Vera Hopkins's role as commentator and witness to or participant in important KPFA or Pacifica events makes her indispensable to this book, which is dedicated to her.

This study began as a doctoral dissertation under the supervision of Vicki L. Ruiz, whose mentorship and guidance have made all the difference in my intellectual journey. I hope this text reflects what she taught me, that ultimately history is about people and their stories. The editor of this series, Robert Dawidoff of the Claremont Graduate University, shook me up when appropriate, calmed me down when necessary, and recited John Berryman by heart. Temple editor Janet Francendese patiently showed me how to make longwinded prose more readable and concise, as did Erica Fox. Elazar Barkan, Janet Brodie, Eric Foner, William Mandel, John Ohlinger, Michael Roth, Susan Smulyan, and Jesse Walker read the manuscript or helped in other ways.

Much of the time I spent working on this project, I felt like a beggar or a burglar. Wandering around California, I confronted ex-Pacificans in their seventies or eighties with painful, sometimes embarrassing, questions and photocopied their private correspondence. Many thanks to the two dozen people who put up with such intrusion, particularly Watson Alberts, Roy Finch, William Mandel, Eleanor McKinney, Richard Moore, and Jerry Shore. Pat Scott, Dick Bunce, and Mary Tilson of the Pacifica National Office in Berkeley opened their doors and their archive boxes to me. By the time I'd recatalogued everything, we'd become good friends. I hope they know how grateful I am for their help. I hope Pamela Burton of the Pacifica Archives in Los Angeles knows as well.

While revising my manuscript for publication, I subscribed to the progressive-radio electronic mail discussion list, which focuses on current Pacifica politics and policy. I cannot say that I always found the experience pleasant, but the list's often heated exchanges helped me clarify my thinking. I owe a debt to its participants. Former KPFA staff engineer John Whiting read the manuscript, generously shared his insights and oral history interviews, and backed me up when I was down. Lincoln Bergman let me use his invaluable oral history of Elsa Knight Thompson. Jeff Land and James Tracy alerted me to important sources. I am particularly grateful for the friendship and assistance of Veronica Selver, who is producing a documentary film about KPFA.

The San Francisco basement where I hoarded tape-recorded interviews is in the home of Sharon Wood, whose work as a documentary film writer inspires me, whose constant love and support sustains me, and with whose son, Jake, I have mastered many Sony Play Station games.

My mother, Rita Lasar, conducted one of the oral history interviews and transcribed another. That was the least of her assistance. I deeply cherish our friendship and the memory of a man we both knew named Theodore. I'd also like to thank my brother, Raphael, and sister-in-law, Karen, as well as Larry Bensky, Darcy Buerkle, Lawrence Chatman (aka D. J. Collage), Gary Coates, Arlette Cohen, Dan Cox, Ilana DeBare, Sherry Gendelman, Marilyn Golden, Amina Hassan, Cliff Hawkins, Thea Hensl, Julia Hutton, Margaret Jacobs, Elaine Korry, Neskah LaFlamme, Peg Lamphier, Jane-Ellen Long, Mimi Lyons, Laurie Nelson, Ken Nightingale, Mark Mericle, Alicia Rodriguez, Sam Schuchat, Abby Smith, Ralph Spaulding, Eugene Stevanus, Emilie Stoltzfus, Tamara Thompson, and Janice Windborne. Thanks also to Olivia and Snowball, Ted the lizard, and the beloved memory of Skittle the rodent. Needless to say, no one mentioned thus far bears any responsibility for the story you are about to read.

Pacifica Radio

The Rise of an Alternative Network

Updated Edition

I

WAR

That extreme Evils are committed today, with no large-scale opposition, by the agents of great nations—this leads me to conclude not, with the liberals and the Marxists, that the peoples of those nations are horrified by these Evils . . . but rather that, on the contrary, these Evils are rejected only on a superficial, conventional, public-oration and copy-book-maxim plane, while they are accepted or at least temporized with on more fundamental, private-levels.

—Dwight Macdonald,
"The Root Is Man"

1)) THE ROAD TO COLEVILLE

I have closed my eyes on the past
As you want it remembered for
The rest of life, called 'forever'.
I was not there. I was away.
At the Poles, in the Amazon.
I am not going to have been
Where you say I was. You fancy
You can force me to have lived
The past you want. You are wrong.

—KENNETH REXROTH,
Kenneth Rexroth: The Collected Shorter Poems

THE PEOPLE who founded KPFA were pacifists. Moved by principles of nonviolence, they refused to fight in the Second World War. They joined organizations such as the Fellowship of Reconciliation and the War Resisters League. They wrote for and subscribed to pacifist newspapers, and they attended antiwar demonstrations and events. A. J. Muste, the most prominent advocate of pacifism at the time, was often quoted as saying that "there is no way to peace; peace is the way."[1] The founders of KPFA wholeheartedly endorsed this as their personal and political credo.

Yet somehow their message did not get through. Even two decades after the creation of KPFA, the Pacifica Foundation's political origins were widely misrepresented. Journalists, even sympathetic ones, described the founders as communists, or liberals, or adherents of some other incompatible perspective. In 1974, for instance, a reporter covering a conflict at KPFA for the *San Francisco Bay Guardian* summarized the station's early history by claiming that the "vocal minorities using the station at that time were generally communists, well-educated and often rich."[2] Vera Hopkins, Pacifica's archivist and historian, asked William Triest, KPFA's first regular announcer, if the reporter's statement was true. "Never, never, never," Triest replied. Although some of the original KPFA staffers had joined a Communist Party (CP) front organization, he insisted that "all the principals were in fact anti-communist in the sense of being anti-authoritarian (not in the sense of being red-baiters)."[3] Indeed, aversion to the Party among Pacifica's first generation sometimes bordered on paranoia. "Our greatest difficulty in those days," recalled another founder, "was the risk that the Communist Party would take over. And we were constantly on guard against this."[4] By all standards their vigilance proved successful. In the 1950s—the Cold War's cruelest years domestically—the Federal Bureau of Investigation scrutinized the Pacifica Foundation for communist influence and by its own admission found little.[5]

Whether Pacifica's early antipathy toward Marxism-Leninism made practical sense, it certainly makes sense historically. People who opposed U.S. involvement in the Second World War could not possibly have functioned as members of the Communist Party. After Germany invaded the Soviet Union in June 1941, the party condemned labor strikes as sabotage and denounced as obstructionist efforts by African American union leader A. Philip Randolph to desegregate U.S. troops. Further, communists who adhered to the leadership of the Soviet-controlled Third International would never have tolerated efforts to resist the draft among its members. Many served in the most dangerous theaters of the war.[6]

Later Pacifica promotional literature sometimes described the organization's founders as liberals, but they did not fit comfortably fit into that category either.[7] Anarchists at heart, the first Pacificans sympathized with the goals of the New Deal but feared liberalism's reliance on an increasingly bureaucratic and militarized state. "We felt that liberals were people who couldn't be counted on," recalled one early Pacifica supporter, "and that when the showdown came, they would be lining up with conservatives."[8]

No one symbolized liberal vacillation more among the early Pacificans than Minnesota senator Hubert H. Humphrey, who championed moderate civil rights legislation one day and voted for the creation of concentration camps for communists the next.[9] They expected liberals to make remarks like novelist and reformer Upton Sinclair made in 1963: "I am also a pacifist, but I supported both of the World Wars. I'm that kind of pacifist."[10] The creators of listener-sponsored radio were not that kind of pacifist. They had refused to serve in the only overwhelmingly popular armed conflict in U.S. history. The Pacifica story begins with a recounting of that resistance.

A Meeting in the Woods

Having graduated from Andover Academy and Yale, Roy Finch was drafted in 1942 while working at the *New York Herald Tribune*. Refusing active duty, he was sent to Coleville, a remote camp for conscientious objectors on California's far eastern border, about seventy miles south of Reno. He would not be released until 1947, when he joined the War Resisters League and resumed his study of the writings of Wittgenstein.[11]

Many pacifists met worse fates in dealing with the selective service system. The decision to grant someone 4-E status was not made by some bureaucrat in Washington, D.C., but by a local official at a draft office. "You went in and said, 'I want to be a conscientious objector,'" Finch recalled, "and he said yes or no. . . . In some places they accepted virtually anybody, and in other places they said, 'No. We're not going to do it. You've got to go to jail.'"[12] Despite Coleville's harshness and lack of electricity, Finch considered himself lucky to have wound up there. A young Berkeleyan named Kerwin Whitnah, who would eventually help raise KPFA's first transmitter tower, had not been so lucky. His board had decided that since Whitnah did not belong to a "historic peace church," he would be sent to the "Greybar Hotel," as COs called it, a penitentiary notorious for its cruelty, on McNeil Island in Washington. "I don't know of any CO who went to McNeil Island who came out emotionally unharmed," another pacifist remembered.[13]

Along with the Mennonite Central Committee and a group called the Brethren, the Quaker-led American Friends Service Committee had negotiated with the Selective Service to operate Coleville. They did so as part of a Civilian Public Service (CPS) program, modeled after the New Deal's Civilian Conservation Corps, that the Quakers ran with the Forest Service.[14] The program supervised, clothed, and fed about twelve thousand men nationwide in 151 camps.[15] The churches saw the camps as an alternative to noncombatant duty; however, many pacifists regarded any service to the government as either participation in war or exploitation.[16] By the time Finch went to Coleville, he had lost respect for even the Quakers, whom he regarded as compromised by their willingness to collaborate with the government. He had only slightly more regard for the Forest Service, which in his view offered Coleville residents little to do that was productive. Mostly they built trails, a make-work activity.

When Lewis Kimball Hill arrived in June 1942, he struck Finch as different from anyone he had ever met before. Hill showed up far better dressed than the other residents. "The guy looked like he had outfitted himself at Abercrombie and Fitch, that kind of a place," Finch remembered. The newcomer was twenty-three, blonde, frail, pale of complexion, and he chain smoked. Finch noticed that Hill had difficulty straightening up in the morning, due, as Finch later found out, to an arthritic condition. Finch marveled at Hill's "amazing mellifluous voice" and his slightly aristocratic manner, made all the more charming because it seemed so natural.

Both Finch and Hill were assigned to late-night kitchen duty, where, during the course of making sandwiches for Coleville's 150 COs, they talked about their favorite subjects: philosophy, politics, poetry, and radio. Hill was consumed with a plan to create a new kind of radio station, one that would promote wide-ranging discussion. He hoped such dialogue would lead to the identification of the roots of conflict and help resolve them. Over time, they began to see the station "as like a living room," where people who had fundamentally different ideas would talk and work out their differences.[17] The formative ideas for the Pacifica Foundation were coming into being.[18]

Lewis Hill had been born on May 1, 1919, in Kansas City, Missouri, to a pair of "empire builders," as his wife, Joy Cole Hill, once put it.[19] His father, Johnson D. Hill, a lawyer, had moved from Missouri to Tulsa, in the Oklahoma territory. While visiting the city of Bartlesville, he met and married Lura Phillips. Lura's older brother, Frank, was soon to become the living symbol of the "self-made" Southwest oil millionaire. A one-time singing barber who married into a prosperous Iowa banking family, Frank Phillips had taken advantage of the breakup of the Oklahoma Indian territory to obtain fields rich with oil. By the late 1920s, the Phillips Petroleum Company, with its chain of "Phillips 66" gas stations along legendary Route 66, had become a byword for Jazz Age prosperity.

Johnson Hill also went into the oil business, and later he bought an insurance company. Young Lewis grew up in an atmosphere of sudden wealth. He spent time at his uncle's majestic ranch in Bartlesville, where Frank Phillips entertained the likes of Hollywood cowboy Tom Mix, Herbert Hoover, and evangelist Aimee Semple McPherson. The famous mansion was noted for its halls filled with medieval sculpture and Frank Phillips's gigantic study. In a letter to a friend, Lewis once described his home life as combining "corporate wealth, romantic ladies and unlimited scotch and soda."[20]

But beyond this lavishness lay fresh and unapologetic corruption. In the year of Hill's birth, Oklahoma had been a state for little more than a decade. Its politics was unstable and bizarre. In 1927, the dapper and bespectacled governor, Henry Simpson Johnston, a member of the Ku Klux Klan, summoned the National Guard to prevent the legislature from convening a special session to investigate charges of graft in the executive branch; two years later the legislature finally impeached him for incompetence.[21] During the later years of the Second World War, Johnson Hill won the speakership in the state assembly on the promise he would investigate charges of kickbacks at Oklahoma State University (OSU); his anticorruption stance began his career in politics. "Father is going to be governor sooner or later," Lewis Hill confidently wrote to Roy Finch during a family visit in 1944.[22] But Johnson resigned as speaker—and cut short his political career—when the Democratic political machine stopped him from firing OSU's president.[23]

By all accounts, Lewis Hill was a precocious child. He played musical instruments with little effort and, according to classmates, often was absent from school yet passed exams easily. Later on he became one of those people who could easily fix a mimeograph machine after others had fumbled with it for hours.[24] Like so many young boys in the mid-1920s, Lewis was fascinated with radio. One historian suggests that during an era when professional career paths had become increasingly bureaucratized, technical activities such as amateur broadcasting allowed boys to prove their virility. When Lewis was six, his older brother, Johnson, Jr., gave him the parts to construct a small crystal radio set, complete with a cigar box. Lewis assembled the kit with ease. This and later displays of technical proficiency apparently did not please Hill the elder, however, who envisioned his son becoming a rugged oil man and carrying on in the family enterprise. In pursuit of this goal, the family sent Lewis to Wentworth Military Academy in Lexington, Missouri. He detested the place and cultivated a lifelong contempt for militarism. Eventually, Lewis fled west to Stanford University, where he studied philosophy and flew airplanes for sport.[25]

At Stanford, Hill embraced the branch of philosophy known as existentialism, concluding that, for better or worse, people live free lives—in that they define themselves and the rest of the world through their own self-perceptions and beliefs. The "reality of society," Hill later declared in a radio broadcast, resides in the individual's "own inward nature, and . . . change in society can only be the product of his own inward transformation."[26] The challenge was how to translate that transformation into a constructive, collective reality. One might have called Hill a pragmatic existentialist. He thought that people made their own realities but that those realities were negotiable. He derived much of this passionate credo from his reading of Søren Kierkegaard, the nineteenth-century religious philosopher with whom he closely identified for most of his life.

Later Pacifica literature would claim that Hill drew his ideas primarily from Gandhian or Quaker thought. Certainly Gandhi influenced Hill's writings and statements, but letters to Finch written after they both left Coleville consisted of page after single-spaced page asserting that "there is perhaps nothing in the world like Kierkegaard, nothing that approaches his tremendous, visible movement through the existential tensions of belief."[27]

In his brief life as a writer, Kierkegaard had posed a single startling question: if God were to suddenly appear, how would one know it was God? Here, Kierkegaard warned, lay the truly radical aspect of Christianity. One did not find evidence of God's existence in external reality but in one's desire for God and for higher meaning. God and godly qualities such as love lay hidden from humanity. "As the quiet lake invites you to look at it but the mirror of darkness prevents you from seeing it," Kierkegaard wrote, "so love's mysterious ground in God's love prevents you from seeing its source."[28] Contact with God required a "leap of faith." One had to create God and then submit to one's creation, as did Abraham when ordered by Jehovah to sacrifice his son Isaac. In daily existence one had to become what Kierkegaard called a "knight of faith."[29] The capacity to create the eternal through belief meant the capacity to construct all of reality through perception and belief. This was Kierkegaard's paradoxical understanding of reality and human life.

To the young Lewis Hill, these ideas proved that one did not need a socioscientific plan like Marxism or liberalism to make a better world; one simply needed to believe and act accordingly. "The mere conception that reality and present being consist in paradox," Hill wrote, "and the dialectical proof that the only possible movement through paradox is a leap, are like a clean broom, all manner of positivist, phenomalist, humanist rubbish is swept out and the way is empty."[30] Hill drew from his studies at Stanford a deeply optimistic belief in the power of the individual to reconstruct human relations. The foundation for this view—and later for his vision of listener-supported radio—was Kierkegaard's contention that one's relationship with others, like one's relationship to God, was based on a willfully constructed self based on faith. Thus, in a sense, one created human reality as one created God. After reading Martin Buber's *I and Thou*, Hill wrote to Finch: "The real crux of the matter, is, as Kierkegaard saw it, that an implacable paradox arises in the absolute existence of Thou through the cognitive act of I. The paradox can only be lived subjectively."[31]

Sometimes this ideology, which placed so much primacy on "inward nature," made Hill's friends nervous. A "philosophy for desperadoes," Finch once said of Hill's interpretation of Kierkegaard,[32] and it was easy to perceive a lonely, radical individualism in Hill's statements. But Hill assured his friends that he didn't mean it that way. Rather, he said, we must acknowledge and accept the realities of others as well as our own. This, for Hill, represented true human relatedness. "Our relationship has often appeared to me to consist in our sharing the tension of an identical paradox from its opposite poles," began yet another letter to Finch in Hill's strangely affectionate style. "Perhaps it is that the poles of a true paradox are interchangeable that we meet so often."[33] Hill put the matter more plainly in a lecture to psychologists in 1952: "As long as I can communicate I can create. As long as I can create I am free."[34]

To Hill, words, pictures, and ideas controlled the world, not the environment or economics. His friend Richard Moore remembers Hill as someone who thought that if one could engage in dialogue with others, one could solve any human problem. "He was not intimidated by anything," Moore recalled, "because what is there in the human being except the human being's perceptions and language?"[35] The small group of writers and artists who later surrounded Hill found his hopeful enthusiasm irresistible.

From Kierkegaard to Gandhi

At Stanford, Hill also became involved with one of the most popular movements of the 1930s: pacifism. Although nowhere in the hundreds of letters Hill composed after the Second World War did he explain why he decided to become a conscientious objector, his close friends thought it was in good part because of his unhappy life at Wentworth Military Academy.[36] Whatever the reason, Hill refused to serve during the Second World War.

In the decade before the war, there had been an upsurge of support for pacifism throughout the Atlantic region. Many pacifists found this ironic, since conscientious objectors had been persecuted during the First World War by virtually every sector of society. Many Americans who had applauded President Woodrow Wilson's intervention into that war now saw nothing that justified the bloodshed. England and France seemed determined to hold onto their empires. The German economy staggered under the terms of a vindictive peace. "Fifteen years ago, came the Armistice and we all thought it was to be a new world," lamented Kansas newspaper publisher William Allan White. "It is! But a lot worse than it was before."[37] Grim exposés like George Seldes's *Iron Blood and Profits* charged that the conflict had been orchestrated by the munitions industry. In 1936, a widely publicized Senate investigating committee came to the same conclusion. Perhaps nothing so symbolized the changing mood of the times than the return of social reformer Jane Addams to public favor. In 1917, as head of the Women's International League for Peace and Freedom, Addams had opposed U.S. entry into the war. For this, the Reserve Officers' Training Corps (ROTC) Honorary Society described her as "the most dangerous woman in America."[38] Yet, by the early 1930s—just before her death—the sage of Hull House basked in what one historian aptly called "sunshine pacifism."[39]

By the mid-1930s, almost everyone—Stalinists, Democrats, Republicans, Trotskyites—had some kind of antiwar stance. But this professed love of peace was a mile wide and an inch deep. In addition to disillusionment over the outcome of the First World War, the pacifist movement had strong roots among the isolationists, led by newspapers such as the *New York Daily News* and the *Chicago Tribune*.[40] Further, by the early 1930s, the Communist Party had entered into its so-called Third Period, during which capitalism, imperialism, and fascism were seen as fundamentally the same. To the Party, "war" meant an imperialist war—most likely against the Soviet Union—distracting the proletariat from its historic task: the overthrow of a deteriorating capitalist world.[41]

In the midst of this ambiguous political atmosphere, a remarkable student movement against militarism and war flourished. On April 12, 1935, some sixty thousand college students engaged in a nationwide strike in which they pledged never to participate in an armed conflict.[42] Even before the strike, antimilitarism had ignited many campuses. In 1932 at the City College of New York, a young communist named William Mandel—who would later play a crucial role in the Pacifica Foundation—attended a tense meeting with the president of the college after he called in the police to break up a student demonstration. The president had stipulated that students could speak at the meeting only if they asked questions. Mandel obliged with a carefully phrased 250-word rhetorical question. School authorities expelled him from the college within the year.[43] On the opposite coast, at the University of California at Berkeley, Richard Moore, a future KPFA staff member, had also immersed himself in antiwar activities. "My position was, one: I don't believe in killing," he later explained, "and two: I was not willing to submit myself to a higher authority whether it was God or the United States of America."[44]

The core of the antiwar sentiment in the mid-1930s was based not in isolationism or communism, however, but in organizations that emphasized spiritual pacifism. No leader so epitomized this tradition as A. J. Muste, described by *Time* magazine as America's "Number One U.S. Pacifist" and spokesperson for a generation of war resisters.[45] Finch, along with pacifist leaders Bayard Rustin and David Dellinger, served as a coeditor with

Muste on the postwar pacifist magazine *Liberation*.[46] Although both Finch and Hill disagreed with Muste on some issues, they recognized his importance to the American peace movement and his role in creating a pacifism that emphasized both spiritual and political goals.

Abraham Joannese Muste lived a life of constant conversion and reconversion. As a minister for a Massachusetts Congregational church, he had opposed U.S. entry in the First World War, a position his congregation found intolerable. Muste turned to and soon became a leader in the Fellowship of Reconciliation (FOR), an organization founded in Britain a few years earlier. Under his leadership, FOR abandoned its apolitical stance and became an exponent of Walter Rauschenbusch's "social gospel" vision of Christianity. FOR activists believed that eliminating economic injustice was a requisite to the struggle to eliminate war and that once both these evils were eradicated, Christ's Kingdom would be approximated on earth. A strong advocate of organized labor, Muste briefly left FOR and joined the Trotskyist Socialist Workers Party (SWP). But this proved to be a brief digression in his spiritual and political development. Two years later, after an argument with Trotsky in Norway, Muste experienced a religious renewal while visiting a medieval church in Paris. Trotsky's revolutionary/materialist analysis had satisfied Muste's desire to engage in political work, but it had left a significant void spiritually.[47]

Muste's dilemmas proved prototypical for the pacifists of his time. How was one to reconcile the need for an inner faith with a desire to fight for the collective good? And how was one to engage in this struggle nonviolently, without having enemies? The answer for Muste and thousands of other pacifists—particularly those who started the Pacifica Foundation—could be found in the living example of the Indian attorney Mohandas Gandhi, whose campaign against British imperialism in India had attracted great interest among religious pacifists in the United States. Gandhi's philosophy—or at least American readings of it—seemed to offer a way to engage in transformative political work not only without advocating violence but also without identifying individuals or classes of people as the enemy. This was certainly Richard B. Gregg's interpretation of Gandhi's works.

During the Second World War, Hill and Gregg, a Quaker lawyer, both served on a blue-ribbon support committee for conscientious objectors. Inspired by Gandhiism in the 1920s, Gregg journeyed to India, where he spent more than half a year with Gandhi at his ashram.[48] Gregg then returned to the United States to reengage himself in the American pacifist movement and write pamphlets and books on Gandhian nonviolence. Gregg's ideas paralleled Hill's understanding of Kierkegaard, and in a 1932 essay, *Gandhiism versus Socialism*, Gregg anticipated Pacifica philosophy.

Like Kierkegaard, Gregg argued that perceptions and beliefs construct reality. He thought that the socialist assumption that classes and institutions determine how the world is governed avoided the central issue: "The real control comes from ideas and sentiments—a scheme of values, a set of ideals or activities which people are induced to desire and accept as right, fitting and praiseworthy." Gregg argued that the words people speak and the symbols they use determine how society works much more than any class or institution. Because society functioned according to what people think and feel, nations ultimately could change only through movements that emphasized moral persuasion rather than violent coercion. For Gregg, Gandhi embodied such a movement as both leader and symbol. By exemplifying the idea of simple living, by making his own clothes, and by performing daily community service for the poor, Gandhi offered an alternative model to exploitative capitalism. "Gandhi's full program tends to restore reality to economic, political and social relationships, and to correct a symbolism which has gone wrong," Gregg wrote. Similarly, Gandhi's program of disciplined nonviolent civil disobedience, or *Satyagraha*, showed the masses that they could have faith in themselves, rather than in symbols of militarism.[49]

Gregg acknowledged that socialism and Gandhiism had many similarities, especially their emphasis on economic leveling. But he predicted that the willingness among socialists to use violence would ultimately produce little more than a new ruling class skilled in the art of repression. "Gandhiism does not talk of the expropriation of the ruling class," he explained. "Instead, it proceeds to demolish the values and symbols which are the source and inner strength of the ruling class."[50] Finally, like Kierkegaard's vision of truth through faith, Gandhiism rejected the idea of objective truth. "Nobody in this world possesses absolute truth," Gandhi wrote. "This is God's attribute alone. Relative truth is all we know. Therefore, we can only follow the truth as we see it. Such pursuit of truth cannot lead anyone astray."[51]

By the late 1930s and early 1940s, Muste and the American pacifist movement had clearly embraced this mode of thought, which satisfied both the desire to be engaged in political change and the need for spiritual growth. American Gandhiism, with its emphasis on spirituality, also attracted the generation of younger pacifists who had joined the War Resisters League. The WRL had been founded in 1925 as a secular sister to the Fellowship of Reconciliation.[52] Many early members of the Pacifica Foundation belonged to the league, including Americo Chiarito, KPFA's first music director.[53] These pacifists had become increasingly uncomfortable with credos that emphasized personal, conscience-oriented opposition to war without addressing the inevitable need for social and political action. The likelihood of another world war only intensified this disagreement.

In 1941, as the United States verged on intervention in both Europe and Asia, Muste reaffirmed his faith in Gandhiism as a political and spiritual path. In the essay "The World Task of Pacifism," he urged his followers to practice pacifism as "a way of life" and as a tool for social change: "A Western non-violence movement must make effective contact with oppressed and minority groups such as Negroes, share-croppers, industrial workers, and help them to develop a nonviolent technique, as Gandhi did in the India National Congress." But the pacifist movement also had to decide what kind of world it wanted. "It must decide how much socialization is possible without the creation either of a totalitarian state. . . . It must not only invent, it must experiment with schemes for a more decentralized, human and cooperative way of living."[54]

Finch and Hill strongly concurred with Muste. "This was the way *we* imagined pacifism," Finch recalls. "We did not think of it as non-resistance; we thought of it as direct-action of a non-violent character."[55] They agreed that oppressive groups such as southern segregationists would sometimes have to be coerced, albeit nonviolently, into agreeing to change. Finch and Hill differed with Marxists, however, in that they believed that persuasion would have to accompany that coercion, if coercion proved to be necessary. This idea that politics had to be done by example, through dialogue and persuasion, through emphasis on spiritual values rather than materialist analysis, and above all nonviolently, would eventually form the ideological basis of the Pacifica Foundation. In 1945, Hill wrote a letter to Finch that hinted at the faith-oriented path they had both taken. "If St. John of the Cross were walking out of Williamsburg this year you would follow him, though at severe expense to your sense of propriety, while if Eugene Debs were doing the same, you would not."[56]

By the late 1930s, American pacifism gained internal coherence but quickly lost political ground. As the Nazi war machine spread across Eastern Europe and war with the Japanese Empire became a reality, pacifism lost supporters on the left and right. In one of a series of devastating *volte-faces*, in June 1941, the CP-USA reversed its anti-interventionist stance after Germany invaded the Soviet Union. This response was critical in convincing Hill and Finch that Stalinists could not be trusted.[57] Similarly, isolationist organizations, such as America First, almost immediately reversed their stance once the Japanese attacked Pearl Harbor.[58] Finally, as Germany began cutting a swath through France by land and then over Great Britain by air, fewer groups opposed proposals to loan ships to the British Navy.

Simultaneously, draft resistance became less popular. In the autumn of 1940, Congress debated the Burke-Wadsworth conscription bill. On the Senate floor isolationist Burton K. Wheeler warned, "If you pass this bill, you slit the throat of the last democracy still living—you give Hitler his greatest and cheapest victory." Nevertheless, Congress passed a law drafting almost a million men into the armed forces, and President Roosevelt signed it immediately.[59]

Pacifists like Muste remained skeptical of the drive toward intervention in Europe. Many of them, Roy Finch and Lewis Hill included, regarded stories about Nazi atrocities as anti-German propaganda, similar to false stories circulated during the First World War.[60] In speeches, Muste reminded his audiences that the European powers had failed to negotiate a just peace after the First World War and that Hitler's racism was hardly unique, since England and France also justified their imperial conquests with racist ideology. Another total war would exhaust Europe and elevate the United States, also a racially segregated society, to imperial superpower status.[61] Finch, Hill, and others thought that a war with Germany would simply set the stage for a much larger conflict, a showdown with the Soviet Union. "We were very clear on this point," Finch remembered. "It was a way by which we would be led into a war against the communists."[62] They also feared that during the war civil liberties would be suspended as they had been during World War I. Muste called for pacifists to press for a negotiated settlement between Germany and the Allies, to use diplomacy to drive a wedge between Hitler and the German people. "There is no cheap and easy way out," he argued. "But the assumption that the German people are a special breed of semi-humans who do not react to love and hate, good and evil, as do other men is patently without foundation."[63]

Surely Muste knew, however, that most of his audience had disappeared. The pacifist movement of the 1930s had staked out an eloquent moral position against U.S. intervention in World War II, but it had no compelling political arguments to explain how nonviolence would prevent the spread of fascism worldwide. By the late 1930s, Reinhold Niebuhr weighed the risks of nonintervention against an inevitable catastrophe. "We can justify the refusal to take such risks only if we believe that peace is always preferable to the exploitation of the weak by the strong," Niebuhr warned.[64] After the war Hill admitted to Finch that even he could not stand firm in this instance. "One of the threads of the pacifist problem today runs back to the early days of the last war," Hill wrote in 1948, his mind now on Stalinism, "they never answered Niebuhr about Evil."[65]

Nonetheless, in the months following the Japanese attack on Pearl Harbor, both men went to CO camps out of strong convictions about the nature of violence. They agreed with Muste, reflecting the teachings of Gandhi, that "your real 'enemy' is not a person, someone whom you can shoot and thus 'solve' your problem,"[66] but learned behaviors that could be unlearned through example. "Lew's attitude was that modern war so far exceeds all talk about traditional honor and right and wrong that it becomes ridiculous to even deal with it in those terms," Finch later said.[67] Although Hill could have easily gotten a 4-F status (medical exemption), he registered as a conscientious objector and went to Coleville.

A View from the Center

After Hill had been at Coleville for about a year, his arthritic condition worsened. Camp authorities transferred him to kitchen duty and had him treated in the infirmary. In October 1943, they released him on 4-F status.[68] He returned to Tulsa to rest and reconcile with his father. Johnson Hill had not approved of his son's decision to become a CO, and, Lewis confided to a friend, had called him a "dirty yellow dog" during one particularly bitter confrontation.[69] The elder Hill was now distracted enough by his involvement in state politics that a rapprochement developed between them. "It will now amuse you to know that the two of us have never enjoyed greater intimacy," Lewis wrote to Finch. "This follows from a recognition of my 'other qualities' and apparently some grudging approbation that, at least, I stuck it out." The easing of the conflict did not loosen the family purse strings, however, and Lewis sought a "dishwashing job" to tide himself over. "It's snowing luxuriantly outside," his letter continued, "the great fat flakes that drift quietly straight down in Tulsa every other year. They lie like money on the ground. I can't escape that allusion, money. I am reminded of how much of it there is, and how it comes as a reward to complacency and honest conventionality."[70] Hill knew he had little time to decide what to do next.

One possibility that loomed on the horizon was a position as salaried lobbyist for the American Civil Liberties Union's National Committee on Conscientious Objectors (NCCO). Nearly twelve thousand conscientious objectors lived in civilian public service camps during the war and more than six thousand were in prison (representing more than 16 percent of the prison population).[71] NCCO officials spoke in behalf of these pacifists and worked to increase the pathetically low wages—eight cents a day—COs received in camps like Coleville.[72]

Hill had already participated in various NCCO activities in Washington even before he'd been given 4-F status. On March 8, 1943, a delegation of pacifist leaders had met with President Roosevelt and pressed for civilian control of parole applications for imprisoned COs. The president had expressed surprise that they were paid so poorly and that many had been incarcerated. "[Roosevelt's] entire reception, in short, was far more cordial and open than anyone anticipated," Hill wrote to Finch. He attributed FDR's sympathy to the fact that Dorothy Detzer—head of the Women's International League for Peace and Freedom—had discussed the COs' plight with Eleanor Roosevelt.[73] Hill was just discovering his affinity for bureaucratic politics and indicated to the NCCO that he wanted to come on board. By mid-January 1944, Hill wrote to Finch on ACLU stationery. "The letterhead indicates my location," he proudly began.[74] The NCCO had hired him as its director.

From Washington, Hill could see all of mid-century American pacifism in action. The NCCO's membership roster, starting with Dorothy Detzer, who handled the committee's public relations department, read like a Who's Who of the U.S. antiwar movement. A feminist, pacifist, and seasoned Washington lobbyist, Detzer had convinced two U.S. senators to conduct an investigation of the munitions industry in the early 1930s. The inquiry persuaded millions of Americans that the United States had joined World War I at the behest of gun manufacturers.[75] Also on the NCCO was Richard B. Gregg, A. J. Muste, socialist leader Norman Thomas, his pacifist brother, Evan (who had been brutally beaten in prison as a CO during the First World War), and Dorothy Day, founder of the Catholic Worker movement.[76] The NCCO job gave Hill the opportunity to travel around the United States, especially to the West Coast, where he paid a troubling visit to a Japanese American internment camp.[77]

Hill was hired to speak out for pacifists in trouble because they walked out of CO camps to go to peace conferences, had gone on strike against Jim Crow segregation in prison, or faced charges of disloyalty because they'd come to believe in pacifism. The case of Henry Weber was typical. A member of the Socialist Labor Party, Weber had naively believed that the army would consider his objections to killing after he was inducted. When he subsequently refused to drill with a weapon in his hand, the officers at his boot camp first court marshaled him and condemned him to hang, then commuted his sentence to life at hard labor, and finally sentenced him to twenty years in prison. Hill hoped to get Weber's sentence reduced to two years but had to settle for five.[78]

Over time, however, Hill began to lose faith not so much in pacifism but in how pacifists expressed their beliefs within the political system; he saw the emphasis on individual antiwar resistance as detrimental to collective efforts toward peace. Although he too sometimes resorted to a dramatic pacifist gesture, Hill left Washington convinced that the pacifist movement had to find ways to communicate with people on their terms, not just in the context of what he increasingly saw as an isolated, self-referential community, bent on dramatic but ineffectual forms of resistance.

"Leavening the Lump"

To many of the "left" pacifists of World War II, as they sometimes called themselves, the CO camp system represented a betrayal by organized pacifism itself.[79] By taking the job of shunting war resisters off to remote areas of the United States and keeping them busy doing nothing of importance, Pacifist organizations, such as the Quaker-led American Friends Service Committee, had become part of the war machine. No one felt this more strongly than Hill's friend and colleague at the NCCO, Denny Wilcher. A nature-loving individualist in the tradition of Thoreau, Wilcher had been playing professional tennis and studying at Yale when the war broke out. At first he had reluctantly filed as a conscientious objector within the CPS system, but later defiantly relocated to Washington, D.C.[80] In 1944, Wilcher was sent to prison, and Hill replaced him at the NCCO.[81]

During the war, Wilcher wrote two succinct articles in *Christian Century* in which he damned the CPS camps as "a rapprochement between the pacifist Christian groups and the secular warring state" that compromised the ability of Protestantism to criticize modern warfare. Wilcher noted that the peace churches ran the camps in only the most superficial sense. Should an objector refuse to go along with camp regimen, the only option the churches had was to turn him over to the government for sentencing. Pacifists had a duty, he said, not to run CO camps but "to witness their opposition to all modern war and concurrently to exert every effort to bring a ministry of relief to those who suffer and to effect reconciliation among those who hate."[82] He refused to cooperate with a thinly disguised agent of the state that denied pacifists their civil rights and forced them to do busywork.[83]

Refusing to cooperate with the CPS system became a badge of honor for many of the pacifists who later became involved with Pacifica. To resist the state was to resist violence and to promote the cause of peace. "As we came into camp for the first time by forestry truck, those of us who had read our Koestler and Kropotkin concluded that we had finally reached Siberia," recalled future KPFA manager Wallace Hamilton. "We could see ourselves as a curiously American form of Narodniki, anarchist revolutionaries who would someday transform the society now given to war, imperialism and potential fascism." As one of their many acts of defiance, some COs turned their sites into miniature bohemias. Known as the "Kasbah," Barracks Four at Hamilton's camp, for example, was filled with Buddhist altars, prints of India, "and a plethora of wandering dogs."[84]

The loneliness of their rebellion can be summarized in a single sentence in *Essay on Civil Disobedience*, in which Thoreau explained why he refused to pay taxes in 1846: "It is not so important that many should be as good as you, as that there be some absolute goodness somewhere, for that will leaven the whole lump."[85] During the Korean War Muste would send the essay to the government in lieu of his taxes.[86]

Leavening the lump proved to be exciting work, and doubtless more interesting than clearing forest trails. At a conference in 1943 in Chicago to plan antiwar activities, COs called on pacifists to refuse to go to the camps, to walk out of them collectively, or to go on strike. In the Gandhian tradition, they sought to make others understand their politics by making an example of themselves: "A government capable of complete understanding of conscientious objection is likely to be a government capable of maintaining peace," they declared. "Conversely, the more understanding and recognition we create for our position, the more surely we are making possible greater freedom for all people and thereby building the world of peace."[87]

Two years later, in 1945, future KPFA manager Alfred Partridge and six other COs walked out of a camp in protest of their conscription. The authorities caught up with them and sent Partridge to a prison in Ashland, Kentucky. Outraged, he refused to cooperate with his jailers and was put in solitary confinement.[88]

In another act of defiance, Elmer John Lewis, an early KPFA treasurer and public affairs director, and other COs at a camp in Minersville, California, engaged in slowdowns "of epic proportions." Ordered to dump leftover beans into a garbage can, one pacifist performed the task bean by bean while onlookers converted the act of resistance into a guess-the-total contest. Another camper took an entire workday to move a cot three hundred feet while two of his colleagues managed to convert cleaning a couple of pots and a table into a two-day exercise.[89] Lewis was still in Minersville on February 2, 1946, when he and eleven other men went on a complete work strike in protest against what they regarded as inadequate living and working conditions. CPS officials arrested and drove them eighty miles to a jail in Red Bluff and then to a prison in Sacramento where bail was set at $500 each.

Writing about the men's imprisonment in a newsletter for pacifists, future KPFA staff member Roy Kepler commented: "There will be a rather stiff cover charge accompanying the floor show that will be put on in the Sacramento Federal District Court at a not-yet-assigned date. Our readers are once again the victims of a solicitation for funds to cover legal expenses, but with ten new cases forthcoming the need for contributions is clear."[90] Kepler had every reason to hate the CPS system. His brother had died in a fire in a CO camp.[91] CPS directors and prison officials probably all agreed to some extent with a jailer who commented to a group of the pacifists that "you c.o.'s may be glad when the war is over but not half as much as I who yearn for the good old days of simple murderers and bank robbers for prisoners!"[92]

By the last year of the war, however, Hill and others had become increasingly skeptical of the value of such rebellion. In a public declaration issued in July 1945 to all CPS pacifists, Kepler, E. John Lewis, and Denny Wilcher argued that by focusing on individual grievances, pacifists had lost sight of the larger goal: "We do not recognize the validity of CPS and therefore will not work for its modification. Our emphasis at all times shall be on the elimination of this precedent of conscript labor."[93]

Hill and John Lewis registered their concerns explicitly during the last and largest of the World War II–era pacifist revolts, the 1946 CO strike at a camp in Glendora, California. On April 24, 1946, the director of the camp announced that he planned to transfer two COs without allowing them to appeal. The next day, forty outraged pacifists went on strike. The director declined to meet them, and within two weeks the number of strikers had more than doubled. They occupied themselves by raising money in nearby towns to send food packages to Europe. On May 18, federal officers arrested six of the strikers and put them in a Los Angeles jail, which other COs in the area began to picket. In addition, they brought attention to the fact that an African American CO had been put in a Jim Crow section of the prison. Meanwhile, the strikers expanded their demands to include payment for work done, the elimination of arbitrary military rule, and accident compensation. Eleven days later, U.S. marshals arrested forty-one more strikers, all of whom started to protest as soon as they were incarcerated in Los Angeles.[94]

Hill did not feel comfortable directing criticism at the Glendora strikers, but, nonetheless, in November 1946, he and John Lewis published an "Open Letter" about their struggle. Hill and Lewis charged that the Glendora pacifists had become too preoccupied with protesting the conditions at their camp. "Your five demands," the letter charged, "are directed exclusively against the more onerous conditions of CPS, while the real issue today is conscription—permanent conscription." As the American people clamored for demobilization, the military lobbied to create a permanent draft. Was it any wonder that pacifist delegations appealing the Glendora case in Washington had met with sympathy from "liberals," who obviously wanted to know how to make CPS more palatable to the leaders of the pacifist movement and its sympathizers? "You are being used as the springboard for a new era of peace church compromise," Hill and Lewis said, concluding their letter with a single-sentence paragraph: "*Is* that the way you want it?"[95]

Hill's impatience with what he saw as the narrow-mindedness of CO camp pacifism and the escalation of the war in the Pacific led him to a bold scheme. During the early summer of 1945, he and Finch began meeting with prominent pacifists on the East Coast, seeking support for the "Japanese Project."[96] Their idea was for twelve "carefully chosen pacifists" to sail across the Pacific Ocean in a small boat, meet with Japanese pacifists in the middle of the sea, and jointly call for an end to the war.[97]

The atomic bombings of Hiroshima and Nagasaki in August 1945 effectively ended the Japanese Project, since the Japanese government surrendered shortly afterward. In a letter to other pacifists, Hill carefully chronicled the aborted campaign, predicting that it would seem "more abnormal as the war recedes" (and, indeed, his friend Finch later called the plan a "hare-brained idea").[98] Hill thought the scheme represented the right way to do politics. It cut beyond all the minutiae of day-to-day pacifism and got to the heart of the matter. Pacifists wanted the war to end; hence, they would prove it by literally sailing into the middle of the conflict and demanding cessation of the hostilities. The plan rescued pacifism from the periphery, Hill argued. It reached "the man on the street" and put war makers where they liked to put pacifists, on the defensive. Most important, the sheer shock value of the plan positively defined pacifism: "It dramatized the desperate need for common people to break through the barriers thrown between them and maintain communication by their own will, against, if need be, the authority of their governments."[99]

Hill later confided his impatience with movement pacifism in a letter to Roy Kepler. So much of pacifist activity, Hill argued, had at its core not the desire to further the pacifist idea so much as to register personal frustration with the system. Pacifists loved to picket this or that event, Hill observed, and to bicker with the police over their right to picket. But in reality they sought "a mass discharge of the individual emotion, that suppurates and swells in isolation," rather than to formulate their thoughts. Unless a movement stood *for* very specific ideas, rather than against a variety of outrages, it could only expect to drift. "Many things, fantastic things, become possible through the definite determination to remain definite," Hill concluded. "Zionism and the Gandhian movement have always had this specificity."[100]

Hill had broken with the pacifists' thesis, expressed at their 1943 conference in Chicago, that by resisting oppressive conditions at CPS camps one implicitly fought for peace. At the end of World War II, he began developing organizing strategies to promote what he called the "pacific idea." Hill wanted to demonstrate to ordinary people through positive example not why a government policy was wrong but why a pacific world was desirable, and, most important, achievable.

Most of the pacifists in Hill's immediate circle agreed with his position, even if they had participated in CO rebellions at one time or another. All of them knew that one of pacifism's failings before the war had been its inability to stake out its own ideological territory. Instead, it had become embedded in movements such as isolationism and communism. Hill and his supporters also agreed that during the war pacifists had substituted dramatic tactics for ideas and vision. John Lewis wrote to Hill in March 1945 that he wanted to see the movement develop more of a socialist ("with a small 's'") orientation but felt that such a perspective had yet to be fashioned. "We constantly find ourselves battling *against* encroachments that appear to threaten progress toward our vaguely held objectives," Lewis lamented. ". . . there is no clearly understood social philosophy of pacifism that is politically relevant, even to pacifists themselves."[101] Kepler expressed this same frustration at about the same time. He wanted to see less "leaping eagerly into the fray of non-cooperation" and more "voluntary group purpose and discipline" in organized pacifism.[102] The "leftist pacifists" of the World War II era found their vision for the future in the short-lived but influential journal *Politics*.

"The Root Is Man"

Born in New York City in 1906, the founder of *Politics*, Dwight Macdonald, had much in common with Hill. As a boy Macdonald attended exclusive private schools—Phillips Exeter Academy and Yale. He then took a writing position at that flagship publication for corporate America, *Fortune* magazine. By the late 1930s, however, he had concluded that the so-called free market system had failed. Ambivalent about Stalinism as well as capitalism, he wrote briefly for the *Partisan Review*, then joined the Socialist Workers Party (SWP). But like A. J. Muste, Macdonald really could belong to no party save his own. Outraged by Trotsky's support of the 1941 Soviet invasion of Finland, Macdonald resigned from the SWP that year. Macdonald concluded, in the words of one scholar, that "something disasterous had happened in his lifetime."[103] This disaster had befallen not only the Nazi Holocaust's many victims but the entire world, indeed, human consciousness. Dwarfed by the bureaucratic state, by modern war, by deterministic ideologies, people were, in Macdonald's view, losing the capacity to know what it meant to be human. In an effort to redefine humanness and figure out how societies might resurrect and nourish it, in 1943, Macdonald started his own magazine.

By the end of the Second World War, *Politics* had become an underground hit, attracting readers on the left and right. In his search for fresh answers, Macdonald printed the writings of a new generation of intellectuals, including cultural critics James Agee and Marshall McLuhan.[104] Many took note of his publication of Mary McCarthy's translation of Simone Weil's "The Iliad, or, the Poem of Force," which eloquently argued that Homer understood the circular nature of violence.[105]

But it is doubtful that any group took Macdonald's magazine as seriously as the era's COs. They liked *Politics* in part because *Politics* liked them. By 1946, horrified at the possibility of an atomic war, Macdonald enthusiastically championed the COs' cause. He saw direct-action pacifists as intellectually minded people taking the decision-making process into their own hands, rather than leaving vital moral questions to the state. He published articles outlining the major issues involved in the various CO strikes, including the walkout at Glendora.[106] Likewise, COs praised Macdonald and his publication in their letters and political statements. After collectively reading a Macdonald essay in 1945, for instance, a group of Philadelphia pacifists all declared it to be "a damn good article and the world is in a helluva shape."[107]

Even after *Politics* folded, Macdonald and his writing retained significant influence. Roy Kepler, for example, took his manuscripts to Macdonald for critical comments long after the journal ceased publication,[108] and one pacifist newsletter continued to print a Macdonald quote just below its masthead: "The crazy and murderous nature of the kind of society we have created is underlined by the atomic bomb. Every individual who wants to save his humanity, and indeed his skin, had better begin to think 'dangerous thoughts' about resistance, rebellion, and the fraternity of all men everywhere."[109]

But Lewis Hill and his circle did not like Macdonald simply because he supported their battles. They took Macdonald seriously because he made sense of the ideas of Richard Gregg and A. J. Muste. Macdonald drew from a concept that quickly gained enormous currency after the war: being "human" or having a "self" required being and communicating directly with other people. This prescription was championed by intellectuals as diverse as Harry Stack Sullivan, Martin Buber, and Hannah Arendt. What made Macdonald's take on this theme distinctly pacifist was his contention that both the modern state and deterministic ideologies, like Marxism-Leninism or corporate liberalism, coerced or tricked people into not listening to each other and thus into not being human. From this refusal to listen emerged people's capacity to resort to or condone mass violence. Macdonald did not arrive at this view from a spiritual so much as a psychological perspective, but that proved sufficient for the COs who read him.

In 1945, Macdonald published a book-length essay in *Politics* entitled "The Root Is Man," which strongly influenced left pacifists. Asserting his desire to see a "free, classless, warless society," Macdonald argued that any effort to find that future in Marxism would come to naught.[110] Marxism, with its positing of values based on historical/economic circumstances, eliminated the possibility of free will and therefore of humanness: "Why not begin with what we living human beings *want*, what we think and feel is *good?* . . . then see how we can come closest to it—instead of looking to historical process for a justification of socialism?" Macdonald asked the reader to consider the possibility that none of the currently assumed political categories—"left," "right," "socialist," and "capitalist"—worked very well. They didn't mean much anymore in a world in which governments could suppress individual liberty in the name of the working class and capitalists produced commodities for the warfare state instead of the free market. In Macdonald's view, the world had evolved into an assemblage of state systems neither capitalist nor socialist, bent on self-aggrandizement and willing to use war, or the constant threat of war, as their tool. Macdonald saw these states as controlled by a new kind of leader who sought power for neither workers nor capitalists but for the state alone. "Bureaucratic collectivism, not capitalism," Macdonald warned, "is the most dangerous future enemy of socialism."[111]

What was to be done? Macdonald called for the pacifist movement to emphasize personal values rather than sweeping materialist or historicist ideologies. He embraced Gandhian uncertainty, telling his readers that they "must learn to live with contradictions, to have faith in skepticism, to advance toward the solution of a problem by admitting as a possibility something which the scientist can never admit: namely, that it may be insoluble." He warned pacifists not to join mass organizations that, by challenging the state on its own terms, would simply replicate the state. Above all, he called upon them to work in small groups in which human emotions could be encouraged. Like Gandhi, Macdonald predicted, after World War II pacifists would once again foment change through example: "Through symbolic individual actions, based on a person's insistence of his own values, and through the creation of small fraternal groups which will support such actions, keep alive a sense of our ultimate goals, and both act as a leavening in the dough of mass society and attract more and more of the alienated and frustrated members of that society."[112]

For the conscientious objector in 1945, "The Root Is Man" illuminated two possible roads. One, taken by pacifists such as Bayard Rustin and James Farmer, would lead to the civil rights movement of the 1950s, in which women and men, through their own heroic example, would promote attitudes of disrespect toward a state-sponsored system of racial inequality. The other road, taken by Lewis Hill and his friends, would lead to the formation of the Pacifica Foundation, to the creation of small educational institutions designed to take a Kierkegaardian leap, that would show—once again by example—that a pacific world was possible, not in the distant future, but in their lifetimes. Imagining the postwar pacifist movement, Macdonald suggested that small groups "would get into the habit, discouraged by the Progressive frame of mind, of acting here and now, on however tiny a scale, for their beliefs."[113] Why not begin with what we living beings want? Macdonald had asked at the beginning of "The Root Is Man." Thus, in a philosophical sense, the editor of *Politics* foresaw the coming of KPFA-FM a mere four years later.

By mid-1945, Hill's commitment to organized pacifism had waned. He still believed in nonviolence, but his enthusiasm for forming a post–World War II pacifist party steadily dwindled. He even rejected the idea, suggested by a friend, of starting a pacifist magazine. "It would be easy to make a weekly digest of all the domestic and international shenanigans which are inimical to a world of brotherhood," he wrote, and went on to vaguely suggest that pacifism needed "a new organ which can place all these events in the perspective of a dynamic, conscious and completely premised program of its own."[114] Hill had begun to realize something he would articulate later on: pacifism couldn't progress as a movement as long as the world perceived pacifists as outsiders, as lonely dissenters without standing in the community. He began to return to the idea that he and Finch had discussed at Coleville: creating a pacifist-controlled radio station that would give consideration to all points of view.

Perhaps this vision stayed with Hill because by the summer of 1944 he had also taken on work as an announcer at WINX in Washington, D.C., doubtless to supplement his salary at the NCCO.[115] Hill had a compelling voice, and after a year he was offered a job as a scriptwriter/announcer for NBC's so-called Blue Network. He sometimes worked all-night shifts at WINX, as on June 6, 1944, when he announced the invasion of Normandy by the Allied forces.[116]

The regimentation and falseness of commercial media appalled him, as exemplified in a story Hill later told friends about the last press conference given by President Roosevelt. FDR came into the conference room in his wheelchair, exhausted, his face ashen. The president then made himself over while reporters watched. All at once, "the cigarette would be lit, and the holder would be tilted at an angle where before that he was slumped in the wheelchair like a dying man."[117] Only then would the cameras be allowed to roll and reporters to ask questions. Hill saw something inhuman in this grim political theater. He found it equally offensive that radio announcers read material they had not written or even thought about. He later told audiences about the test WINX gave job applicants. Each received a page of sentences that had correct syntax but made no sense. The prospect had to read the page several times, first solemnly, then comically. How, upon mastery of this process, Hill later asked, "can one possibly maintain an ordered discrimination of values? How does one remember, beyond the consuming cynicism of such an art, any posture of actual belief?"[118]

Eventually, Hill's discomfort with this system forced him to part company with WINX. On May 29, 1945, while on the air, someone handed Hill a story he felt was false. He later wrote to Finch that it referred to "the people at Tule Lake," the site of a concentration camp for Japanese Americans.[119] It will never be known what Hill disliked about the story, but he refused to read it and quit his job. "[I] only beat them to the punch," he told Finch. "It was exciting, and I'm very glad to be out of that particular doldrum."[120]

Hill did have one positive experience at WINX. One day management told him to report to the station's public relations department so someone could write up his biography. Upon walking into the PR office, Hill met a woman named Joy Cole, who was arguing with another employee about the futility of war. Hill and Cole quickly discovered that they had much in common, both personally and politically. Both came from old American families: Hill's from colonial Virginia, Cole's from New England. Cole could recall family tales of her ancestor Susannah Adams doing secretarial work for President John Adams. Brought up in a comfortable section of Syracuse, New York, Joy Cole had been told from an early age to live up to her heritage and background, to contribute to society.[121]

After a short period of dating, she and Hill "bustled into a judge's chambers" and were married. "Last Tuesday, my friend, I went and did it," Hill boasted to Finch on November 3, 1944.[122] The ceremony seems to have been very modest, indicative of two people much too busy saving the world to indulge in ostentation. After they were married, Joy Cole Hill took on the task, among other projects, of writing for the *Conscientious Objector*.[123]

BY 1946, Lewis Hill's work on behalf of COs was over. His efforts to help pacifists face their greatest challenge in twenty-five years had changed him politically. He no longer thought that pacifism as a movement could survive solely by reacting to events. Like Richard Gregg, Hill rejected the notion that political revolution could precede a change in consciousness. Rather, pacifists would have to demonstrate the possibility of peace, not simply demand it. In Hill's words, they would have to abandon the practice of "imposing a specific fiat upon the ethical without having first awakened its necessity." For this reason, Hill rejected Leninist-style vanguard strategies. "The concept of class revolution in America is utterly bankrupt," he later declared. "Equally bankrupt is the puerile notion of creating an awareness of crisis by entering the community from the outside at the top of one's lungs, with a crummy propaganda sheet." Hill sought mechanisms for bringing about what Richard Gregg had described as an ethical transformation, proving the validity of the pacific idea not in some historically imagined future but in the present. He looked for strategies that would teach people about pacifism through living example: "Basic institutions [that] will represent not merely political ideas, but, in a most active sense, a superior aggregate of modern culture. Its institutions will not merely symbolize, but actually effect [*sic*], the wholeness of the political problem."[124]

Subsequent generations of Pacifica radio staff would invent terms that obscured this unashamedly utopian vision. They would call Pacifica "underground" radio. The COs of World War II, however, had had enough of the underground. They wanted the light of day. Later writers would also describe KPFA as "alternative" media. But the founders of Pacifica did not see their philosophy as an alternative but as the only possible way. Terms like "free-form" radio meant nothing to a generation of people who knew that "freedom" offered the most terrible choices. At the end of the Second World War, the institution that would gradually invent all these words did not yet exist. To create it, Hill returned to the only place in the United States where he thought such a project might thrive: the San Francisco Bay.

2)) The Pleasures of the Harbor

We must become singers, become entertainers. We must stop sitting on the pot of culture. There is more of Orpheus in Sophie Tucker than in R. P. Blackmur; we have more to learn from George M. Cohan than from John Crowe Ransom.

—Jack Spicer,
"The Poet and Poetry: A Symposium"

In early 1946, Lewis and Joy Hill moved to San Francisco, where they rented an "old flat with a bedroom" on Shraeder Street, a thoroughfare sandwiched between the Haight-Ashbury District and the eastern rim of Golden Gate Park. Joy took a position managing a garage, supporting Hill as he looked for work as a radio announcer. He had explored a number of possibilities, among them a position in Los Angeles offered by "a wealthy octogenarian Wallace liberal" as the radio director of an educational foundation. There was a still a chance, he wrote to Finch, "of camping with the networks and independents in the city until a position opened," but nothing had panned out yet. Work had become scarce as scores of returning GIs claimed their old positions in the Bay Area. Eventually, he would find another "dishwashing job," this time as an announcer for radio station KYA in San Francisco, but at the moment his heart wasn't really into job hunting.[1] After his experiences with WINX in Washington, he had become less hopeful about influencing the policies of another station "from within" and more determined to get his own operation off the ground. "I've decided to start the thing right now," he wrote to Finch, "and expect to spend the next three to four weeks getting together a complete and rather detailed sketch of a proposed operation, including all technical, financial and corporate data." By May, Hill had outlined the basics of the station he had in mind for the Federal Communications Commission in Washington.[2] Soon after that he produced the first fundraising prospectus for his project.

A "Closed Shop Empire"

The poet Walt Whitman had once dubbed New York "the most radical city in America."[3] But for all its social and intellectual turbulence, New York never elected a labor leader for mayor. San Franciscans did in 1910, when they turned over City Hall to P. H. McCarthy, the head of the city's all-powerful Building Trades Council. The relative remoteness of San Francisco combined with its desirable port and post–gold rush economy created unparalleled opportunities for working-class people. In New York immigrants competed for jobs and housing, whereas in San Francisco skilled labor, particularly in the building trades, seemed always in short supply, creating a favorable climate for union organizing. When local contractors wanted to hire workers, they politely applied to McCarthy's council, whose bureaucrats informed them how much they would pay in wages. San Francisco had become, in the words of one historian, a "closed shop empire."[4]

The devastating earthquake of 1906 only enhanced the favorable situation for carpenters and bricklayers, who built a thriving plebeian culture that exempted itself from Victorian moral standards. When Mayor McCarthy promised he would convert San Francisco into the Paris of the Pacific, local upholders of decency knew exactly what he meant, and they didn't like it at all. They already regarded the town as Parisian enough with its "Barbary Coast" of saloons, amusement parks, and brothels.[5] The city of "good food and cheap prices," a young Charlie Chaplin called it after his first visit in 1910.[6]

Indeed, by midcentury, San Francisco was a place where events almost impossible anywhere else in the United States could take place, where the fantastic indeed emerged through definite determination to remain definite. In 1934, just twelve years before the Hills took their comfortable apartment on Shraeder Street, the city's longshore workers struck against a corrupt system that required them to pay off shift bosses to obtain employment. On Thursday, July 5, the major shipping companies attempted to break a picket line on the city's Embarcadero waterfront with a phalanx of police and hired thugs. Workers on the nearby Bay Bridge, then under construction, ducked as shotgun bullets whizzed past their heads. From the hills of the city, thousands of San Franciscans watched in horror as bluecoats assaulted scores of picketers, murdering two in the process. After about ten thousand people marched in a funeral procession for the martyrs of "Bloody Thursday," a coalition of unions called a general strike. For three days in mid-July almost the entire population of the city ceased work, until the shippers agreed to practically all the demands of the union.[7]

This victory created a sea change throughout the Bay Area, as residents emerged from the experience with a unique sense of the possible. Emboldened by grassroots support, unions penetrated the Bay Area economy. Worker militancy combined with cooperative trade unionism to form a way of life in San Francisco. The motto of the International Longshore Workers Union summed up this attitude: "An injury to one is an injury to all."[8] The community existed to defend and enhance the life of the individual. No politician, conservative or liberal, dared question this tradition, no matter how radical the rhetoric of union leaders. When Angelo Rossi, the mayor during the general strike, died in 1966, Harry Bridges, who had led the remarkable walkout, gave the eulogy. Bridges had nothing but respect for Rossi, he told reporters: "We had our bitter fights but there was never a doubt in my mind that he honestly represented his class and, whenever we reached agreement, his word was good."[9] Such talk came easily to the chief of the longshore workers, as well as to Sidney Roger, his press secretary, who later served as a commentator on KPFA.[10] Unlike most American cities, the populace of San Francisco often regarded the actions of the city's labor council as more significant than those of City Hall.[11]

This spirit of cooperation and heightened sense of the possible also attracted a stream of social visionaries to the Bay Area. They established oddly named utopian colonies up and down the state—Fountain Grove, Icaria Speranza, Kaweah, Llano del Rio, and Altruria. Lewis Hill and the leaders of these early ventures bore similarities in both politics and temperament. Although often espousing the solidarity inherent in unionism, many of these visionaries rejected the concept of class struggle, hoping, instead, that their projects would serve as social models.

Several of these social experiments made a strong impression on Hill, particularly those espousing the cooperative movement, the work of Alexander Meiklejohn, and Theosophy, a worldwide spiritual community with a devoted following on the West Coast. The first Pacificans had many Theosophist relatives and friends. Elsa Knight Thompson, who in the late 1950s joined KPFA as its public affairs director, came from a family "sort of split down the middle between rock-bound Presbyterians and Theosophists." At the age of eight, Knight Thompson met a friend of her uncle named Annie Besant, one of the international leaders of Theosophy. "She said that I had come back at this time in history to be what she called one of the forerunners of a new kind of human being that was coming," Knight Thompson later recalled. "She said that these new people, this new way of life, would arise in Northern California."[12]

Theosophy had its origins in the teachings of Madame Helena Petrovna Blavatsky, a woman of southern Russian origins whose writings emphasized the unity of all life. Drawing much of her teaching from eastern religion, Blavatsky emphasized that such unity depended on recognition of the uniqueness of each person. "Act individually and not collectively," she wrote. "The Theosophical ideas of charity mean *personal* exertion for others. . . . Political action must necessarily vary with the circumstances of the time and with the idiosyncrasies of individuals."[13] Led on the coast by the charismatic Katherine Augusta Westcott Tingley, California Theosophists promoted the "Universal Brotherhood of Humanity" through their emphasis on the spiritual nature of each human being. Many Theosophists also shared enthusiasm for Edward Bellamy's utopian writings, particularly *Looking Backward.*[14]

Denny Wilcher became familiar with Theosophy in the late 1940s through his wife, Ida Shagaloff, a painter, dancer, and member of the United Lodge of Theosophists in Los Angeles.[15] Before meeting Wilcher, Shagaloff had been involved with Henry Geiger, a conscientious objector at Glendora, a Bellamy socialist, and a Theosophist intellectual.[16] Hill was introduced to Theosophy through his correspondence with Geiger, who in 1948 started to publish his own fortnightly journal called *MANAS*.

Read by many members of the early Pacifica Foundation, *MANAS* served as a kind of intellectual mirror image for the foundation by sounding unashamedly idealistic themes that Hill also emphasized. "Today's problems are neither theological nor scientific," the premier issue opined, "they are *human* problems, and need to be conceived and addressed in human terms." In a true democracy people had to take each other seriously enough to "think things through," as Geiger liked to put it, in a cooperative fashion. Geiger saw in such cooperation a process that would bring out the inner self in each person and that had as its ultimate end the nonviolent construction of better values. "Democracy operates collectively only to the extent that its meaning is understood individually," Geiger explained. Like Hill and Dwight Macdonald, Geiger saw the possibility of such a human revival residing "with intelligent minorities — the undismayed few who are always found on the fronts of the human struggle, whose natural work is with the growing tips of the social organism."[17] The staff of the Pacifica Foundation followed the essays in *MANAS* throughout the 1950s. In the summer of 1949, a short notice in the journal complimented the fledgling radio station for its news department, "which faces honestly the limitations of news sources available to radio, yet assumes editorial responsibility for what is presented, and how it is presented."[18]

Educator Alexander Meiklejohn shared Geiger's emphasis on dialogue but had populist sympathies that attracted him to broader forums of expression. In 1953, a Meiklejohn speech on the First Amendment—broadcast over KPFA—would win the station a national award and define its opposition to McCarthyism.[19] By then, he and Hill were friends.[20]

Born in 1872, the son of Scottish socialists, Meiklejohn grew up in Rochdale, the birthplace of the English consumer cooperative movement. Immigrating with his family to Rhode Island, he studied philosophy and quickly made his way up the academic ladder, becoming president of Amherst College in 1911. Meiklejohn's willingness to tolerate campus opposition to U.S. intervention in World War I made him unpopular with powerful forces in the administration.[21] By in the early 1920s, he had moved on to the Experimental College at the University of Wisconsin. There he abolished courses. Students underwent an open-ended two-year program dedicated to the study of ancient Greek and modern American history. "Freedom is possible in a community," Meiklejohn argued, "only when all the members of the community are so disposed in mind and so equipped in intelligence that the action they will take when free shall be such, not only that it will not interfere with another, but will contribute to the freedom of every other; when every member has the same purpose in mind."[22]

When the Experimental College collapsed during the early years of the Depression, Meiklejohn went west to organize a school for working-class adults. The San Francisco School of Social Studies charged no fees and assigned its students both Plato's *Republic* and Thorsten Veblen's *The Vested Interests*. It operated on the premise that the capitalist system had lost any sense of social responsibility, explained Helen Meiklejohn, Alexander's wife, and sought to help students "understand and control the social order in which they live." To this end, the school admitted the memberships of entire union locals, such as the Bakery Wagon Drivers and the International Ladies Garment Workers' Union.[23]

While the San Francisco school actively solicited unionists, the directors sought to avert class strife, emphasizing conflict resolution instead. During the 1934 general strike, for example, the school came under serious fire from the community. "Every partisan group either wanted the School to serve its purposes," one instructor recalled, "or feared it was lent to service of the opposing group. Some saw its curriculum as too radical; others saw its sponsors as too respectable. The School's task was to get both those parties into its study groups and make them talk together."[24]

At the same time, the co-op grocery movement spread throughout the

Bay. Lewis Hill looked to community-based cooperatives as the hope of the future and an alternative to state socialism. "When it is made clear that peaceful, democratic revolution can be carried out without the aid of the Kremlin," he wrote in 1945, "the revolutionary potential of the unemployed may be realized." Hill opposed more large-scale reforms that "parade as humanitarian socialistic changes while actually strengthening the state controls of private capitalism." The left, he urged, should organize "direct action projects to put a new economy of decentralized, democratic socialism to work"—agricultural co-ops, worker-consumer management of industries, and local public works projects. He called for locally controlled economic planning boards.[25]

"The original idea was to make [KPFA] a co-operative," Joy Cole Hill recalled. "The San Francisco area was selected because co-ops abounded" throughout the region.[26] Indeed they did. In 1936, the year Hill came to Stanford, a group of Palo Alto scholars and businesspeople founded the Consumers Cooperative Society, basing their operation on the so-called Rochdale Plan. Seeking ways to stretch their Depression-sized incomes, the cooperators bought bulk groceries and distributed them in a basement store. Within three years the society had an annual sales rate of $75,000 and 345 members. Meanwhile, in Oakland, the congregation of a Methodist church pondered ways to develop a more Christian system of distribution. They formed a buying club that within a year had local depots and chapters in Alameda and Berkeley as well. The East Bay's tightly knit community of Finnish immigrants had a similar club.[27]

The presence of these unique ventures—schools, unions, cooperatives, spiritual movements—both influenced Hill and reflected his thinking. He would draw upon their traditions in creating the Pacifica Foundation.

Recruiting from the Renaissance

By war's end an entire generation of poets and artists—many of them conscientious objectors assigned to work camps in California—had migrated to San Francisco. They had often visited "the City" during leaves from their camps and found the region's visionary politics and natural environment irresistible.[28] Their ranks included the Dominican lay brother and printer William Everson ("Brother Antoninus"); poets Jack Spicer, Kenneth Patchen, and Robert Duncan; early feminist balladeer Helen Adam; and the painter John Hartmann, with whom Hill became friends in Coleville. Their populist sympathies could be traced to the title of one of their most important journals, *Illiterati*, printed in a CO camp at Waldport, Oregon. During the war *Illiterati* published the poetry and prose of many

COs, including Hill and Finch.[29] Issue 4 boldly announced the journal's intentions: "THE ILLITERATI PROPOSES: CREATION, EXPERIMENT, AND REVOLUTION TO BUILD A WARLESS, FREE SOCIETY; SUSPECTS: TRADITION AS A STANDARD AND ECLECTICISM AS A TECHNIQUE; REJECTS: WAR AND ANY OTHER FORMS OF COERCION BY PHYSICAL VIOLENCE IN HUMAN ASSOCIATIONS."[30]

Remembered as the "San Francisco Renaissance," these poets were a close-knit community who drank at the city's great bohemian hangout, the Black Cat Cafe on 710 Montgomery Street.[31] They wrote poetry to be read out loud, to be performed for each other, and strove to become themselves *through* each other. "What is it that makes a precious bond between two people if it is not some sudden fusion of thoughts," asked a 1944 editorial in *Illiterati*, "expressed or unexpressed? Mind and body, if not one, are inescapably allied: fusion of thoughts create bonds of personality."[32]

These writers, most of whom would broadcast on KPFA in the 1950s, drew their literary models from the most unexpected sources. "We must become singers, become entertainers," Jack Spicer declared in 1949. "We must stop sitting on the pot of culture. There is more of Orpheus in Sophie Tucker than in R. P. Blackmur; we have more to learn from George M. Cohan than from John Crowe Ransom."[33] They committed themselves to what cultural scholars sometimes call the poetics of place. "We firmly held to the view that we would never surrender and go to New York in order to be published or anything like that," one participant recalled. "This was a *West Coast* artists group."[34] Unlike New York writers, one of these poets bragged, San Francisco writers did not just talk about proletarians, they *were* proletarians. "[Proletarian culture] is dominant," he wrote in 1957, "almost all there is."[35] Feeling a deep affinity with their cause, in 1946 Lewis Hill approached San Francisco's poets for help with his radio project. He knew, however, that to gain their support, he'd first have to win over their undisputed leader, a difficult man named Rexroth.

Several generations of KPFA listeners knew Kenneth Rexroth as the station's witty book reviewer. But in the years just after the Second World War, this remarkable poet held sway over the so-called Libertarian or Anarchist Circles of San Francisco. These poets, artists, and performers modeled themselves after the members of anarchist communes and got a steady diet of anarchist ideology from Rexroth himself. "Such was the passion of his anarchist knowledge and beliefs that you could leave his presence believing that he had had one-on-one discussions with Kropotkin," recalled his friend Richard Moore.[36]

Rexroth was born in 1905 in South Bend, Indiana, to a family of feminists and socialist reformers.[37] When both his parents died, a relative took Kenneth to Chicago, where he soaked in the culture of the city during the early 1920s. Hyperliterate and socially adept, he dropped out of public school and insinuated himself into some of the finest salons in Chicago. There he listened to discussions among the likes of Clarence Darrow, Eugene Debs, and Carl Sandburg. But to Rexroth, the anarchist speakers at Bughouse Square were far more interesting.

Already committed to the black flag of anarchism by his late teens, Rexroth took a job writing for local newspapers to support his poetry and painting. When the economy began to decline in the late 1920s, he joined the communist-led John Reed literary club movement. But his anarchist spirit could not stomach the phony patriotism of the American Communist Party during its Popular Front period. After Hitler's election in Germany in 1932, worldwide communism determined that its respective parties must support those industrial democracies capable of defeating fascism. Rexroth grimaced at the sudden unveiling of portraits of George Washington at CP meeting halls.[38] Having moved to the West Coast by the time the United States entered the war, Rexroth joined in the Fellowship of Reconciliation's efforts to protect Japanese Americans from local hostility. Like other socialist-pacifists, Rexroth believed that U.S. intervention in the war would produce "something a lot worse than a heavy fog in a blacked-out London. We have got to keep hands joined, or we will never get out on the other side."[39] When summoned by his local draft board, Rexroth filed as a conscientious objector. He wound up working as an orderly in a mental institution in San Francisco, where he attempted to liberalize treatment of the patients.[40]

By the war's end, Rexroth had established himself as a respected writer and poet in San Francisco, where younger COs admired his experience, talent, and radicalism. But perhaps because his political goals remained so distant, or because he still lived on the economic margins, he became bitter and self-righteous in his forties. Jack Kerouac immortalized him as "Reinhold Cacoethes" in his novel *The Dharma Bums*, which ends with Cacoethes holding forth at a writers gathering, where he condemns everyone in sight. "By God, I'm the only good one here. At least I've got an honest anarchist background," the character declares. "At least I had frost on my nose, boots on my feet, and protest in my mouth."[41] This characterization may have appeared unkind, but it was accurate. "I was always luckier than anybody else because I knew more about what I was doing," Rexroth once told a magazine inteviewer.[42]

Rexroth held court at his Libertarian Circle meetings, which usually took place at the studio of Richard Moore, an ex-University of California at Berkeley poetry student. Moore had managed to avoid either induction or the CPS experience simply by telling the truth at his selective service board examination. Just before reaching draft age, the ballet company of José Limón and May O'Donnell had recruited him as a dancer because the war had created a shortage of experienced men. At his induction interview Moore was asked to declare his profession. "I'm a poet," Moore replied. "But how do you make a living?" a board official asked. "Well, I'm a ballet dancer," he elaborated. A troubled clerk led the potential draftee to a room where another examiner placed a paper towel on a chair before asking the young man to sit. "Do you have an anal fixation or something like that?" Moore asked. Ignoring the question, the official got the point: "Would you follow a direct order if it was given to you by your commander in chief?" The poet/ballet dancer thought for a moment. "It would depend on what the order is," he replied. As the clerk scribbled a few comments on a form, Moore sneaked a glance. He had been classified 4-F—"psychotic/neurotic." Freed from the obligation to serve his country, Moore converted his flat into part of an underground railroad for COs who went AWOL from their camps. They usually stayed at Moore's place on their way to Big Sur. "They thought they could hide out in the wilds there," he later recalled, "and they would get arrested by the FBI agents in about two weeks or so."[43]

One afternoon, shortly after they arrived in the Bay Area, Lewis and Joy Hill showed up "unannounced," as Rexroth later put it, at a Libertarian Circle meeting at Moore's house. "[Hill] had the most haunting eyes I've ever known on anybody. I mean the eyes were *that* kind of penetrating," Alan Rich, an early KPFA music director, later remembered.[44] "He was a tall thin man with a long dead white face and a soft, propulsive manner of speaking," Rexroth recalled.[45] Older anarchists, as well as Richard Moore and a young radio producer named Eleanor McKinney, made up a large portion of the audience. Granted a few moments to speak, Hill presented his thesis. Society had undergone "a great structural change," giving pacifists far more effective means of communication than "street meetings and little pamphlets." It would not be difficult at all, Hill suggested, to put together a listener-sponsored radio station, cooperatively run, with a Bay Area-wide signal, unencumbered by commercials.[46]

Unfortunately, Hill's penchant for sociological jargon made him less than completely effective. "It was difficult enough for the younger college educated people to follow," Rexroth later wrote. "For the elderly Jews, Italians and Spanish—who after all had been reading revolutionary theory all their lives—it was totally incomprehensible." Indeed, a civil rights leader later remembered Hill's name coming up in a conversation with Bayard Rustin. "They say you can't understand what he's talking about," he joked.[47] It also didn't help Hill's cause that he showed up in an expensive sharkskin suit, trench coat, and fedora hat. "Lew probably reminded them of an FBI agent," Moore recalled.[48]

Rexroth and his entourage scoffed at Hill's proposed radio project. "Radio isn't political activity," one of them declared. "Political activity is in the barricades."[49] Rexroth told the Libertarian audience that radio was an inherently inferior medium, turning everything into *kitsch*. How? Why? Hill calmly asked, demonstrating his knack for wearing down the resistance of an adversary with a steady stream of gentle, but persistent, questions.[50] After some discussion, much of the group's skepticism for the proposal subsided. Joy Hill affectionately shook her finger in Rexroth's face: "That will teach you to argue with my husband!"[51] Hill left the meeting having generated some interest in his project, even from Rexroth, who ultimately would read his autobiography over KPFA's airwaves.

Through encounters like this, Hill gathered a small circle of activists willing to devote time and energy to his project. Most were former COs with some broadcasting experience or ties to the local co-op movement. Without question, Eleanor McKinney, witness to his Libertarian Circle presentation, counted as his best find during this period. McKinney worked for NBC radio and had just finished coordinating the network's coverage of the 1945 United Nations conference in San Francisco. Creative and ambitious, she shared Hill's daring spirit and would prove his staunchest ally throughout the Pacifica Foundation's first difficult decade.[52]

In a letter to Finch, now living in New Rochelle, Long Island, Hill revealed the extent to which his thinking mirrored the surrounding culture. To be effective, Hill said, the pacifist movement needed to keep several points in mind. First, "the need is for a general coordination of many activities, including witnessing but tying together especially affirmative and creative activities." Hill saw culture not as an end unto itself but as a means to communication and ultimately social change. Like the editors of *Illiterati,* Hill distrusted "tradition as a standard and eclecticism as a technique." Hill then reiterated what he saw as the crucial principle of organizing, that any undertaking must "begin on the basis of personal relationships with a small group acting in mutual confidence."[53] For Hill, political work had to be personally satisfying. This sense of community, profoundly antithetical to the approaching Cold War suburban experience, represented the central tenet of Hill's pacifism. It also represented a crucial aspect of the Bay Area's political culture. From the days of the utopian communities of

Altruria and Kaweah through the general strike of 1934 and the co-op movement, San Franciscans had always found their sense of self through community rather than isolation.

It was in this context that on the evening of October 7, 1946, Lewis Hill and four former COs met for dinner at Breen's Cafe, a hangout for employees of a local AM station, KYA, where Hill sometimes worked as a news announcer.[54] These five people had already declared themselves the incorporators of the Pacifica Foundation in early August. Now they elected Hill chairman and appointed several other officers. Having made a commitment to go forward with their proposed radio station, they ate their meal and spoke of the many tasks before them.[55]

II

DIALOGUE

While we live, we cannot escape difference. Rapid communication, the products of invention, the heterogeneity of experience, all force us to deal with those who differ from us."

—VERA HOPKINS,
"Tolerance"

3)) Utopia in Richmond

The engineer and I will be in Washington in two weeks. I'll write from there. And now let us all kneel.

—Lewis Hill,
writing to a friend (1947)

One night after first meeting Lewis Hill, Eleanor McKinney had a "vision dream," as she later described it. It was early 1947. McKinney had spent the evening wondering whether to get involved with Hill's radio project. Suddenly, the journalist aroused from a deep sleep, aware that she still lingered in a half-dream state. Before her appeared not one but three dreams unfolding simultaneously, each as if hovering on a mountain range. Astonished, McKinney awoke in a mild shock, but the stories in her dream stayed with her like a trio of poltergeists. Now, however, they appeared on a linear path, one behind the other. Fully awake, McKinney considered what her vision meant. Time, she decided, like other spatial arrangements, represented a subjective rather than an objective reality. McKinney now saw this subjectivity as a barrier to greater understanding. "You just know the living reality that our consciousness is truly capable of knowing all that is, simultaneously," she explained, "but that as a human being we have to walk through our bodies from the past to the future."[1] People needed institutions that helped them transcend such limitations, such impediments to true communication, she concluded. McKinney literally followed her dreams. This one told her to join the Pacifica Foundation.

Born a year after the conclusion of the First World War, Eleanor Mahon grew up as the daughter of a Tennessee Presbyterian minister. Her father taught her Latin, and she spent much of her time reading the novels of Louisa May Alcott. A cache of pacifist literature also made a strong impression on her. "So at about the age of thirteen or so I began to have a feeling, a poetic sense that I had a purpose and it had to do with educating and with being against war," she later recalled, "with trying to prevent it."[2] At nineteen she eloped with a man named John McKinney, with whom she moved to San Francisco and then divorced.[3] Seeking work, McKinney found that, like so many other cities during the war, San Francisco was bereft of employable men. She applied for a position at the local NBC affiliate. The editor who interviewed her recognized the depth of her knowledge and hired her almost at once. To McKinney's astonishment, she received not an entry-level position but the task of directing a weekly celebrity interview show. "In one fell swoop I'd skipped about twenty years of hierarchy and got this wonderful job."[4] McKinney went on to coordinate NBC coverage of the San Francisco United Nations conference in 1945. She and her new husband, Richard Moore, were regulars at the Black Cat café. Remembered by Roy Finch as a sort of "pre-1960s flower child," McKinney began to study various forms of psychology and mysticism, including Jung and the mythologist G. I. Gurdjieff.[5]

Like other early participants in Pacifica, Eleanor McKinney Hill had utterly utopian expectations for the radio station. She saw the project as nothing less than a way to transform humanity. "As you know the [Pacifica] group is animated by a splendid desire to save the world, . . . "Hill wrote only half-jokingly to a friend in 1947. "I personally begin to feel as though I were on my tenth crusade (which as a matter of fact, by count, is somewhat accurate)."[6] But in the process of planning this world-transforming radio outlet, the creators of listener-sponsored broadcasting had to convince an organization that had little interest in pacifism in the legitimacy of their project. Affiliated with the Department of Commerce, the Federal Communications Commission (FCC) held undisputed legal sway over the airwaves. Lewis Hill faced a formidable challenge. He had to outline a plan for both a pacifist/anarchist radio station and an FCC-approvable radio station. He had to write promotional literature for his hypothetical signal that appealed both to a Washington bureaucracy and to the Bay Area pacifist community.

Hill possessed the skills to write an effective proposal, but it would take time and effort. From 1946 to 1949, Hill wrote five lengthy fundraising "prospectuses" aimed at both the government and potential donors.[7] Having spent a year in Washington speaking up for obstinate men who had refused to fight the "good war," Hill probably found this process somewhat less daunting, but the task before him still required considerable patience.

He knew that on paper he would have to create a pacifist and a liberal radio station at the same time; he would have to emphasize pacifist ideas and dialogue as the path to peace, but also fairness and individual rights.

With time, however, these differences became blurred. Hill's need to comply with the requirements of the corporate/liberal state moved him to deemphasize the foundation's role as a source of direct pacifist advocacy, not to mention a hotbed of former COs. Thus, even before KPFA actually went on the air on April 15, 1949, the foundation's mission had become publicly ambiguous.

The 1946 Prospectus

Lewis Hill wrote the first prospectus for Pacifica in July of 1946 in his apartment on Schraeder Street. Later that year he mimeographed copies of a slightly altered second version, which he gave to Pacifica fundraiser Denny Wilcher, who traveled around the country with them.[8] Hill began by elaborating on something he had said earlier: that advocates of nonviolence had to reach beyond the pacifist inner circle. War resisters, "especially since 1939—have been made to feel their severe impotence in the surge of public affairs outside their subscription and mailing lists." Pacifists needed to move beyond intellectual appeals or "ivory-towerism," as the prospectus put it, which had done little to alter public opinion. "Average beliefs have their form and interpretation in matters close to home, in the events of the neighborhood and city," he wrote. "In the average man, on whom war prevention depends, the sense of right action is not a sense of large philosophical orientation, but one of a familiar and satisfying adjustment to the people and institutions in his immediate environment." The task for pacifists, therefore, was to speak of peace not only through lofty principles but also through constant reference to "familiar things," indeed, to become familiar to the community by serving it as a radio station. "Pacifica Foundation," Hill wrote in a single-sentence paragraph, "has been organized to begin this job."[9]

Pacifists somehow had to link their ideals to the world of daily life. That world, often only dimly perceived by the full-time radical, consisted of the great majority of people who did not live for politics and could not be reached by those who lived for nothing else. "It matters whether the man who writes, or works in the shipyard, is a pacifist," Hill wrote to Roy Finch several years later, "but as to the man who is first, last and only a pacifist—it doesn't matter at all that he is a pacifist."[10]

The prospectus went on to print in full what would become the most important single document in the organization's history: article II of the Pacifica charter, which outlined the five purposes of the foundation. The most important of these purposes, stated in section (c), committed Pacifica to what could be called the principle of pacifist dialogue: the idea that peace emerged not out of polemics but out of the process of diverse groups of people communicating with each other. The Pacifica Foundation promised to "engage in any activity that shall contribute a lasting understanding between nations and between individuals of all nations, races, creeds and colors; to gather and disseminate information on the causes of conflict between any and all of such groups; and through any and all means available to this society, to promote the study of political and economic problems, and the causes of religious, philosophical and racial antagonisms."[11]

To Pacifica's founders, a lasting "understanding" between nations, races, or individuals did not mean that the parties involved had arrived at an objective truth but simply that through the exchange of language they had come to know each other better—as "humans," rather than through some other ideological category, such as race, nationality, or class. "We really believed in the power of the word as the source of identity in human beings," Richard Moore later explained.[12] This knowledge, the first Pacificans hoped, would lead to the peaceful resolution of conflict.

"The other side of the word 'understanding' is nonviolence, that you can solve all human conflict if you relate, if you communicate," recalled Eleanor McKinney. "If you do that in small communities and the communities grow and grow, it can apply to nations."[13] Understanding did not so much represent a quest for knowledge as a human practice that both led to peace and was itself peaceable. In 1946, the first Pacificans' faith in communication could not be shaken. Richard Moore remembered a skeptic asking Hill what he would do if Nazis broke into his house and pointed a gun at him. "I'd try and talk," Hill replied.[14]

The 1946 prospectus then described how pacifist dialogue would play itself out in the city Lewis Hill hoped would become his radio station's host. The fundraising document proposed the construction of a thousand-watt AM radio station in Richmond, an "East Bay" city about five miles north of Berkeley. Since 1941, Richmond had been transformed, in the words of one historian, from a "dull industrial suburb" to a classic war boomtown. Home to an oil refinery and a Ford plant before the conflict, after the bombing of Pearl Harbor it drew thousands of Mexican Americans, African Americans, and Oklahoma migrants to the town's hastily assembled Kaiser Shipyards. Twenty-four thousand people lived in Richmond in 1941; nearly five times that many lived there three years later.[15]

The creation of the radio station represented an opportunity, Hill argued, to show working-class people, many of them veterans, how pacifism worked in action. The prospectus noted that a stark social division existed in Richmond between the eighty-five thousand recently settled war workers and the "old guard," who frequently reacted with hostility to new civic projects. The document promised that the Pacifica Foundation would sponsor many forums and "gripe sessions" at which Richmond residents could discuss the drastic changes taking place in their city, as well as the resultant racial tensions. "Roundtable" discussions would be devoted to peaceful ways to reintegrate returning veterans of many races into Richmond society. "In addition to Negro and Mexican groups," Hill wrote, "the Japanese-American population returned from internment camps represents an outstanding context for penetrating discussion of human relations."[16]

Hill predicted that industrial growth in Richmond would lead to bitter factional and ideological fights among unions. These disputes would center on rivalries between leaders of the Congress of Industrial Organizations (CIO), whose "broader social philosophy" advocated militant, industrial unionism, and the older generation of more conservative trade unionists. The station would promote principles of nonviolence among workers, the prospectus promised: "Its forums will throw constant attention upon the ethical aspects of the labor movement in its origin, the fellowship of workers, and the disastrous effects of war on labor's independence. The widely recognized urgency for introduction of non-violent techniques and philosophy into the labor movement will have here a fundamental testing ground."[17]

After his years with the NCCO, Hill believed that only pacifist institutions intimately connected to a community could effectively proselytize nonviolence. He sought ways to preach pacifism not through a "crummy propaganda sheet," as he once disdainfully put it, but through a source an audience would come to see as part of their daily lives and culture. Thus, the prospectus also outlined how the radio station would reach the community culturally by sponsoring study groups and drama-writing workshops as well as providing public space for musicians.[18] The station would also recruit its audience through the airing of folk and popular music. Hill noted that much of Richmond's population had recently arrived from the Southwest. Most radio stations in the area, he argued, exploited the musical tastes of these groups by providing a few professional bands, "playing a degenerate juke-box hoe-down."[19] Pacifica's radio station, seeking to maintain the "loyalty of the great majority who prefer dance records," would also play popular music but would offer a much more expansive range of choices—including recordings of indigenous folk music and live sessions from the region's many folk music festivals. Seeking to make "a concerted bid for the audience of the migrant labor group," Pacifica radio would also broadcast Saturday-night folk dances from the Richmond civic auditorium.[20]

True to the strategy Hill had developed just after the war, the station he envisioned would promote pacifism in two ways. First, through dialogue, it would demonstrate the viability of peace in practice. Second, it would introduce listeners to a challenging ideology in the context of familiar and pleasurable sounds. Like the editors of *Illiterati*, who refused to understand culture as an end unto itself, the first Pacificans saw music, poetry, and drama as the facilitator of "a much more fertile ground for the ideas that we all had about war and peace."[21] Dialogue and pacifism in context—these two approaches represented the heart of Lewis Hill's strategy of war resistance. "When war resistance appears in the same context as another phase of the same authenticity, it is not only met with respect—it goes deep."[22] Hill also knew, however, that he had to present arguments for his radio station that would meet with Federal Communications Commission approval, including how the station would meet government licensing requirements. That meant that he had to come to terms with the Mayflower decision.

The Mayflower Decision

By 1941, the Roosevelt administration had appointed all of the FCC's commissioners. They watched nervously as conservative businessmen bought radio stations as platforms for their virulent anti-New Deal views. Aware of the limited powers Congress had given the FCC, the commissioners nonetheless kept careful track of industrialists such as George A. Richards of WJR, Detroit, mentor to demagogic "radio priest" Father Charles Coughlin.

That year, the commissioners saw their chance to wield influence. A proposed new radio network in Boston, called the Mayflower Broadcasting Company, had challenged WAAB's license in that city. Mayflower charged that the station's owner, a conservative magnate named John Shepard III, took openly biased positions on controversial questions and broadcast political endorsements without giving equal air time to opposing points of view.[23] After receiving assurances from Shepard that he would avoid further editorializing, the commission issued a policy statement: the right of the individual listener to hear more than one point of view over the air remained superior to the right of individual broadcasters to "support the candidates of his friends" or to regularly broadcast his favorite opinions. The individual broadcaster could not play the role of "advocate" over a public utility like the airwaves. "Freedom of speech on the radio must be broad enough to provide full and equal opportunity for the presentation to the public of all sides of public issues," declared the commission. "The public interest—not the private—is paramount."[24]

To gain FCC approval, Hill would have to demonstrate how the Pacifica Foundation intended to further the commission's policy of fairness. He did not feel entirely comfortable with this task, however, and in the 1946 prospectus tried to avoid the matter. Hill knew that although his radio station would present many points of view, it would also advocate both pacifism and war resistance. In light of the Mayflower decision, how was he to justify this?

After summarizing the Mayflower decision in the July 1946 prospectus, Hill noted that in the last year the commission had given broadcasting licenses to unions, cooperatives, "and other primarily ideological groups whose clear-cut purpose [was] to express a point of view." He then concluded that in granting licenses to these groups, "no formal reversal of the Mayflower Decision has been announced, but the practice of the Commission has in effect discontinued its operation." In the revised November prospectus, this sentence was changed to "the Commission in this respect seems unquestionably to have modified its operation. . . . Considering these facts, the Foundation anticipates no difficulties involving cancellation of its license to broadcast as its program of direct commentary and analysis develops."[25]

But, in truth, Hill anticipated plenty of difficulties and so sent a copy of the prospectus to Jerome Spingarn, a pacifist scholar and advocate of radio reform. Spingarn served as adviser to Senator Glen Taylor of Idaho, who would soon fill the vice-presidential slot with Henry Wallace in his 1948 bid for the presidency.[26] Spingarn's first act as an adviser was to sternly warn Hill that he had been mistaken in suggesting that the FCC planned to scuttle the Mayflower decision. "I would therefore suggest that you withhold from circulation further copies of the prospectus. They might be used to prove that you do not intend to give full and fair opportunity to all sides in public discussions."[27]

Hill honestly didn't know how to handle this problem and decided to lay out his ideological dilemma in the next version of the prospectus, written in January 1947. He now admitted that even if the FCC had given some radio licenses to blatantly biased groups, the commission's primary concern was still "with fair and objective discussion of controversial matters, as opposed to the censorship of all but one opinion over a single radio channel." But even the pursuit of dialogue could have an ideological agenda, Hill observed. What if the proposed radio station offered its own analysis of some labor dispute and then invited listeners who disagreed to join a roundtable discussion of the conflict? Couldn't the station be accused of violating the Mayflower decision anyway, not only because it offered its own analysis of the dispute but because it advocated dialogue regarding the matter? "It would appear that the sponsorship of any general concept of human relations," he wrote, "or even of such a concept as democracy itself, would be forbidden to a licensee by the Mayflower Decision."[28] Where did the advocacy of peaceful resolution of conflict end and the search for "balance" and "fairness" begin? Here lay the borderland between pacifism and liberalism.

Hill confided that he expected further discussion with the FCC before the matter could be settled entirely. Lewis Hill the pacifist knew that advocacy of dialogue represented not only a quest for objective truth but a moral stance. You believed in something specific on the moral scale if you believed in getting people to talk and reason with each other, if you wanted to get to the root causes of violence. In the 1947 prospectus, however, Hill the liberal also assured possible backers that he understood the problem in the FCC's terms. "The whole object of the Foundation's educational program in the field of public affairs and social problems is to study these matters, and to help the public to study them with exactly that freedom from exclusiveness and partisanship which the FCC lays down as a condition for use of radio channels."[29] The dilemma momentarily tabled, Hill went on to explain how the proposed station would support itself, particularly how it would deal with commercials and the problem of "commercialism."

The Promise of Radio

The 1946 prospectus opened by explaining how the Pacifica Foundation would promote dialogue in behalf of peace. A Pacifica pamphlet produced in 1947 entitled *The Promise of Radio* introduced the mission of the proposed station in very different terms: "If you are satisfied with today's radio broadcasting, this booklet is not for you. Chances are, however, that you are among that growing number of Americans who are becoming increasingly critical of the caliber of radio advertising and the quality of programs which are occasionally inserted between the commercials." The brochure also suggested that the reader might be part of a minority group "whose views are seldom, if ever, aired." Finally, the opening statement finished off the list of malcontents with the kind of person the 1946 prospectus began with, someone actively seeking "a pacific world in our time." These were the kind of people who would "want to read this outline carefully."[30]

The Promise of Radio set forth the priorities listed in the 1946 prospectus in reverse. The prospectus appealed to a pacifist audience first and to a liberal audience second. Written after Hill's exchange with Jerome Spingarn, *The Promise* foreground fairness and public service, in opposition to exclusiveness and commercialism, as the primary goal of Pacifica. It emphasized the idea of pacifist dialogue only secondarily. The piece specifically deemphasized the presence of pacifists in the foundation. So zealous was Hill to obscure his own pacifist history that he modified his brief vita at the end of the brochure. *Promise* listed him as "Director, Washington office, American Civil Liberties Union." This description might have prompted a reader to believe that Hill was the director of the Washington office of the ACLU. Rather, he ran the group's office in Washington for conscientious objectors and nothing else. Chances are Hill phrased his job title in this ambiguous way not to exaggerate his influence within the ACLU but to obscure the fact that he had filed as a CO during the war. In fact, *The Promise of Radio* identified no member of the foundation as a former CO or CPS camp resident. The personnel list mentioned one Pacifican as a former "designer and builder of short-wave transmitters, National Park Service."[31] How he became involved with the park system was not explained.

Hill exhibited equal selectivity in his correspondence describing the foundation's goals to prospective fundraisers. "Pacifica Foundation was formed last year by a group of c.o.'s with a compelling desire to find new educational outlets for the peace movement," he told one potential supporter.[32] To a U.S. senator, he put it differently: "The group which has come together to form Pacifica Foundation are mainly professional radio people."[33] In fact, the early staff fit both these descriptions. Hill knew that his project had potential support not only from pacifists but also from liberals who had long been critical of commercial broadcasting and looked to the FCC for regulatory relief.

To appreciate the politics of these early critics of mass media requires a basic understanding of radio's first years.

"Drunk and Disorderly"

From the 1920s onward, many social reformers saw radio as a potential cure for the deteriorating politics and culture they saw around them. Writing in 1924 for *Century Magazine,* Bruce Bliven predicted that radio would enable the citizenry to make calmer political decisions by producing a new kind of politician — one who gave speeches "possessed of a quiet, logical persuasiveness."[34] By the early 1930s, this seemed like a pipe dream. Somehow the promising new medium had become host to cheap comedy, big-band crooners, and banal thirty-second advertising spots. Even early radio pioneers expressed disgust. In 1931, Lee DeForest, who had earned the name "Father of Broadcasting" after inventing the radio receiver, publicly declared his desire to disown the title. "I'm disgusted and ashamed of my pet child," he said, calling commercial broadcasting "a national disgrace."[35]

By 1934, despite its best efforts, the radio reform movement could boast few victories. In the early 1930s, a coalition of educators, clergy, and journalists called for the government to reserve a large percentage of bandwidth space for public broadcasting. To their minds, 1930s radio had been destroyed by an unholy alliance of corporations and the masses — easily seduced by the most crass commercial product. After ten years of domination by corporations, the airwaves had become "drunk and disorderly," as advertising copywriter James Rorty declared. Radio had been taken over by an oligopoly. "That means," Rorty wrote, "not merely that time-on-the-air cannot be had, except from relatively insignificant independent stations, for criticisms and attacks upon the policies and performances of these corporations, but that the *status quo* of business and finance in general is protected from such attacks." Rorty argued that under the privatized "free-speech" system, created in the 1920s, censorship abounded on the airwaves. Commercial broadcasting stations permitted no criticism of a sponsor's product, the subject of birth control had been completely banned, and little if any sympathetic discussion about unionism was tolerated.[36]

But when it came time for the reform movement to compel the system to change, Rorty and his associates could threaten little more than that a boycott by the better sort of listener. "Advertisers consistently offend large sections of [radio] audiences — the most civilized sections — people who are properly and sensibly cynical, not merely about radio advertising but about advertising in general, so cynical are they that their comment is not to write a protesting letter to the broadcasting station but to tune out the station and in many cases to secede from the Great Radio Audience."[37]

Scattered, elitist, and politically isolated, the broadcast reform movement accomplished little. In 1934, as Congress deliberated the law that would create the Federal Communications Commission, several reformers convinced Senator Robert Wagner of New York and Representative Henry Hatfield of West Virginia to add a rider that would reserve 25 percent of all radio channels for nonprofit broadcasters. The effort was hopelessly outclassed by the network broadcasting lobby, as was an attempt to establish federally subsidized radio stations managed by civic leaders. Big radio had completely consolidated its hold on the airwaves, convincing the public that network advertising reflected the "American" system of doing business.[38]

The American system went into full gear during the Second World War. President Roosevelt responded to public pressure by slapping corporations with a 90 percent surtax on war profits, turning America's economic royalists to their accountants in despair. The bookkeepers gave excellent counsel: take the surplus profit, spend it on advertising, and deduct the price tag as a capital expense. Shortly after the war, the FCC initiated research that proved all too true a sarcastic comment in *The Promise of Radio* about radio programs being breaks between commercials. FCC agents documented that a station in San Antonio, Texas, ran almost seventeen commercials an hour during a sample week—one every three and a half minutes. And a station in Toledo, Ohio, ran nothing but commercials during the 6 P.M. dinner hour. Even worse, the commission found that thousands of stations routinely refused to broadcast network-produced public affairs shows available to them for free.[39] As public outrage over these developments reached another high point, the FCC knew it had to issue an even stronger statement than its Mayflower ruling.

In 1943, the Roosevelt administration appointed Clifford C. Durr to the FCC. The brother-in-law of Supreme Court justice Hugo Black, during the McCarthy era Durr would find himself on a public list of alleged communist sympathizers. In 1946, however, he enjoyed enough influence to persuade the commission to issue the so-called Blue Book report on fairness in broadcasting. Produced with the assistance of future Pacifica Foundation attorney Harry Plotkin, *Public Service Responsibility of Broadcast Licensees* decried the predominance of advertising on the airwaves and called for more balanced public affairs programming. FCC officials called it the Blue Book because, at Plotkin's wise suggestion, it had been printed with a blue cover—red being the only alternative at the government printing office.[40] The Blue Book once again called on broadcasters to deal evenhandedly with matters of public controversy. "Probably no other type of problem in the entire broadcasting industry is as important or requires of the broadcaster a greater sense of objectivity, responsibility and fair play," the FCC declared two months before Hill came out with his first prospectus. "Accordingly, the carrying of such programs in reasonable sufficiency and during good listening hours is a factor to be considered in any finding of public interest."[41]

The FCC's response to the postwar crisis of the airwaves seemed fully in line with the general approach of the New Deal era. Congress and the FCC refused to sanction what would have in effect been a government-administered public-access zone on the airwaves. Instead, the commission offered guidelines to the broadcasting industry that it enforced only in the most extreme cases. As historian Alan Dawley argues, the New Deal avoided policies that emphasized the genuine redistribution of resources. Rather, its programs offered reforms without tampering with the idea of "free enterprise." The Social Security Act, to cite only one example, did not tax the wealthy to aid working-class retirees but, instead, administered an insurance program for individuals. Thus, what frequently began as movement-based approaches wound up as policies designed to save capitalism from its own worst impulses. The U.S. government could have, like England, responded with a state-chartered radio system. Instead, it published the Blue Book. "You can pretty much do what you want," the document said, in effect, "just avoid an overemphasis on advertisements and give the people you criticize on your station a chance to talk back." This policy, which conservatives damned as Bolshevism, actually substituted for the more far-reaching measures that radio reformers had proposed. Nonetheless, the Blue Book spoke to the sentiments of a frustrated constituency who regarded themselves as enlightened radio listeners, seeking an alternative to crass commercialism.

From the start, Hill and his friends would have liked to be able to tell potential backers that their proposed radio station would operate without commercials and rely entirely on listener subscriptions. Unfortunately, a practical question kept coming up. Where was the station to derive steady income until it had a faithful audience? Thus, on January 31, 1947, Hill wrote a memorandum accepting the prospect of advertisements on KPFA, with the assumption that ads would gradually be eliminated within five years.[42] "The Foundation has adopted an advertising code which will, it believes, eliminate the most objectionable features of today's radio advertising," *The Promise of Radio* said, "—excessive commercialism and bad taste." No more than one-third of the air time of the station would ever be available for sponsorship. No commercials would be allowed during news broadcasts. No advertising would be accepted that "makes irritative or excessively repetitious use of names, slogans or catch-phrases, singing, music, or sound effects." In other words, neither the first prospectus nor *The Promise* said anything about the station being noncommercial. "Primarily," *The Promise* concluded, "the Foundation represents a group of persons who desire to make use of first-rate talent through radio and other media for the purpose of furthering understanding among men."[43]

In the first two years of the Pacifica Foundation, Lewis Hill directed his fundraising appeals to both pacifists and liberals. Their concerns sometimes diverged and sometimes overlapped, but the first Pacificans viewed them differently. The pacifist community sought a radio station that would carry pacifist ideas beyond the hallowed inner circle of activists and intellectuals to the "average" person, on whom peace depended. The liberal community sought radio that might reform an increasingly commercialized mass culture. Both groups saw dialogue on the airwaves as crucial, but for different reasons. The pacifist saw dialogue as the way to achieve a "pacific world"—as a way to both advocate and demonstrate nonviolence. The liberal envisioned dialogue in more rational terms: as a practice that promoted fairness, balance, and equal opportunity. The pacifist wanted to reach out to the average person. The liberal often saw the average person as an impediment to enlightened broadcasting. Hill had stood at this ideological crossroads once before when he fought bitterly against "liberals" who wanted to turn CPS strikes into struggles for better conditions at the camps, rather than a campaign to eliminate military conscription itself. During the war he had drawn a clear political line; now, needing the approval of the government and wanting to reach out beyond the pacifist in-crowd, Hill cautiously worked between the lines.

The extent to which Hill and his colleagues appreciated the precarious nature of their ideological balancing act surfaced in an internal memorandum circulated just before their fledgling radio station began operation. Probably written by Hill, it summarized the foundation's fundraising history thus far. The memo characterized the true nature of the Pacifica project as "an attempt to carry a radical war resistance program into a mass medium," making possible "a more and more intense cultivation of the interests of common people in resisting war." The principals behind the effort remained all too aware, however, that funds for a program represented in this way would prove very limited. Using language that gained them access to a wider range of resources—largely among "the more enlightened and disillusioned liberals"—they made their appeal "based on the widely appreciated need for better radio programming." The organization had thus created a "double personality," the memorandum confessed: "In its total representation to the government and our professional assistants, the project has appeared as a purely 'liberal' undertaking within the code of governmental liberalism." This bifurcated strategy worried the founders of Pacifica, the circular acknowledged. The document called on the organization's main participants to keep in mind the tension between "temporizing in order to gain confidence" and the "ideological purity, so much demanded of us if the project is actually to escape the ordinary end of causes when they are institutionalized."[44]

As the Pacifica Foundation applied to the FCC to establish an AM station in Richmond, its organizers knew that they enjoyed only partial control of the process necessary to accomplish even their short-range objectives. In early March 1947, Lewis Hill nervously readied himself to present a formal case for licensing before the commission. By then, the foundation had collected nearly $8,000 in donations.[45] "I doubt if there was ever a thousand dollars before that could be described as an act of faith," he wrote to a friend who had just sent the foundation a check for that sum. "The engineer and I will be in Washington probably in two weeks. I'll write from there. And now let us all kneel."[46]

4)) The Two Percent Solution

It was agreed that it will be necessary at first to aim at a smaller more exclusive audience than originally envisioned.

—Pacifica Foundation Radio Committee minutes, March 5, 1948

In the second week of March 1947, Lewis Hill presented the Pacifica Foundation's case to the FCC in Washington.[1] He then returned to San Francisco for a series of follow-up hearings with the commission. That the foundation had an active audience with the FCC greatly strengthened its credibility with potential funders. By the close of the San Francisco hearings, on April 2, the organization's assets had multiplied fourfold, to nearly $32,000.[2] Denny Wilcher busied himself "digging for treasure in the East," in Hill's words, while Eleanor McKinney worked the San Francisco elite.[3] One day she lunched with the wife of a local millionaire, who shortly afterward sent Pacifica a contribution. Included in the donation was a note informing McKinney that the contributor had asked the Federal Bureau of Investigation to check the journalist's background.[4]

Pacifica's fundraisers were often equally suspicious of potential donors, particularly "progressives" associated with Henry Wallace, whose 1948 presidential campaign received considerable aid from the Communist Party. The fundraisers also kept their distance from prominent liberals, such as Carey McWilliams, the highly regarded editor of *The Nation* and a Wallace supporter. "General decision was to hold off on seeing Carey McWilliams until all possible funds have been drawn from traditional sources," read the minutes of an early meeting.[5] "Traditional sources" sometimes meant prosperous Quakers but more often "well-to-do liberal types," as Hill described them to a friend. Most of these liberals had invested in victory bonds during the war, Hill observed, and, "perhaps a little conscience stricken," were now eager to support other causes again.[6]

The steady stream of good news came to a halt in June, when the FCC formally denied the Pacifica Foundation an AM license at its requested frequency. The commission claimed that the foundation's desired signal would come 30 kilocycles too close to both NBC- and CBS-owned stations broadcasting in the Bay Area.[7] "The rule," Hill bitterly explained to a friend, "which will protect the big established metropolitan interests by denying, presumably, applications like ours."[8] Indeed, the networks had lobbied heavily against licensing the Pacifica signal.[9]

After the bad news, members of Pacifica's radio committee hired a high-priced technical consultant to see if a different signal could be found, but this inquiry came to naught.[10] AM network radio had saturated the San Francisco Bay Area, shutting Pacifica out of the market. Members of the foundation decided to suspend further fundraising while pondering their next move. "If you'll forgive the cliché," Hill wrote, "we're down but not out."[11]

For the foundation to continue attracting support, it would have to obtain an operating license from the FCC. The only other option was to apply for an FM license. But, as everyone connected with the foundation also knew, taking the FM route would present many problems. FM broadcasting had been in existence for almost a dozen years, but its future remained in doubt. The last thing Hill wanted was to marginalize his project, yet his options were few.

The need to build an FM station compelled the Pacifica Foundation to move even farther from the goals outlined in its original prospectus and to conceptualize its audience in more elite terms. Like other radio reformers, Hill knew the story of FM radio all too well, the tale of a promising technology held hostage by corporate subterfuge.

Radio's Second Chance

On a November night in 1935, a group of skeptical scientists gathered in mid-Manhattan to hear Edwin Howard Armstrong of Columbia University outline the possibilities for a new kind of broadcasting called "frequency modulation." Affectionately referred to as "The Major" after his stint in the First World War, Armstrong had already distinguished himself as a pioneer in the development of radio. Having given his talk, Armstrong signaled to his assistant. The sound of a radio receiver filled the air, searching for the signal of Armstrong's own station, W2AG. When the frequency finally came in, the inventor's audience sat in hushed amazement. Never before had they heard anything like this on the radio.[12]

W2AG broadcast perfectly clear silence. It was, as one historian wrote, "a dead, unearthly silence, as if the whole apparatus had been abruptly turned off."[13] The Major's assembly knew that they sat just above Times Square, one of the noisiest places in the world. Three subway lines ran megavolt-powered trains beneath their feet.[14] A radio signal in the area carried by the amplitude modulation, or AM system, would be thick with the *bête noir* of the broadcaster: static. Anything from a lightning bolt to a neighbor's cranky refrigerator could produce the infuriating crackle that reduced a symphonic transmission to inaudible hash.[15] Yet Armstrong's station had unprecedented clarity, broadcasting the pouring of a glass of water and the deep reverberation of an Oriental gong.[16]

Some of the technicians in Armstrong's audience became true believers that night, but others knew that it would take a fortune to develop a commercially viable FM technology competitive with the already entrenched AM system. The Major understood this as well, and so the next day he provided a personal demonstration of FM for his old associate, David Sarnoff of the Radio Corporation of America (RCA). While Armstrong was developing his innovations in radio technology, this Russian émigré had worked his way to the top of RCA, turning it into the world's most powerful radio manufacturing company.[17] Sarnoff heard Armstrong's case and appeared cordial. But if the latter saw in Sarnoff the financial champion FM needed, Armstrong was strongly mistaken. Sarnoff thought like an entrepreneur, not a scientist; certainly FM would improve the quality of the airwaves, but would it enhance RCA's profit margin to spend millions of dollars to make its entire product line compatible for FM, a technology for which RCA owned no patents?[18] Besides, Sarnoff had his sights set on what he saw as a far more powerful broadcasting innovation. By 1935, RCA engineers had already designed the first commercially viable machines that received visual images over the airwaves. Sarnoff viewed FM broadcasting as a threat to television, using up frequency signals that RCA engineers hoped to reserve for future TV stations.[19]

Armstrong and other promoters of FM realized only gradually what was happening, or, more accurately, not happening. While amateur and small commercial FM stations took to the airwaves, big radio made no attempt to promote FM broadcasting.

The final outrage was played out at an infamous series of FCC hearings at the American Museum of Natural History in New York City. As the Allies headed for Berlin in 1945, many critics of commercial broadcasting arrived at the museum dreaming of a parallel broadcasting universe true to their vision of superior culture. Surely, these reformers imagined, the possibilities inherent in FM could no longer be denied. But when the presidents of NBC and CBS arrived, they brought with them engineering consultant Kenneth Alva Norton, who announced that he had made a remarkable discovery. Sunspots, Dr. Norton explained, seriously distorted FM signals at the low range of the broadcasting spectrum. The only solution was to reallocate FM to the ultrahigh portions of the wavelength scale, the region from 88 to 108 million cycles per second (megacycles), where FM stations broadcast to this day. Armstrong and his colleagues were aghast. This would require all extant FM stations to retool their equipment to new frequencies, a process that would take years and cost millions of dollars.[20]

Not only did the FCC accede to this drastic adjustment, but it suddenly developed a mania for equality among FM stations. Following the recommendations of a CBS executive, the commissioners restricted to a modest 1,200 watts the amount of broadcast power any FM post could command. CBS argued that such a plan would create a level playing field for FM stations. In fact, as historian Tom Lewis notes, the ruling pauperized them, reducing FM to a state of commercial nonviability.[21]

Armstrong and his allies strongly suspected that the sunspot theory served an unspoken agenda: RCA wanted FM out of the lower radio spectrum so it would not interfere with television receivers. Their suspicions of government collusion were confirmed in 1946, when Charles Denny, head of the FCC, took a position as vice president and general counsel of NBC. A year later Kenneth Norton publicly admitted that his sunspot theory was wrong. Thus concluded, in the words of one scholar, the beginning of FM's "economic, or, perhaps more correctly, 'uneconomic,' history."[22]

Meanwhile, on the opposite coast, Lewis Hill, still smarting from the denial of his AM signal, grimly pondered the museum debacle. "Its closest analogue in recent years is the cynical, industry-sponsored decision on the FM spectrum," Hill wrote to a friend. "Hang them all by their lower inlays, anyhow."[23]

Ironically, the museum hearings only steeled the determination of FM advocates. Charles A. Siepmann, a former employee of the British Broadcasting Company and a consultant for the FCC, stood prominently among their ranks. Siepmann's book, *Radio's Second Chance*, summarized the hopes of post–World War II radio reformers. Like early broadcasting critics such as James Rorty, Siepmann decried corporate-controlled radio stations for refusing to provide high-quality local programming and relying on advertising. He saw hope for the future in FM. First, FM had inherent competitive edge because of its superior sound. Second, five thousand additional radio stations could appear nationally on the FM dial. "It is as if a new continent had been discovered," he wrote, "with room for all and opportunity for each." Finally, Siepmann urged readers to watch out for "the little man with the large view," the most likely candidate to develop FM's possibilities. "A number of nonprofit organizations," he predicted, "not out for money but for legitimate publicity, may be able to afford the cost of constructing and operating stations catering for their particular clientele."[24]

After reading *Radio's Second Chance*, Hill understandably saw himself in Siepmann's vision. He dispatched Roy Finch and Wallace Hamilton in New York to contact the author, then wrote to Siepmann himself, inviting him to serve on the foundation's advisory council. Normally cautious in his solicitations, Hill took an unusually confident tone: "When you have had time to decide upon this matter," he wrote, "and to satisfy yourself concerning the Foundation's group and its objectives, there are a number of problems we should like to take up with you."[25] Doubtless the first among these was how to entice listeners when most people did not even own an FM receiver. Furthermore, how would Pacifica find advertisers willing to purchase airtime for the meager FM audience? If these didn't represent sufficient obstacles, there was David Sarnoff's impending new product to consider. "What worries me is only that television is bound to land with an enormous splash out here in a little while, and where will that leave FM, Class A FM, in particular?" Hill wrote to a friend in Los Angeles.[26] *Radio's Second Chance* did not provide answers to such questions. In truth, nobody in the Pacifica group knew in 1947 exactly how they would solve these problems. They only knew that, having made many promises in exchange for more than $30,000, the Pacifica Foundation needed some kind of radio license to stay afloat. Approximately two-thirds of the organization's large donations existed in "escrow" form, to be released only when the foundation received a license from the FCC. For the moment, getting an FM license would have to do.[27]

Seeking an FM license would greatly enlarge the number of channels from which the foundation could choose, but it would add a more immediate conundrum: was Richmond the appropriate place to start the station? Unlike AM radio, FM belonged to a small, affluent, and formally educated group of radio enthusiasts. The Pacifica Foundation, Hill wrote to Denny Wilcher in June 1947, must direct itself "to a mass audience," seeking "mass effects." Deprived of access to a mass radio signal, the Pacificans knew they'd have to redefine their listener base. "It was agreed that it will be necessary at first to aim at a smaller more exclusive audience than originally envisioned," the Pacifica Radio Committee resolved in a subsequent meeting.[28]

On September 16, 1947, the executive membership of the foundation authorized Hill to submit an application for a permit to construct an FM station four miles south of Richmond, in Berkeley.[29] This meant developing a new fundraising prospectus, which Hill wrote and released in May 1948. Hill frankly explained why Pacifica planned to operate from Berkeley rather than Richmond—according to the 1940 U.S. Census, Berkeley's estimated 28,210 occupied dwellings contained nearly twenty-seven thousand home radio receivers. "There can be little doubt that the city now has and will continue to have more FM sets per capita than nearly any other city in the United States," Hill concluded.[30] Although walking distance from Richmond, Berkeley was worlds apart from its blue-collar North Bay neighbor. Once again, external influences compelled the foundation to modify its mission.

Berkeley Then . . .

Later generations could not imagine Berkeley without looking through a prism created by the city's formative 1960s experiences: the Free Speech Movement and the People's Park uprising. In 1946, however, there was no "People's Republic" of Berkeley, only a conservative East Bay town of about one hundred thousand residents. An alliance between business and the administration of the university ruled the town. Robert Gordon Sproul, UC Berkeley's president, promised not to build more dormitory space for its nearly twenty-two thousand students in return for the city keeping out of the university's business.

In 1955, Berkeley elected Claude Hutchison, the grandson of slaveholders, mayor of the city. His ascendance reflected local white unease over the growing African American population employed by the local shipping industry and settling on the western edge of town. As late as 1963, after a plucky group of council members passed a fair-housing act, an enraged coalition of conservatives had the law repealed through popular referendum.[31] The university employed more Nobel laureates than any other campus in the world. But beyond the liberal veneer associated with almost any college town, Berkeley was run, in the words of one longtime KPFA subscriber, "by the downtown businessman for the downtown businessman. That was it."[32]

Both the 1946 and 1948 Pacifica Foundation prospectuses emphasized the need for pacifists to reach people on their terms. But the tone of the 1948 opening statement changed. No longer did it speak of communicating with the "average man, on whom war prevention depends." Now it spoke only of reaching the "individual" and made many references to far less average groups of people. The document noted, for example, that there were several military stations near Berkeley, housing thousands of officers, who would "constitute one of [the station's] most interesting sounding boards." The prospectus also boasted that Pacifica would broadcast to a wide variety of scholars: Stanford in Palo Alto, Mills College in Oakland, and San Francisco State College. "Of profounder import," the document continued, ". . . the KPFA audience will include not only many of the country's best artists and scientists, but specifically those scientists who have had, and continue to have, the major role in manufacturing [and] 'improving' the atom bomb." The prospectus noted that the Pacifica Foundation had already initiated discussions with members of the Northern California Association of Scientists for Atomic Education about conducting a series on nuclear weapons. "If the moral conscience of the American physicist needs stimulation," the paragraph concluded, "KPFA is in a position to offer one important stimulus."[33]

Prior assurances that the station would play music directed to a working-class audience were deleted. The 1948 prospectus stated that KPFA's musical inspiration would come primarily from the faculty and students at Berkeley, Mills College, and the San Francisco Conservatory. KPFA's director of music would be a "finished instrumentalist," knowledgeable in music history and theory. "The performance standards for this music will be the highest," promised the text. "The types of music broadcast, both live and by transcription or recording, will be concert, recital, and folk exclusively." Popular records were no longer mentioned.[34]

Like the earlier prospectus, the Berkeley document gave considerable attention to the need to influence labor unions. The 1946 version had called for programs on labor history with an emphasis on the effectiveness of nonviolent tactics. The 1948 prospectus noted with disapproval that most Bay Area broadcasters reported on labor only as "a protagonist of conflict, the antagonist of 'business.'" Workers currently had only one alternative to this kind of reporting, the text noted. "Unfortunately the only press and radio sources of consistent and comprehensive labor reporting are either controlled by the Communist Party or Stalinist in inclination." It was time for some source to add labor news to the general picture in "fair and realistic proportion."[35]

Up to this point, none of the literature produced by the first Pacificans had mentioned their historic antipathy to the CP. Now they did, albeit with some discomfort. An internal memo expressed concern with the extent to which the foundation had "compromised" itself by appealing for assistance to the anticommunist Americans for Democratic Action. Pacifica, the memo admitted, had "acquired obligations to the kind of liberals who are not at all disillusioned but are busy preparing for war with Russia, recently discovered to be the new look in 'fascism.' "[36]

Despite these misgivings, the early Pacificans probably felt more at home with their new approach to community outreach. Minutes to the foundation's 1947 spring meetings raise doubts about the extent to which their hearts were in the Richmond project. Almost a year after Hill had drafted the prospectus, another internal memo reported that the organization had done "practically nothing" to establish links with Richmond's public schools, labor unions, or civic groups. "Despite some efforts at gaining a knowledge of the inner workings of Richmond," the circular continued, "we are still novices in this field."[37] And indeed, for all the emphasis on reaching out to the "average" person, Eleanor McKinney later fondly remembered KPFA as a place for artists, poets, and intellectuals. "There was nowhere where people, as it were like ourselves, could meet, talk to each other, listen to each other's poems, talk about what we believed on all issues: nonviolence, art, literature. It was like creating a place where we could be with people like ourselves," she explained.[38]

The Richmond prospectus had called for pacifists to venture beyond their "subscription lists," but the need to target an FM rather than the broader AM audience validated a comfortable shift back to old ways. As for Hill, a few months after the first Berkeley prospectus had been circulated, he wrote that KPFA's immediate future depended entirely on marketing the station to a university audience. This strategy, he boasted to an attorney in Washington, had gotten "persons in High Places" firmly committed to working with the station. "Our forecast is based on talking turkey with campus people," Hill explained in the summer of 1948. "'Prestige accounts?' Precisely, because that is what the FM audience is made for at this moment. As the audience broadens its economic base, we can broaden with it, with caution. But our first job, and our best chance to keep the lead with the future audience, is to grab the loyalty of the present audience."[39]

Having resolved to target the campus community, the Pacifica group moved quickly to realize its ultimate goal of obtaining a FCC permit authorizing the construction of a low-power FM radio station. In January 1949, Hill, McKinney, E. John Lewis, and the other Pacificans met at the

Berkeley home of Eleanor McKinney and Richard Moore and reviewed the project's budget. After expenses, the organization had a grand total of $13,120.75 for the construction of its station. The group knew that such a sum would prove inadequate for ongoing operation of even the scaled-down station they now had in mind. They also knew that they'd have to spend most of that capital on station equipment, leaving virtually nothing for such untrivial details as their salaries.[40] But after two years of fundraising, they could no longer justify further monetary appeals without creating something to show for the money they'd already collected. Two proposals lay on the table: one to scrap the project and send checks back to most of the donors, the other to "take a leap in the dark"—as McKinney put it—to build the station and raise additional funds at the same time.[41]

Having resumed his education at Berkeley, Moore sat studying Latin in the next room. Suddenly he heard a round of applause. He poked his head through the door and asked what had happened. "We've decided to put the radio station on the air!" McKinney told him.[42] The foundation's principals had concluded that they had no alternative but to move forward. They ruled unanimously to commit themselves to the construction of a 550-watt "interim" station, capable of demonstrating what the organization stood for. After pondering call letters such as "KBAY," the group decided to stick with the signal ID that they had already been using in promotional literature. A week after that meeting, Hill found a site for KPFA: an office suite perched on the sixth floor of a University Avenue building—just a short walk from the Berkeley campus and downtown.[43] By then the group felt confident enough to issue a public statement predicting that the station would go on the air within three months.[44]

Several days later, Pacifica hired Edward Meece as its chief construction engineer. Meece had spent some of the war years at a CO camp in Kashockton, Ohio, and from there had gone to work at an acoustic research laboratory in Boston. From Boston Meece next went to Columbia University, where he took radio production courses.[45] Meece brought many talents to Pacifica, among them a knack for locating used broadcasting equipment. Soon secondhand components began to arrive from all parts of the country. In fact, in 1949, the foundation bought only two machines new from a distributor, one of them a fifty-foot mounting transmitter tower from War Surplus, which members of the staff hauled up to the roof and installed themselves.[46]

Several skilled carpenters were then hired to supervise a crew of more than thirty volunteers, who constructed KPFA's studios.[47] All this took up the first fourteen weeks of 1949, leaving the foundation's suite unfinished on April 14, the day before broadcasting was scheduled. On the evening of April 14, KPFA's leadership brought in several cases of beer to recruit volunteers to stuff loose asbestos fibers into the back wall of the main studio.

The next morning a somewhat hung-over crew staggered in.[48] At one o'clock in the afternoon, two hours before the station went live, the carpets for Studio A suddenly arrived. As staffers frantically unrolled and installed them, Lewis Hill and Richard Moore—now recruited as an announcer—positioned themselves before microphones. As the moment of truth—three o'clock—arrived, Meece nervously approached a young volunteer named Gertrude Chiarito. The former postmaster of Elkton, Oregon, she had married pacifist composer Americo Chiarito during the war. Hill had recruited Gertrude and Americo to KPFA in 1947, Americo as the station's music director; she, as an accountant. "Please," Meece told Gertrude, "you've got to help me." He led her into the control room and handed her a set of instructions. Then he climbed up to the roof to stabilize the antennae, which had been receiving unwanted signals. Just before three o'clock, he shouted down from the transmitter, "Throw on the switch that says 'Lew'!" Chiarito looked across the studio board and saw the marked lever. She watched as the clock reached exactly three o' clock, threw the switch, and pointed to Hill, as per her notes.[49]

Hill began talking about the Pacifica Foundation's mission, and after that Moore hosted the station's first music program, entitled "Anglo-American Folk Ballads."[50] The staff and volunteers sat around the studio complex shocked and exhausted. Some were crying, and one volunteer sat drinking liquor straight from a bottle.[51] As the initial euphoria was wearing off, the phone rang. Perhaps responding to an on-air appeal for feedback, a local FM listener had called in to report that, from where he lived in Berkeley, KPFA's signal was coming in just fine. "We just sat there in [that] control room grinning," McKinney later recalled. "You could have lit up the whole room on the strength of those grins."[52] Having regained some of their composure, McKinney and Hill returned to the eternal task of fundraising. The Pacifica Foundation had spent nearly all its capital reserve on construction. It had barely enough money to keep KPFA running for a month.[53]

Remarkably, considering that the station had few subscribers, practically no advertisers, and operated on a signal that few Bay Area residents could receive, KPFA stayed on the air for well over a year. Local jazz record collector Phil Elwood later recalled with amusement how his mother cheerfully gave a donation to KPFA only to discover that she couldn't tune into the station without an FM receiver.[54] The press offered warm but skeptical support, especially for KPFA's strict advertising code, which one Bay Area newspaper columnist predicted would "lead the station to an early death."[55]

Propelled by good intentions, the Pacifica Foundation had inadvertently designed its first trial balloon to run out of air quickly. At $10 a subscription, KPFA had too small an operating fund for the station to keep up with monthly expenses. And although Hill boasted in fundraising documents of KPFA's far-reaching FM signal, Meece knew that the station's FM frequency had little range around the cities in the East Bay, let alone in San Francisco. "I could just barely pick it up on Broadway in Oakland with an old pilot tuner," Meece later admitted. In reality, the station's first signal was directed primarily into the Berkeley Hills, the most affluent but least populous or ethnically diverse part of the city. "You were lucky in 1949–50 if you could hear KPFA at all," wrote Vera Hopkins years later, when the truth could be told without losing a contribution.[56]

By New Year's Eve of 1949, KPFA's on-air appeals and mass mailings had induced a mere 115 Berkeley residents to mail in subscriptions. Unable to rely on a regular pool of subscribers, the staff exhausted itself by trying to provide programming while running an ongoing fundraising drive. Although more than $22,000 in capital contributions came in to the station in 1949, operating expenses consumed this harvest faster than it could be reaped. By February 1950, KPFA had incurred a deficit of nearly $10,000. "It should . . . be noted that the lack of adequate funds during KPFA's first ten months has imposed severe personal sacrifices on the staff members," a station memo noted. In other words, Hill, McKinney, and Moore had already established that grim nonprofit radio tradition: postponing salaries to keep the station operating.[57]

On July 5, 1950, Hill, Richard Moore, and Gertrude Chiarito made a last-minute on-the-air appeal for funding. By then station debts had grown to $13,378. The three admitted to listeners that the station now ran almost entirely on unpaid labor, each member of the "paid" staff having donated an estimated $2,000 of his or her time. Somehow, Hill explained, the station had to get past this crisis. "Aided by many," he told the audience, "[we have] lifted ourselves by our bootstraps just about as far as it's possible to lift anything by that method." If those who tuned in to KPFA did not take the financial initiative, Hill warned, the station would go off the air in a matter of weeks. Models of gentility, the first Pacificans never would have thought to suspend regular programming and exhort listeners to call in with their pledges, as listener-sponsored stations do today. Instead, the trio made polite requests. "I'd like to suggest that if anyone has at all the intention of supporting this present plan why I would certainly like to hear from each and every one of you," Moore said.[58]

Such courteous appeals concealed the fact that KPFA really did verge on collapse unless new funds arrived quickly. Desperate attempts at economy, such as mimeographing rather than typesetting the station's fortnightly program, *Folio*, proved of little value.[59] Some staffers could no longer participate in the project and live functional lives. Pacifica treasurer E. John Lewis, Hill's old pacifist ally, left the station after his wife, Dolly, suffered serious complications during her second pregnancy.[60] In fact, by early August, almost everyone had quit out of economic necessity, except Hill and McKinney.[61] The station was careening toward bankruptcy and no one could stop it; at least they could keep the situation from getting worse. On August 4, the executive membership resolved to take the station off the air that Sunday, August 6—five years to the day after the bombing of Hiroshima put an end to Hill and Finch's Japanese project. Ten days later, a grim Committee of Directors debated whether to put KPFA up for sale.[62]

But then, confirming the adage that you don't know what you have until it's gone, listeners who had come to rely on KPFA banded together to save the station. Hill and McKinney met with about 150 of these supporters and appraised them of KPFA's immediate future: the station couldn't go back on the air again until it had raised more than $6,000 to pay off back wages and debts, another $24,000 so the station could operate for eight more months, and nearly $10,000 to purchase a more powerful transmitter.[63]

To Hill and McKinney, the challenge seemed insurmountable. To their relief, the members of the audience thought otherwise and immediately pledged $2,300 to the station.[64] A newly formed "KPFA Campaign" organized into teams and held recruitment meetings as far north as Marin County and as far south as the Santa Clara peninsula.[65] This amazing grassroots movement, which had a strong presence in local co-ops and Unitarian churches, conducted a door-to-door campaign that reached approximately three thousand people. Nearly $22,000 was raised for the foundation, and soon the station's short-term financial needs had been met.[66] After nine months of silence, KPFA returned to the airwaves in the summer of 1951 with one thousand subscribers, money in the bank, and a new transmitter twelve times more powerful than its predecessor.[67]

Hill knew all too well, however, that as encouraging as the fundraising campaign had been, the donations that had been collected were not enough to keep the station alive for long. Once back on the air, KPFA faced the same dilemma as before: the staff could not recruit a steady supply of subscribers and provide good programming at the same time. "The lack of funds has made any kind of promotional activity impossible, in consequence of which the very tiny and almost accidental FM audience has remained static."[68] KPFA required enough capital to liberate its core staff from the quotidian task of begging for at least two years, long enough to improve the quality of the station. With this goal in mind, Hill set about soliciting support from the biggest "prestige account" in the history of the modern world.

A "Philanthropic Stew"

Before 1947, the Ford Foundation had served as a local charity in the Michigan area. The fund supported the Detroit Symphony Orchestra, a hospital, and the Henry Ford Museum, a fourteen-acre rest home for old automobiles and trolley cars. Mr. Ford himself distrusted philanthropy. "Give the average man something and you make an enemy of him," he is quoted as having once said.[69] But in 1947, after Ford died, his heirs faced a unique problem. Having just been bequeathed the largest privately controlled corporation in the country, they could expect to pay inheritance taxes of more than $300 million. To finance this bill, they would have to sell huge amounts of Ford stock, greatly diminishing their authority within the corporation. Finding this unacceptable, the Fords kept the voting stock and gave the other 90 percent to their foundation. The staff of the Ford Foundation moved into a manor in Pasadena, California, which they affectionately named "Itching Palms." A journalist given the task of writing about the foundation described it as "a large body of money surrounded by people who want some."[70] In 1951, Lewis Hill decided to become one of those people.

Hill probably sensed opportunity when the news got around that Paul Hoffman, past president of the Studebaker Corporation, had been named head of the Ford Foundation.[71] Hoffman had just completed a stint as co-administrator of the Marshall Plan, the United States' anticommunist relief effort in postwar Europe. The Ford Foundation's stated goals in 1949 seemed tailor-made for Pacifica's targeted audience. A report for Ford that year outlined goals I, II, and IV as "The Establishment of Peace," "The Strengthening of Democracy," and "Education in a Democratic Society." Hoffman told a reporter that he personally wanted the foundation to discover what had to be done to secure peace. "You are either going to have a war or peace, and I think we all want peace," he explained. "What we have to know are the conditions that must be created to make such a peace possible. There are some things Russia must do and some we must do and some the other countries must do, but we don't know what they are." [72]

Hoffman hired a bevy of liberal-minded functionaries who shared his views.[73] One was W. H. Ferry, or "Ping" to his friends. The son of the chairman of Packard Motors, in later years Ferry would organize think tanks with names like ExPro, the Exploratory Project on the Conditions of Peace.[74] After the war Ferry worked as public relations director for the political action committee of the Congress of Industrial Organizations. He did some publicity work for Ford but was unpopular with his supervisors. Ferry then found employment with another early Hoffman ally, Robert Hutchins, whose Fund for the Republic, a liberal Ford Foundation spin-off, took on the thankless task of confronting McCarthyism.[75]

Hill sought Ping Ferry out and probably found him as accessible as did journalist Dwight Macdonald, who later wrote a book about the Ford Foundation. Ferry, Macdonald discovered, had a direct phone line and no intervening secretary outside his office door. Above his desk was a flower embroidery with the words "Feel Free" on it; matchbooks with the same motto were scattered about the office.[76]

Hill first met with Ferry at the University Club in New York City. It appears that these two errant sons of corporate wealth got along splendidly. As usual, when Hill went to New York City, he stayed with Roy Finch. The ex-CO recalled his friend returning from the meeting and bursting into his apartment.[77] "Finch," Hill exclaimed, "would you believe there are people in this world who have a problem getting rid of money? . . . We've got to make it more easy for them!" [78] At that meeting, or soon after, Ferry or someone within the foundation's orbit directed Hill to a Ford subsidiary, the Fund for Adult Education (FAE).

The FAE was run by a former sales manager for Studebaker. After wearying of selling cars, C. Scott Fletcher had worked his way up to president at Encyclopedia Britannica Films. The FAE declared as its primary goal the development of "mature, wise, and responsible citizens who can participate intelligently in a free society." By 1955, it had spent $25 million pursuing this task. The people who ran the Ford Foundation, it should be remembered, had made their living selling things. It was not surprising, therefore, that many FAE grants were used to finance the production of educational commodities: records, books, films, pamphlets, and other consumer "study aids." Hoping such products would foster group discussion, FAE officials also funded the production of films with titles such as "Room for Discussion" and "How to Organize a Discussion Group."[79] It is not hard to see why Hill was so enthusiastic about the Ford subsidiary. KPFA and the FAE certainly seemed perfectly matched. Indeed, by 1951, Hill and company had so tailored the station to the UC audience (complete with UC administrators as members of the sponsoring committee) that he wondered how the FAE could turn them down. The station, in Hill's words, was "nothing but an Adult Education Project" and had already gone a long way in its literature to define itself as an educational station, if for no other reason than to convince the IRS the foundation deserved tax-exempt status.[80] In fact, KPFA had already worked with the FAE, broadcasting the discussion meetings of the Great Books Foundation, which received more than $750,000 from the fund.[81]

If on the surface the FAE seemed to project a sort of do-gooder logic, the fund dispensed its largesse with one primary concern: to encourage what its administrators regarded as critical thinking, "as opposed to passive acceptance of ready-made opinions."[82] Like many liberal thinkers of the time, Ford's leaders concluded that the mass movements of the recent past and present—fascism, Stalinism, McCarthyism—derived their strength from a paucity of critical thought, particularly regarding individual rights. Hutchins called his Fund for the Republic a "court of reason" or, in more desperate moments, "a small island of sanity in a McCarthyite world."[83] Hutchins and other Ford Foundation funders sought to disseminate what they saw as the values of a few among the many. Hutchins and Hoffman wanted Americans to feel and think freely. After they had done that for a while, Ford's leaders hoped Americans would conclude, as did they, that liberal, capitalist democracy represented the best of all possible worlds.

Understanding the thinking of his potential benefactors, Hill wrote a funding proposal that tailored the mission of the Pacifica project to the views of Ford's administrators. The grant won the Pacifica Foundation $150,000 from the FAE in 1952.[84] Almost as important, however, the final report Hill wrote for the fund became Pacifica's defining text and the single piece of writing for which he would be remembered. Turning the goals of the Richmond prospectus upside down, Hill argued that listener-supported radio depended not on reaching the many but on winning the sympathy of a self-conscious elite.

The central message of Hill's book *Voluntary Listener-Sponsorship: A Report to Educational Broadcasters on the Experiment at KPFA* surfaced in a short document called "The Theory of Listener-Sponsored Radio," published in 1952 in UC Berkeley's *Quarterly of Film, Radio, and Television.* In his last paragraph, Hill said, almost as an afterthought, "The survival of this station is based upon the necessity of voluntary subscriptions from 2 per cent of the total FM audience in the area in which it operates."[85] In *Voluntary Listener Sponsorship*, Hill elaborated on this formula, turning it into something of a natural law of radio. He argued that the 2 percent formula could apply to any listener-supported radio station in the United States. If, for example, the total number of FM households in the San Francisco Bay Area were projected to be 375,000 in 1954, and the station's operating budget was held to the "lowest possible minimum" at $75,000, then 2 percent of the FM household population, or 7,500, would have to contribute $10 in subscriptions to finance the station. Hill presented a table illustrating the income a typical listener-supported AM station could derive based on this formula. In New York, a listener-subscriber station would enjoy a $592,000 annual budget, based on there being nearly three million AM radios in the area; in Chicago, such a station would bring in $352,000.[86]

These apparent showers of wealth obscured a difficult question: how exactly did he arrive at the 2 percent figure? Why not 1 percent? Or 3? Hill made reference to the fact that 2 percent corresponded to the "standard deviation in many survey and polling systems" and then insisted that he arrived at the figure on the basis of "simple arithmetic."[87] More likely, though, Hill's approach had its foundation in pacifist arithmetic. Since Thoreau's 1846 *Essay on Civil Disobedience*, the notion that a determined few could have far-reaching impact had been fundamental to pacifist thinking. In 1930, Albert Einstein, at that time an ardent advocate of war resistance, gave his famous "two percent" speech at a conference in New York City. "Even if only two percent of those assigned to perform military service should announce their refusal to fight," the physicist said, "as well as urge means other than war of settling international disputes, governments would be powerless, they would not dare send such a large number of people to jail."[88] Now Hill borrowed such logic to make credible the proposition that people would voluntarily pay for radio shows that they could have for free.

But not everyone would have to pay for radio, Hill explained, just some people. And what kind of people would they be?

> As a general rule, it is persons of education, mental ability, or cultural heritage equating roughly with the sources of intellectual leadership in the community who tend to become voluntary listener sponsors. . . . It is thus clear that the 2% theory, when we speak of supporting serious cultural broadcasting by this means, represents also *a way of extending the legitimate functions of social and cultural leadership*. Obviously, to earn systematic support from the community's

intellectual leadership, the listener-sponsored station must give the values and concerns of that leadership an accurate reflection at their highest level.[89]

This same writer had once said that war prevention depended on reaching the average person through the presentation of the familiar. The phrase "war prevention" did not appear in *Voluntary Listener Sponsorship*; neither did words such as "pacifism" or "peace." Instead, the text presented the world of listener-subscriber radio as a promising haven for the enlightened few and, even more significantly, as a bastion of personal freedom. "Within [KPFA] itself, and within its broadly defined program policies," Hill wrote, "the staff members were endowed with unusual personal freedom in the selection and creation of program materials. The station was quite free from any influences, direct or otherwise, which supervened on the imagination and discretion of the persons responsible for broadcasting."[90]

As we shall see, this was anything but the case. In Hill's Ford Foundation literature, however, personal liberty in the pursuit of high culture became the Pacifica Foundation's central quest, replacing broad-based dialogue and intercommunication. For several generations of community radio activists and scholars, Hill's book offered the definitive representation of the Pacifica Foundation. Few seemed to notice, however, that the text read primarily as a report to the biggest liberal megafund of its time. As he had with the FCC, Hill had redefined Pacifica's mission in order to move the organization forward.

Did the first Pacificans wholly subscribe to Hill's version of their project? Richard Moore, who managed several public television stations after working for Pacifica, always admired his friend's ability to tailor his "propositions depending upon whoever the signified is" but never thought that the Ford application and its resultant text revealed Pacifica's goals. "It is an economic fact of life that there is a relatively small percentage of the general population who are both willing and able, and it takes both, to contribute [to listener-sponsored radio]," Moore later said. "Nine times out of ten the argument that is most convincing is that what we are doing reflects 'your' values, and that these values will be made available to the community at large that can't pay for them."[91] Ironically, it was the Ford literature, not the Richmond prospectus, that became Hill's principal contribution to the idea of public radio.

As for the Ford Foundation, at the end of fiscal year 1952, its leaders surveyed their many endowments and saw that they were good. Martin Quigley, chief of publicity at Ford's Pasadena headquarters, reviewed the season's grants and then wrote a long poem entitled "Philanthropic Stew, a Recipe Derived from an Annual Report of the Ford Foundation." The first two lines of this doggerel made reference to a work in progress unfolding in the city of Berkeley: "Take a dozen Quakers — be sure they're sweet and pink — /Add one discussion program to make the people think."[92]

After six years of begging, organizing, and scrounging, the Pacifica Foundation had proved it could deliver on its central promise: the birthing of a unique radio station. There had been many setbacks, but the founders of listener-supported radio exemplified Lewis Hill's "definite determination to remain definite." Never dwelling on the obstacles, the first Pacificans had by 1952 mastered the fine art of walking around problems. When the station could no longer survive on its own, the community rushed in to offer support. When that did not suffice, Pacifica's staff persuaded a wealthy foundation to provide the capital funding KPFA so desperately needed. Thus, for its first five years, benefactor-supported not listener-supported radio, more accurately characterized the Pacifica project.

The question of whether to air commercials resolved itself naturally. In the first months on the air, practically nobody sought to advertise on KPFA. The business office gave some advertising time to the station's landlord, possibly in exchange for a discount on the rent.[93] After that, the staff abandoned the idea of advertisements, tasteful or otherwise, altogether. Besides, Pacifica's attorneys had by then explained that the IRS would never clear the foundation for nonprofit tax status if KPFA ran commercials.[94] By the mid-summer of KPFA's first year on the air, the station's leadership had resolved that the station would pursue what Hill described as a "sink-or-swim" listener-subscription plan. The payoff for this particular leap came relatively quickly. About three weeks before Christmas 1949, the organization received notice from the IRS that the Pacifica Foundation had been granted tax-exempt status.[95]

The Pacifica Foundation had survived, but its methods of survival came with a price. Desperate for capital contributions and government cooperation, the organization's fundraisers had cast a wide net and had presented Pacifica in many ways to different camps. "KPFA is designed to become *one thing to all people*," the Berkeley prospectus declared, "the source of the area's most incisive and continuous examination of public affairs, and of its richest and most consistent unfolding of musical and dramatic values."[96] On the surface, this ambitious statement described two goals. Beneath the surface, the foundation had already represented itself as having many goals, some quite contradictory.

As we shall see, at its core, the primary goal remained the same: a demonstration of pacifist dialogue. But to whom was this demonstration to be directed, the "average" person or the influential policy maker? A "mass audience" or the educated cultural connoisseur? Attendees of "vast jitterbug arenas" or patrons of chamber music concerts? Did the first Pacificans create KPFA to reach out to the masses or as an avenue of internal communication, a voice for the San Francisco Renaissance? More important, why did the founders of Pacifica believe in dialogue? Because they thought it promoted peaceful human relations, or because they thought it led to a "balanced" understanding of civic questions?

Even before KPFA went on the air, its parent organization had made many compromises, leaving the central purpose of the organization shrouded in ambiguity. After the station began broadcasting, Pacifica announcers often boasted that as an advertisement-free station, KPFA was protected from the need to appease commercial influences. But this freedom did not protect Lew Hill and his band of utopians from the strict ideological requirements of the liberal corporate state. Nor did it inure Pacifica from the influence of the class able and willing to pay for commercial-free FM radio. Ironically, the absence of advertising revenue and the scarcity of paying listeners had made the foundation hungrier for "prestige accounts" and willing to redefine itself in elite terms.

Was there any social force that could hold the Pacifica Foundation to its original vision: to offer a demonstration of nonviolent dialogue that ventured beyond the pacifist in-crowd? That established links between those few who had refused military service during the good war and the great masses of "average" people on whom the prevention of war truly depended? A revitalized pacifist movement, more sophisticated about identifying its allies, might have been the answer. Such a social base might have protected Pacifica from the influence of nonpacifist philanthropy. A pacifist external presence also might have kept the early Pacificans—constantly struggling to keep their project afloat—mindful of the larger picture. For all their ambivalence about earlier war-resistance strategies, Hill and his friends certainly wanted a pacifist movement to reemerge after the defeat of fascism. But as the early clouds of the Cold War gathered on the horizon, it became clear that the movement they had grown up with not only faltered but verged on extinction.

5)) 1949

By and large, [pacifists are] more interested in their particular field of study, their family, their record collections, their comfortable homes, their correct and genteel friends than they are in challenging people to think anew on the great issues of war and peace.

—Roy Kepler,
"Report on Country-Wide Trip"

As the first Pacificans struggled to keep their radio station on the air, a stunning realignment of world politics took place. During the struggle against fascism, the United States and Soviet Union had been staunch allies. Now they were rivals. The pacifists of the late 1940s saw both camps as equally immoral. Dwight Macdonald argued that modern states inevitably fought for no reason than to legitimize their internal authority. The Pacifica Foundation's 1948 prospectus grimly noted the impending crisis in the opening statement of its text: "[A] world resounding with belligerent propaganda moves again towards war."[1]

One might have expected such an atmosphere to provide fertile territory for the pacifists at KPFA. The opposite proved true, since the peace movement could not resolve a double-edged problem. First, how could pacifists oppose U.S. aggression abroad—especially in the postcolonial world—without implicitly supporting their former allies, the communists? Second, how could pacifists denounce Stalinism without aiding the emerging Cold War consensus at home? Domestically, pacifists found themselves torn between their desire to protect Stalinists and fellow travelers from government repression and their apprehension of Stalinism itself. They had not forgotten the Communist Party's sudden support of U.S. intervention in Europe once Germany attacked the Soviet Union in 1941.

Communists, declared A. J. Muste in 1949, "use deceit and violence at the behest of the Party; they do conceal and lie about membership in the Party; they do penetrate organizations of all kinds for ulterior purposes and without hesitating to resort to the most egregious chicanery."[2]

Pacifists also opposed the Soviet Union on moral grounds. As a student at Berkeley High School, CO and early KPFA volunteer Kerwin Whitnah read Vladimir Tchernavin's 1935 exposé of the Russian forced labor camp system entitled *I Speak for the Silent Prisoners of the Soviets.* "From that time on I knew that there was a terrible hoax going on," he recalled, "that [Russia] was the 'brave new world.'"[3] KPFA's staff also perceived communists as inflexible in their thinking, awaiting Party instructions before making decisions. "Communists when they were on KPFA individually wouldn't change their minds about anything," recalls Eleanor McKinney. "They had rote thoughts."[4]

In the international arena, pacifists detested the use of anticommunist rhetoric to overthrow democratically elected postcolonial governments. Yet they also thought that Soviet socialism posed a genuine threat to the peoples of the world. They did not agree with the "progressive" supporters of 1948 presidential candidate Henry Wallace that Americans should accept Soviet communism as a fact of life. To put it simply, these pacifists were sincere anticommunists. Unlike conservative Republicans, they did not oppose communism to discredit unions or civil rights organizations. They simply saw Stalin's socialism as no more acceptable than the national security state emerging around them at home.

What, then, represented the third way—the path between totalitarianism and corporate imperialism? Postwar American pacifists had no answer. "What is lacking among the formal pacifists is a sufficient cause and an orientation of responsibility; perhaps fundamentally, imagination," Lewis Hill wrote in 1948. "The dilemma of Stalinism cuts through every pacifist hypothecation like the Sword of Fire. I feel an abysmal despair on behalf of many former hopes."[5] The collapse of organized pacifism had serious consequences for the Pacifica Foundation, forcing the organization to define pacifism alone, rather than as part of a mass movement.

"Radio Is Doomed"

While some pacifists put their hope in radio as a way to encourage peaceful dialogue, television, a far more powerful broadcast technology, overwhelmed the cultural landscape, bringing the voice and face of the state into every living room. The first TV sets went on sale in 1946. By 1952, the populace owned fifteen million video receivers and spent their evenings watching such programs as Ed Sullivan's *Talk of the Town*.[6] "The country has never experienced anything quite like it," *New York Times* reporter Jack Gould declared. Gould, who would later follow Pacifica affairs for the *Times*, found that in many cities close to half the population had stopped going to movies on a regular basis. Theaters closed down in record numbers: 134 in Southern California, 64 in Chicago, 71 in eastern Massachusetts. B movies faced a particularly serious crisis. "You can't charge for mediocrity any more, when everybody can get it at home for nothing," commented one despondent film exhibitor. Restaurants, amateur team sports, the local tavern—involvement in all these institutions declined.[7]

As TV viewing increased in popularity, nothing fell faster than radio. Even the most sagacious observers did not realize how quickly radio's empire would collapse. Noting the decline in advertising revenue, George Voigt, a writer for the *San Francisco Chronicle*, suggested that local sponsors deliberately invested in television to bring down radio advertising rates. "It doesn't make sense for them to abandon radio for television and it won't make sense until there are many more homes equipped with TV sets," he said.[8] But TV manufacturers hastened to put inexpensive sets on the national market. During KPFA's first two years on the air, the Pacific Coast represented the second fastest-growing television market in the United States, outranked only by the Northeast. By 1956, three out of every four West Coast households owned a TV set.[9] Radio broadcasting networks earned $134 million from ad accounts in 1948; the sum dropped to $103 million five years later. Meanwhile, revenue for TV advertising skyrocketed, from $2.5 to $172 million in nearly the same period.[10] A week after KPFA went on the air, a reporter for *Look* magazine bluntly gave this assessment: "Radio is doomed."[11]

The impact of television on the sale of FM receivers proved of particular significance to the Pacifica Foundation. U.S. radio manufacturers produced approximately 1.4 million FM receivers in 1949. By 1954, that figure declined to 130,000.[12] The problem of how to broadcast to a community of people who did not own FM receivers would plague KPFA throughout the 1950s. As the decade progressed, KPFA would also find itself competing not so much with commercial radio—as its founders had envisioned—but with TV.

Meanwhile, militant anticommunism effortlessly took possession of the political landscape. In 1949, genteel New Deal attorney Alger Hiss faced trial for lying to Congress about classified documents he allegedly passed to the Soviet Union. Ten prominent Hollywood screenwriters began prison terms for refusing to discuss their political backgrounds with a congressional committee.[13] In the winter of 1950, Wisconsin senator Joseph McCarthy claimed he possessed the names of no less than 205 State Department employees who were communists.[14] In the summer of that year, Americans followed the arrest, trial, conviction, and eventual execution of Julius and Ethel Rosenberg for spiriting atomic secrets to the Soviet Union. And on June 25, the country committed ground forces to the Korean peninsula, initiating a conflict that in less than two years would consume the lives of nearly forty-five thousand Americans.[15]

Closer to home, the supposed threat posed by communists dominated Bay Area newspaper headlines. During KPFA's first two months on the air, union leader Harry Bridges, voice of the 1934 general strike, faced federal charges of perjury for allegedly lying to immigration authorities about his relationship with the Communist Party. After an eighty-one-day trial, a grand jury found Bridges guilty and sentenced him to five years in prison. Then, on July 26, 1951, ten FBI agents broke into the San Francisco office of Communist Party newspaper editor Al Richmond, who later would often appear on KPFA, and led him out of the building in handcuffs. Setting his bail at $75,000, the government charged Richmond and eleven other California CP leaders with violation of the Smith Act, which made it illegal to advocate the violent overthrow of the government. A jury quickly found the defendants guilty, sentencing them to half a decade in prison.[16]

Just before KPFA went on the air in April 1949, the state senate passed a law requiring every public college professor in California to sign a loyalty oath. Under the bill, introduced by Jack Tenney of Los Angeles, academics would have to swear they had never been members of any group mentioned in the attorney general's subversive organization list. Alarmed at this harsh legislation, the board of regents of the University of California offered a milder "anti-communist affirmation" as a substitute. Hundreds of Cal Berkeley teachers lost their jobs after refusing to sign the statement.[17] Some professors—veterans of the First or Second World Wars—found infuriating the assumption that their patriotism could be verified only by a written document.[18] Two future Pacifica Foundation presidents became embroiled in the controversy. In 1949, college lecturer Hallock Hoffman received an anticommunist oath statement requiring his signature with his real estate bill. In response, Hoffman took Los Angeles County to court and published a polemic entitled *Loyalty by Oath: An Essay on the Extortion of Love.*[19] UC Berkeley professor Harold Winkler simply refused to sign the "anti-communist affirmation." Cal officials fired him, then gave his name to local newspapers.[20]

Appearing during the early years of the Cold War, television greatly enhanced the power of the state. On May 5, 1949, TV station KGO in San Francisco launched itself like a battleship. A Catholic archbishop, an Episcopal bishop, and a rabbi appeared in the founding telecast, and following their blessing, California governor Earl Warren gave a fifteen-minute address. Viewers then settled in to watch the first of a twenty-six-part documentary series based on General Eisenhower's *Crusade in Europe*.[21]

The idea of television functioning as an assistant to the state came easily to network executives, many of whom had served as high-ranking communications officers during World War II.[22] During the 1930s, network radio had broadcast a relatively diverse range of political opinion. Civil libertarians such as Roger Baldwin and socialist/pacifist Norman Thomas had often expressed their views on discussion shows, such as *America's Town Meeting of the Air*, addressing topics such as "Which Way for America—Fascism, Communism, Socialism, or Democracy?" NBC television's updated version of the program, called *American Forum of the Air*, rarely permitted the broadcast of left-of-center thought. Typical was its August 19, 1950, debate over domestic communism between Senators Karl Mundt and Hubert Humphrey. Mundt, who would later participate in an investigation of the Pacifica Foundation, described communists as saboteurs. Humphrey declared that "all patriotic and freedom loving, decent Americans [are] anti-Communist."[23] TV also offered hundreds of civil defense programs that seriously suggested that one could survive a nuclear attack in a well-built basement. "They'll be plenty of suffering, plenty of misery, broken homes, death—dangers that used to belong only to soldiers," one televised government film explained. "But we've got to be able to take it and come back fighting."[24]

It was in this political climate that war resisters strove to achieve the preeminence they had enjoyed in the mid-1930s, when college students across the country had gone on strike against militarism. Thousands of COs had developed close bonds during their years in CPS camps. But after the war, the pacifist movement proved far less unified ideologically. In 1945, Roy Finch and other pacifists organized a conference in Chicago for the purpose of merging groups devoted to "wartime resistance, socialism, militant labor unionism, consumer cooperation, and racial equality."[25] A preamble to the conference articulated ideas expressed in the Pacifica Foundation's early fundraising prospectuses: "We must break away from the Marxist alternative of dealing with large numbers of people (or large institutions like trade unions) and move towards a concept of working in terms of the total life pattern of a few."[26] The contradictions were already evident. No sooner had the conference begun than its organizers came out both in favor of and against unions.

Lewis Hill participated in the event and sent a public letter to those in attendance. Like Dwight Macdonald, Hill saw opposition to the modern state as the primary task, as that entity "which must be conquered first," but only "through the conditioning of individuals in a sense of their solitary responsibility for the values of freedom."[27] Ninety-five activists, responding to Hill's appeal, met in early February 1946 and declared themselves the "Conference on Non-Violent Revolutionary Socialism" [CNVR]. Their program rejected state socialist methods, while emphasizing support for worker cooperatives and community control of the means of production.[28] But except for picketing the United Nations as a tool of imperialism, CNVR accomplished little in its single year of existence. A classic example of what seasoned conference goers call "resolutionary socialism," the 1945 Chicago event spread its ideological net too wide, appealing to pacifists who wanted to emphasize mass protest and those who wanted to focus on building cooperative institutions.

In the May 1946 edition of the CNVR's bulletin, Hill suggested that many of the conference's declarations had been contradictory.[29] A minority of participants gave the conference "the right emphasis to its basic attitude of rebellion," but they also created the false impression that at the gathering's last hours they had forged a consensus on social, economic, and political principles. "As everyone remembers," he wrote, "the twenty or thirty people still on the floor [by that time] were extremely sleepy." In fact, they had built little more than "an exploratory group with an indefinite periphery." Hill urged the participants at the conference to meet again the following February and to maintain their "ideological commitment to war-resistance and to the use of non-violence in preference to violent means of action." Beyond that, he suggested allegiance to the CNVR "should entail no commitment whatsoever to the form and theory of the resolutions voted at the first Conference."[30]

As Hill had already noted to his friends, pacifists during the war had spent too much time fighting the CPS system and too little developing a larger purpose. The open-endedness of his proposed coalition reflected an appreciation of this weakness. Hill knew that all the radical-sounding resolutions in the world could not prevent the majority of uncertain

CNVR delegates from becoming discouraged and abandoning the coalition. Hence, he sought a fragile unity based on the one principle that had united pacifists during the Second World War: nonviolent resistance.

Attempting to build a more coherent program, in April 1948 about 250 pacifists met once again in Chicago for an appropriately entitled "Conference on More Disciplined and Revolutionary Pacifism." This meeting took a more explicitly Gandhian tone. Its participants called themselves Peacemakers and spoke less about local workers councils and more about resistance to the Truman administration's new draft registration act. "We call on youths to refuse to register or render any service under this iniquitous law and on all others to support youth in this non-violent non-cooperation," an early circular declared.[31]

But soon the same schism emerged between those who supported various forms of communalism and those who desired a broader political approach. Not surprisingly, younger activists like Dave Dellinger, whose ideas had been formed during the CPS era, sought to build new cooperative institutions.[32] A. J. Muste and others wanted pacifists to rebuild a mass movement against militarism and social injustice. By 1952, this division had become pronounced. At an executive committee meeting that year, the group broke into two factions, one led by Bayard Rustin and Muste, the other led by Dellinger and War Resisters League leader Ralph DiGia. The gathering went on for hours. Finally, Rustin lost his patience. "This is getting us nowhere," he exclaimed.[33]

In fact, both strategies faced severe difficulties. Muste and Rustin correctly observed that a pacifist wave of small-scale social experiments might satisfy personal needs but would do little in the short run to challenge the militarist state. The road to rebuilding a pacifist mass movement, however, also stood blocked by socialist/pacifist antipathy toward the Soviet Union. The pro-Soviet coup of Czechoslovakia and attempts to blockade Berlin from the west tested the faith of pacifists and their supporters. Many advocates of nonviolence, including Dwight Macdonald and Evan Thomas, simply could not withstand the complexity of the moment and resigned from the WRL. How, Macdonald asked, would nonviolence save West Berlin from the Russians?[34] In correspondence with Macdonald, Roy Kepler found himself repelled by the editor's now near fanatical anticommunism, exemplified by Macdonald's frequent references to "Stalinoids." "I do not agree with you that Stalinists are 'not human,'" Kepler wrote to Macdonald in 1949. ". . . If you think that of them, then there is not much humanly possible to be done in the situation. You are faced with the idea that all that is left is to destroy these sub-humans." Unable to answer such concerns, Macdonald abandoned activism altogether, embracing cultural criticism instead. He shut down *Politics* and gave a talk in May 1949 entitled "Goodbye to Utopia" during which he declared hopeless any "consistent systematic pattern for understanding reality."[35]

Meanwhile, as Hill and the rest of the early Pacifica group became more deeply involved in their radio project, they gradually lost touch with the national pacifist scene. By the fall of 1947, Hill confessed to Finch that he no longer recognized the names of many participants in CNVR. Hill had become increasingly skeptical of the organization's future but very much wanted to keep in touch with pacifist events. Upon learning, only secondhand, about the conference on "More Disciplined and Revolutionary" pacifism, he expressed dismay that one of the workshops had emphasized the development of pacifist-controlled media. "As you know the Pacifica project for two years has been developing what is no doubt the only mass medium pacifists have or will have for some time to come," he wrote, "yet none of us was so much as informed that the conference would occur, nor has anyone yet received direct word about it." This, Hill declared, "will serve, I suppose, as a last straw."[36]

Hill had contradictory expectations of pacifism in the late 1940s. On one hand, he wanted some kind of pacifist mass movement to prosper; on the other hand, he sympathized with those who believed that a new revitalized pacifism depended on the creation of decentralized experimental communities. But by 1950, the Pacifica Foundation's relationship with organized pacifism had become so distant that Hill decided to contact Muste himself. "Dear A.J.," he began. "I am writing to obtain advice and, if possible, some help in settling the problems of the Pacifica radio project."

> A prime expectation, which proved to be quite naive, was that the individuals and organizations roughly comprising the "peace movement" in America would many of them view such an undertaking as fundamental to the advancement of a peaceful society and would accordingly assist in its capitalization.
>
> In our experience with very few exceptions organized pacifists have neither supported nor encouraged the project. . . . I seek your advice on the possibility of continuing and developing the Pacifica project, and particularly on the chance that with the ground of experience and evidence which KPFA now provides some renewed effort to interest the pacifist community in its capitalization might be undertaken.[37]

Hill apparently did not understand that by the time he wrote his letter, the pacifist movement had largely disappeared. Although various Dellingerian experiments thrived around the country, they had become isolated and marginal. In 1949, just before migrating to the West Coast, Roy Kepler undertook a national survey of groups that affiliated themselves with Peacemakers; hardly any survived. Many ex-COs, Kepler found, had gone into college teaching or private pursuits. "By and large," he wrote, pacifists he met seemed "more interested in their particular field of study, their family, their record collections, their comfortable homes, their correct and genteel friends than they are in challenging people to think anew on the great issues of war and peace."[38] Most pacifists who remained active followed ex-COs Bayard Rustin, James Farmer, and Jim Peck into the early civil rights movement. In 1939, *Time* had bestowed on A. J. Muste the title of "Number One U.S. Pacifist."[39] A decade later it would not have occurred to a magazine editor to identify such a person. Not until the late 1950s, under the influence of organizations such as the National Committee for a Sane Nuclear Policy (SANE) and Women Strike for Peace, would movements against militarism again enjoy influence in the United States.[40]

The Pacifica Foundation had become a cadre organization without a revolutionary movement. Not a single prominent pacifist leader of the era belonged to the "KPFA Sponsoring Group" in the early 1950s.[41] Had the nation's most important pacifist organizations come forth with regular financial assistance, leaders like A. J. Muste and others might have enjoyed greater influence over the foundation's policies, perhaps even sitting on the organization's sponsoring board. A stronger socialist/pacifist presence at KPFA might have forced the organization not to waver on its original commitment to reaching the "average" person with a message of nonviolence. The more active input of groups like the War Resisters League might have called into question the long-term wisdom of Hill's "prestige accounts" strategy. But the sources of such input no longer existed on any meaningful level. Organized pacifism could not see its way out of the morass of the Cold War. Its participants had moved on to new political fronts or retreated to personal worlds. During the Peacemakers debate between Muste and Dellinger in 1952, the organization's secretary announced that the group had a budget of just $1,000. "Today," Dellinger lamented, "there is no place for rebels to go."[42]

This is not to say that Hill and the rest of the early Pacifica group had broken faith with pacifism. They continued to see the station as a model for pacifist dialogue. But that dialogue would now take place in the context of an insular university town. Its parameters would be defined by women and men cast adrift from what might have been a popular movement forging its way between Stalinism and corporate imperialism. Pacifist dialogue properly understood would not play itself out before dock workers and machinists in Richmond. It would perform before Berkeley's cautious upper middle class, raised to adulthood during depression and world war, enduring a cruel political inquisition by day, broadcast on television by night. For that audience, KPFA would serve less as an agent of change and more as a refuge from the storm.

6) A Hedonist's Millennium

During the eight years that I was at KPFA I don't remember taking a single day off. . . . Whatever I may have felt about individuals at the station, whatever hassles I may have felt, it had just gotten to the point where it was the only place where I really lived. It was like one of those plants that you buy in the five-and-ten—when you take them out of water they dry up and when you turn them back into water they turn green overnight.

—Alan Rich,
"Pacifica Is Twenty-Five"

For its creators, KPFA represented an experiment in dialogue and reconciliation. The staff would provide programming that advocated and demonstrated the viability of a pacific world in the present. Rather than simply lecturing about pacifist politics, KPFA would ingratiate itself within the community by offering a "familiar and satisfying" array of cultural programs. Pacifist thought and peaceable process would function as an integral part of the daily life of listeners. This approach flowed from many influences, from Gandhiism to existentialism to the writings of Dwight Macdonald.

But like all significant movements for change, the organizers of this experiment planned their revolution in one way while the objects of their reform experienced it in another. Most of KPFA's first listeners had not spent years in CPS camps. Although many admired Gandhi, they did not necessarily subscribe to anarchist/pacifist ideas or want to change the world. Most remembered the humiliations they and their families experienced during the Depression. Berkeley poet and KPFA listener Adam David Miller recalled years during his youth in South Carolina when his family had almost no income.[1] Richard Moore remembered watching his solidly middle-class parents sell their furniture to avoid the poorhouse.[2] Many listeners now aspired to academic or professional careers. As it became clear by the mid-1950s that California's Cold War economy would stave off another economic collapse, the last thing KPFA's audience wanted to sign up for was a pacifist Great Awakening. The KPFA community certainly wouldn't have turned down a "pacific world" in their time, but short of that, they'd gladly settle for a good time, for economic security, a chance to engage in personal exploration, and the good things in life—classical and "international" music, fine literature, different cultures, stimulating ideas.

For these pioneers in radio listening, KPFA represented a windfall, an oasis in a desert of crass commercial fare. Once they realized what had come into their lives, they volunteered and raised money until KPFA became their own institution as much as Lewis Hill's. The first journalists who wrote about the Pacifica Foundation teasingly described it as an "egghead" organization and a "highbrow's delight."[3] But KPFA broadcast a different version of highbrow culture from that of previous generations. Having lived through the New Deal era, KPFA's educated, middle-class audience had inherited a deep appreciation not only for Mozart string quartets but for what they saw as the "authentic" cultural expressions of the economically disinherited. Thus, KPFA staffers thought nothing of scheduling the music of Leadbelly and Liszt for the same afternoon, an act of cultural blasphemy in an earlier age. To the foundation's inner circle, KPFA broadcast culture in the pursuit of principle. But for the station's first listeners and volunteers, a community of middle-class hedonists if ever one existed, KPFA broadcast culture in the pursuit of pleasure.

The First Subscribers

It would be an understatement to describe KPFA's first audience as very educated. In 1956, the staff received nearly two thousand responses to a questionnaire it mailed to subscriber households. (The station had about 4,250 subscribers at the time.) Of these respondents, 98.7 percent said they had graduated from a secondary school, 82 percent had finished college, and more than 70 percent had gone to graduate school, 22.5 percent for at least four years.[4] These listeners also earned more money than the average Bay Area resident. More than half declared their annual income at between \$4,000 and \$8,000. Only about 20 percent of the entire Bay Area's "experienced civilian labor force" made such a claim on their 1950 federal census form.[5]

But prosperity did not temper the caution with which these radiophiles lived their lives. Even an anecdotal look at a small group of KPFA listeners reveals a cautious generation, satisfied with their newfound careers and not eager to overtly disturb the status quo. Neil MacGregor, for example, had grown up in territorial Alaska, where his father served as a U.S. marshal in a fishing village; young Neil went to elementary school with Norwegians and indigenous North Americans. "There weren't that many MacGregors," he recalled. After his parents lost everything in the Depression, the family fled to Modesto, California, to live with relatives. Neil picked fruit with migrants from Oklahoma and attended junior college in Yuba City. One day he noticed a poster at the college's front office—the government needed help with its tree disease control project. MacGregor signed on and wound up working in a forest camp, a welcome respite from the "hot, sticky peach orchards" of Yuba City.[6] After serving for several years as a radio engineer during World War II, MacGregor returned to the states to earn a degree in forestry. Eventually the Forest Service put him in charge of disease control for all the national parks in California. Macgregor moved to Berkeley and opened an office in San Francisco.[7]

Neil MacGregor arrived in the Bay Area hungry for a better life, and to him that meant immersing himself in culture. "I came to Berkeley a very naive person," he remembered, "culturally naive."[8] He'd been exposed to a smattering of what he wanted while stationed in Naples, where he attended the opera every night. But MacGregor felt he had a lot of catching up to do. So did his wife. The daughter of a civil engineer, Marilyn Russell wanted to major in English literature at Oregon State College, but no such program was available. Shortly after the war, she'd been accepted to some of the best universities but on the condition that she wait a year so that they could privilege the huge wave of returning veterans. Not wanting to go home to her parents, Russell changed her major to education so she could stay at Oregon State. After she and Neil married and moved to the Bay Area, she took a position as secretary for the German department at UC Berkeley.[9]

Neil and Marilyn eagerly embraced the culture of the Bay Area. They attended the Elmwood, an art-film theater where Pauline Kael sold tickets and wrote short incisive descriptions of each movie. They frequented the City Lights bookstore in North Beach, run by poet Lawrence Ferlinghetti. Then one day Marilyn listened to KPFA at a friend's house. "It sounded good. It sounded interesting," she recalled. In fact, Marilyn and Neil were so impressed with what they heard that they sent KPFA money even before they owned an FM radio. Subsequently, they learned that any listener who pledged at a special rate would receive "the Subscriber"—an FM receiver custom built for the Pacifica audience. The MacGregors got their "Subscriber" and became regular listeners through the 1950s and 1960s.

Neil's loyalty to the station was unshakable. At one point, an East Coast forestry service made him a generous offer. "I said, 'No. We can't move away from here. We can't get along without KPFA,' "he recalled. "I know I literally said words like that."[10]

Like the MacGregors, novelist Dorothy Bryant entered adulthood seeking an escape from a world of limitations. Bryant had grown up in the Mission District of San Francisco during the Depression. Her parents were from an Italian factory town. Her father worked as a car mechanic; her mother—the only high school graduate in her family—had a job as a bookkeeper. Bryant knew nothing about North Beach and the San Francisco Renaissance. "I was a Mission girl," she recalled. "I was a working-class daughter of immigrants." At the age of twenty, she had a husband and children of her own.[11]

But Dorothy's parents respected education and encouraged her to complete her bachelor's degree at San Francisco State, then get a teaching credential. While at State, she studied with political science professor Louis Wasserman, the author of the popular book *Modern Political Philosophies and What They Mean*. Wasserman represented a window to the world for his students. "He was very devoted to teaching people like me who came from these working origins and didn't know anything," Bryant recalled.[12]

After graduation, Bryant taught English in a private high school that had become a haven for radicals, some of whom were probably trying to avoid the loyalty oath requirement at state schools. She found their company liberating. "I wanted to identify with these other people," Bryant remembered, "these people I met who were pacifists, who were politically left."[13] In 1957, a colleague approached Bryant and asked if she would subscribe to KPFA. Proudly, she told him that she already did.[14]

By that time, Alan Klinger had been listening to KPFA for close to a decade. Born in Sheridan, Wyoming, in 1918, Klinger had already seen much more of the world than most ranch hands. His father's cattle business had gone bankrupt during the Depression. Searching for a secure environment for their son, the family shared him with relatives in Los Angeles.[15] Perhaps influenced by his mother—a pianist who had studied in Europe—Klinger developed a passion for languages. At Pasadena Junior College and UC Berkeley, he studied French, German, Spanish, Russian, and Latin. Subsequently, during the war, the army sent Klinger to a

German language studies school in Minnesota, then to Luxembourg to interrogate Nazi POWs. As a reward for his service, Klinger received a seven-week leave in Paris, where he attended an army sponsored intensive language program. "Nothing to do but study French all day," Klinger fondly recalled. "The evenings were free, and as far as being a student goes, that was the most golden period that I can ever remember."[16]

Sometime around 1943, during basic training at Fort Ord, Klinger met a man named Harry Partch while walking along the beach. An inventor of unique musical instruments, Partch would become a key figure in the avant-garde musical scene of the 1960s. Partch introduced Klinger to a circle of friends who put him in touch with Eleanor McKinney. Klinger and McKinney shared an interest in spiritual questions, especially those raised by the psychologist Carl Jung, and developed an ongoing correspondence. "There was a mutual recognition of Jung being so right on," Klinger recalled, "you know 'E' and I were both interested in what can loosely be called self-discovery. You know, the deepening of awareness beyond the intellectual."[17] Eventually, Klinger made his way back to Berkeley, just in time to help raise KPFA's transmitter. He rented a small cottage behind the home of McKinney and Richard Moore and became a regular KPFA listener.

For Bryant, Klinger, and the MacGregors, KPFA represented a way station from the provincial to the cosmopolitan, a smorgasbord of possibilities for a post-Depression intelligentsia. Neil MacGregor recalled his stunned sense of delight as he listened to KPFA for the first time in the early 1950s. "I thought, 'My God, this is something that can really change things, because nothing [else] like this exists."[18] If KPFA didn't transform the world as Lewis Hill and his friends hoped, it walked hand in hand with a generation of people who wanted to make their lives more than just materially good. What drew these people to the station? First, KPFA broadcast what its listeners experienced as innovative ideas within an array of socially familiar contexts. Second, the station offered a vision of the world that encouraged personal exploration to a cautious, upwardly mobile middle class.

The Children's Hour

Like most radio broadcasters in the early 1950s, the first Pacifica programmers assumed that their station served families. Indeed, like a family themselves, the staff ceased broadcasting between 6:00 and 7:30 P.M. to have dinner.[19] By 6:00, most staffers wanted to stretch their legs and eat. But the break concept also "partook of the idea," William Triest recalled, "that between 6:00 and 7:30 most households were engaged in other activities and they weren't about to listen to what we had to offer."[20]

KPFA's staff frequently had dinner at a restaurant called Edy's, located right beneath the station's matrix of rooms. "We spent a lot of time there drinking coffee," Gertrude Chiarito recalled. "We were always together. It was no wonder we got irritated with each other at times. But in general, we got on pretty well."[21]

Pacifica's first programmers also sought to use the airwaves to address the concerns of families. In its first year, for instance, KPFA devoted one out of every six broadcast hours to programs for children.[22] Aside from the fact that, as dedicated social reformers, the early Pacificans wanted to inculcate their values among the young, most of KPFA's personnel were parents themselves.[23] Further, by the early 1950s, the San Francisco Bay Area was awash with toddlers. According to the federal census, while the number of people in the area grew by 53 percent between 1940 and 1950, the increase in the percentage of children ages three to nine registered at 76 percent.[24]

The value of scheduling family programming became apparent by 1960, when the census reported that nearly one-third of the Bay Area population was younger than eighteen and one out of every five Berkeley residents fourteen or less.[25] The 1956 survey of KPFA listeners revealed that nearly half were parents, and more than half that group had as many as four children.[26] The point of children's programming seemed self-evident. "We just felt that programs available to children were so poor," Eleanor McKinney remembers. "We wanted our children to have good things to listen to."[27] This meant shows that broke through inhibitions and encouraged personal exploration. Like the pediatrician Benjamin Spock, author of the 1950s best-seller *Baby and Child Care*, Pacifica's decision makers believed that children ought to be subject to fewer restrictions. Influenced by the writings of Carl Jung, they wanted to encourage children to "become themselves," a process requiring the exploration of ancient myths revealing fundamental human qualities. With all these missions in mind, KPFA's staff recruited a unique array of children's programmers, including a strange man named Jaime de Angulo, unique even among them.

An interesting process led the first Pacificans to this devotee of Native American folklore. During the Second World War many West Coast conscientious objectors went AWOL and found refuge in Big Sur, California's beautiful coastal community. There they visited writer Henry Miller, who had set up temporary headquarters in the area and declared himself a pacifist. A literary inspiration to the pacifist community, Miller corresponded with ex-CO and KPFA volunteer Kerwin Whitnah and with Roy Finch.[28] Eleanor McKinney also saw Miller on occasion. "I used to sit on Henry Miller's back and give him massages and hear all his wonderful stories and laugh," she recalled.[29]

On top of a hill called Partington Ridge, near where Miller lived, resided a doctor, who also struck up a friendship with McKinney. He scoffed at Miller's ideas and branded them naive ("if you can believe that," McKinney later commented).[30] Certainly no one could qualify as more worldly than Jaime de Angulo. Born in Paris in 1887 to Spanish parents, de Angulo emigrated to San Francisco in 1906 and experienced the earthquake of that year. Intrigued by the mystique of the West, he worked on California ranches and made himself over into a cowboy. With the entry of the United States into World War I, de Angulo enlisted in the army and was sent to Johns Hopkins Medical School. Subsequently, he graduated as a psychiatrist with a marked taste for Native American folklore.[31]

In the 1920s, de Angulo moved to Berkeley and befriended the anthropologists Alfred Kroeber and Franz Boas at the University of California. As her husband's reputation as a folklorist grew, de Angulo's wife, Cary Baynes, became a disciple of Jung and began to translate the psychiatrist's works into English. Mabel Dodge Luhan, the Taos, New Mexico, salonist of the 1920s, kept correspondence with de Angulo, and the novelist D. H. Lawrence either envied him or was sexually infatuated with him, depending on which reminiscence one reads. When McKinney found de Angulo on the shores of Big Sur, dying of cancer, he had achieved international renown for his dedication to the representation of Indian lore. Ezra Pound called him the "American Ovid."[32] Readers of Robinson Jeffers suspected that de Angulo served as one of his literary models. The poet Robert Duncan served as his live-in typist.[33] McKinney saw a golden opportunity. In 1949, she asked de Angulo to read his stories on KPFA.

What made Jaime de Angulo such an effective children's storyteller was his capacity to convey the thinking of the indigenous peoples of the American West in a way that Berkeleyans could experience as utterly authentic. The charm and believability of his tales emerged from his skill at bringing to life from indigenous creation myths a universe in constant metamorphosis. KPFA listeners found in de Angulo's playful cosmology a refreshing alternative to their own world. This above all else convinced educated people who possessed only indirect knowledge of Indian life that his stories were genuine. "[de Angulo] was for real," Alan Klinger later declared. "He was a falcon of a man; completely spontaneous gut level." [34]

De Angulo reveled in his personal version of Indianness. Long before it became trendy, then banal, then politically incorrect, he wore the perceived accoutrements of the West Coast Native American range rider: headband, jeans, and a huge belt knife.[35] So fascinated was de Angulo with the Berdache holy men of the Pueblo—who dressed as women—that he sometimes practiced transvestitism, walking the streets of San Francisco in stockings and high heels. de Angulo took female hormones, ostensibly to treat his cancer, so that by the last years of his life he had full female breasts.[36] Few of KPFA's listeners knew much about this, or that the doctor sometimes showed up for on-air reading sessions so drunk he could barely turn the pages of his manuscript.[37] Nor did they know that de Angulo was about to die a slow and agonizing death. All they heard was an elderly man, with his matchbox drum to keep rhythm, speaking in an avuncular voice of a world in which all forms of life came from one source—unified yet interchangeable at the same time.

"I am going to tell you about the adventures that happened to the little boy Fox, and his sister Quail, and their mother the graceful Antelope, and their father Bear, who was very strong, but sometimes he was grumpy," de Angulo announced to his radio audience in a 1949 program. One dawn, he began, Fox-boy and Old Man Coyote got into an argument over who created the world, the boy being under the impression it had been created by Coyote. No, Coyote firmly explained. Marum'da forged it from armpit wax and pipe carvings. Satisfied with this answer, Fox-boy went off to hunt rabbits and wound up getting ambushed by a group of hunters. His enemies delayed their attack, arguing whether to kill or capture him. Finally, one hunter wondered if Fox's father might be a medicine man. "My father is not a medicine man," Fox declared, "but my grandfather is one. My grandfather is Coyote Old Man!" The hunters laughed. Coyote Old Man was *their* grandfather too! "I guess you must be our cousin," they cried. Finally the hunters found Coyote among the Ant Tribe and he assured everyone that they were all his children. That night they danced until dawn in the great Hall of the Ant People. "When the grown-ups came out it was near noontime," de Angulo concluded, "and Fox had already traded his bow and arrows for a spear and a hat with antennae." [38] Thus concluded the tale of a boy fox, descended from a coyote, the son of a bear and an antelope, who turned himself into an ant—the story told by a European man who became a psychiatrist, then a cowboy, then an Indian, then a woman. A forgiving world of limitless possibilities—this was the message the Pacifica Foundation wanted children to hear, no one more than KPFA volunteer Flora Arnstein

Born in San Francisco in 1885 to a comfortable German-Jewish family, Arnstein had a regular KPFA program called *Pony Pegasus.*[39] It might be a bit of an exaggeration to describe her as an advocate of "children's liberation," but not by much. This teacher of children's writing experienced her own life as an ongoing process of recovery from the constraints of her late-Victorian upbringing. At the age of one hundred, Arnstein consented to an oral history interview in which she described unpleasant exchanges with her father as if they had just occurred. For years, she told her interviewer, she hadn't been able to listen to music on radio or television. Suddenly she realized why. It was because she associated music with "him"—her father. "He took me to concerts," Arnstein explained, "he took me to operas, and liked my playing because he whistled all the tunes I'd played. But he never praised me. I would have given my right eye to have him say, 'You did that nicely,' or 'You played that well.' When I realized this I was able to listen to music again."[40]

In 1915, the educator Maria Montessori came to San Francisco to give a series of lectures. Arnstein attended her talks and agreed with Montessori's contention that true learning required desire as well as discipline. "It was the first time I had heard of any educator who had equated interest with learning," she recalled. "Learning was always something you threw on people, but interest had nothing to do with it."[41]

Five years later, Arnstein helped inaugurate the Presidio Open Air School, an experiment in progressive education.[42] Arnstein felt that adults too often told children what to think and feel. She recalled with delight a discussion she had with her friend Erik Erikson, the child psychologist and author of *Childhood and Society*, for whom she sometimes worked as secretary. One afternoon a rebellious student from the school arrived at Erikson's San Francisco office for counseling. Among other offenses, she came to class dressed in a boy's shirt and jeans "before any girls wore them," Arnstein remembered. After the psychologist had seen the patient, Arnstein asked him what was wrong with her. "Nothing," Erikson said. "What do you mean nothing?" she asked. "Well," the psychologist replied, "she only hates her mother."[43] Like Erikson and Thomas Jefferson, Flora Arnstein thought that a little rebellion was sometimes a good thing.

On *Pony Pegasus*, Arnstein urged children to express what they really thought about their lives. The educator read poetry and explained it in a way children might understand. Children in turn sent her their verse and she read that as well.[44] KPFA's programmers wanted their young listeners to see everyday life not as a call to obedience but as a chance for creativity. A folk singer named Lori Campbell epitomized this spirit with the "kitchen orchestra" she regularly brought to the airwaves. Arriving at KPFA with eggbeaters and other common cooking tools, Campbell led children in song while accompanying them with devices they could find at home. The September *Folio* of 1951 announced the premiere of a new Campbell offering, the "Swapping Song," performed with chair rungs and sticks.[45]

So intent was Arnstein on delving into early consciousness that in her seventies she published an autobiographical novel entitled *No End to Morning*, based on her recollection of her childhood. "The Family was One," an early section of the manuscript began. "It had existed from all time, it would exist from all time. It was one because it hung together. The members quarreled sometimes, but no quarrel lasted. To Grandma a lasting quarrel was the unforgivable sin."[46] Nothing bad lasts forever. That is what the first KPFA programmers told children four years after the conclusion of the biggest war in history.

Josephine Gardner, official storyteller of the San Francisco Recreation Department, shared Arnstein's desire to help children sort out their feelings.[47] "Once upon a time there was a man who had two sons, . . ." began Gardner in an early KPFA broadcast. Her voice had a compelling edge. Patient and grim, it hinted at a working-class, Irish American background.[48] "And the older one was all right, but the younger one was very quiet. They called him 'Dumbling.' One evening," Gardner continued, "their father told his older son to go to the churchyard and borrow a spade from the sexton. The boy refused. 'Oh, father,' he said, 'I don't want to go across the graveyard in the night. It makes me shiver.' Dumbling looked up. 'Shiver?' he asked. 'How do you shiver?' His brother responded with contempt. 'Oh, Dumbling, you are a fool! Anybody knows how to shiver! You'll learn how to shiver when you learn how to be afraid!' Dumbling could only admit his ignorance. 'Afraid?' he asked. 'What's afraid?'"

In Gardner's remarkable tale, Dumbling wanders through the world trying to figure out how to shiver. The sexton gives him work digging graves, but still Dumbling doesn't shiver. So Dumbling hitches a ride with a carter, who takes him to a gallows where six thieves hang by their necks. Even when Dumbling sets one of the bodies ablaze while trying to start a fire, he does not experience the desired response. Finally Dumbling learns that a local monarch has a challenge that might do the trick. The king owns a castle in which treasure is hidden. He promises half the booty, plus marriage with his daughter, the princess, to anyone who can locate the treasure. Unfortunately, because terrifying things happen within the building, no one dares spend the night. Dumbling, of course, agrees to take on the task. That evening, while in bed at the castle, a screaming old man with a four-foot beard attacks Dumbling. "I'm going to kill you!" cries the man. After a long chase, he corners Dumbling. "Aren't you afraid?" the old man asks. "You should be shivering with fright!" Dumbling replies as always: "Shivering!? How do you shiver?" His attacker rejoices. "At last I've found a man who isn't afraid! Now I can go away!" He shows Dumbling the castle's treasure room and the king honors his agreement.

"You would think [Dumbling] would be happy," Josephine Gardner suggested. "But oh no. Every day they heard nothing but 'When am I going to learn how to shiver?'" Finally, the princess, now married to Dumbling, loses her patience. One morning, as Dumbling sleeps, she goes to the garden, scoops up a bucket of freezing pond water, and dumps it over her husband. Dumbling leaps out of bed, "shivering with cold," and demands an explanation from his wife. "Oh, Dumbling," the princess exclaims. "You always say you want to know how to shiver. Now you're shivering!" Dumbling cannot restrain his delight. "This is shivering?" he said. "Now I can shiver?"

Eventually Dumbling inherits the king's throne. "And he was the best king they ever had. He was perfectly happy. He knew how to shiver," the storyteller concluded. "But he never did learn how to be afraid."[49]

Some parents did not appreciate Josephine Gardner's ways of metaphorically encouraging children to sort out the emotional categories adults presented to them: love, hate, fear, shivering. Understandably, they expressed alarm at the more grizzly aspects of her prose. Indeed, an early Pacifica progress report conceded that Gardner's stories had set off an "area wide controversy on the significance of fairy stories to children."[50] This was an understatement. A tale about a man who sliced off the king's head, dipped it in a bucket three times, and returned it to its still-alive owner proved a little too much for some parents. At this point, program director Eleanor McKinney, who had undergone Jungian therapy, came to the rescue. She quickly summoned Jungian analysts to the station, explaining that "it is exactly these kind of symbolic violences that children experience that help them grow mature in their psyches."[51] The trauma of the world cannot be hidden from children, KPFA's staff believed. Better to help them sort out their feelings through stories, a process Richard Moore called "deep learning."[52]

Often the station inadvertently invited such controversy. The summer

1949 edition of the *Folio* promised that children's programming would serve as an alternative to the crude fare decried by Radio Listeners of Northern California, which had just completed an experiment of the kind that public-spirited organizations seem never to tire of replicating. The group catalogued the children's programs broadcast by one network station for seven days and, not surprisingly, heartily disapproved of what they found. "During this week," KPFA's subscribers learned, "they heard thirty murders committed, contemplated, or implied. Other crimes enacted or described in the same programs included blackmail, arson, housebreaking, kidnapping," and so on. As an alternative to this chamber of horrors, the *Folio* promised listeners "a children's theatre, a children's chorus, musical broadcasts by and for children," and "serial dramas of worthwhile material."[53] Some parents, expecting arcadia, became confused when they heard tales of ritual decapitation and little boys setting corpses afire. In theory, the Pacifica Foundation stood for peaceable things. In practice, KPFA encouraged its audience to let go a little. Nowhere was this informal credo more evident than in the music department.

Hybrid Highbrow

Former conscientious objector Americo Chiarito served as KPFA's first music director. The son of an Italian cabinetmaker, Chiarito had studied psychology and music at New York University. His assistant at KPFA, Alan Rich, studied in UC Berkeley's graduate music department. Rich had attended Boston Latin School and then briefly attended Harvard as a premed student before pursuing music criticism.[54] Rich also worked for a record importer, who sometimes assigned him tasks in California. A stay in San Francisco convinced him to relocate to the West Coast. Once settled, Rich studied for an M.A. in music, "specifically to become an educated music critic, which I regarded as a rare phenomenon at the time."[55]

Chiarito and Rich set out to establish KPFA as a mecca for classical performance and composition. "My idea was to present the full range of music," Chiarito remembered, "from very early music to modern music and everything in between, without being bound by ideas of having bestseller programs like Beethoven's Fifth and Schubert's Unfinished."[56] When Chiarito quit KPFA in the early 1950s, Rich took his job, adopting a more cautious approach. He made no secret of his disinterest in pacifism, describing himself as a "non-political person." Like other relatively recent additions to the station, Rich had little to do with Hill's inner circle and thought Hill was somewhat out of touch with KPFA's day-to-day operations. "It's like Christianity," he later explained, "you can state a belief or a principle way up there, and then when you come to implement it, you find . . . that progress consists of three steps forward and two steps back."[57]

Rich understood that however Hill defined KPFA's formal mission, people still listened to radio to hear good music, presented well. Like Chiarito, he thought that contemporary music should not to be "quarantined" from European music composed before the twentieth century. He wanted listeners to experience the explosion of modern composition in the 1950s as part of "a stream of music that went from medieval times to the present or the immediate future."[58]

Alan Rich was the perfect music director for KPFA. He sought to make classical music, especially contemporary classical music, accessible to his audience. Sometimes he put on a snobby front. "While I am music director at KPFA, there will be no Tchaikovsky played at this station," Dorothy Bryant fondly recalled Rich declaring during a broadcast.[59] But neither was he an avant-gardist, contemptuous of the subscription symphony crowd. Listeners, Rich believed, came first. "The final perfection of an art work, the last link in the chain of reflections, is the person whom the creator reaches with his art," he once wrote. The listener or viewer "is the reason why arts exist and in a very real way, therefore, the clearest mirror of the arts."[60]

A look at KPFA's classical music schedule on Tuesday, August 11, 1953, illustrates these priorities. In the evening the station offered *First Concert* at 6:05, followed by *Second Concert* at 9:15, with a live performance of a classical piece sandwiched in between. That day, Rich managed to fit Bach's *Sixth Brandenburg Concerto*, Franck's *Symphonic Variations*, contemporary composer David Diamond's *Round's for String Orchestra*, Bach's variations on "Von Himmel Hoch" for organ, and works by Schoenberg and Poulenc into a four-hour period that also included news, commentary, an interview with a marine biologist, a discussion of national politics, and a ten-minute program entitled *Miscellany*.[61] Such scheduling, which anticipated the format of subsequent public FM radio stations, legitimized new music by placing it with works of the previous two centuries. But the most daring aspect of KPFA's music format in the 1950s was the station's willingness to break a taboo firmly established during the First World War. KPFA's staff juxtaposed classical compositions with music in other styles, most notably folk and jazz. Sing outs, blues performances, and jazz sessions frequently aired on KPFA after a performance of the most serious Bach cantata or Mozart piano sonata.

To be sure, the rigid separation of "highbrow" and "lowbrow" cultural expression had begun to break down in the 1930s under the influence of an American intelligentsia that identified with both "the classics" and the populist politics of the New Deal. Its followers attended the plays of Clifford Odets and admired the voice and persona of the communist baritone Paul Robeson, who sang both opera arias and African American spirituals on the same platform. This alliance between academics, classically trained musicians, and indigenous performers would soon lead to the folk music revival of the 1950s.

In the Bay Area, artists and writers associated with the San Francisco literary renaissance made a point of rejecting high culture as an end unto itself (or "tradition as a standard," as *Illiterati* put it in 1945). A story illustrative of their attitude involves a 1953 lunch conversation between Lewis Hill and Jon Rice, the first program manager for San Francisco public television station KQED. Hill asked Rice about his goals. Rice proudly answered that KQED would soon broadcast a televised series on Shakespeare. Hill paused a moment, then posed a rather strange question, especially in light of KPFA's reliance on British Broadcasting Company versions of Shakespearean plays.[62] "Jon," Hill asked, "do you like Shakespeare?" Hill's colleague was unprepared for this blunt inquiry. No, he finally confessed, he didn't. "I had never admitted that I didn't like Shakespeare," Rice later commented. "But I'd also never been asked."[63]

Such a question could never have come from someone who regarded love of the Bard as the moral duty of a well-bred person. The first Pacificans sought a middle ground between the commercialized fare of network radio and the highbrow world so obviously the property of the American ruling class. They found their alternative in what they saw as the authentic expressions of the people—folk music, blues, and jazz—and in performers such as Pete Seeger and Woody Guthrie. They often argued among themselves over what constituted "true" folk music; one such debate was described in an early edition of the KPFA Folio: "One theory maintains that folk songs have a communal origin. Another theory maintains that only the individual can create a song and the community absorbs and alters it after its original creation." On one point all KPFA programmers agreed, however: "Folk songs differ from the average popular song which is written to conform to popular taste and to put money into the purse of the writer."[64]

Although Hill and his inner circle took a theoretical interest in these questions, in practice they left folk, blues, and jazz programming to others.

At first, the station's managers tried to entice jazz pianist Dave Brubeck to host a show on KPFA. When he declined, they turned to an energetic young record collector named Philip F. Elwood.[65]

The son of an agriculture specialist at UC Berkeley, Phil Elwood was raised on old left culture. As a teenager he attended folk concerts at the left-wing California Labor School, haunted record stores, and corresponded with other jazz and blues enthusiasts. Phil's older brother enlisted in the army during the war, expecting to serve in a specialized training program. He wound up in the infantry instead. The news of his death in Europe devastated the family, particularly Phil's father, who died shortly after. The younger son decided to approach military service pragmatically, by enrolling in naval ROTC at Cal. "It seemed quite sensible to do anything to keep out of any active military activities," Elwood explained. "And it also turned out that I stayed in my hometown for two and a half years of the war, barracked on campus, but that didn't hurt."[66] During his ROTC service, Elwood kept in contact with friends who had filed as conscientious objectors, particularly those in Denver, "where there was essentially a huge fascist camp that battered COs into either joining up in the military or going to prison."[67] Elwood's concern for his CO friends and for civil rights in general intensified. So did his interest in jazz.

By the end of the war, twenty-year-old Elwood had developed what he described as a "casually national" reputation for collecting jazz records. So knowledgeable had he become on Dixieland and blues that the owner of a local record store contacted KPFA and suggested that Elwood be given a show.

Beginning in 1952, Elwood's program became a regular feature on KPFA. Not surprisingly, station management at first wanted him to stick to early forms and avoid more contemporary styles. KPFA's early audience reacted cautiously to anything even remotely like popular music. In fact, when asked what kind of music they never listened to, respondents to KPFA's 1956 listener survey overwhelmingly answered jazz, followed by full-length opera.[68] But Elwood's programs were carefully scripted and prerecorded, giving them a feeling of authority. He took advantage of production talent among the students at nearby public schools, some as young as twelve, trained in studio engineering work by Gertrude Chiarito.[69] "They were the kids with the big watches in school who hated gym and never brushed their teeth, and knew all about the insides of radios," Elwood recalled. "Nowadays they'd be computer hackers."[70] Furthermore, his on-air comments about the records he played reflected a broad knowledge of

American history, which he taught at local high schools and community colleges.

By the late 1950s, Elwood enjoyed a loyal following among KPFA listeners. A survey conducted in 1960 found his name elicited more responses than that of any other music deejay.[71] Soon his influence would land him a job as critic for the *San Francisco Examiner*.[72]

While Elwood's jazz programs attracted an older audience, KPFA's first folk music programs were designed for children and teenagers. William Triest discovered two boys from Berkeley High who excelled at guitar and song, and he and Gertrude Chiarito put them on the air for fifteen minutes each week. After their class schedule changed, Chiarito broadcast their performances in a special live midnight program on Saturday nights. "I'm going to leave you on the air tonight," she warned her protégés. "I'm not going to sign off at midnight as I usually do. . . . So be careful, don't say anything you shouldn't and just go right ahead with what you are doing."[73] All night long the phones rang with praise from enthusiastic listeners. The staff decided to make the show a regular feature, appropriately called Midnight Special.

Eventually one of the teenagers, Barry Olivier, received authority over the program. Olivier invited a wide range of folk singers, including Pete Seeger and John Fogarty, to appear with him in the late hours of Saturday night. Soon Midnight Special became a regular stopping-off place for aspiring young performers, many of them students at a local high school run by the Quaker American Friends Service Committee.[74] After Olivier moved on to other projects, Chiarito reclaimed the show. Gradually, Midnight Special evolved into a kind of incubator for the "San Francisco Sound," the merging of musical traditions such as blues and bluegrass with then-popular singing and performance styles. Chiarito encouraged spontaneity and worried less about the competence of her guests than had Olivier. "Didn't matter how bad they were," she recalled. "At that hour of the night, who cared?"[75]

Nevertheless, she occasionally made quite a find. In 1961, one of the show's regulars, a musician named Phil Lesh, said he'd encountered some promising new talent at a bookstore-coffeehouse in Menlo Park, south of San Francisco. Owned by Roy Kepler, who had by then resigned from KPFA, the pacifist meeting and reading center functioned as a miniature Greenwich Village for high school and Stanford students. One of the center's regulars was the son of a Spanish-born club owner and Dixieland musician. José Ramón Garcia's passion for the musicals of Jerome Kern inspired him to name his son Jerry. By the late 1950s, Jerry Garcia had developed an original banjo and guitar style, derived in part from his fondness for the singing group the New Lost City Ramblers.[76] Following Garcia's performance one evening, Lesh convinced him to record a demonstration tape for Gertrude Chiarito. "This guy could have a show all to himself" was Chiarito's response on hearing the recording. Henceforth, the future leader of the Grateful Dead, one of the most influential musical ensembles of the late twentieth century, would become a regular on Midnight Special.[77]

KPFA's commitment to both authentic and high culture was also reflected in the two classical composers the Pacifica Foundation appointed to its advisory board. Darius Milhaud, a world traveler, took delight in tango and jazz; Roger Sessions, a classicist, achieved renown as a "composer's composer." Both shared a deep love of the pleasures of musical community.

Having barely escaped the Nazi occupation of Paris, Milhaud arrived in the Bay Area in 1940 with an invitation to teach at Mills College in Oakland. Even as a teenager in pre–World War I France, his compositions simultaneously delighted and offended audiences. "It sounds just like Arab music!" protested a listener after hearing an early string quartet. "This is hot stuff!" countered one of the violinists.[78] By the 1940s, Milhaud had established an international reputation for scores that combined Latin/Dixieland rhythms, classical orchestration, and amusing titles, such as *Le Boef sur le Toit* (*The Cow on the Roof*). At home at the Paris Conservatory or in a Harlem nightclub, he championed a cosmopolitan nationalism that acknowledged both the formal, the regional, and the specific. "I am a Frenchman from Provence, and by religion a Jew," read the first sentence of his 1953 autobiography.[79] Milhaud loved his job at Mills, especially the students. "They do not look upon composition as something solemn or momentous," he observed, "but rather as a subject like any other, not reserved for exceptional beings, but something to be done with greater or less success, and always with ease and gusto."[80]

Roger Sessions, by contrast, labored in a constant state of seriousness. Indeed, his mother, a feminist magazine writer from Boston, sometimes referred to young Roger as her "serious baby."[81] Born in 1896, Sessions studied music at Harvard, producing an essay entitled "Wagner's Opinions of Other Composers" for the school's music journal and composing a "monstrous fugue with all sorts of modulations" for his counterpoint class.[82] While Milhaud embraced popular culture and spontaneity, Sessions looked upon composing as something "solemn and momentous." An unabashed Europhile, he championed traditional forms: the symphony, the sonata, the contrapuntal mass. Sessions sometimes went so far as to warn his students against putting too much emphasis on compositional "color" or "sonority."[83] The titles of his more adventurous works aptly illustrate his temperament: *The Black Maskers, The Trial of Lucullus*, and *Montezuma*.

After spending some years in Europe living on fellowships, Sessions took a teaching position at UC Berkeley after the war—just as the loyalty oath controversy exploded. As a boy he had opposed American entry into World War I; now he bristled at the inquisitorial mood about him. Did he believe in "private enterprise"? someone asked him. "Of course," Sessions flatly replied. "Composing is the most private enterprise there is."[84]

Roger Sessions exerted his greatest influence on KPFA through five of his students, who, inspired by their teacher's quiet intensity, took it upon themselves in 1946 to organize a group called the Composer's Forum. One of these activists, Leon Kirschner, became a regular presence at KPFA and a significant force in the experimental music movement of the 1960s. The Composer's Forum held gatherings throughout the Bay Area at which it premiered works by Hindemith, Schoenberg, and Stravinksy.[85] Its leaders opened their doors to musicians and nonmusicians alike. KPFA volunteer Adam David Miller belonged to the group and attended its concerts. "They were wonderful gatherings," he remembered. "[The Forum] thought of culture as something that belonged to the people; they wanted to make it available to everyone."[86]

On June 11, 1949, Chiarito, Rich, and the Composer's Forum coordinated KPFA's first special music event: the California premiere performance of Bela Bartok's *Sonata for Two Pianos and Percussion*. The cash-poor station went so far as to put a two-inch advertisement in the radio section of the *San Francisco Chronicle* announcing that the performance would be broadcast at 9:00 P.M.[87] As the piece concluded, Rich heard faint but constant noise from the office. "The performance was so exciting and got so many people worked up that the phone began ringing as it was over, begging us to repeat it," he recalled. "So we just went on and did a repeat performance of the half-an-hour-long work."[88] It was this kind of free-wheeling attitude that so endeared KPFA to its first generation of subscribers. No one symbolized KPFA's cross-mixing of cultural hierarchies more than the station's resident opera expert: a beer-drinking, card-playing, pulp fiction editor who, unimpressed with the genre's formal trappings, wandered about the station in his stocking feet.

Every week one of the architects of modern science fiction hosted a program entitled *Golden Voices*. An early station engineer remembers the man arriving with his records securely tucked under a towel, then taking off his shoes and stretching out over the studio control board.[89] Anthony Boucher began his life in Oakland in 1911 as William Anthony Parker White, the son of one of the East Bay's few women doctors.[90] From his college years, White aspired to a career as a playwright and student of high literature. In 1934, he completed an M.A. in German at UC Berkeley. His qualifying essay—"the shortest master's thesis in the university's history," he later bragged to a biographer—was entitled "The Duality of Impressionism in Recent German Drama."[91] By then, White had mastered at least four languages besides English. When his playwrighting career fell short, White fell back on translating, manuscript editing, and writing mystery novels.[92]

Conscious of how differently his professional life had turned out, White decided to fashion a new identity for himself. A devout Catholic, he selected Anthony as his first name and the maiden name of his French grandmother, Boucher, for his last. Having established a dual identity for his dual literary career, White threw himself into the task of translation and Boucher dedicated himself to the improvement of popular literature. White introduced American readers to the writings of Jorge Luis Borges, while Boucher wrote and published detective fiction and "fact-crime" articles. The latter persona also reviewed books for the *New York Times*. In 1949, Boucher and a publishing executive capitalized on the growing national mania for science fiction by putting out their own sci-fi monthly. *The Magazine of Fantasy and Science Fiction* became the premier vehicle for the postwar fantasy short-story writer. Science fiction proved the perfect venue for a writer dedicated to tastes both erudite and plebeian. Boucher reveled in his two-sided self, leaving his friends to ponder which side was the more authentic. "I can stump the highbrow critics with allusions to Caractacus/A ploy that I've perfected by a plenitude of practicus," he wrote in a short bit of autobiographical doggerel.[93]

Anthony Boucher did not represent the soul of KPFA in the 1950s by virtue of what he did but by virtue of who he was: an alienated aesthete dedicated to the pursuit of private pleasures. He listed his "major non-professional interests" as "historical vocal records, football, basketball, rugby, Elizabethan drama, Gibsons," and "dark beer."[94] He and his wife lived in a modest house in Berkeley filled with orange crate boxes, which he used for filing manuscripts.[95]

Like so many KPFA programmers in that era, Boucher interacted with his listeners in a variety of social settings. Marilyn MacGregor came to know him because Boucher presided over one of the few Sherlock Holmes societies that opened its doors to women. She remembered nervously attending a meeting of Boucher's "Scowrers and Molly Maguires" annual Sherlock Holmes birthday dinner one night, having agreed to read a Baker Street version of "Twelve Days of Christmas" for the group. To her dismay, the "Bodymaster" seated her right next to Boucher. "I was paralyzed with awe by his knowledge of music, his knowledge of science fiction, his writing, *everything*," MacGregor later recalled. Boucher and the master of ceremonies took pity on her distress and arranged for her to read between the soup and the salad ("so you can enjoy your dinner," the MC explained). After MacGregor read her pastiche, Boucher leaped to his feet. "This is the finest debut I have ever heard!" he declared. "It must be published in the *Baker Street Journal* and read every year at the birthday dinner!" And so it was.[96]

Neil MacGregor often listened to Boucher on KPFA and read his reviews of mystery novels in the *San Francisco Chronicle*.[97] "[Boucher] personified the kind of person who attracted me to KPFA," MacGregor later said. This attraction had little if anything to do with what Boucher thought about politics. Although there is no evidence that this remarkable editor espoused pacifism in any way, he, like so many early Pacificans, both detested the repressive political climate of the 1950s and despaired of finding a way to effectively challenge it. In 1953, the high moment of Senator Joseph McCarthy's career, Boucher revealed the depth of his pessimism in a short story entitled "The Other Inauguration."

The tale began on the evening before the first Tuesday in November of 1984, in the study of a very discouraged Berkeley historian named Peter Lanroyd. Writing in his journal, Lanroyd surveyed the recent history of the United States. He described as "The Great Years" the period between 1952 and 1976, "when we had, almost for the 1st time, honest 2-partyism." Unfortunately, by that last year, a new party had emerged, the "American" party ("The bastards!" Lanroyd wrote. "The simple, the perfect name."). The American Party represented, in Lanroyd's opinion, the combined strengths of two demagogues: Huey Long and Joseph McCarthy. McCarthy failed, the historian wrote, "because he attacked and destroyed but didn't give." He did not appeal to mass self-interest. "But add the Long technique, every-man-a-king, fuse 'em together," and you had the perfect totalitarian movement, a party that seemed on the verge of winning tomorrow's national election.[98]

The next evening, as Lanroyd sulked before his television set, the American Party's presidential candidate swept the election. "From now on, folks," beamed a jubilant TV commentator, "it's Americanism for Americans!" Lanroyd poured himself a drink and then "went to hunt for a razor blade." Just before taking drastic action, however, he noticed that his neighbor's light was still on. Cleve, a researcher on psychic energy at the university, was still up working in his study. Lanroyd decided to drop in for a visit, and Cleve met him at the door with an alcoholic beverage. "Have this, old boy," Cleve said. "I'll mix myself another. Night for drinking, isn't it?"

As the two disappointed liberals inebriated themselves, Cleve slowly explained to Lanroyd that he had a plan. Over the past ten months he had perfected not only time travel but the applied alteration of the past. In a series of little experiments, Cleve had even doctored various aspects of the once present with profitable results. Although skeptical, Lanroyd listened. Then he realized why he had never been able to win at craps with his neighbor. Cleve had always gone back a few seconds and adjusted the dice! "We can not only travel in time," the engineer now explained to the historian, "we can rotate into another, an alternate time. A world of If."[99]

After a few warm-up experiments, the two resolved to ensure the latest election had a more acceptable result. They traveled back in time and got to work, eliminating highly placed collaborators with the American Party with a few "well-planned parliamentary maneuvers." They reorganized their favorite national organization, the "Free Democratic Republican Party," to make it politically stronger, and returned to the present. On January 20, 1984, the two watched television as the new president of the United States, a judge with a solid background in civil liberties, took the oath of office. "Lanroyd and Cleve beamed at each other and broached the bourbon," the story concluded. Satisfied, Lanroyd returned to his journal. "I'm the first politician in history who ever made the people vote right against their own judgment!"[100]

Like Lewis Hill, Anthony Boucher dreamed of using a machine to change the course of history. In Hill's case, the machine was real—a radio transmitter. But Boucher could not imagine so concrete a solution. Like many Berkeleyans, he had no idea how to improve the grim Cold War landscape. From Boucher's doorstep, the American people seemed incapable of preserving their democracy, and those in the know appeared powerless to hold the American people in check. The best Boucher could do was concoct a fantastic device that would protect his fellow Americans from their own worst impulses, a contraption he and a friend could operate while drinking at home. This genteel editor—with his science fiction magazine, his poker games, and his opera collection—embodied the culture KPFA helped create in the early 1950s, a culture of refuge. He represented a radio audience that experienced the world as a problem taken out of its hands, carved up between senators from Wisconsin and commissars from the Kremlin. While the first KPFA subscribers thought politics was a fascinating subject, they did not know what was to be done. In this spirit, they carefully listened to the station's public affairs broadcasting.

What Is to Be Said?

For the inner circle at Pacifica—Lewis Hill, Eleanor McKinney, and Richard Moore—public affairs programming represented a delicate challenge. While they all felt strongly about pacifism as an idea, they adhered to the first Pacifica precept: KPFA should demonstrate the viability of a pacifist world not through propaganda but through practice. KPFA's listeners should be convinced of the viability of peace not through the repetitive broadcasting of certain political positions but through the experience of hearing people of different ideological backgrounds relate to one another. The first Pacificans distinguished between "pacifism and the peaceful resolution of conflict," Richard Moore recalled. "We were devoted to a process. Not an ideology (even though each of us possessed an ideology!)."[101] The paradox, as Moore's statement suggests, was that although these broadcasters believed in dialogue, they also wanted this dialogue to result in KPFA listeners reaching certain conclusions about crucial issues of the day. The early Pacificans wanted people to be free, and to agree freely with them, on most matters of importance. Privately, KPFA's public affairs staff strongly identified with the goals of organized labor and cooperatives, anarcho-syndicalism, the fledgling civil rights movement, and, of course, pacifism. No one believed in dialogue more than Lewis Hill, but he listened like someone who had made a bet on the KPFA-sponsored debate between novelist and Communist Party fellow traveler Howard Fast and James Murray of San Francisco Americans for Democratic Action. "I only regret that Murray was perhaps too much the gentleman," he wrote to a friend.[102]

Hill took pride in the anarcho-pacifist speeches broadcast on the station. Occasionally, he delivered one of his own. In October 1949, Hill went on the air to praise a French pacifist who chose prison rather than fight in that nation's war against Indochina. He also approvingly cited an article by Bernard DeVoto in which the *Harper's* editor urged Americans not to cooperate with FBI loyalty investigations. "The FBI is a contemptible institution and the whole country knows it, despite its constant propaganda," Hill told the KPFA audience. " . . . DeVoto's solution is the only one. It is always the only solution in relationship with the state which violates the integrity and conscience of man. Refuse to cooperate. Say, No. Say, I for my part will not."[103]

How was a group of radio broadcasters who believed in active nonviolent resistance to encourage a "free" dialogue that kept anarcho-pacifist concerns high on the agenda? KPFA solved this dilemma quite ingeniously. Anyone capable of coherently representing a political point of view—from far left to far right—could speak. Once seated in Studio A, however, they would be asked pacifist/anarchist questions. Thus, KPFA expressed its agenda not so much by restricting who spoke on the air as by controlling the questions guests had to address.

The station sponsored several ongoing panel discussion shows, each of which centered on a single problem. KPFA listener Adam David Miller recalled participating in an early discussion on religion in which three points of view were represented. He and two other UC Berkeley students who lived with him at the local YMCA took on the roles of the atheist, the believer, and the agnostic.[104] Usually, the discussions addressed more overtly political concerns. In 1949, The *KPFA Round Table*, for example, ran a program entitled "Is the Atomic Age Destroying Our Civil Liberties?" The show included a commander of the local American Legion post, a Mills College history professor, a UC Berkeley biophysicist, and a member of the San Francisco Lawyers Guild. "Can World Government Be Achieved in Our Lifetime?" pondered a panel that included a member of the Daughters of the American Revolution.[105] It didn't matter how much the American Legionnaire declared atomic weapons to be compatible with individual rights, or how much the Daughter damned world government as an anti-American plot. The pacifists who planned these programs always won, because, unlike anywhere else in the broadcasting universe, they always decided on the topic of the hour. That is why who appeared on the programs was probably less important than the questions the moderator asked. In fact, staff went to great lengths to invite public figures whom they no doubt detested. A letter of invitation to state senator Jack Tenney stank with a politeness that must have come hard to its author, a CO who had spent time in prison during the war. "The bills which you have introduced in the state legislature on loyalty oaths, particularly as they would affect State employees at the University of California, have resulted in considerable discussion through the Bay Region," E. John

Lewis wrote to Tenney in 1949. "To our knowledge, you have not had the opportunity of explaining your position on this subject on any radio station in this vicinity." Would you care to appear, Lewis asked, on a KPFA program entitled *The Challenge Table,* in which a prominent public figure "is confronted by two or three questioners seeking explanations of the stand taken by the speaker on current issues."[106]

Subsequent generations of KPFA listeners experienced what they heard on the station as calls to action. Berkeleyans during the free speech movement and People's Park uprising of the 1960s regularly tuned into KPFA for news of demonstrations and meetings. But the first Pacifica subscribers listened to political debates more or less as they consumed the music, radio dramas, and children's readings the station broadcast. Judging by the letters they sent to the station, they drew intellectual pleasure from these discussions, rather than guidance for public citizenship. None of these listeners promised to *do* anything on the basis of what they heard, except to continue to listen. "May I compliment you on your distinguished musical programs and particularly on the highly literate and enlightened commentaries," one subscriber said. "It is indeed refreshing to know that it is still possible to get commentaries on such an elevated level after being forced to listen to the banalities, the hysterical and sensational outpourings of the run-of-the-mill newscasters who practically monopolize the air."[107]

The sense of powerlessness these listeners felt came across in a 1952 panel discussion entitled "Is Free Speech Still Free?" Asked why the right to speak might be considered important, one of the panelists gave an answer that hinted at Anthony Boucher's pessimism. "Free speech as far as I'm concerned means free hearing," explained Lawrence Sears, a Mills College professor. "That seems to me relatively unimportant in a totalitarian nation. But in a democracy where all of us play some role, no matter how indirectly remote in the formulation of our policies, it's of desperate importance that we hear all sides of an issue if we're going to decide wisely."[108]

The first KPFA listeners cherished their right to hear. They also felt the indirect remoteness of their lives. In interviews, neither Alan Klinger, Dorothy Bryant, or the MacGregors mentioned taking any public action as a result of tuning into KPFA in the 1950s. Like many loyal listeners, Bryant did not know then that the station was founded by pacifists. These radio consumers viewed themselves, at least at that point in time, as concerned spectators. For the Pacifica Foundation's inner circle, dialogue had the potential to save the world. But the first Pacifica subscribers sought not global transformation but a stable, predictable world, the kind of "honest 2-partyism" society that fictional historian Peter Lanroyd longed for. When asked about their political leanings, 76 percent of the listeners who answered the 1956 survey described themselves as "liberal," while only 11.4 percent said "conservative" and 12.4 percent said "left-wing."[109] For the first generation of Pacifica subscribers, dialogue promised reassurance, if nothing else. In a world of demagogues and fools, at least somebody somewhere carefully thought things through.

Dreams and Realities

One Christmas Eve in the early 1950s, KPFA volunteer and UC physics major Watson Alberts tuned into the station for the evening news. Former CO Wallace Hamilton, a recent addition to the staff, was serving up the day's events. Hamilton had already established a reputation as one of the station's more spontaneous programmers. "Here's the important news tonight," Hamilton announced. Then he read the first verses from Luke[110]:

> And there appeared unto [Zacharias] an angel of the Lord standing on the right side of the altar of incense.
>
> And when Zacharias saw him, he was troubled, and fear fell upon him.
>
> But the angel said unto him. Fear not, Zacharias; for thy prayer is heard and thy wife Elizabeth shall bear thee a son, and thou shalt call his name John. . . .
>
> And Zacharias said unto the angel, Whereby shall I know this? for I am an old man, and my wife well stricken in years.
>
> And the angel answering said unto him, I am Gabriel, that stand in the presence of God; and am sent to speak unto thee, and to show thee these glad tidings.
>
> And, behold, thou shalt be dumb, and not be able to speak, until the day that these things shall be performed, because thou believest not my words, which shall be fulfilled in their season.[111]

At about the same time, Eleanor McKinney had another vision dream. This one represented not the promise of the foundation but its fruition. In her sleep, McKinney saw the long stairwell leading up to KPFA's second-story studios on Shattuck Avenue. Strange as it might seem, some of McKinney's fondest memories took place in this dusty corridor. There she heard the remarkable piano playing of composer Henry Cowell wafting from the music studio. There her three-year-old son had once playfully flung himself in midair and been caught by her friend Pete Seeger. Normally one faced a blank wall at the top of this stairwell and turned to the left to pass a receptionist's desk. In her dream, beyond this barrier, McKinney saw the shimmering light of millions of tiny diamonds. She perceived a huge building in the haze, then saw clearly. "It was an awesome sight and an awesome feeling," she recalled. Before her stood Chartres Cathedral in France, which McKinney had carefully studied for years in picture books.[112] Like this historic structure, a survivor of centuries of political change and war, the Pacifica Foundation had become a monument of hope for its creators, a living demonstration of the possibility of a millennium of peace.

But the Pacifica Foundation's first listeners bore a remarkable resemblance to Zacharias, who prayed that his wife, Elizabeth, might bear not a prophet but simply a son, who loved incense and temples but did not think they would truly summon angels and who, confronted by the presence of the eternal, fell back in mute fear. KPFA's first listeners sought the good things in life, not the divine. KPFA represented a refuge where intelligent people played good music, where college students sang songs of the folk, and where, at the end the day, the right people always won the debate. "During the eight years that I was at KPFA I don't remember taking a single day off," Alan Rich recalled. "It never occurred to me to take a single day off because whatever I may have felt about individuals at the station, whatever hassles I may have felt, it had just gotten to the point where it was the only place where I really lived. It was like one of those plants that you buy in the five-and-ten—when you take them out of water they dry up and when you turn them back into water they turn green overnight."[113]

Adam David Miller shared in this rarefied experience. A student of English literature at Cal, he too enjoyed the plays, music, and cultural events KPFA broadcast. Like many KPFA listeners, Miller had grown up in the shadow of the Depression and served in the military during the Second World War. But his perception of KPFA in the 1950s was different in one crucial way: Miller counted as one of the few African American volunteers at the station in its first decade of existence.

Miller's path to Berkeley had been circuitous. Seeking escape from the segregation and poverty of South Carolina, he had fled to New York and joined the navy during the war. At first the navy sent Miller to a small officer training school in Washington State. "They saw me and decided it was not the place for me," Miller later explained. So the navy transferred him to a training program at Cal. The city of Berkeley was no racial paradise in the late 1940s, but Miller found it preferable to Washington. "I could walk down the streets and not be looked at. I could walk in and out of places, most of them, and be served. And I could be in school, in classes, where most teachers didn't assume I would fail."[114]

One day while waiting on line in Cal's cafeteria with several other navy men, one of the food service attendants took notice of Miller. She said she was proud of "us Negro lads" and promised that soon she would purchase a house in Berkeley on Carleton Street, in a white area. When Miller and his friends returned from the service, would they like to rent rooms from her at nominal rates? Through correspondence, Miller later found out that the real estate transaction had been predicated on the hope that local officials would not identify this light-skinned woman as black. Once they did, discriminatory housing practices slammed the door shut on her purchase. Returning to Berkeley after his tour of duty, Miller discovered that his cheap apartment near campus did not exist. Perhaps feeling a sense of obligation to her faithful sailor, the woman offered Miller the basement of her mother's home near downtown Oakland. There he lived for eight months before finding a place in Berkeley: the local YMCA.[115]

Miller pursued a master's degree in literature at Cal. He moved with relative ease through the various cultural institutions that surrounded Berkeley academic life, such as KPFA and the Composer's Forum. "I was made to feel welcome," he remembered. "I was not looked down on in those gatherings. I was a university-trained person. And I knew the language and I knew the iconography." Years later—well over a decade after a series of difficult conflicts brought considerable ethnic diversity to KPFA—Miller reflected on the station's founders. He drew from a discourse largely unknown to the Berkeley of 1953. "You have to understand how Eurocentric or white folk see themselves," Miller explained. "They don't see themselves as anything special, though they are very special. They have a history of conquest and domination and all the privileges that flow from that. . . . So [the founders] didn't see themselves as intellectual and special, although they were intellectual and special."[116]

Forty years later it would be impossible for KPFA listeners to look back on the station's first days without referring to the multicultural struggles of the 1970s and 1980s, when white liberals learned that power would have to be shared in Berkeley as well as in Mississippi. The first listeners and staff members at KPFA were indeed privileged. They enjoyed the privileges that flowed from their whiteness, from their education, and from the economic windfall about to come with the Cold War.

In the late 1940s, however, Dorothy Bryant, Alan Klinger, and the MacGregors did not know how the future would unfold. Bryant, who did not begin to write until she was thirty, did not know that she would eventually become a significant novelist.[117] Neil MacGregor did not know that he would preside over the preservation of California's forests. Most of KPFA's subscribers did not know that they would enjoy long academic or professional careers. In 1950, the KPFA community knew only that they had seen poverty, and world war, and in some cases the insides of CO camps and prisons. They understood that they lived in a country where it was effectively against the law to say anything praiseworthy about certain foreign governments. They knew that if they refused to sign certain documents, they could be fired from their jobs. The first Pacifica community was indeed an elite, but it was a unique elite. When Lewis Hill and his friends spoke of pacifism in Berkeley, they indeed spoke as insiders, not as outside agitators waving a "crummy propaganda sheet." But the community they spoke to possessed a specialness that distanced it from American society. Leery of television, of "mass culture," of the harsh realities of politics, Pacifica's discriminating listeners huddled together against the Cold War. Fleeing the past and uncertain of the future, these cautious pleasure seekers found their millennium in the present. Deeply alienated—"disengaged," as one of their peers would put it—they desperately sought fresh interpretations of the outside world.[118] Four remarkable KPFA commentators told them what they wanted to hear.

7)) Three Gurus and a Critic

However much I may be impressed by the difference between a star and the dark space around it, I must not forget that I can see the two only in relation to each other, and this relation is inseparable.

—Alan Watts,
This Is It, and Other Essays on Zen and Spiritual Experience

They revolutionized Zen Buddhism. They cheerfully endorsed enemy governments. They offered mentorship to a generation of great poets. They reinvented movie criticism. Alan Watts, Felix Greene, Kenneth Rexroth, Pauline Kael—these were the most prominent among the first KPFA commentators. From the early 1950s, these four intellectuals offered a vision of the world so unique that sometimes even KPFA's staffers could hardly believe their ears. They wore monks' robes and chain-smoked. They invented theories of culture while whining about their sex lives. Brilliant and self-absorbed, they loved to make trouble.

Yet for all their egotism, each of these pundits remained true to the Pacifica Foundation's fundamental mission: to expand the possibilities for dialogue and the sources of information. These commentators cherished intense discussion, albeit on their terms. They understood that they lived in an age of containment, when middle-class Americans had withdrawn into what one historian called "the psychological fortress" of the suburban nuclear family.[1] These four personalities, ranging in age from their mid-thirties to their early fifties, all remembered earlier days, when socialist, pacifist, feminist, and anarchist ideas were openly discussed. Each now sought to entice his or her listeners into a uniquely fashioned representation of the wider world, to draw them closer to the foreign and threatening, to bring them into imagined contact with the Other.

West Meets East

Shortly after KPFA returned to the air following its first financial crisis, Richard Moore, Eleanor McKinney, and Lewis Hill decided that the station needed a program on Eastern thought—Buddhism and Zen in particular. "The idea was that we should try to get away from the Eurocentric perspective, Eurocentric culture, and Eurocentric religious systems," Moore recalled. Having given Moore the job of finding a host, he concluded that only three people could adequately perform the task. The first, scholar D. T. Suzuki, lived in New York City. The second, writer Christmas Humphries, resided in Great Britain.[2] The third at just about that time was driving west in a state of personal and professional disgrace. In February 1951, Alan Wilson Watts arrived on the coast with a new wife and two children by previous marriage. He probably felt relief at having escaped the eastern winter, but his sudden appearance had little to do with the weather. Watts fled from scandal. For six years this English-born clergyman had distinguished himself as the most unusual Episcopal priest in Chicago history. He later admitted that he had chosen the priesthood "because it was the only formal role of Western society into which, at that time, I could even begin to fit."[3] But even this occupation ill suited him, and in 1950 his life began to unravel. His first wife had begun writing to the Anglican bishop of Chicago, complaining that Watts had declared monogamy outdated, was having affairs, and practiced sadomasochism. Distressed by these confessions, she became involved with one of her piano students. Upon disclosing this new relationship to her husband, she expected outrage. Instead, he heartily expressed his approval and suggested that both the student and his own lover move into the combination home and chapel where the Watts family lived. This indeed took place; Watts's wife even had a child with her student. Finally, she wrote to the bishop that she could bear the situation no longer and secured an annulment of the marriage in Nevada.[4]

When asked by his Anglican superiors about these developments, the priest declared himself unrepentant. He had embraced the church, Watts explained in a letter, out of nostalgia and a desire for security. The logic of Christianity no longer spoke to him. The Christian philosophy of sex encouraged the individual to "foster a simulated love which is fear in disguise." As for the rituals, Watts could stomach them no longer. "I can understand worship as an act of thanksgiving for God's love," he wrote, "but the formularies of the Church make it all too plain that it is likewise to be understood as a means of spiritual self-advancement."[5]

In the summer of 1950, Watts resigned from the Episcopal Church. In a surprisingly friendly reply to this announcement, the bishop said that he was "grateful for all you tried to do for good in your ministry, and I commend you to the justice and mercy of God."[6] By the late 1950s, Watts had become, for many KPFA listeners, something of a god himself.

After settling in the Bay Area, Watts took a position with the American Academy of Asian Studies in San Francisco. Shortly after that, Richard Moore invited him to present a commentary on KPFA. The two met at 3:00 P.M. for a studio recording. Moore asked if Watts wanted to read from a prepared script. "Oh, no," Watts replied. "I'll talk. You let me know what time it is." After Moore turned on the tape recorder, the ex-minister began his commentary. He spoke with remarkable calm, always taking time between sentences, and produced a flawless speech—fifteen minutes to the second. Moore was astonished. "Have you got any more of those?" he asked.[7]

Watts's philosophy on Zen could be summarized as follows: the most important thing humans can experience is their oneness with the cosmos. "However much I may be impressed by the difference between a star and the dark space around it, I must not forget that I can see the two only in relation to each other, and this relation is inseparable," he wrote. The self, Watts argued, is an illusion, an artificial construct that keeps the individual from appreciating the joys of connectedness. "'Cosmic' consciousness," Watts explained, "is a release from self-consciousness, from the feeling that one's organism is an absolute and separate thing, as distinct from a convenient unit of perception."[8]

Watts did not say anything particularly new up to this point; he simply reiterated a version of Zen wisdom that Eleanor McKinney had experienced in her first vision dream. What made Watts's ideas so popular was the way he believed one came to Zen—that is, very easily. In Watts's mind, there existed two false paths to enlightenment. One he called "square Zen"—the belief that a person achieved a Zen-like state through years of study and rigorous meditation. Square Zen erred in its "quest for the *right* spiritual experience, for a *satori* which will receive the stamp (*inka*) of approval and established authority," he warned. "There will even be certificates to hang on the wall."[9] Yet, despite his private hedonism, Watts also rejected "Beat Zen"—the embrace of Zen as a revolt against conventionality, as exemplified in the writings of Jack Kerouac. "Because Zen truly surpasses convention and its values," Watts explained, "it has no need to say, 'To hell with it,' nor to underline with violence the fact that anything goes."[10] One had to neither drop out nor go to graduate school to master

Zen. One simply had to consider its basic precepts and experience joy daily. "The central core of the experience seems to be the conviction, or insight," he said, "that the immediate *now*, whatever its nature, is the goal and fulfillment of all living."[11] Watts urged his listeners to "cherish both the angel and the animal"—to connect with the universe through bodily experiences as well as through Zen study and practice. Writing that "the saint-sinner and the mystic-sensualist is always the most interesting type of human being because he is the most complete," he surely must have been thinking of himself.[12]

Alan Watts represented the perfect middle-class Zen master. You could take his version of Zen anywhere: home, school, or work. More important, Watts brought the foreign home and made it seem safe. Taking pains to evade confrontational politics, Watts just skipped the Cold War, preferring, in his effortlessly Zen way, to bypass recent events in his representations of the East. Listening to his gentle voice on KPFA, one forgot about Mao and Pearl Harbor when thinking about China and Japan. These nations did not harbor enemies, his lectures suggested. They represented the homes of ancient philosophies and wise teachers. Despite KPFA's expressed desire to transcend Eurocentrism, Watts made no secret of his orientalism, his Westernized version of the East. Watts wrote in his autobiography that as a child he had taken delight in the costumes and rituals described in Sax Rohmer and Edgar Wallace's *Fu Manchu* novels. "While other boys dreamed of becoming generals, cowboys, mountain climbers, explorers and engineers, I wanted to be a Chinese villain. I wanted servants carrying knives in their sleeves, appearing or vanishing without the slightest sound. I wanted a house with secret doors and passages . . . with jade idols and joss-sticks, and with sonorous gongs." In his later years Watts often wore a Japanese kimono and noted that when he traveled to Japan people thought him old-fashioned and funny.[13] A slender man, fond of drink and rarely without a cigarette or pipe in his hand, Watts embodied a genteel version of the Other that supported well-worn imperial stereotypes yet challenged the xenophobia of the Cold War.

Watts's Zen philosophy made exoticized concepts seem plausible. People in the West worry about death too much, Watts told his listeners in 1953. Death doesn't bother the Chinese because they understand that the "aware" self represents nothing but a long series of memories. The commitment to this self represents a commitment to those memories, which continually slip away from us as the past recedes. Attached to the aware self, the Westerner remains in a constant state of anxiety over its decaying contents. The Chinese, by contrast, understand that the true self exists in what Watts called the "now" or the "eternal moment": "Insofar as that point of view is ingrained in a culture, there is not the same concern at all for the survival of the individual." He then blithely slipped reincarnation into the argument. Eventually the true self dies, is reborn, and "suddenly you wake up again—as a baby or some other kind of conscious being with no memory of the past." You may have lost the "you" implicit in Western memory yet still retain the sense of being, of existing. So cheer up, Watts explained, "you might be anybody."[14]

These arguments had a disturbing edge. Watts's characterizations of the East came uncomfortably close to the orientalist claim that "life is cheap" in the Third World. Yet he also deserved credit for encouraging the breakdown of national barriers. If you could be anyone, you could communicate with anyone; perhaps you could even coexist with anyone. Such ideas had subversive implications during the heyday of domestic anticommunism, implications another KPFA commentator chose to politicize.

"When asked what nationality I am, I find myself hesitating because nothing I can say would really be true," wrote Felix Greene in the "Author's Note" to his book *A Curtain of Ignorance: How the American Public Has Been Misinformed about China.* Born in Berkhamsted, England, in 1909, educated at Cambridge, Greene immigrated to the United States during the Great Depression and took odd jobs, such as driving a truck. He then went back to England, ran for a seat in Parliament, worked for the British Broadcasting Company, and returned to the States. Looking back on it all, Greene noted that he'd lived half his life in the United States, married an American woman, and was raising an American child. "So," he asked his readers, "what am I?"[15]

The answer was that Greene was English, precisely because of his particular style of internationalism—that at-home-anyplace attitude that came naturally to a people who had, until recently, controlled a considerable portion of the world. Like so many of the journalists who preceded him—J. A. Hobson and Evelyn Waugh, to name a few—Greene possessed an insatiable desire to go into the unknown and return with news that challenged the status quo. Hobson brought news from South Africa; Waugh, from Ethiopia; and Greene, from Mao Tse Tung's China, making him, in the words of Vera Hopkins, "one of the most popular broadcasters ever to use the KPFA air."[16]

In his introduction to *A Curtain of Ignorance*, however, Greene neglected to mention an important personal detail: he imported furniture for a living.[17] Perhaps he omitted this fact because he disliked capitalism and found his aptitude for it embarrassing. Long before his first visit to

China, in 1957, Greene made no secret to KPFA listeners that he sought a new kind of society. "Western competitive capitalism has given us a world that from any other perspective is unbelievably lavish—" he told them in 1959, "but it has failed in one primary respect—it has failed to give us healthy and satisfying human relationships."[18]

The alienation and isolation Greene saw in American life both fascinated and repelled him. In 1955, Greene gave a talk on KPFA entitled "The American Woman," in which he described an encounter with a woman whose groceries he offered to carry. In response, she fled across the street. Ignoring the possibility that his subject might have had a bad experience with strangers, Greene labeled this "a uniquely American incident" typical of "a society which has none of the homogeneity of the older cultures which allows strangers to be less threatening."[19] Greene wanted people to be closer to one another, to regain a sense that he thought the world had lost, a "fellow feeling, a mutual liking and trust that flows in thousands of almost invisible little currents but which make a man feel that he belongs, with no need at all to be watchful or competitive, or tough." Competitive capitalism stood in the way of this feeling, Greene insisted, thwarting the "unlived lives and unlived experiences" that people carried within them.[20]

Greene took advantage of his British passport in 1957 to journey to communist China, an option then forbidden to Americans. Three years later, he conducted the first filmed interview with the premier of China, Chou En-Lai.[21] What struck Greene almost immediately, he told KPFA listeners, was the discrepancy between Western reports of famine and tyranny and what he saw. Defending China became his mission. Somehow, communism there was different. If some journalists insisted that Chinese communism destroyed the family, Felix Greene bore witness to the contrary. "In fact," he said on the air in 1959, "anyone who knows China and the traditional closeness of family life there would realize that any attempts by any government to break up the family would be doomed to failure."[22] If Western reporters insisted that authoritarianism was widespread on the mainland, Greene cited the ownership of guns among Chinese peasants. He claimed that resistance to Maoism in Tibet stemmed from reactionary religious sentiment among locals and a revolutionary overzealousness that Peking's leadership had already curtailed. As for reports of famine, in *Curtain of Ignorance* Greene described in detail the abundant farmers markets he saw. He insisted on the availability of consumer goods and dramatic gains in the Chinese economy as a whole, and contrasted his impressions with stories in *Time* magazine and the *New York Post*. "The reports seem to me to bear so little relationship to this country that I happen to be in," he wrote. "The real gems of misreporting are sometimes passed around at Western dinner parties or among the Western diplomats here for the laughs, but the rest are usually passed off with a shrug."[23]

This biased journalism represented the source of U.S. hostility toward Mao, Greene argued. "The people of America have responded to world events in a perfectly rational and predictable way *given the information with which they have been provided.*" Greene believed Americans would better understand the world if they were separated from their newspapers and television stations. A later Pacifica commentator, Noam Chomsky, would turn this assumption into a science and himself into almost a deity within Pacifica's cultural universe, but Greene developed the idea first. The American people, he explained, "being basically generous," deserved no blame for their own and their government's hostility to China's new government.[24] Greene did not measure too carefully the basic generosity of a people who had yet to end segregation — even in Berkeley. He offered analyses that a middle-class, university-educated audience could accept: U.S. foreign policy would be resolved not in the messy world of mass movements and party politics but in a struggle between elites over who would control the flow of information to the populace.

Most important, Greene wanted KPFA listeners to consider his perspective on China because he thought he'd found the antidote to Western individualism there. "What makes China so significant is the entirely new ground she is breaking in terms of human relationships and cooperative endeavors," he explained after returning from his first trip. "Nothing that has happened anywhere else can be compared to it."[25] In the peasant communes and close-knit Chinese family, Greene saw a better future for everyone. In a pamphlet entitled *The New Human Being in the People's Republic of China,* the furniture merchant drew upon his KPFA talks to extol Chinese society as the next stage in human evolutionary development. "What we all long for, surely," he wrote, "is to be a part of a society that doesn't divide us from one another, which releases us from the prison, the small, boring world of me; which allows us to be members of a community in which we do not have to push ourselves."[26]

As U.S. military involvement in Vietnam escalated, Greene's rhetoric became harsher, as exemplified by the title of one of his books: *The Enemy: What Every American Needs to Know about Imperialism.*[27] But in the 1950s, Felix Greene, like Alan Watts, made the foreign feel safer for the Berkeley listener, albeit with an overtly political edge that the Zen scholar avoided. While Greene and Watts focused on the East, another KPFA commentator made the entire world his spiritual home.

The Omnivore

"I hope in time to be able to get the hum out of this dingit," a voice grumbled across the KPFA airwaves. "But so far I haven't been very successful. There's a little orifice that says 'hum adjustment' on it. . . . I'm sorry. After all the immense trouble we went to get this thing to France we seem to be back pretty much where we were in San Francisco a year ago."[28] These were the opening words of Kenneth Rexroth's November 20, 1958, KPFA broadcast, recorded from his temporary home in Aix-en-Provence, France. Even when relaying broadcasts from his cumbersome tape recorder across the Atlantic, Rexroth brought the same spontaneity to his work that he brought to everything else—although he hated to listen to himself. "It gets worse as I get older," he told a friend. "I play back tapes and shudder—sounds like a B gangster picture."[29]

Rexroth was without question an acquired taste. The poet Phillip Levine recalled tuning into KPFA from a motel room during a 1957 road trip. The program he heard "consisted of one man with an extraordinarily affected and ponderous professorial voice reminiscing on the famous people he'd known personally." He nonetheless found the speaker's depth of knowledge irresistible. In a single discussion Rexroth referred to Gertrude Stein, Carl Jung, Robinson Jeffers, Isaac Bashevis Singer, Luis Companys, and Tu Fu. "I was so excited I had trouble sleeping that night," Levine wrote, "and once again rose and dressed in the dark."[30]

By 1951, Rexroth had overcome his theoretical objections to radio and begun a show on KPFA modestly entitled *Books*, devoted to "mature nonfiction, high-brow literature, scholarly works, fine arts, orientala, poetry."[31] The collaboration of this anarchist poet and KPFA coincided with his slow rise in American letters and his mentorship of the poets associated with the Beats. By the mid-1950s, he had with some discomfort won a reputation as something close to their senior adviser, publishing an essay in 1957 entitled "Disengagement: The Art of the Beat Generation" in which he praised the Beats for challenging the isolation and anomie he saw in traditional Western aestheticism. "No avant-garde American poet accepts the . . . thesis that a poem is an end in itself," Rexroth argued, "an anonymous machine for providing esthetic experiences. All believe in poetry as communication, statement from one person to another."[32]

But like Alan Watts, Rexroth felt uneasy with the nihilism of some of the Beats, particularly Kerouac. He feared the cultural impact of the "emptied out hipster" and saw an implosion ahead. "I believe that most of an entire generation will go to ruin—" he predicted—correctly, in Kerouac's case—"the ruin of Celine, Artaud, Rimbaud, voluntarily, even enthusiastically."[33] Moreover, Rexroth, who had come to adulthood in the faddish 1920s, saw in the Beats' emphasis on image and lack of introspection the potential for commercial co-optation. He knew how marketable nonconformity could be and how easily nonconformists without carefully thought-out principles could be induced to sell to the highest bidder. "I think that since you have never been to America," he told the English writer Colin Wilson on KPFA, "you do not realize the degree of conformity that exists and the way this devours even its rebels. It's got a place for them right away."[34]

Reflecting the thinking of the first generation of Pacifica commentators, Rexroth distrusted freedom for its own sake. He wanted free speech to do something worthwhile, to bring people into conversation with each other and those they perceived as threatening. Rexroth shared with Alan Watts a deep desire to be "one" with the universe. In his autobiography, which Rexroth read on KPFA, the poet recounted various episodes in this quest, including his first "visionary" moment at the age of four in front of his home in Indiana while a hay truck drove by: "An awareness, not a feeling, of timeless, spaceless, total bliss occupied me or I occupied it completely, an awareness of the true, everyday nature of reality. . . . This seemed to be my normal and natural life which was going on all the time and my sudden acute consciousness of it only a matter of attention."[35] Watts recalled a similar epiphany at the age of seventeen while reading the prose of D. T. Suzuki. "I annihilated and bawled out every theory and concept of what should be my properly spiritual state of mind, or of what should be meant by ME," he wrote. "And instantly my weight vanished. I owned nothing. All hang-ups disappeared. I walked on air."[36]

Watts seemed to stay on air, however, on an abstract and logical plane, at least as he presented himself on the airwaves. In contrast, Rexroth delighted in both Buddhist philosophy and a kind of earthy internationalism—to be one with the world by going to it, standing in solidarity with it, and, above all, reading about it. "Somewhere around my twelfth year I acquired the questionable accomplishment of being able to read absolutely everything. Perhaps this is a vice or neurosis, but I still have it," he boasted on KPFA.[37]

Rexroth probably did know more about world politics than almost any other programmer at the station. He did not share Greene and Watts's optimism about the future. Forty-four and still broke when KPFA went on the air, Rexroth had seen too much to believe a spiritual breakthrough was imminent. Sometimes this pessimism seemed overwhelming. The powers that be, he wrote, "are pushing all this pretty/Planet, Venice, and Palladio/ And you and me, and the golden/Sun, nearer and nearer to/Total death. Nothing can stop them."[38] But if Rexroth had little hope for the human race, he still yearned for knowledge and experience, and he communicated this to his listeners. For all its disappointments, the world, Rexroth told his audience, existed to be known rather than to be feared. Furthermore, while Rexroth never shied away from sharing his anarchist sympathies with listeners, his radicalism had an irresistibly erudite quality. Somehow, he never addressed the dirty business of actually overthrowing the U.S. government and setting up an anarchist society. By the 1950s, his had become a politics of interpreting society rather than changing it, and that too made him appealing to KPFA's audience.

An article profiling Rexroth in the *KPFA Program Folio* in 1958 showcased his literary and artistic accomplishments and completely omitted his association with the communist-led John Reed movement or Rexroth's role as a conscientious objector during the Second World War. The farthest the essay would go was to say that "Mr. Rexroth" had, through his commentaries, "aroused intense reactions over the years," usually over capricious remarks about various writers.[39] Indeed, Bay Area literati scheduled parties to coincide with his Sunday-night broadcast so that revelers could listen to his outrageous assessments of great literature present and past. "It's been a long time since I got worked up over the overeducated conversation of the Karamazov brothers," Rexroth declared one evening, adding that "I read Melville only when paid."[40]

Outrages real or perceived aside, when Kenneth Rexroth reviewed books on KPFA, all cultures, ages, and subjects seemed to converge into one place. The poet regarded the lands and peoples beyond the borders of the United States with anything but suspicion—a voracious longing would be more accurate. Rexroth knew that the fundamental assumption of the Cold War—that huge portions of the world could somehow be "contained"—was absurd. Like Watts, Rexroth modified old imperial arguments to make the Other seem less foreign and hostile.

Reviewing William Appleman Williams's *Tragedy of American Diplomacy* in 1959, the poet complained that Williams told only half the story of U.S. expansionism. Williams argued that behind a veneer of Wilsonian idealism, U.S. foreign policy represented a quest for markets abroad.

According to Rexroth, this thesis ignored the fact that much of the world had historically embraced the imperial gesture for its own purposes. "It is self-evident that contrary to cheap propaganda nobody really shoots British cottons into the markets of Africa with gattling guns," Rexroth explained. "The natives wanted them. The thing that the sentimental Social Democrat . . . refuses to face is that the imperialized peoples like imperialism." Anticipating the theories of W. W. Rostow, Rexroth argued that when postcolonial nations embraced Marxism-Leninism, they did so to embark on a process of development that would enable them to "build a capitalist culture of their own."[41] Let those people out there choose their own path, the poet implicitly counseled. In the end they will choose ours.

Rexroth's KPFA program on New Year's Day 1959 remains typical of his work. It included a swipe at Dame Edith Sitwell's *Atlantic Book of British and American Poetry*, which he insisted showed insufficient knowledge of Middle English verse. "It makes you realize how poorly educated that Bloomsbury generation were," he opined, "and of course they were so proud of being so very well educated." Then came a discussion of Conrad Brandt's *Stalin's Failure in China*. "Every Chinese student that I knew at the University of Chicago and elsewhere was killed in those years," Rexroth intoned. "Every Chinese student, male or female, without exception." Then onto Elena Zarudnaya's translation of Trotsky's *Diary in Exile*. "It's a good personal picture of Trotsky," Rexroth, who detested any kind of vanguardism, explained, "absolutely confident and incorrigibly narrow. Not as narrow as Lenin or Stalin but I would say less sensible. . . . It is a portrait of a man who certainly should have stayed off politics."[42]

Rexroth had no difficulty combining these somber subjects, however, with an enthusiastic endorsement of *The Fossil Book* by Caroll Lane and Mildred Adams Fenton. "Kids, of course, just love fossils and I thoroughly recommend it," he cheerfully explained—with one qualification. Rexroth, a passionate hiker, regretted that the text did not include a directory of fossil beds in the United States. He suggested, however, that such a guide could be purchased from the California State Bureau of Mines. "Every rock collector and fossil collector and nature study enthusiast and Boy Scout should have [*The Fossil Book*]," he concluded.[43] Here was the perfect literary sage for KPFA's audience, an accredited radical with a gentle voice who could talk about the Bloomsbury group, imperialism, Lenin, and Trotsky in one breath and tell his listeners what to get their Scout nephew or niece for Christmas in the next.

When Rexroth died in 1982, the world literary community mourned his passing. Services were held in temples in Tokyo. On KPFA's memorial,

Lawrence Ferlinghetti, a frequent commentator himself, confided his suspicions that Rexroth was "hovering over us at that moment, in the form of a giant Monarch butterfly dreaming it's a Chinese philosopher."[44] Kenneth Rexroth departed from the KPFA scene beloved, admired, and remembered well. The station's first film critic did not.

The Movie Lover

On December 8, 1962, Pauline Kael let the station have it. She'd been reviewing movies for KPFA since 1953 and, as she made clear that day, had lost her patience for what she saw as the complacency of the station's programmers, managers, and listeners. In recent reviews Kael had demanded a community-wide discussion of how KPFA did business, and she'd been ignored. Now she segued into that subject while dismissing the film *Ivan the Terrible*. "Whenever I ask people who love [the film] to explain to me what it's about," she said, "they come up with some rather mysterious answers. It's almost like asking them why they think KPFA is so great."[45] Kael was particularly incensed by the way the station manager, Trevor Thomas, had responded to a letter from a listener who felt Kael deserved praise for being critical of KPFA. Thomas had sent the writer an official Pacifica document, which Kael read during her program, that described the structure of the Pacifica organization. It concluded with an only slightly veiled request for continued financial support.

Calling this response "doubletalk worthy of a congressman addressing a constituent," Kael lamented that it was all but impossible to communicate with KPFA without being asked for money. And for what? "Dithering discussions. When you consider how dull much of the programming is, a casual listener would have to be a martyr to keep the station on in the hopes of getting something that interested him." Kael confided that nothing had changed as a result of her demands for reform. "Apparently they prefer to overlook the matter," she said, "as if I made a bad sound at the dinner table." Having attacked everyone else, she concluded her show by attacking her audience:

> And you I suppose will go on guiltily turning your dollars over to this station, feeling that with each contribution that you are a better person for it. You're paying off the liberal debt. You feel as if you're really doing something even if no one will tell you exactly what. It's all a big union of self-sacrificing dedicated staff and self sacrificial listeners. A kind of osmosis. They give you guilt. You give them money. And the more guilt they give you, the more you need to assuage your guilt by giving them money.[46]

Kael's charges were, for the most part, unjustified and unfair. In its first fourteen years on the air, the station had published numerous reports about its structure, finances, and goals. As we shall see, during the 1950s KPFA had gone through a series of painful and very public controversies over how decisions should be made. Indeed, during much of Kael's tenure at KPFA, the institution functioned far too often like an open book, broadcasting its internal battles on the airwaves.

But Pauline Kael was just doing her job. Since anyone could remember, she had taken on the task of shaking people up, especially people who thought they had everything all figured out. Born in 1919 in Petaluma, California, the daughter of Polish-Jewish immigrant ranchers, Kael studied philosophy at UC Berkeley, flirted with Trotskyism, and joined the campus debating team. "She would use her considerable wit as a weapon," recalled Richard Moore, one of her classmates. "She would say things which, by the nature of what she said, would be devastating to the person who heard it."[47] Her professors urged her to study law or earn a Ph.D., but by then she'd become "art crazy," as she said later, spending her free time at theaters and jazz clubs. Following the war, she met James Broughton, one of the poets associated with the Rexroth circle. The two lived together briefly but separated before their daughter was born. They also attempted some collaborative film projects, but with scant success. Kael "never felt at ease with experimental cinema," Broughton later wrote. "She deplored little theater, little magazines, little films. She valued the big time, the big number, the big screen."[48] A hint of Kael's assessment of that relationship may have surfaced in a radio skit she later produced for KPFA entitled "Orpheus in Sausalito." The play takes place in "a handsome flexible house in the Sausalito Hills," circa 1949. "Richard Trowbridge," a poet in his mid-thirties who speaks with a pronounced Ivy League accent, returns home to his partner, Beth Thomas. "Well, dear, it won't work," Trowbridge announces. "The analyst made it perfectly clear today. You are my mother all over again." Thomas appears unimpressed. "I don't understand," she says. "How does it make anything clear to say you feel I'm your mother? I thought analysis was supposed to help you get over the feeling that every woman was your mother?" This remark throws Trowbridge into a panic. "You see! You see! That's just like her! As soon as I get everything straightened out and know where I am you attack me and get me all confused again. It was all so clear when I came in the door."[49]

As KPFA's movie critic, Kael saw it as her mission to stand by the door and disabuse the world of the notion that anything could be straightened out with the aid of some revered or fashionable theory. Like Dwight Macdonald, she thought that any "consistent systematic pattern for understanding reality" denied reality its due. Reality, Kael believed, could be discovered only through experience, feeling, and, most of all, courage. Like Watts, Rexroth, and Greene, Kael brought a foreigner to the KPFA audience. In her case, it was not a country, a political ideology, or a spiritual path but a popular culture that the station had religiously avoided before Kael arrived on the scene. KPFA played no rock 'n' roll, songs from Broadway musicals, and certainly no country music. Its drama and literature department staff read no popular novels or magazine articles on the air. Like the radio critics of the 1930s and 1940s, to the KPFA community popular music and culture represented a corrupt alliance between the easily misled masses and the powerful corporations that controlled the culture industry.

Almost alone in pursuing popular culture at the station, Kael introduced this outsider to KPFA's audience in the form of the movie. To a certain extent she made the movie more acceptable by focusing on "the cinema" (although she hated that word), especially foreign films that met with the approval of KPFA's well-educated audience. But she also ventured into the realm of the Hollywood blockbuster, favorably reviewing films such as *West Side Story*, *Lolita*, and *The Day the Earth Stood Still.* She even praised Jerry Lewis's performance in *The Nutty Professor.* As the manager of Berkeley's most popular repertory film theater, the Cinema Guild, she championed films such as *Touch of Evil* and *Unfaithfully Yours.*[50]

What made Kael so daring, however, was not only that she explored a medium consumed by the masses but that she detested all the middlebrow/left-wing objections to taking in a Hollywood movie rather than attending a folk song benefit. Kael thought that liking a work of art purely because it carried a socially redeeming message represented a form of self-abuse. A "blur of embarrassing sentimental pseudo-biblical pseudo-commentary," she said of *The Grapes of Wrath.*[51]

Kael wanted her audience to own up to who they really were, not who they thought they should be. Her reviews invited KPFA listeners to think about themselves. "In Bergman's modern comedies, marriages are contracts that bind the sexes in banal boredom forever," she explained in one broadcast. "The female strength lies in convincing the man that he's big enough to act like a man in the world, although secretly he must acknowledge his dependence on her."[52] Like Watts and Rexroth, Pauline Kael searched for that "moment," that sensation of connectedness with others and with the world. But Kael found hers not in anarchism or Zen but in a dark movie theater, where she sought a visceral sensation, a feeling of élan, which she once described to her listeners as "what a man feels when he is working at the height of his powers and what we respond to in a work of art with the excited cry of 'this time he's really done it,' a response to his joy and creativity, to his achievement."[53]

Like Watts, Kael trusted her senses. She measured a film's success by its ability to convey a deeply felt truth, rather than by well-worn intellectual or political agendas. She had nothing but contempt for the so-called *auteur* school of film criticism, associated in the United States with Andrew Sarris. Sarris, Kael charged, spent so much time trying to find the authorial links between two movies by the same director that he never explained whether the pictures were any good. Kael saw this approach as the height of alienation. "The ideal auteur is a man who signs a long-term contract, directs any script that is handed to him, and expresses himself by shoving bits of style up the crevasses." She also kept a portion of the KPFA audience on edge by condemning the socially conscious criticism of Sigfried Kracauer and the so-called committed critics of Britain. Their literary corpus, she charged, had produced little more than "a form of Stalinist thinking," especially when they condemned as "fascist" one of her favorite films, Elia Kazan's *On the Waterfront*, in which the principal character testifies before a government commission investigating a corrupt union.[54]

As one might expect, KPFA listeners either loved or hated Kael, and she did nothing to discourage this reaction. In her mid-thirties when she joined KPFA, she disclosed her intimate self in her film criticism, "trying to avoid saphead objectivity," as she later wrote in the *New Yorker*, and letting her listeners in on "what sort of person was responding to the world in this particular way."[55] Movies *were* the world to Kael. She saw talking about movies as a way to connect with people and with that world. Kael demanded discussion and wasn't above jarring her audience into joining it, as this opening salvo to her KPFA review of *West Side Story* indicates:

> Sex is the great leveler, taste the great divider. I have premonitions of the beginning of the end when a man who seems charming or at least remotely possible starts talking about movies. When he says, 'I saw a great picture a couple of years ago—I wonder what you thought of it?' I start looking for the nearest exit. His great picture generally turns out to be *He Who Must Die* or something else that I detested—frequently a socially conscious picture of the Stanley Kramer variety. Boobs on the make always try to impress with their high level of seriousness (wise guys, with their contempt for *all* seriousness).

Kael then reported that she had recently met a man (a "really attractive Easterner") who told her that he'd very much enjoyed *West Side Story*, and so she went to see it, to "learn if this man and I were really as close as he suggested or as far apart as I feared."[56] When Kael's listeners wrote to the station about her broadcasts, they clearly responded to her as much as to her reviews. Her letter writers demonstrated that even in the Bay Area what historian Elaine Tyler May calls the culture of "sexual containment" had taken hold: the idea that women were least subversive to society when kept within an eroticized marriage.[57] One KPFA listener wrote to suggest that perhaps if Kael found a husband she might lose that "nasty, sharp bite" in her voice. A single mother, Kael had little patience for such criticism. Before this new "Freudianized" age, Kael responded, women received praise for their chastity; now they had to marry to be taken seriously. Either way a woman can be nothing without a man, and sex, she observed, "or at least regulated marital sex—is supposed to act as a tranquilizer." A man wrote in to ask why, if she knew so much about film, she didn't go out and make one. "But first, you will need a pair of balls," he advised. On air, Kael always called her letter writers John or Jane Doe. Responding to "Mr. Dodo," (in honor of his "two attributes"), Kael reminded her audience that you "don't have to lay an egg to know if it tastes good" and suggested her detractor cease thinking with his "genital jewels." Following this display of feminist *riposte*, Kael could not resist flirting with her audience. Thanking some listeners for their flattering fan mail, she made a request. Please, she asked, don't tell me this is the first time you've written a fan letter. "Don't say it," she begged, "even if it's true. You make me feel as if I were taking your virginity—and it's just too sordid."[58]

Kael left KPFA in disgust in 1963. She departed after a particularly bitter broadcast during which she confessed that the listener hate mail had become too much for her. Kael had tried to open discussion about the quality of programming at the station, and in her opinion had gotten slapped for it. "Liberals always talk about pressures to conformity," she lamented, "but there's a KPFA kind of conformity too. If you're ever going to do something about the 'out there,' I think you should start right here. It looks like a pretty good Augean stable to me, encrusted with sincerity and cant."[59] Some suspected that Kael left because she resented never having received payment for her commentaries.[60] But her remarks hit home nonetheless. The first Pacificans had created an insular culture, one, like any other, with heroes, demons, and taboos. Perceiving itself as an island of sanity besieged from without, the station could sustain only limited criticism from within. "The typical KPFA listener seems to regard criticism of the station the way a Chamber of Commerce man regards an attack on the profit system," a genuinely offended Pauline Kael concluded. "'Go back where you came from.' *Holy cow!*"[61]

The "Man at the Door"

In the summer of 1952, Lewis Hill spoke at a conference of the Mental Health Society of Northern California, held at Asilomar, Pacific Grove. He titled his talk "The Private Room" and addressed what he saw as the great problem facing the modern world: privacy. In the prosperous, suburbanized present, most people enjoyed unprecedented access to this commodity, Hill observed. "No average man in history has had such a private room, even for a holiday. The image of the self is reflected back to the self from a half-dozen shiny appliances that would have caused the average man of the eighteenth century to say his prayers." Hill saw considerable potential in this privacy. Never before, he argued, did human beings have such power to fashion their individual selves. "We possess ourselves, we inhabit the chamber of our consciousness, with an altogether new sense of its identity."[62]

But Hill also saw danger. This commodity had been bestowed upon society with a price: the decline of a "communal value system. Its very privacy seems to be in proportion to a general decline in common holdings. The room itself appears as the only remaining repository of values capable of commanding belief." As Americans grow more comfortable with this arrangement, Hill suggested, they will become increasingly intolerant of a presence he called "the Man at the Door." This unwanted visitor could be anyone or anything, from a critical friend to an aggressive foreign nation. Whatever the Man's specific purpose, "he will aim, in each case, to disturb in some measure the ability to see the self's image clearly and confidently." In a privatized world, KPFA's manager warned, the response to this unwanted guest will be a general slamming shut of doors. To Hill the pacifist, this condition was intolerable.

> As long as I can communicate with [others], and they with me, there remains the prospect of our living together, and of our making out of our differences and likenesses an integrated, productive community. As long as I can communicate I can create. As long as I can create I am free. And conversely, as long as I am able to receive the communication of others I am able to grow. But if this fundamental condition is eliminated, I am not free, I cannot grow, I cannot create.[63]

While Lewis Hill believed in the sanctity of the "solitary individual," as he once put it, he saw such rights as the minimal condition necessary to lead a productive life. Freedom meant not just the right to talk but the willingness to consider the most unwanted voice, even the voice of the Man at the Door—"that composite threat to well being which ranges from the toothpaste ad to the nightmare of an alien enemy stinging us to death,"

Hill explained. "The door, so it seems to me, must be opened, the threat admitted, and communication with its sources restored, before our dilemma is likely to be alleviated."[64]

In their own ways, Alan Watts, Felix Greene, Kenneth Rexroth, and Pauline Kael fulfilled this mission. Using unique sources of information, they encouraged their listeners to communicate with those perceived as threatening. They opened doors, although the landscapes they disclosed often said as much about themselves as the world beyond. Each in his or her unique fashion tried to show Cold War America a way out. But as we shall see, the adventurous fare KPFA offered in its first decade posed a challenge not just to the "Establishment," as it came to be called, but to the Pacifica Foundation itself. Although KPFA's commentators spoke in the name of dialogue, theirs could also be interpreted as "dissenting" voices. Although KPFA could be understood as a site for trans-ideological exchange, it could also be understood as a protective haven for those with controversial ideas, a reserved space for the ostracized and the ignored. Although the Pacifica Foundation's mission could be defined as a search for a "communal value system," it could also be interpreted as championing the solitary right of the unpopular individual to speak. Two roads loomed ahead. How would Pacifica choose which to take?

1. Alan Watts's talks about Eastern philosophy on KPFA won international renown and a dedicated following in the San Francisco Bay Area. Pacifica stations continued to broadcast his commentaries for years after he died in 1973.

2. Harold Winkler (front left) oversaw the expansion of Pacifica from one radio station to three. Here he joins actor Vincent Price (front right) and KPFK board member Bill Butler for a day of special programming in 1959.

3. William Mandel and two friends during a KPFA marathon

4. Lewis Kimball Hill

5. Elsa Knight Thompson moderating a discussion with three Pacifica stalwarts. On the far right sits Alfred Partridge, former World War II conscientious objector and KPFA general manager. Next to him is seated UC Berkeley educator Frank Nugent Freeman, Lewis Hill's staunch ally. On the left, foreground, KPFA board member Henry Elson listens to Freeman's remarks.

6. Her back faced to the audience, Pacifica children's programmer Stella Toogood tells a story to a live studio audience in 1955.

7. Writer, critic, opera lover, Anthony Boucher offers his thoughts on music to the KPFA audience.

8. In his brief career as a KPFA programmer, folklorist Jaime de Angulo won a dedicated listenership.

9. A late-1950s panel discussion at KPFA

10. It was the fate of Pacifica president Trevor Thomas to guide the foundation through its most perilous hour: subpoena and investigation by the FBI, the Senate Internal Security Subcommittee, and the Federal Communications Commission in 1962 and 1963.

III

DISSENT

Suppression is always foolish. Freedom is always wise.

—Alexander Meiklejohn,
"The First Amendment: The Core of Our Constitution"

8)) Palace Revolution

Domination is the means of change.

—Richard Moore,
interview with author

Raymond Pierce of the *San Francisco Call-Bulletin* did not like KPFA. He did not approve of its staff interviewing reporters from the Communist Party's *Daily People's World* or reading children's stories in which animals said, "There is no God, only nature." Perhaps Pierce had a tip that he needed to tune in on the evening of April 22, 1954, when KPFA's new manager, Wallace Hamilton, introduced the first of a series on "Various Conceptions of Freedom."[1] What the reporter heard so alarmed him that he took drastic action, setting off a long, difficult debate about responsible programming. A bitter, very public factional fight already wracked the station. Now, behind the reporter's action, and the fight, lay a crucial question. Which kind of broadcasting should Pacifica embody? The kind that promoted dialogue or the kind that promoted dissent?

As Pierce listened, some light jazz guitar music floated across the airwaves, then a voice: "Well, I'll call myself Red. I'm thirty-four years old. I've been a viper, which is to say that I've been smoking marijuana since the summer I turned seventeen." Red said he worked in the building trades, then got to the point: "During the time that I have smoked marijuana, I have become convinced that the only problem, really, that the American people are faced with concerning marijuana, is that you got a good thing here and if you get caught using it you'll get put in jail. I think it should be established that all of us here are for it, right?"

A pause, then a somewhat reluctant "yeah" came from another male voice. Red obviously felt the need to prod his associates. "Right, Lola?" he asked. "Yeah," someone responded. "Louie? Sam?" the moderator demanded. "Right," both men chimed. "All right," Red declared. "Now, where were we?"

By this point it had to be clear to any listener over the age of twelve that the four people in the studio were stoned. As the show drifted on, they boasted that, because they smoked pot, they never suffered from hangovers. Lola cautioned the listeners not to smoke marijuana seeds because they produced headache. "We should direct our efforts to the problem immediately at hand," Red insisted, "which is getting the police off our backs." But even he could not resist sharing his scheme to get a cigarette company to lobby for the legalization of marijuana in exchange for the right to market joints. "I don't think of [pot] as a drug," he added. "I think of it more like Coca-Cola."[2]

As the sound of someone sucking from a pipe could be heard, Raymond Pierce of the *Call-Bulletin* did what he thought he had to do. He called the East Bay's state narcotics bureau, then accompanied a police officer to the station. They demanded a copy of the tape from the station manager, who offended the reporter by insisting that the police return it as quickly as possible. "It's a fascinating program," Wallace Hamilton said (or "blandly explained," according to Pierce). "We're going to replay it Sunday morning at 11 A.M."[3] The police quickly declared the marijuana show a menace to the public. "Anybody who hears it who is on the fence would certainly be put over on the wrong side," a spokesperson told the *San Francisco Chronicle*.[4]

The next day, Edmund Brown, the attorney general and future governor, issued a statement condemning "those who seek to minimize the effects of marijuana." His assistant told reporters that Brown had no intention of returning the tape to Hamilton, since it had been classified as a public nuisance.[5] Meanwhile, various law enforcement agents hung around KPFA's offices, making volunteers nervous. The police never found Red, Lola, Louie, or Sam. KPFA's management had arranged with the quartet not to be given their names. The four had recorded their show late one evening when nobody was at the station.[6] On the morning of Brown's statement, jazz programmer Phil Elwood walked up the stairs to KPFA's offices with his daughter while several police officers flashed their badges. "You work here?" one asked.[7]

By this time KPFA's directors realized that the station's subscribers deserved an explanation. On Saturday, April 24, Pacifica management broadcast a statement defending the program "as an important social document of interest to all who seek a sincere and enlightened understanding of the narcotics problem." The announcement made the debatable claim that at no time had the four vipers advocated an "unlawful act." Finally, the broadcast emphasized the station's right to dissent: "KPFA has a particular responsibility to its listeners' sponsors to offer them free expression, which may not always be available through commercial media deriving some part of their income from advertising." The communiqué also announced that Attorney General Brown had returned the tape to KPFA. Brown had also asked KPFA not to rebroadcast the show, and the station's management had decided, at least for the moment, to comply with his wish.[8]

Unfortunately, police action soon represented the least of Wallace Hamilton's problems. Two weeks after the broadcast in question, at least twenty-three members of the Pacifica Foundation's sponsoring board resigned in protest. Begun by Lewis Hill as a small coterie of advisers, by 1954 the board had become a virtual Who's Who of the Bay Area cultural establishment. Among the resignees were former League of Nations staff member John Bell Condliffe; choral conductor and Leonard Bernstein protégé Madi Bacon; and Daniel E. Koshland of the Levi-Strauss Corporation, who had personally donated $1,500 to Pacifica in 1948.[9] The most ominous resignation was that of Frank Nugent Freeman, dean emeritus of UC Berkeley's School of Education, the campus adult extension division. Freeman told the *Call-Bulletin* that the marijuana broadcast confirmed his apprehensions about the Hamilton administration: "We feared there would be some errors made in management," Freeman explained. "The marijuana broadcast was a realization of those fears." Those who resigned concurred with Freeman. In a joint statement, they declared that "the incident itself, with the station's statements concerning it, further confirms our lack of confidence in the group now in charge of the station."[10]

Who was Wallace Hamilton? How had he come to the position of KPFA manager, a job Lewis Hill enjoyed only a year earlier?

In some ways Hamilton fit in well at KPFA. Like Hill, he came from a conscientious objector background. Hamilton's philosophy of free speech, however, differed fundamentally from that of Hill, Eleanor McKinney, and Richard Moore. The latter group, in essence, thought that KPFA should always offer a counterpoint of perspectives. Hamilton and the people who sided with him believed that the station should not be afraid to billboard unpopular points of view from a one-dimensional perspective. This now-besieged manager thought that KPFA should side with the underdog, with whom he identified.

In the long run, Hamilton's vision won favor with the Pacifica Foundation. But in 1954, KPFA wasn't ready for his kind of broadcasting. Hamilton's views on free speech become clearer when one examines his life.

A View from the Margins

Born in 1919 in New York City, Wallace Hamilton was the son of a doctor and a prominent civic leader. In the late 1930s, he enrolled at Harvard to study medieval history.[11] During his senior year, Hamilton began to take an intense scholarly interest in the body, especially the body of the social outcast. For what was probably his senior thesis, he chose the subject of leprosy and the Christian church. The first page of the paper, entitled "Combustio Leprosorum: A Historical Reconstruction," showed a photograph of a leper. "Looking carefully at the frontispiece," Hamilton wrote beneath the picture, "What are your reactions?—Horror?—Fear?—Pity? Those, your reactions, are the basis of this thesis. In that subtle mixture of involuntary emotion, you catch the foundations of intolerance far better than through any written description."[12]

After graduating cum laude in 1941, Hamilton worked as a publicity assistant for a hospital fund in New York.[13] Then the Second World War changed his life.

Following the Japanese attack on Pearl Harbor, Hamilton filed for 4-E status. He found the CO experience isolating and frustrating and admitted years later to having second thoughts about the self-righteousness with which he and others declared their pacifism. "America, in 1940–41 was confronted with some gruesome alternatives of action," he wrote. "Even then, the choice to enter the war had to be pushed upon the country by the massive fact of the Japanese attack on Pearl Harbor. America was a reluctant dragon. But, once incited, it was ferocious. We saw the ferocity, but not necessarily the reluctance."[14] In 1942, however, Hamilton desperately wanted to prove his fealty to the pacifist cause. Lewis Hill chose to serve that cause by moving toward the center of power: Washington, D.C. Hamilton headed in the opposite direction, moving to the periphery instead.

After spending a freezing winter at a CO camp in the White Mountains of New Hampshire, Hamilton took work as an orderly at Massachusetts General Hospital. He spent countless hours in the emergency room, then produced hundreds of pages describing the patients he saw: "Otis Edgarton was 73 years old, an unemployed machinist with ca [cancer] of the esophagus," began a typical entry. "They had taken out his trachea in what

I think was called a whipple procedure. There was a tube that came out of his lower esophagus and appeared just above his collar bone—between his colar [sic] bone and the lower part of his chin there was nothing."[15]

In 1946, Selective Service gave Hamilton his demobilization papers. He immediately burned his draft card, mentioned this action on his resume, and took employment as a publicity agent for the World Council of Churches.[16]

In 1952, Hamilton was in Los Angeles when Lewis Hill approached him via mutual friends. Just after the war, Hamilton had helped Hill make some contacts in New York City on behalf of the Pacifica Foundation. Now Hill asked if he would consider a job as public affairs director for KPFA. Hamilton was not Hill's first choice, he wrote to Finch. Hamilton was "an aggressive fellow with many bright spots but not enough," Hill explained. "The total effect is of a protective cynicism and a self-conscious and rather waggish bombast which are still fresh enough to make the college paper."[17] All of Hill's old CO comrades had declined the public affairs position, however, so Hamilton would have to do. "The man is human," Hill wrote, "and there is our hope."[18]

Two wives, three children, and two decades later, after Wallace Hamilton had returned to New York City and come out as a gay man, he looked back on the perspective that he brought to broadcasting at KPFA. He remembered editing almost one hundred hours of interviews with Native Americans into four radio programs. Repeatedly, the interviewees said that the demoralized older generation seemed unable to offer any positive guidance to their children. At fifty-four, Hamilton empathized with this dilemma. "Like the California Indians, the younger gays, 'the children' of the gay community, are left . . . nowhere," he observed in his 1973 book, *Christopher and Gay: A Partisan's View of the Greenwich Village Homosexual Scene*. "And also, like the California Indians, the older people of the community, bearing the weight of a tradition of centuries of oppression are also . . . nowhere. Doesn't it seem reasonable to suggest that if we could build an intergenerational transmission system that works, both groups might get . . . somewhere?"[19]

Lewis Hill felt badly for Native Americans. Wallace Hamilton identified with them. Therein lay the difference between the two. Hamilton did not share Hill's philosophical distance from the world. He was, like so many of KPFA's listeners, a genteel free spirit, committed to whatever personal exploration one could get away with in 1952. He did not see himself, as did Hill, as the architect of a system of pacifist dialogue but as a purveyor of adventurous ideas. Hill had created KPFA to make the pacifist case from the inside, from a position of respect within the community. In his zest for freedom, Hamilton did not fully appreciate the carefully balanced system he had inherited. He thought like an outsider, because, deep inside, he was an outsider. As Hamilton's influence within the station grew, Hill became alarmed. KPFA volunteers liked Hamilton. Many of them, such as Phil Elwood, found Hill and his "high-flying, high-falutin' ideas" remote and unfathomable.[20] Hill, Richard Moore, and Eleanor McKinney decided that they had labored too long to see their creation undone by newcomers. By any peaceful means necessary, they would take the station back from Hamilton and his followers, preserving the primary mission of KPFA as they understood it: to foster communication, not freedom.

After Lewis Hill's departure from Pacifica, there came a generation of programmers who believed in the absolutely "free" KPFA of the 1950s—a halcyon era when programmers could say whatever they wanted without interference from management. "Free Speech, First Amendment Radio," they dubbed Pacifica.[21] This slogan had its origins in a widely praised 1953 address by Hill's friend Alexander Meiklejohn made before a congressional committee. The famed educator entitled his talk "The First Amendment: The Core of Our Constitution." Meiklejohn's oration, broadcast on KPFA during the height of the McCarthy era, challenged the notion of the "subversive" activity or idea. Meiklejohn spoke with an eloquence that first-generation Pacificans found irresistible. "Whatever may be the immediate gains and losses," he declared, "the dangers to our safety arising from political suppression are always greater than the dangers to that safety arising from political freedom. Suppression is always foolish. Freedom is always wise."[22]

Lewis Hill certainly concurred that Congress should take no action to control speech at KPFA. That, he believed, was his job. The first Pacificans tolerated adventurous radio up to a point, then made it clear that the pacific world in their time had rules just like anyplace else.

Alan Rich discovered this when he criticized a local conductor. For a "fairly consistent" period, Rich told listeners of his music review program, Enrique Jorda, director of the San Francisco Symphony, was "driving the symphony into a hole in the ground." Rich broadcast these comments during a feud between the music critics at the *Chronicle* and the *Examiner* over Jorda's competence. They infuriated industrialist Harold Zellerbach, who took considerable philanthropic interest in the symphony.[23] Zellerbach contacted Hill and told him that Rich's remarks did not enhance KPFA's fundraising prospects. "Lew presented me with this not exactly ultimatum but 'don't-you-think-you-ought-to' situation," Rich recalled, but when the criticism of Jorda continued, Hill became alarmed. Rich arranged for influential members of the Bay Area musical community to talk to Hill about the controversy, and only then did he withdraw his demand for silence.[24] Others did not escape Hill's scrutiny so easily.

One afternoon in May 1951, while attending to station business, Hill turned on his office audition speaker to check the evening's programming. After listening for a few minutes, he began pacing about the hall. Roy Kepler, who had a weekly commentary show on KPFA, appeared to be committing "first-class libel." He was rebroadcasting taped excerpts from statements made a week earlier by a member of the Daughters of the American Revolution, who had participated in a panel discussion on UNESCO, while adding his own remarks "on the lady's mentality and the state of the world." Kepler's behavior, Hill later wrote to Finch, represented "a shocking discourtesy to one who had accepted in good faith the station's invitation to appear in discussion."[25]

At the conclusion of Kepler's diatribe, Hill rushed into the studio and made an on-air apology to the woman "on behalf of the entire staff." He then met with Kepler to explain why he had taken such drastic action. To his dismay, Hill couldn't convince his old CO comrade that any ethical error had been committed. Later, Americo Chiarito criticized Hill for presuming to speak for the staff. He later recalled Hill's reply: "If, as chief officer of this organization, I cannot assume a common concern for the essential dignity of the individual, what can I assume?"[26]

Several years later, a man who identified himself as a member of the "Progressive Left"—strongly suspected of being a member of the Communist Party—asked KPFA for some commentary time. He said he wanted to talk about loyalty oaths at the University of California. On May 14, 1953, the executive membership of the Pacifica Foundation met to discuss the matter. The station, Hill suggested, should encourage any "independent" critique of American society, but he had examined the man's script and had forwarded it to an official at UC Berkeley. Both Hill and the official agreed that a "personal attack" on UC Berkeley president Gordon Sproul should be removed from the text. The committee concluded that the "Stalinish Marxist point of view should be honestly expressed and *identified* to have a valid place in the entire spectrum of political positions in the air. The need to make an announced distinction between the views of the Commentators and the fact that they in no way reflect the station's viewpoints was discussed."[27]

Perhaps the most dramatic evidence of Hill's cautious approach to broadcasting took place during one of the most important free-speech trials of the century. In the first week of June 1957, the San Francisco police department arrested poet Lawrence Ferlinghetti and his assistant for selling copies of Allen Ginsberg's poem *Howl for Carl Solomon* at their City Lights bookstore in North Beach. A florid exposition celebrating the drug-induced sexual adventures of Ginsberg's circle of friends, *Howl* condemned suburban, Cold War America in the most explicit terms. "What sphinx of cement and aluminum bashed open their skulls and ate up their brains and imagination?" Ginsberg asked. "Moloch!"—the ancient Semitic god to whom children were once sacrificed—came the answer. "Moloch! Moloch! Robot apartments! invisible suburbs! skeleton treasuries! blind capitals!" Authorities regarded this literary extravaganza, with its references to poets "who let themselves be fucked in the ass by saintly motorcyclists," as well beyond the protection of the First Amendment.[28] "The Cops Don't Allow No Renaissance Here," reported a newspaper as the police confiscated most of the first edition of *Howl*.[29]

While the book dealer faced trial, KPFA sponsored a panel discussion about the Howl controversy. With Lewis Hill moderating, the staff assembled Ferlinghetti, literary critic Mark Schorer, a civil liberties attorney, and a librarian. Hill began by announcing that listeners would first hear the poem in question read by its author. Hill also explained that Ginsberg, who had made the recording several months before the controversy for a "very late" program, had deleted several passages of the poem "for radio broadcast." In addition, KPFA had seen fit, "in consideration of the hour at which this broadcast occurs," to edit out various words from the poem "simply as a matter of taste." With that, KPFA listeners heard a version of *Howl* on the air.

Ginsberg's omissions were for the most part gracefully executed. The KPFA edits were not. Before the age of digital audio, engineers deleted words from magnetic recording tape with scotch adhesive, a metal editing bar, and a razor blade. The station's extractions were audible and awkward. A listener following along with the text could tell what had been adulterated. Hill assured his listeners that despite the alterations, they would hear "the full essence of what has provoked the San Francisco police department." This was double-talk. The edits clearly obscured the sexual meaning of certain passages. "With waking nightmares, alcohol and cock and endless balls" became "with waking nightmares, alcohol and endless balls." Those who "ended fainting on the wall with a vision of ultimate cunt and come eluding the last gyzym of consciousness" now did so "with a vision and come eluding the last gyzym of consciousness." In fairness, it was not always clear whether KPFA or the author had altered the text. An amusing reference to "the whole boatload of sensitive bullshit" was deleted and, as a result, the word "religions" got kicked from one stanza to another.[30] Lewis Hill, the war resister and poet who had once told KPFA listeners to say no to the FBI, had clearly compromised with government censors and local bluenoses.

After Ginsberg had finished reading, Hill began the discussion by mentioning that "in the preparation of this program KPFA spoke on the telephone with the principal figures in the case *contra* Mr. Ferlinghetti," namely, the heads of the police commission and juvenile squad. None of them, Hill observed, were willing to appear. "We are therefore confronted by the fact . . . of agreeing with one another, fundamentally, upon the issue of censorship posed in this case. And for that reason, let us hope that our program can confine itself principally to information, rather than mutual congratulation upon our agreement upon the issue."[31]

Hill did not see freedom of speech as a right to be defiantly celebrated for its own sake. He saw it as a means to get different people to talk to one another. If that did not happen, no movement toward a "lasting understanding" or a "pacific world" had taken place. Hill struggled to guide KPFA toward what he saw as the larger goal: pacifist dialogue properly understood, to protect the station from those who would make it a vehicle for diatribes, exercised in isolation from one another. Hill viewed the very word freedom with suspicion. " 'Freedom' must be considered in our definition of listener sponsored radio," Hill wrote in his report to the Ford Foundation, boasting that KPFA's staff members "were endowed with unusual personal freedom in the selection and creation of program materials." But even in the listener-sponsorship model, "the degree of independence within the broadcasting operation—as to its particular programming choices—is a matter of concept and delegation."[32] By 1953, the problem of who would conceptualize and delegate at KPFA preoccupied Hill more than ever.

Such questions worried others as well. Richard Moore became uneasy about Alan Watts and the longshoreman philosopher Eric Hoffer, who also offered commentaries on the station. Watts was slowly transforming himself into a "showman," in Moore's opinion, a role that would become obvious when Watts commenced broadcasting on KQED television in San Francisco. "I began to become more and more aware of the fact that coteries and groupies and followers and cult members were naturally following Alan Watts," Moore recalled. "I felt that there was an imbalance which

Alan was unable to correct with any skepticism of his own role or teaching." Moore distrusted the uncritical adoration his words provoked. "There was too much unquestioned data being absorbed," he later said.[33]

Farewell to Anarchy

In October 1952, Lewis Hill decided to act on his concerns. He proposed to the executive membership that the organization fundamentally reform the way it did business. Although KPFA still remained a small operation, it had expanded considerably since 1949. There were now 2,340 subscribers, promising an annual income of nearly $25,000.[34] Once run by a tiny crew of adherents to the pacifist cause, the station enjoyed a much larger staff and a steady stream of volunteers. The community that Hill wanted pacifists to lead now insinuated itself into the very structure of KPFA. Hill bluntly asked at an October 9 meeting that, as the executive director of the foundation, he be given "the authority to organize the staff and operate the station." Two restrictions would limit his authority. First, the Committee of Directors would have the power to consent to staff changes that required an increase in the station's budget. Second, the committee had to approve staff dismissals.[35] Despite these limitations, Hill's proposal amounted to an effort to win considerable jurisdiction, especially given the potential for hiring that accompanied receiving the Ford Foundation grant.

The sixteen people who listened to Hill at that meeting responded to his ideas, for the most part, with undisguised hostility. Resentments long endured suddenly found expression. Various staff members claimed that a "Triumvirate," consisting of Eleanor McKinney, Richard Moore, and Hill, controlled KPFA. Roy Kepler very likely bore responsibility for this label. The former CO had studied the history of the French Revolution in the late 1940s and eventually wrote a somewhat overheated history of his experiences at KPFA entitled "The Terror during the KFPA Revolution: A Chronicle of Division and Dissent."[36] The Triumvirate, it will be recalled, consisted of three liberal aristocrats who formed a power bloc during the creation of the French National Assembly in 1789.

Hill acknowledged that he did enjoy more power than anyone at the station. "The only healthy approach," the minutes quoted him as saying, "was to define the delegation of authority within the democratic system in a way which would conform to the practice of similar organizations."[37]

KFPA did not, however, conform to the decision-making practices of similar organizations. Its internal structure, designed by latter-day anarcho-syndicalists, was based on one principle. "The people who did the broadcasting," explained Richard Moore, "made the policy decisions."[38] The Pacifica Foundation's anarchist structure had been drafted in early December 1946 by its five original incorporators, all former COs. The by-laws created a persona called the executive member, defined as anyone who worked for the foundation: "The ultimate control of this corporation shall be vested in the Executive Members who shall exercise such control in regular and special Executive Membership meetings." Pacifica's by-laws commanded the executive members to gather and elect from among themselves a five-person Committee of Directors, entrusted with managing the "business and property of the corporation." The directors, in turn, chose the foundation's four officers: a chairman, vice chairman, secretary, and treasurer. The chairman presided over executive membership meetings and acted as chief administrative officer.[39] From the earliest days of the foundation, Hill had occupied this post.

The language of the foundation's by-laws empowered everybody and nobody to do everything and nothing. It gave someone who regularly answered the phone at the station the right to object to how the next fiscal quarter's debts were amortized. Further, the person making this decision had no instructions as to whom she or he was responsible. A director's simplest decision could be overruled by a group of cranky executive members, or a director could do whatever he or she wanted until the station's excruciatingly democratic process caught up with the fact that the director had overstepped his or her bounds. The director frequently had to resort to such bureaucratic relay races, since the by-laws did not authorize anyone to give orders. Hill complained at the October 9 meeting, for example, that he sometimes "felt powerless" to get other Pacifica staff to attend to what he saw as crucial tasks.[40] Thus, he often did them himself. As is frequently the case in organizations with such structures, power tended to flow to whomever attended the most meetings and did lots of work. In practice, because Lewis Hill and Eleanor McKinney had stuck with the project longer than anyone else, they enjoyed considerable authority at the station. McKinney's husband and Hill's friend Richard Moore also devoted most of his time to KPFA. Thus, the trio's sinister reputation as a Triumvirate flowed from only the best intentions.

Wherever the Triumvirate label came from, it doomed Hill's proposal, and it was easily defeated. Perhaps in an effort to assuage their leader's feelings, someone suggested a largely meaningless substitute proposal that passed, authorizing the executive director to make "permanent" hires (whatever that meant in 1952), "subject to the previous confirmation of the Committee of Directors." The next day, October 10, Hill informed the staff that he had handed in his resignation. After that, business as usual at KPFA took a holiday.[41]

Over the next twenty months, Hill threatened resignation or actually resigned on no less than five occasions.[42] At least seven other people resigned twice. At one large meeting, most of the station's executive members resigned simultaneously.[43] "But finally they pulled themselves together and had a meeting of everybody including the resigned people, and voted that it didn't happen," wrote one bemused Pacifican to a friend. The staff held two or three meetings a day. "We Never Close," participants joked.[44] Programmers circulated petitions against Lewis Hill, or for him, or simply signed statements pleading for someone to fix everything. Before attempting to summarize this time of troubles, however, it is first necessary to step outside the immediate scenario and develop a wider understanding of the problem.

"The Very Nature of Genius . . ."

When Lewis Hill demanded that his colleagues give him traditional executive power at KPFA, he invited upon himself what the political philosopher Jürgen Habermas calls a "legitimation crisis" at the foundation.[45] The first Pacifica staff adhered "fiercely," as Richard Moore later put it, to the anarchist idea that a small community of friends could run KPFA in a nonhierarchical fashion.[46] Not a few colleagues in the 1952 executive membership privately agreed with Hill that this decentralized system no longer worked. But by calling for the end of anarchy at KPFA, Hill forced his colleagues to choose between him and an ideology. Since the ideology didn't function very well, Hill's request was not unreasonable. But a further question remained: what new ideological apparatus would make obeying Lewis Hill feel meaningful?[47]

Hill could not say that he had to control KPFA because he owned it, or because he could manage it profitably. He didn't own it, and besides, KPFA represented itself as a "nonprofit," collectively run corporation. Nobody and everybody owned it, and Pacifica literature often boasted that KPFA had been created to transcend the profit motive in broadcasting. In reality, Pacifica went out of its way to obscure to the public and itself that the station was very much a profit-seeking institution. That the station did not sell commercials in no way detracted from this reality. More accurately, KPFA could be characterized not as a noncommercial station but as a mono-commercial station, since it regularly broadcast a commercial about its noncommercial self. "This is Vera Hopkins, KPFA subscriber from Lafayette," began a script for one such "plug." "As we well know, there is no agency to foot the bill of subscription radio except the subscribers themselves, who must perform the financial function of a commercial sales department in paying this bill. . . . Decide *your* share in this enterprise and mail your check, a substantial one if possible, to KPFA, Berkeley 4."[48] Pacifica's pacifist/anarchist culture rendered its participants unable to recognize this statement for what it was, a commercial for a commodity-producing operation that ran on debits and credits like anyplace else. Hence, Hill could not appeal to his legitimacy as a competent manager, even less to his legitimacy as its proprietor.

Nor could Hill point to a democratic mandate. First, his October 9 proposal sought to limit, rather than enlarge, the range of democratic decision making at KPFA. Second, the foundation went out of its way to disenfranchise its most important constituency: station subscribers. Fearing the "public with [its] mass attitudes," the foundation's original by-laws gave KPFA subscribers no formal voice in the organization. KPFA was "like a magazine that you subscribe to," Eleanor McKinney recalled. "If you like it you subscribe. If you don't, don't."[49] In fact, the foundation sometimes put individuals on its advisory board who neither contributed nor subscribed.[50]

Hill also could not establish his legitimacy by declaring himself the person who best stood for the foundation's original ideological mission. Hill certainly had a clear sense of his goals for Pacifica. By 1952, however, the foundation had represented its mission so differently to various groups that its core goals were interpreted in starkly variant ways. By choosing one fundraising document over another, one could declare KPFA a pacifist station reaching out to the average person; an "apolitical" station dedicated to representing all points of view; an elite, "cultural" station dedicated to the humanities; or the voice of the angry war resister seeking social justice. With postwar pacifism dormant as a movement, the Pacifica Foundation had nowhere to turn for meaning but itself, or, more accurately, its selves. Hill had no choice but to resort to the only form of legitimacy he still enjoyed: personal legitimacy, based on his charisma and class.

A small but intense cult of personality had emerged around Hill after KPFA went on the air. His associates often idolized him. Hill was "so brilliant mentally," Pacifica attorney Norman Jorgenson recalled, "that usually in discussions he was anywhere from five to ten jumps ahead of you."[51] Sometimes his admirers even felt the need to record their awe into the foundation's minutes. "What I am saying is that Hill is not and cannot be a successful chief executive," declared volunteer programmer Robert Schutz during one crisis meeting. "And I dwell upon this because it is of the very nature of genius to accept no limitations."[52]

Such remarks had their roots in Hill's true brilliance, but the atmosphere that surrounded Hill also played a crucial social function. At a time when nobody could be certain that listener-sponsored radio would work, elevating Hill's mental powers to an almost mythical level gave the close-knit Pacifica community the confidence to move forward. In the years when KPFA had hardly any subscribers, at least the foundation could boast that it had a resident genius.

Hill knew this when he threatened to withdraw from the project. But he did not appreciate how much KPFA had changed. An informal survey found that by August 1953 only four people in the executive membership had been on the scene during Pacifica's formative years. Nearly 70 percent had begun working at KPFA in 1950, a year after the station had gone on the air.[53] Although these more recent staffers admired Hill, they chafed at his efforts to control their activities. They experienced KPFA not as a carefully managed experiment in dialogue but as a vehicle for the expression of personal freedom. To them, Hill represented obstruction rather than leadership.

Three days after Hill's first resignation announcement, a nervous Committee of Directors, which included Wallace Hamilton, met to resolve the crisis. The directors issued a statement expressing hope that Hill might reconsider his decision.[54] At the next executive membership meeting, on October 14, discussion of Hill's restructuring ideas became deadlocked and the members decided that the entire Committee of Directors should resign and new elections be held on the spot. Wallace Hamilton received more votes than anyone else and kept his position on the committee.[55] Faced with the reality of Hamilton's ascendance, Eleanor McKinney's friend Alan Klinger, who had taken a half-time bookkeeping position at KPFA, also handed in his resignation.[56] Hill saw his potential allies quitting. The time had come for strategic retreat.

On November 19, Hill circulated a letter throughout the organization saying that although staff control of policy "has not worked very well," he would concede the matter for the present. "I am convinced that the only way out of this frustration is, in a sense, farther into it—not to abandon the principle but to try it in new ways." One concern remained, however: management of the Fund for Adult Education grant. This, he suggested, would necessitate his return to the chairmanship of the foundation as soon as possible. On December 9, a tired executive membership resolved to deal with staff conflicts "on the level of personal relationships" instead of "by changing the By-Laws and the definition of Executive Membership." Richard Moore managed to get a resolution passed declaring that the chief administrative officer would have the "responsibility and authority to organize and administer the staff of KPFA." This nice-sounding statement—which said nothing about hiring and firing—received the hearty approval of the executive members. With this, Hill sneaked back into his directorate position.[57] Round One had ended.

The station had more than just interpersonal problems, however. In January 1953, Richard Moore completed a financial report indicating that by May the foundation's Fund for Adult Education grant would be completely spent. He projected a deficit through the summer of about $12,000. To make up for this shortfall, KPFA's staff had to generate one thousand more subscribers in the first quarter.[58] Once again, the first Pacificans were racing against time. To both Moore and Hill, this impending financial crisis further highlighted the question of who had authority over personnel matters. To them, a decentralized decision-making system guaranteed that the station's ongoing financial crisis would be ignored.

With the arrival of summer, the atmosphere at the station once again deteriorated. Just before Independence Day, Hill wrote to Pacifica's attorney confiding his frustration. "A majority of the members, like very ideological people everywhere, are so much committed to a particular tree that the forest is obscure and frightening," he said. "I have . . . found myself, more than once negotiating a grant or arranging activities for the station which, under attack by a minority of the group, its majority might fail to support altogether."[59] To another friend, Hill confided despair: "I have tried hard, but I cannot get it. There is too much ideology, too much hate."[60] He resolved to test the limits of his authority once more, this time with disastrous results.

On July 6, Richard Moore convened yet another "special" meeting of the Committee of Directors, which included all of Hill's friends: Eleanor McKinney, staff member Charles Levy, and the Chiaritos. Moore read a memorandum from Hill in which he announced that his resignation would be effective on the last day of the month. The group, which did not include Wallace Hamilton, then resolved to ask Hill to reconsider. The directors also expressed their support for a "staff reorganization and budget" based on "reductions in operating expenditures."[61] A day later Hamilton learned that he had been dismissed. The Dance of Resignations began once more as Hamilton's friends Watson Alberts and William Triest resigned in protest of his dismissal. "Since a purge is in progress," Triest wrote, "I am sure that the Committee will understand my wish to be numbered among the purged."[62]

This clumsily staged crisis resulted in an uproar at the station. The Committee of Directors met yet again.[63] Unable to agree on what to do, they had no choice but to call a meeting of the entire executive membership for July 9. Staff and volunteers packed the station's main meeting room, which was extremely hot, thanks to "body heat generated by animosity," as Richard Moore later recalled.[64]

Now that Hill had resigned, Pacifica Vice Chairman Moore faced the possibility of becoming KPFA's new general manager. What he saw were people, largely led by Wallace Hamilton, who sincerely believed that KPFA could function as a collective and who thought they could do it without Hill. Moore thought otherwise. Without Hill's leadership, he feared, KPFA would drift from one set of pet ideas to the next, serving no one except "a very small percentage of Berkeley upper-middle class people with disposable incomes."[65] Moore called for a vote: did the Pacifica Foundation's executive membership support his role as acting administrator, his efforts to reorganize the staff, and the return of Hill to the foundation? The members deliberated and then voted against Moore seven to six with two abstentions. He resigned on the spot.[66]

To his amazement, Moore discovered that Hill, who had not been at the meeting, considered his resignation a terrible blunder.[67] With Moore gone, the Hill group had only one person left in power, Eleanor McKinney, who functioned as secretary on the Committee of Directors. Recognizing that Hill's resignation had been a ploy, Hamilton unleashed a bureaucratic *blitzkrieg*. He immediately notified the *San Francisco Chronicle* that Hill had resigned and had Alan Watts announce the news on KPFA, making it impossible for Hill to undo his decision.[68]

The directors met the next day and, by majority vote, elected Hamilton chairman of the foundation and passed a resolution forbidding Hill to sign any more checks.[69] A group of them then met with McKinney to discuss her future as secretary. How can you hold office for a Pacifica Foundation whose leadership you do not support? they asked while demanding her resignation. "If I do that," McKinney countered, "then Pacifica won't represent different points of view. If we don't embody it in the body of Pacifica, how can we claim to be representative of those points of view that are actually there?" This sagacious response infuriated Alan Watts, who had little patience for women who got in his way. The Zen philosopher thrust himself in front of McKinney, his face beet red. "Principles are all very well until they don't work and then you throw them out!!!!" he screamed.[70] The directors left, met elsewhere, and fired McKinney.[71]

Finally, Hamilton and his followers committed a strategic blunder. They signed a declaration promising to quit their jobs if Hill ever returned to Pacifica management.[72]

The Triumvirate had been deposed. Hamilton gathered his troops and, according to one observer, made a brief statement in which he proudly described KPFA as "an experiment in anarcho-syndicalism."[73] The mirror opposite of Lewis Hill in temperament, Hamilton thought that KPFA should not just demonstrate the possibility of pacifist/anarchism but raise the black flag at its masthead. In 1957, the Quaker publication *Fellowship* ran a piece by Hamilton entitled "False Gandhianism." A picture of Hamilton lined the cover, with the caption "Wallace Hamilton, Gandhian." "Protest, it seems, is a bad habit that the Indians picked up, while pushing the British out of India," Hamilton sarcastically wrote. "Now that the mission has been accomplished, protest should be contained, as Gandhi's portrait is contained, in a proper framework."[74] Hill indeed believed that pacifism needed a framework. He knew that nobody would ever really believe in pacifism simply because somebody on the radio claimed it was a good idea. The possibility of peace had to be demonstrated, not just advocated. The possibility of dialogue had to be planned, not just left to serendipity. Wallace Hamilton did not grasp this, and now he had Hill's job.

For both the Hill and Hamilton camps, that paradoxical question had returned: how do you encourage people to speak and think freely yet arrive at *your* conclusions at the end of the day? On July 10, 1953, the answer at KPFA seemed all too clear: Sometimes you can't. Sometimes people won't freely come to your conclusions, and when that happens—if you really want things done your way—you've got to resort to bureaucratic force. "One of the fatal errors, in my judgment," Roy Kepler later wrote, "was the original KPFA assumption that 'we all agree.' . . . Hence, when (very quickly) differences arose they had no alternative to going at it personally with bared breasts."[75]

Richard Moore watched the events of the next few months and learned the lessons of a lifetime. "I learned of the uses of power within institutions, the importance of effecting change through the aggrandizement of power, all those nasty little things that government and institutions function by," he later recalled. "I learned that domination is the means of change."[76] Thus concluded Round Two.

Hill was now furious, and in his rage he revealed his class bias. He had resigned, he wrote to Finch that summer, in the hope that KPFA's staff might resolve its structural problems in his absence. Now he faced rebellion by "a stenographer, an announcer, a maintenance engineer, [and] a subscription clerk, long confronted by the impossible task of deciding intricate policies out of ignorance, and thus long habituated to the kind of group participation in which A votes no because nasty B, who quarreled yesterday about the carbon paper, votes yes."[77]

It was time to strike back, and Hill—the nephew of an oil tycoon, a man who felt at ease with CEOs and Washington lawyers—knew what to do. On July 12, Hill sent a memorandum to the entire KPFA staff. The original structure of KPFA has proven a disaster, he declared. It put the station into the hands of people who did not have the experience to run it. Even worse, implied Hill, ignorance now took its orders from opportunism. "Trade on the more superficial aspects of KPFA can produce remarkable results;" he warned, "but I fear those results, or the cynic's toy, the memorial of betrayal which they might preserve."[78]

One financial detail remained that those who now controlled the station seemed to be forgetting. Pacifica still depended on monies from the Fund for Adult Education, which had recently bestowed yet another $30,000 KPFA to produce cultural programs for the National Association of Educational Broadcasters (NAEB). The FAE, Hill reminded his colleagues, had been given a 50 percent lien on the market value of KPFA in exchange for its largesse. "The present situation has made the note governing this lien immediately collectable," he suggested. He planned to undertake a "complete reorganization including, as necessary, the staff, if the FAE continued its note."[79] To further panic his opponents, Hill instructed Richard Moore to return a check for half the NAEB grant to the FAE's director, Scott Fletcher. "It is the intention of the FAE to review the prevailing situation at KPFA," Moore wrote in a memo, "before deciding on any further action with respect to their existing commitments to the Pacifica Foundation."[80] Perhaps emboldened by these developments, Eleanor McKinney announced that she had never been legally fired. "The present 'Executive Membership' and 'Committee of Directors' have no legal authority to make any public announcements," she declared, "and if they continue to do so will be liable for the consequences."[81]

KPFA now existed in a state of institutional deadlock. Hill functioned as a kind of government-in-exile, while Wallace Hamilton operated the station with the blessing of a thin plurality of its staff. The schism put tremendous pressure on at least one intimate relationship, that of Gertrude Chiarito, who initially supported the Hamilton group, and her husband,

Americo, who resigned in disgust as music director. The couple split up that year.[82] The Hill and Hamilton camps now played bureaucratic chess, circulating petitions, competing for the attention of the FAE, and talking to listeners. By late July, groups of subscribers had begun holding meetings in support of Hill. Vera Hopkins attended one of their meetings. "Lew's idealism was contrasted to Hamilton's use of the station as a 'tool,'" read her notes. His "biased news" left a "bad taste at the end of each day."[83] The trenches deepened with each passing hour.

Six Wise Men

Shortly before the end of July, however, Alan Watts sent Hill a six-page letter in which he buried an offer. After reflecting on Chinese philosophy and Far Eastern attitudes toward democracy, Watts finally got to the point: would Hill consider submitting the controversy to "some sort of impartial and friendly arbitration."[84] "The various sensibilities and assumptions you advance regarding my 'position,' views and the like, are in error. I have no wish to reply to them," Hill replied. He signed off with the words "With amazement" above his signature.[85]

Despite this cold response, the Hamilton group continued to push the idea of mediation. They knew that Hill represented KPFA's "one chance," William Triest's wife, Rose, wrote to a friend, given "the monies that are so decoratively attached to him by the Ford Foundation."[86] Hill had already demonstrated that he had the confidence of Scott Fletcher of the FAE, who had yet to agree to renew funding if Hamilton ran the Pacifica Foundation. Hill also enjoyed the crucial support of Frank Freeman of UC Berkeley, who presented a petition to the Hamilton group calling for Hill's restoration.[87] While Hamilton and his followers technically ran the station, they had no access to Hill's "prestige accounts"—the philanthropists and foundation men who kept KPFA alive through its first few years of existence.

On August 3, the Committee of Directors passed a resolution calling for a "complete investigation of the situation at KPFA," to be conducted by "three impartial people" approved by the committee "and also by Lewis Hill if possible."[88] Realizing that time was on his side, Hill refused at first to respond to any invitations. Arbitration had now become a popular idea with the staff, one volunteer wrote to Hill in mid-August. She and others had resolved that such a committee should include someone with community affairs experience and a psychiatrist "so that neurotics will be detected at once."[89]

Seeing that the mediation strategy had taken on a life of its own, Hill moved quickly to influence who would do the mediating. On August 10, he sent the directors a letter demanding that a place on the mediation committee be reserved for his friend Frank Freeman. In addition, Robert Schutz had begun to come around to Hill's side, proclaiming in a memo that he had been wrong to vote against Hill in June and welcoming Freeman's influence.[90] On August 11, Hill added further pressure by dispatching another letter to the FAE: "I refrain from addressing to you an analysis and evaluation of the problems at KPFA which . . . you might be embarrassed to receive," he wrote. These communiqués had their intended effect, delaying the arrival of grant checks.[91]

In late September, the Committee of Directors issued a press release announcing that it had agreed on a "structure committee" that would decide the fate of the Pacifica Foundation. All hailed from liberal, well-established Bay Area institutions: John May of the San Francisco Foundation; Karl Olson, minister to San Francisco's Pilgrim Congregational Church; Roy Sorenson, general secretary of the city's YMCA; wealthy UC Berkeley political science professor Harold Winkler; and Ernest Besig, chair of the local chapter of the ACLU.[92] The committee also included former anthropologist Gregory Bateson, who worked at Veterans Hospital in Palo Alto. A prolific writer, Bateson would soon become one of the architects of the so-called human potential movement. Like Hill, he regarded ideologies with skepticism. People, Bateson thought, would be better off if they didn't believe in things so much. "If, of two nations, each comes to believe in the hostility of the other, that hostility is real to this extent and to the extent that each acts upon its belief," he wrote two years earlier. "But it is unreal—and there is therefore always some hope for international affairs—in so far as the belief is conceivably reversible."[93] Nobody connected to the pacifist/anarchist politics of the San Francisco Renaissance had been invited to play a role in designing the new structure for the Pacifica Foundation. Indeed, all six persons came from traditions that regarded social hierarchy as a fact of life.

The structure committee took about three months to complete its work. Perhaps sensing a waterfall ahead, staff members showed little enthusiasm for its presence. Watson Alberts, a friend of Wallace Hamilton, recalled feeling a sense of futility while being interviewed by Gregory Bateson. "I felt it was psychobabble," Alberts later commented. "I came away thinking: 'You know, this has accomplished nothing.'"[94] The committee thought otherwise. On February 10, 1954, it released a report that all but endorsed Hill's proposed organizational reforms. The report described the foundation's decision-making process as a "nightmare" and concluded that "the existing structure . . . is not merely clumsy and awkward but so bad that sane persons participating in it could only exhibit bizarre behavior."[95] The main recommendation was found in the section of their summary entitled "Station Manager." It read as follows: "[The station manager] shall have authority to hire and fire members of the staff. Staff members shall have the right to appeal dismissals to the Committee of Directors in a manner to be prescribed by the Committee of Directors."[96]

Under the proposed changes, executive members would have little formal say in who actually worked at KPFA. Hill had won, and everybody knew it. Hamilton and his Committee of Directors met several days later to ponder their dilemma. Six learned men had, at their behest, called for the end of anarcho-syndicalism at KPFA. The directors issued a mild statement of gratitude for the panel's work but suggested that the report's conclusions were "beyond the instructions given to the structure committee."[97] They then issued a set of counter by-laws that reified the status quo.[98] This stubborn, conservative response could only have raised further questions about the Hamilton group's capacity to govern. What kind of management created a blue-ribbon panel, then categorically rejected its advice?

Meanwhile, the atmosphere at the station deteriorated. Listener subscription rates stagnated.[99] By September 1953, Robert Schutz openly charged Hamilton with censoring anyone who expressed sympathy for Hill. "This is not a democracy!" Schutz wrote to his peers. "It is not the democracy required by the by-laws. The 'loyal opposition' is, to the best of my knowledge, excluded."[100] Each day, Eleanor McKinney doggedly marched into her office at the "ogre's den," as she now described the station, accomplishing what she could given her limited status.[101] When Hamilton angrily demanded that Alan Rich give up his studies at Berkeley if he wanted to keep his job at KPFA, Rich quit and went to Europe.[102] By April 20, 1954, KPFA's management could not even agree with Ernest Besig, chair of the structure committee, on the procedure for debating the committee's proposals.[103]

It was in this context that Red, Lola, Louie, and Sam went on the air to talk about their favorite drug. Within days after the broadcast, Hill's allies moved quickly to scuttle an already rapidly sinking ship. The critics of the program, almost all Hill supporters, sent a flurry of letters to local newspapers, including the *San Francisco Chronicle* and the *Call-Bulletin*. While factional politics played a role in this round of the struggle, there were clearly philosophical differences between the Hill and the Hamilton groups. Those who supported Hill wanted him back, not just because he stood for centralized leadership but because he favored dialogue-oriented free speech. Those who defended Hamilton sought a less controlled version of listener-supported radio, one that allowed dissenters free reign. For two months, the KPFA community debated this issue. When the smoke cleared, those favoring dialogue emerged victorious, at least at first glance.

The Final Round

Eleanor McKinney now led the public battle against the Hamilton group. If KPFA seriously wanted to explore the marijuana question, she wrote to the *San Francisco Chronicle* in May 1954, the station should have aired a program exploring all aspects of the question. Hamilton's marijuana show reeked of "dilettantism," she said. "I myself was shocked by the human indifference which would expose users of an illegal drug to possible prosecution for the sake of satisfying a 'sociological' curiosity." That, McKinney explained, was why she and other executive members had issued a statement protesting the one-sided nature of the marijuana show.[104] The program "failed to distinguish between freedom and license," the statement charged, and indicated that Hamilton did not appreciate the Pacifica Foundation's true mission. "In defending the action," the signees declared, "the chairman is reported to have [implied] that the station exists solely for 'minorities' and an 'intelligentsia.' On the contrary, the station was founded in 1949 for the purpose of providing a cultural service to all the people of the Bay Area regardless of what majority or minority they belong to."[105] No document indicates that Hamilton actually made such a statement. But the people who signed this declaration meant what they said. KPFA, the station's *Folio* had declared just a few months before all the troubles began, "is our own miniature *polis*, a community of people concerned with the same problems that are shared by the community around us, regionally and in the world at large. It is our hope that the KPFA community can 'discuss' any of the human problems in the whole sense, not just as the narrow interest of some specialized view."[106]

The most serious protest, however, came from Frank Freeman, who, perhaps miffed at not making the structure committee, submitted a formal complaint to the FCC in which he asked the commission to take "remedial action" against KPFA's management. It is one of the ironies of Pacifica history that the first demand for a government review of its operations came from a member of the organization's advisory board on behalf of the institution's founder. Although the commission made no discoverable effort to discipline KPFA on the basis of Freeman's complaint, Hamilton's staff was forced to devote considerable time to a reply. Freeman charged Hamilton's administration with reckless mismanagement and denying the station's critics access to air time. The document used Hill's public statements against Hamilton as evidence of the latter's alleged malfeasance. Finally, the complaint reiterated what had by now become something of a mantra: that a number of marijuana smokers, "without context or critical discussion," had "extolled the sensations produced by this drug and urged its legalization."[107]

The beleaguered Hamilton supporters countered that, in fact, they did see KPFA's mission differently than Hill and his followers. In defending his actions, Hamilton took to the station's airwaves. "There are those in America now . . . who fear freedom, and may fear it particularly when it is projected by personality and conviction," he observed. "There have been economic analyses and even psychiatric analyses of why people fear a naked idea. It seems embarrassing sometimes. Inept sometimes. Injudicious sometimes. But it is there, and those who hold to reality confront it."[108] Alan Watts used his commentary time to join the fight, pledging KPFA would continue to support "adventurous and intelligent broadcasting—giving freedom of speech and a 'fair say' to unpopular, as well as popular, causes, whether political, moral, or cultural."[109]

The most honest public defense of the marijuana show came from Anthony Boucher, who offered his perspective just before beginning a program on soprano Geraldine Farrar. The science fiction editor supported the decision to broadcast the marijuana program because it was a "wonderfully illuminating crimino-social documentary." "The meaningful effect of the program was anything but the advocacy of marijuana-smoking," Boucher somehow concluded.[110]

While Hamilton, Boucher, and Watts took to the airwaves to defend the program, subscription director Kepler handled the angry letter writers. "You have done a great deal of talking about your decidation to freedom of expression," wrote one irate listener. "However it appears to me that freedom for the sake of freedom is a rather adolescent goal." Since Kepler's responses were not broadcast, he could be more candid. "The defense of the program was not that it was the best program that KPFA had ever done," he told the correspondent, "but simply that the station had the right to do it, even though it was controversial."[111]

Ironically, people on both sides sometimes agreed that, in practice, Hamilton's KPFA was not very different from Hill's station. Freeman even expressed as much in a letter to the *Chronicle*.[112] But the controversy over the marijuana program forced both sides to publicly define themselves in contrast to the other. The Hill group argued that dialogue about controversial matters should take place entirely within the universe forged by the station's broadcast sound. All programming decisions had to be made with careful supervision; nothing could be left to chance.

The Hamilton group, by contrast, saw KPFA's role as contributing to a larger dialogue, a conversation between the station and the rest of society. Mainstream America would supply the conventional ideas and KPFA would supply the "adventurous" ones. The Pacifica Foundation would offer up the voices others feared to broadcast, and those on the other end of the transmitter would, through their reactions, provide the other half of the discussion. For KPFA to fulfill this mission, caution had to be relaxed. Proponents of such a sense of listener-supported radio would obviously resent a strong managerial structure. Whether Hamilton and his supporters understood it or not, they had, through sheer political necessity, invented what later would be called "alternative radio." Little did the announcer, subscription clerk, and maintenance engineer know—as their world crashed down around them during the summer of 1954—that they, not Lewis Hill, represented the future.

By early August, the Hamilton group had been completely outflanked. Much of the Pacifica community believed, perhaps correctly, that KPFA verged on collapse. The foundation's main benefactor, FAE, continued to withhold desperately needed money. The institution's revered creator lived in exile, demanding that the current leadership step down. A panel of experts had, at the current Committee of Directors' invitation, recommended that Hill's ideas be implemented. The foundation's executive office now waited for Hill's return. Only formalities delayed his arrival, and they were dispensed with quickly.

On August 4, a group of Hill supporters and disillusioned Hamilton followers arrived at an executive membership meeting ready to end KPFA's civil war. They passed resolutions calling for the creation of a new position entitled "President of Pacifica Foundation and of Radio Station KPFA." In unambiguous language, the proposal gave the person in this post authority over personnel and budgetary matters throughout the organization. Next, they offered this position to Hill. Having replaced the king before deposing him, the opposition informed the Hamilton group that the Corporation Code of California stipulated that the majority of a membership could at any time vote out the institution's entire Committee of Directors and hold new elections immediately. Everyone present then voted in a five-person directorate that included Eleanor McKinney and Robert Schutz. Wallace Hamilton was not included.[113]

Hamilton and his remaining supporters gathered for a private meeting. A year and a fortnight earlier they had signed a statement promising to resign from KPFA if Lewis Hill ever returned in a leadership position. Now, true to their word, Hamilton, Roy Kepler, William Triest, and two others offered the station two weeks' notice on their staff positions.[114] "In all my life I have never seen so many fanatic disciples, Tallyrands, and emotional women gathered into one organization," one of the resignees bitterly declared. "And what is most amazing is the way they all pretend to the highest ethical principles while engaging in the most vicious Machiavellian activities."[115]

In late August someone announced on the air that Hill had accepted the position of president of Pacifica.[116] A few months later Alan Rich returned from Europe. Composer Robert Erickson, who now held the position of music director, offered Rich his old job as music programmer. "I discovered that there had been a palace revolution at KPFA," Rich recalled.[117]

With this simple phrase—"Palace Revolution"—Rich summarized the price Hill and his allies had paid to recapture their radio station. They had restored KPFA to their original pacifist vision, but they had done so through the bureaucratic equivalent of brute force. They had used their influence with the Bay Area's wealthy and powerful to squeeze KPFA's finances dry. They had resorted to disingenuous gestures such as phony resignations. They had capitalized on a programming blunder that they might have committed themselves. Put metaphorically, Hill and his allies had shaken the ship of Pacifica until their enemies fell out. Dialogue had won the day by other means. The *polis* had become a palace.

In all fairness, the Hill group had few other options. The first Pacificans had created an institution that offered its leaders no conventional means to establish their legitimacy. A plutocracy that spoke in the language of democracy, a business that spoke in the language of pacifist/anarchism, the Pacifica Foundation had been designed for a political economy that did not exist: a stateless society of anarcho-syndicalist cooperatives. In the absence of a pacifist political presence, Hill and his friends reached out to their one surviving ally: liberalism, the liberalism of academics like Frank Freeman, the ACLU, the Ford Foundation, and the FCC. These institutions sought not a pacific world but a "fair and balanced" world in their time—a world without loyalty oaths, a world where distinguished professors who voted for Adlai Stevenson would not be red-baited. Certainly these represented decent goals. But in their zeal for financial and political support, the first Pacificans failed to create an institutional structure that would transmit the original Pacifica idea to future generations.

On October 30, 1954, a newly reinstalled Lewis Hill went on the air and acknowledged that he and his associates had made some rather dire projections about KPFA's finances. The situation looked much better now, he said. Although KPFA's subscription rate had gone into "disastrous decline," it had picked up again and the number of subscribers was now at about thirty-three hundred. Furthermore, the executive membership had met the day before and elected a new committee of directors that included Dean Frank Freeman, Ernest Besig of the ACLU, Harold Winkler of UC Berkeley's political science department, Robert Schutz, and himself.[118] In 1946, Hill had supped at Breen's Cafe with a directorate of conscientious objectors. Now in their places sat lawyers and bureaucrats who had helped Hill defeat his opponents, most of them ex-COs themselves.

Among those ex-COs, Hill probably disliked Roy Kepler the most. After Kepler resigned his staff position, Hill personally instructed the postmaster to cease forwarding Kepler's KPFA mail to his home address.[119] The ill will was mutual. For many years, any mention of KPFA or Hill would send Kepler rushing to his typewriter. When, some time after Kepler's resignation, a columnist for the *Chronicle* praised the station for what he saw as a shift to a more balanced perspective, Kepler sent Hill a two-page single-spaced diatribe. "As a former promotion director of KPFA I must take exception," Kepler wrote. "The station would be the first to insist it has not changed its programming policies, which have always included viewpoints left, right and center."[120] In reality, Kepler, like so many of his peers, could barely tolerate the existence of the right and center, let alone the vast majority of Americans. "The common man is now free; he has the vote, a job and can even get a college education," he declared in a 1953 commentary entitled "The Vulgarian Revolution." "So what does he do with it all? He buys a shiny car, a shiny refrigerator, a TV set, and indulges himself in the popular culture; that is, soap operas, Bob Hope, Mickey Spillane, and Marilyn Monroe."[121]

Kepler, like Wallace Hamilton and so many others, instinctively experienced KPFA as a refuge from America, far less as a transformative force. The Hamilton group represented those who thought that the station's primary mission lay in the promotion of individual rights, in particular the right to dissent from American culture. For the Hill group, freedom and individual rights represented the foundation's secondary mission, the necessary precondition for the first: peaceable communication among human beings. This misunderstanding had reached a crisis, and the crisis had been resolved, albeit crudely. KPFA's staff and followers could now misunderstand the station's original mission all they wanted, as long as they remembered who was in charge. Pacifist dialogue now depended almost entirely on the personal authority and health of its charismatic creator. In the summer of 1954, as the McCarthy era began its slow decline and fall, KPFA's mission and its founder had become one. He and it ruled in splendid isolation. With his departure, nothing could be guaranteed.

9)) Room for Dissent

Most liberals think that if you can find the middle of anything and you can squat there, that somehow or another virtue has been achieved.

—Elsa Knight Thompson,
quoted in *Elsa Knight Thompson: A Remembrance*

On KPFA's eighth birthday, Lewis Hill went on the air to talk about the station's history. It wasn't a very good program. His voice sounded tired and depressed. Reading from an early KPFA progress report, one he had probably written, he detailed in dry technical prose a series of transmitter difficulties that had caused KPFA to go off the air for three days during its first weeks of broadcasting. Finally the engineers got the problem under control, he said, and the operation was "trouble free thereafter." The president of the Pacifica Foundation paused. "Anyone who has listened to KPFA for some years or followed its history will surely find the last sentence in this description amusing," Hill commented. " 'Trouble free,' indeed."[1]

Hill went on to summarize the financial history of the station. In 1949, KPFA had gone on the air with a cash reserve of $1,700. "Eight years later, it's a little less than 1,700 dollars." Nonetheless, he promised, the station would survive: "It just goes to show, as someone remarked lately, what can happen when a crazy idea is joined with sufficiently stubborn dispositions. Now there are about fifty-three hundred subscribers, so here's to ten thousand. The real difference between now and then is that we know now that it can be done."[2] It was April 15, 1957.

With that said, the inventor of listener-sponsored broadcasting signed off and went back to business—the business of living in agonizing physical pain. Hill's spinal arthritis had gotten out of control. Standard medicine in the 1950s offered no effective therapies for this malady, although some practitioners prescribed a "wonder drug"; a large dose of cortisone injected into the areas where the arthritic experienced discomfort gave considerable short-term relief but also produced psychosis and depression.[3] Even worse, the patient could become addicted or need ever-larger doses to experience remission.[4]

By the time of his broadcast, Hill's physicians had been giving him "monster shots" of cortisone, according to his wife, Joy. At one point, a treatment so affected Hill that people on the street thought him drunk and the police almost arrested him for disorderly behavior.[5] He disregarded his friends' warnings about cortisone,[6] and Gertrude Chiarito suspected that when he could no longer get it from his physician, Hill obtained the substance in nonprescription form. At KPFA, Hill's interactions became increasingly bizarre. Chiarito later recalled a conversation with Hill in the hallway during this time. "I have to talk to you, you're the only person I can trust," he said. "What do you do when everyone is against you?" Hill asked later. Chiarito tried to reassure her friend of almost a decade, but without success. "It finally got to the point where you were so afraid to talk to him," she remembered. "Because you knew that he was misinterpreting anything you said in his paranoia."[7]

Pandemonium had become part of daily life at KPFA, although only newcomers noticed. In April 1957, Elsa Knight Thompson arrived for her first day as a volunteer. "I got to the station, and I walked up some grimy stairs into this incredible lobby" and sat on a "great lumpy sofa with springs sticking out of it," she later recalled. "God, it was a terrifying mess." To her horror, Hill had just fired her contact at the station. Having lost the day's battle, her friend invited her for a drink and summarized everything he disliked about Pacifica radio. "Are you advising me not to volunteer?" Thompson asked. "Oh, no," he responded. "I think you should do it by all means."[8]

By then, Hill appeared at the station less often. One day around that time, KPFA commentator Sidney Roger ran into him during a visit to the Russian River, near where Hill lived. Roger recalled that he looked terrible. When he asked Hill how he was doing, Hill replied that he had retired.[9] Because Hill valued his privacy above all else, most people did not know that he lived in a state of crisis. In the summer of 1956, he had taken a medical leave from the Pacifica Foundation. He had suffered a "slight stroke" and needed to rest, his secretary told the public.[10] This statement represented a half-truth. Hill did need to rest, but not because of a stroke. Over the summer he had tried to commit suicide with sleeping pills. He was recovering from the attempt.[11]

Hill was in deep trouble and nothing could be done for it. He desperately needed to reach out to friends, but his relationship with those he loved had become tenuous and strained. Lewis Hill, advocate of dialogue, did not know how to open himself up and talk. He knew how to write six-page letters patiently explaining why he was right and someone else was wrong about foundation policy. But he could not admit that he needed help. In 1957, Hill remained the person who had, in 1948, expressed his contempt for pacifists who sought from political activity "a mass discharge of the individual emotion, that suppurates and swells in isolation, by rubbing it hard against other swollen emotions; and when they get that relief they are likely to go home temporarily satisfied." It was no coincidence that the arthritic Hill used metaphors of muscular and neurological pain in his prose. That he could not empathize with the simple need to express anger in the face of catastrophic events revealed the extent to which he had come to terms with his own emotions. Seeing everything in intellectual terms, he lived in a state of deep isolation. By 1957, Hill, in the words of the person who knew him best, "had run out of any place to look except his own head."[12]

Meanwhile, the station moved from crisis to crisis. By 1957, a new group opposed to Hill's leadership had formed around Felix Greene. They saw themselves, as had Hamilton's supporters, as reformers attempting to democratize the foundation. It probably did not help that insiders like Alan Rich regarded them as "sort of dopey little people who would feed [Greene] information about how unhappy everyone was."[13]

In early December 1956, Greene and his followers had issued a scathing report claiming that KPFA suffered from pervasive mismanagement and had become top-heavy with salaried staff. The document all but charged Hill with incompetence, suggesting that he had little awareness of day-to-day activities. When Greene's text received less than the enthusiastic response he had expected, he dispatched an open letter to the executive membership. The "unhappy situation" at KPFA, he believed, would never improve as long as "Mr. Hill is in charge of its management." Greene advised his colleagues that if the situation had not rectified itself upon his return from a trip to Europe, he would take legal action.[14]

Some months later, a small congress of listeners confronted Hill. They wanted to know why, if KPFA claimed to be their *polis*, they lacked the right to formal voice on station policy. Hill sat uncomfortably at a meeting while the delegation of subscribers made the case for "suitable representation to be agreed upon" by the directors. "It is an idea of civic-minded kinds of groups," he patiently explained, "that the democratic process has to go on for something socially to go on. KPFA is not that kind of a group."[15] In 1957, Hill still believed that if the Pacifica Foundation made its editorial decisions by subscriber vote, its capacity to encourage dialogue would last as long as the week's weather.

Some days later, Pacifica's Committee of Directors met to discuss a case involving two employees in the subscription department whom Hill had recently fired. The dismissed workers had appealed Hill's decision to the committee and asked a union business agent to represent them. One employee even began picketing the station. Vera Hopkins later recalled having to maneuver around him to get into KPFA's studios. On July 29, when the committee met with Hill to discuss the matter, he insisted on his right according to the by-laws to decide personnel questions. Instead, the directors resolved to extend severance pay for both employees for another ten days and to study the problem further.[16] According to observers, Hill seemed relaxed, even cheerful, as he left for home that day.[17]

On the first day of August—three months after Hill's thirty-eighth birthday—Joy Hill, out on some errand, could not reach her husband. She called the proprietor of the local general store and asked him to drop by their home and check on things. The grocer discovered Lewis stretched out in the front seat of his green Ford sedan; a garden hose had been extended from the exhaust pipe into the front seat. The vehicle had run out of gasoline, but the ignition key was still switched on. Hill had left behind a brief poem: "Not for anger or despair, but for peace and a kind of home." An ambulance and then a coroner were summoned. Word went out to astonished pacifist households throughout the country. "I am sorry to report that Lew is gone," Denny Wilcher wrote to a stunned Roy Finch. "He took his own life at Duncans Mills a few days ago."[18]

The awful news appeared in the *San Francisco Chronicle* the next day.[19] Publicly, the foundation issued a flurry of fine generalities in praise of Hill. Privately, Hill's friends and associates hastened to protect KPFA from the potentially disastrous impact of his suicide. Joy Cole Hill and Richard Moore rushed to the summer camp where the Hill children were staying, alarmed that the youngsters might first hear about the tragedy on the radio.

Meanwhile, the woman who had become an expert at picking up the foundation's pieces took the position of general manager pro tem. Eleanor McKinney and Alan Rich sat by KPFA's phones for the next few weeks, assuring worried creditors that the station would stay afloat even without Hill's leadership.[20] KPFA's management suddenly had to prove to the Bay Area community that the foundation was more than Lewis Hill. They accomplished this with a carefully concealed ease. Despite the fact that to thousands of KPFA listeners Hill represented the soul of Pacifica, on the day-to-day level the station had evolved beyond dependence on any one person. Now Hill's colleagues did something that their departed friend and teacher would have heartily commended: they parlayed the public's concern over his suicide into an enormous economic windfall for the station. A feature article in the *Folio* appeared following Hill's death: "To all of those who have staunchly supported KPFA as listener-sponsors, the staff and administrative bodies of Pacifica Foundation announce that, with your help, the station will remain on the air and will continue as a solvent institution"[21] KPFA quickly organized what was perhaps its first on-air marathon fund drive.[22] Checks from concerned subscribers flowed in. By September, McKinney reported that what had been a $10,000 deficit had been transformed into a net balance of more than three thousand dollars.[23]

The greatest conceptual challenge, however, was how to explain Hill's suicide. A pacifist had killed himself. A man who believed that technology could help make people more human had rigged a machine to end his own humanness. Several generations of Pacifica programmers who knew little if anything about Hill's inner life seized upon the most satisfying explanation: Pacifica's endless squabbling had driven Hill to the edge. Various superficial signs supported this conclusion. A *Chronicle* reporter had quoted Joy Hill as saying that her husband "had been depressed by what he regarded as 'a series of failures.' "[24] At least one of the members of the Committee of Directors, Russell Jorgensen, came away convinced that Hill committed suicide because of the deadlocked personnel meeting of a few days before.[25]

Years later, after calm reflection, practically everyone who knew Hill well agreed that his deteriorating health prompted his demise. Hill had first tried to kill himself in the summer of 1956, when events at the station were at a comparative lull. Although the often difficult atmosphere of KPFA certainly affected him, it alone would never have driven him to suicide.[26] But to the larger Pacifica community, Hill's death became a metaphor for the sacrifice and not infrequent insanity associated with leadership at a community radio station. This became the master narrative of Hill's final days. "I Know Why Lewis Hill Committed Suicide," wrote one exasperated Pacifica staffer in a program guide article some years later.[27] No one contributed more to this myth than community radio pioneer Lorenzo Milam, author of a guide spuriously entitled *Sex and Broadcasting: A Handbook on Starting Community Radio Stations.* For his book, Milam interviewed Gertrude Chiarito, who confided a dream she had about Hill shortly after his death. Milam insisted that her vision told "you and me all about the crazy madmaking tearapart weirdness which is the community of community radio." In her dream she heard a pounding on her door one rainy evening. Chiarito hurriedly ran downstairs. There she saw a drenched Lewis Hill standing at the door. In her sleeping fantasy she expressed amazement at his presence. "Why, Lew," she said. "You can't be here. You're dead." The rain poured down Hill's face. "No," he replied. "I'm not dead. It's just a rumor, spread by my enemies." Milam's interpretation of this dream did not include Chiarito's opinion, expressed in a subsequent interview, that Hill's poor health and the impact of cortisone had done irreparable damage to him. This explanation, awful in its simplicity, was too painful for the Pacifica community to bear.[28]

Whatever people believed caused Hill to end his life, the tragedy marked a significant turning point in Pacifica Foundation history. Even if he had survived the summer of 1957, Hill probably would not have been able to prevent a fundamental shift in Pacifica policy. His departure further facilitated the emergence of a new generation of programmers who redefined the foundation's objectives. The central political experiences of these staffers had not taken place in pacifist student clubs during the 1930s and in CO camps during the Second World War. They had learned their lessons as victims of McCarthyism or, in one case, as a witness to European fascism. Unlike Lewis Hill and the young Dwight Macdonald, they believed in the legitimate existence of a left and a right in world politics and aligned themselves with the former. Although they paid verbal homage to KPFA's original precepts, the station they created was very different in practice. For them, the fundamental struggle was not to preserve the Pacifica Foundation as a center of intercommunication but as a zone of broadcasting where "unpopular" ideas could be expressed. The more daring these producers became in the pursuit of this goal, the more the national security state reacted with threats and investigations. Such measures only emboldened these broadcasters, convincing them of the just nature of their cause. In their hands the vision that Wallace Hamilton had once stood for—which saw dissent and the adventurous celebration of individual rights as the organization's primary mission—now came to fruition. Between the autumn of 1957 and the winter of 1964, the Pacifica Foundation invented alternative radio.

The Philosopher/Businessman

Shortly after Lewis Hill's death, Pacifica's presidency fell to a member of the 1954 structure committee, Harold Winkler. Born in 1914 to a wealthy family, Winkler took a Ph.D. in political science at Harvard University.

After completing his dissertation, entitled "The Way Is Freedom," he worked for the Council for Democracy, run by *Time* magazine editor Henry Luce. On his vitae, Winkler described the organization as dedicated to combating "hysteria which threatened democratic U.S. institutions." Nothing so far made Winkler appear very different from prior Pacifica administrators. Unlike earlier staffers, however, when Japan attacked Pearl Harbor, Winkler did not declare himself a conscientious objector. Instead, he joined the navy, served on a carrier in the Far East, and returned with a Bronze Star.[29] A nonpacifist liberal had been chosen to lead the Pacifica Foundation. Early KPFA fundraiser Denny Wilcher, who replaced Hill as Roy Finch's West Coast correspondent, nervously took note of this fact and that he had not been asked to assume the presidency himself. "There has been a sequence of events here which has led me to do some hard thinking about Pacifica," he wrote Finch on November 7. "In brief, I fear that in retrospect, with Lew's death, we have ended by permitting the liberals . . . and to a great degree . . . the academic liberals to take over."[30]

Two qualities doubtless distinguished Winkler from other academics in the eyes of Pacifica's inner circle. First, he had refused to sign a loyalty oath at UC Berkeley while teaching political science there in 1949. In August 1950, when the university dismissed him from his post, it made a point of identifying Winkler to the press as an "oath rebel." Newspapers across the state noted Winkler's distinguished navy record during coverage of his firing.[31] "We are living in a period of the most bitter controversy since the war between the states," he told a gathering of teachers in 1953—a battle between the "belief in individual freedom and the belief one is entitled to claim citizenship only if one shrieks to disguise one's hatred of Russia."[32]

The second quality that distinguished Winkler from other academics was that he was rich. After his dismissal from Berkeley, he joined the statewide Group for Academic Freedom, which organized against the oath, offering loans and placement assistance to anyone who defied it.[33] Winkler certainly did not need a loan. In 1951, he donated $340 to the cause, making him one of the organization's biggest personal contributors.[34] By 1960, Winkler had served as director to several large corporations and, after leaving Pacifica, chaired an important taxation study group for the California state senate.[35] Pacifica had put its future in the hands of a philosopher-businessman, someone who sought not a pacifist world in his time but the protection of liberalism from anticommunist repression.

During his tenure at Pacifica, Winkler oversaw the expansion of the radio network to three times its former size. By the year of Lewis Hill's death, the foundation had already made significant inroads toward establishing a second station in Los Angeles. Shortly before his death, Hill began correspondence with a journalism instructor at Pomona College, about sixty miles east of Los Angeles. Years later, Terry Drinkwater would enjoy national acclaim as a correspondent for CBS News. In the mid-1950s, however, he managed Pomona's student-run radio station. By February 1957, Hill reported that Pomona had agreed to move its frequency down the dial to make space for what would become Pacifica station KPFK.[36]

Ex-CO and fabric manufacturer William Webb raised funds for the station for several years.[37] After Hill's death, however, Webb came into conflict with the new leadership at Pacifica. He had understood that KPFK would operate in alliance with Pacifica while preserving its own independent nonprofit status. The members of a consortium of KPFK supporters that included Hill's old CPS comrade Theosophist Henry Geiger had made the same assumption.[38] Winkler, however, had other plans. As his contribution to the 1954 structure committee report suggested, the professor had little sympathy for anarchist-style decision making. One day a member of the KPFA staff declared that she didn't like dictators. "Well, I'm a dictator and you get along with me," Winkler cheerfully replied.[39]

By the early 1960s, Winkler had centralized Pacifica's system of governance, removing staff members from the foundation's board of directors and persuading the executive membership to "vote itself out of existence," as one observer later put it.[40] After a series of acrimonious meetings, Webb publicly denounced what he saw as a strong-arm strategy to control KPFK. "The Pacifica project has always implied to me certain philosophical premises about the human spirit," he wrote in a mid-January 1959 letter of resignation. "I am frankly disturbed that, on an organizational level, somewhat removed from the actual programming, there appears to be a blindness to these cherished concepts."[41] Hill, however, had already largely abandoned such premises. Certainly a case could be made for a network being controlled by one foundation. Why had Hill and his associates gone through the trouble of initiating plans to start KPFK if not to formally extend Pacifica's influence? With Webb's withdrawal, Drinkwater and KPFA programmer Gene Marine took over the operation. KPFK went on the air on July 26, 1959.[42]

The process by which WBAI in New York City came under Pacifica control must have been more to Winkler's liking. One day in 1959, someone called Winkler and asked if the foundation would like to own a radio station in Manhattan. At first Winkler thought the call was a joke. Russian-born millionaire Louis Schweitzer had to repeat the offer several times before Winkler believed him. When Winkler realized that Schweitzer's offer was genuine, he quickly dispatched Eleanor McKinney and Alan Rich to supervise WBAI's daily operation.[43]

An eccentric executive with the Kimberly-Clark Corporation, Schweitzer took pleasure in controlling his personal environment by purchasing large portions of it whenever possible. According to Pacifica lore, when Schweitzer's union barber refused to cut his hair shortly after quitting time, the magnate bought the shop and gave it to the coiffeur on one condition: the millionaire could get a haircut whenever he desired. In similar spirit, he purchased WBAI-FM so that he could regularly listen to classical music. Ironically, Schweitzer became disillusioned because of WBAI's success. During a citywide newspaper strike, WBAI managers found they could sell all the advertising they wanted, turning a record profit for the frequency. Schweitzer, however, hated what he heard: crass, commercial broadcasting. "I realized right then, when we were most successful commercially, that it was not what I wanted at all," he later said. "I saw that if the station ever succeeded, it would be a failure."[44] Few could have predicted in 1960 when "BAI"—as subscribers fondly called it—became a Pacifica station, that it would soon win world renown as the frequency that cheerfully broke every rule in broadcasting.

By the first year of the new decade, Winkler had established an impressive record as the foundation's second president, although his centralizing measures initially generated opposition and resentment. In retrospect, however, Harold Winkler's main contribution to Pacifica history can be summarized in the recruitment of a single man.

The Dissenting Scholar

William Marx Mandel first learned about KPFA during a trip in February 1950 from his home in New York City to the Bay Area. Although only thirty-three, Mandel was already an expert on Soviet culture and politics. His father, a Russian-Jewish emigré, had participated in the 1905 revolution. Father intended to name his son Karl but instead named him for his brother Willy, who had died several days before the boy's birth. Shortly after the Bolshevik triumph, an enthusiastic Mandel *pere* brought the family back home to "help build socialism," as he put it. He joined American exile William "Big Bill" Haywood in the founding of the American Industrial Colony in Siberia. Young Bill attended the University of Moscow for a semester, studying biochemistry, before the family returned to the United States.[45]

Mandel continued his education at the City College of New York, where he joined the Young Communist League. The Communist Party also hired him to teach courses on Marxism-Leninism at its school in New York. Quite by chance his duties required him to pay a visit to the American-Russian Institute, which produced a quarterly journal on Soviet affairs. Mandel asked if it needed help, successfully translated a test essay entitled "Physics and Marxism" from Russian into English, and was hired on the spot. As the Second World War began, this obscure party intellectual suddenly found himself surrounded by suitors. He did translation and background analysis for *Life, Time,* and United Press International and taught area studies for the Army Specialized Training Program at Syracuse University. By 1944, he had amassed enough information to publish his first book, *The Soviet Far East and Central Asia.* Shortly after the war, he accepted a fellowship at Stanford's Hoover Institute for Slavic Studies.[46]

But familiarity with contemporary politics in communist Asia proved hazardous to academics in postwar America, even those who did not belong to the Party. In 1950, Joseph McCarthy denounced Owen Lattimore as "an extremely bad security risk," even though he had headed the Office of War Information's Pacific operations division during the war. Lattimore spent years appearing before hostile congressional committees and grand juries and could not publish another book in the United States until 1968.[47] By 1950, Mandel had been blacklisted by everyone except pacifists and communists.[48] He hung on as a research assistant for the explorer Vilhjalmur Steffansson, who was producing a ten-volume encyclopedia on the Arctic.[49]

Then, while visiting the Bay Area, someone asked Mandel if he'd like to talk about Soviet affairs on KPFA. He mentioned the invitation to some of his communist friends, who immediately advised him not to go. "They're Trotskyists," they said.[50] Mandel ignored this warning. By that time he had lost his Hoover position. "The notion of not accepting an opportunity to air one's views under those circumstances I thought was crazy," he later recalled.[51]

At the station, Mandel met with Robert Schutz, who was working on his Ph.D. in economics at Berkeley.[52] Schutz had a reputation as a hostile radio host. "He would really push people," Adam David Miller later recalled.[53] Schutz led Mandel into an on-air studio. Their conversation often sounded more like a job interview than a discussion. "Good afternoon, sir," Schutz began, "you are an author, lecturer. Tell me a little bit about your education and background, will you please." Mandel explained as delicately as he could that his academic career had been destroyed by Mc Carthyism. The interviewer seemed unmoved. "Now," Schutz continued, "what are you doing besides living on your royalties?" Mandel responded by describing his research on the Soviet Arctic, explaining the commercial concerns the Soviets had with the Arctic Ocean. Perhaps wanting to liven up the interview, Schutz asked Mandel what the communists were doing in the north, "militarily speaking."[54]

At this point, Mandel launched into the kind of response he would give to any such question for the next four decades. "Frankly," he began, "my impression is very little." The Soviets did not represent anything like the threat Americans had been led to think, he said. Long-range bombers were the only sensible weapons to place in that area, and the Soviets "have never believed in the efficacy of long-range bombers." Beginning what younger, less patient KPFA programmers would later on describe as a "Mandelian monologue,"[55] the scholar offered a lengthy rundown of Russian aerial capabilities since the late 1930s. The Soviets had almost an ethical aversion to strategic bombing, a military position in which they had become quite invested, Mandel suggested. The Russians "just don't believe in bombing civilian populations en masse. They didn't do it in World War II at all."[56]

Schutz did not know what to make of this. "Well," he stumbled. "I'm listening to you. . . ." But he was listening to his guest in 1950. In California, Richard Nixon had just won a seat in the Senate by issuing a report (on pink paper) allegedly proving that his rival, Helen Gahagan Douglas, consistently voted the Communist Party line. Up and down the state, academics, civil engineers, and tax clerks busily signed declarations promising never to join a group that said nice things about Russia. Yet here in KPFA's studio sat a well-spoken person with credentials suggesting that the men who ran the Kremlin based their military policy on scruples.

Mandel returned to New York and his work as a translator and research editor. After the government devastated his academic career, he chose to make himself into a public symbol of resistance, in the hope of encouraging others to do the same. His first attempts did not live up to his expectations. In 1952, the Senate Internal Security Subcommittee, which would later play a crucial role in Pacifica history, subpoenaed Mandel for having written *The Soviet Far East and Central Asia.* Mandel chose to play the reasonable man at the hearing, rationally arguing with the senators at every turn. The next day he scanned the newspapers for coverage and to his disappointment found nothing. After self-publishing a short book about the exchange (entitled *Man Bites Dog: Report of an Unusual Hearing before the McCarran Committee*[57]), he pondered what had gone wrong. "The lesson," Mandel later explained, "was that in dealing with these people, dealing under those circumstances, you hang them by their own petard." Next time, he vowed, he would come at them "with both fists flying."[58]

The next opportunity came on March 24, 1953, when Senator McCarthy summoned Mandel to appear before his committee. By then the tradition of turning an anticommunist hearing into free-speech theater had been well established. The so-called Hollywood Ten, a group of defiant screenwriters subpoenaed by the government, had excoriated the House Committee on Un-American Activities in 1948. Mandel studied their speeches, as well as the courtroom remarks of communist George Dimitrov, tried by the Nazi Supreme Court in 1932.[59] He decided that he too would offer the sword.

On the day of the hearing, McCarthy's counsel Roy Cohn conducted testimony while the senator kept to the background. Cohn began by requesting Mandel's name. "My name is William Marx Mandel," Mandel declared and then, offended that the committee had identified a previous witness as Jewish, he expressed his desire "to make clear that I *am* a Jew." This took Cohn completely by surprise. "You are a *what*?" he asked. "I am a Jew," Mandel reiterated. "So am I," Cohn parried, "and I don't see that that's an issue here." "Well," Mandel shot back, "a Jew who works for McCarthy is thought of very ill by most of the Jewish people." Seeing that he had stepped into a trap, Cohn quickly cut Mandel off. "Are you a member of the Communist Party?" he demanded. "My dear sir," Mandel replied, using his favorite salutation for men he didn't like, "I have never consulted with the Communist Party in any manner regarding the writing of the four books I have written." Cohn interrupted him again with the same question. "I'm going to answer your question, sir," Mandel continued, "under my privilege in the Constitution, but I'm going to answer it in my own way. This is a book burning. You lack only the tinder to set fire to books as Hitler did twenty years ago and I'm going to get that across to the American people!"[60]

It went on like that for quite a while, a cat contending with a very obstreperous mouse. At one point Mandel accused McCarthy of driving a staff member of the Voice of America to suicide. Later, ready to throw Mandel out of the building, McCarthy ordered a security guard to stand by. The entire proceeding had been televised for two hours.

Mandel's testimony had the intended effect. The next day the *New York*

Times printed an article about his firefight with McCarthy and Cohn.[61] But even this did not satisfy Mandel. He asked sound engineer Tony Schwartz, who would later do TV commercials for Jimmy Carter, to produce a vinyl recording of the event, complete with a network-style narrator and annotation by Mandel himself.[62]

Ironically, Mandel took the Fifth Amendment on Cohn's question (excusing himself from possible self-incrimination), thinking he still belonged to the Communist Party. Preoccupied with its survival in the aftermath of the Smith Act trials, which had forced the Party leadership underground, the organization had never bothered to tell Mandel that it had expelled him around late 1952. Mandel never knew why he was purged, although he suspected it was because he was willing to work with other left groups. Then one day in 1956, shortly after Soviet premier Khruschev's speech denouncing Stalin, a large, husky man appeared at Mandel's apartment door. He turned out to be the Party's new section organizer and he invited Mandel back into the fold. Having digested the news of his expulsion, Mandel thought about the offer for a minute and politely declined, although he would not speak of this conversation for decades. In 1958, attracted to the relatively unsectarian atmosphere of the San Francisco Bay, he and his family moved to Berkeley. One day a mutual friend introduced Mandel to Harold Winkler, who asked him if he wanted a regular program on KPFA.[63] Thirty-four years after Winkler had left the station, Mandel would still be talking about Russian politics on KPFA's airwaves.[64]

For those KPFA listeners who disliked William Mandel, he represented the epitome of the anti-anticommunist, the polemicist who demanded his constitutional right to praise a country without constitutional rights, to distort information about the Eastern bloc in order to deny fodder to Cold War reactionaries. Mandel "did a lot of lying on KPFA. He knew better," Sidney Roger later said. "I could have done better. The difference is that he lied, and I avoided."[65] In reality, Mandel's talks on the Soviet Union startled KPFA listeners more because of their complexity than their perceived dishonesty. Mandel certainly did not "avoid" difficult questions; in times of crisis, he shocked listeners with his impassioned briefs in support of communist policy. As late as 1982, he offered critical defense of the Polish communist government's crackdown on Solidarity, describing the dissident group as led by "wild men" with "no program but destabilization."[66] More often than not, however, Mandel simply wanted to expose his listeners to another side of Soviet life. In his many talks and interviews on the subject of Soviet society and politics, he brought home to KPFA listeners a single message: the USSR represented a very complicated place; its peoples, who belonged to many cultures and spoke many languages, did not spend their waking hours concocting ways to overthrow the U.S. government. Their lives were preoccupied with issues that had little to do with the West, or even communism, for that matter.

Mandel brought in guests who compared conditions in Soviet and Iranian Azerbaijan, or visitors from Central or Far Eastern Asia. He once interviewed Basque exiles from the Spanish Civil War, sent to the USSR as children. Long before multiculturalism became fashionable, he wanted his audience to see beyond the West's monoethnic image of the Soviet Union, and eventually published *Soviet But Not Russian: The "Other" Peoples of the Soviet Union.*[67] Sometimes, as in a program broadcast in July 1960, Mandel answered questions from listeners who had sent him mail. His responses were simple and frank. Can a family of three—husband, wife, and child—live comfortably in the Soviet Union if only the husband works? asked one subscriber. Not by American standards, responded Mandel. How much electricity is available to each Russian? asked another. "I would say, roughly, about one-fourth as much as to each American." Has there been much debate over the death penalty? No, explained Mandel. "There has been no public discussion (when I say public discussion, I mean discussion that reaches the press in any form) on the death penalty any more than there has been on alternatives to foreign policy. This, thus far, has not been permitted."[68]

To his admirers, William Mandel represented the embodiment of Cold War dissent. It did not matter so much whether they entirely agreed with his opinions. What counted was that in both thought and action Mandel categorically refused to cooperate with the pervasive anticommunist discourse of his time, which sought not to discredit communism but liberalism. He openly defied both government committees and the vast daily outpouring of learned and plain language that represented the Soviet Union as a threat to the "free world" and nothing else. To much of Mandel's audience, the specific content of his words mattered less than their oppositional nature. "Mandel completely opened my eyes unto the world of Soviet communism," poet Lawrence Ferlinghetti later declared. "I had no idea about it except what I read in the *New York Times* up to that time."[69]

Courageous and determined, Mandel flourished at KPFA, where the simple desire to hear certain points of view proved more urgent than the need to completely agree with them. Neil and Marilyn MacGregor distrusted him. Neil thought Mandel was preachy and sometimes imitated

Mandel's radio personae. "*I am William Mandel*," the longtime KPFA subscriber mockingly intoned. "*I have been to Russia. I can speak Russian. I know more than you do, and I am going to set you straight on this!*" But they listened, nonetheless. "We wanted to know what was going on," Marilyn later said, "what different people thought about different things."[70] In the late 1950s, Mandel probably represented the only "different" Sovietologist broadcasting in the United States. To the KPFA listener, he became indispensable. By 1959, a subscriber survey revealed that Mandel was by far the most popular commentator at the station.[71]

Whatever people thought about Mandel, no one could dispute that his boldness signaled a shift in the political mood. By the time he arrived at KPFA in 1958, domestic anticommunism faced a serious crisis, and not just in Berkeley. Joseph McCarthy had destroyed his career by clumsily attempting to impeach the army for allegedly harboring communists. The Supreme Court had weakened the Smith Act. The University of California had repealed its loyalty oath requirements. A resilient culture of opposition to red-baiting now flourished throughout many regions of the country. Urban audiences flocked to hear comedians like Lenny Bruce defiantly mock the repressive climate of the Eisenhower era.

In the early 1950s, the enemies of McCarthyism contented themselves with the gentle protests of their patron saint: twice presidential candidate Adlai Stevenson of Illinois. But by the late 1950s, many Americans had lost patience with respectful entreaties to men they regarded as crude opportunists. If freedom was, in fact, "always wise," as Alexander Meiklejohn had declared in 1953, then the time had come to be free. Now the politics of inquisition was denounced from the highest levels. In 1959, no less than former president Harry Truman described the House Committee on Un-American Activities as the "most un-American thing in the country today."[72] From Phil Elwood's perspective as a community college instructor and jazz radio deejay, he could sense the change: "There was a noticeable uneasiness across the land."[73] Mandel represented KPFA's symbol of this uneasiness, but the station needed someone to harness its energy. Unknown to most of the staff, she had already arrived.

Mission to Berkeley

After Elsa Knight Thompson's first difficult day at KPFA, she tried to get along as best she could in the factionalized atmosphere at the station. The staff noticed that she had gone for a drink with someone Lewis Hill had just fired. Not surprisingly, Hill's supporters shunned her, while his enemies took an interest in her work. One afternoon, however, Hill suggested they have lunch and she told him her story.[74] After that, he took her more seriously.

When Elsa Knight Thompson died in 1983, politicians, entertainers, and intellectuals sang her praises. "We should all give thanks to the good lord that we had an Elsa Knight Thompson among us all these years," telegraphed rock 'n' roll promoter Bill Graham. The writer Theodore Roszak agreed: "Elsa used radio the way it was meant to be used: to discover issues and empower people." "She combined tradition with openness toward the new in life," recalled Tom Hayden. "She was one of the bright spots of my years in Berkeley." Even the most powerful politician in California paid homage: "The ancient Greeks tell us that when a good person dies their goodness lives on," eulogized Congress member Phillip Burton. "Elsa Knight Thompson was just that, a good person."[75] These celebrities had listened to Knight Thompson's broadcasts on KPFA for years, or had been interviewed by her. To them, she represented the epitome of progressive radio broadcasting, the journalist who brought the highest standards to the liberal cause.

Those who knew Knight Thompson personally also admired her work, but remembered her differently. "I think that it would not be unusual to say that I was afraid of Elsa Knight Thompson," admitted Phil Elwood years later.[76] "I worshipped her and was terrified by her," confessed Alan Rich. "Sometimes simultaneously. Sometimes by turns."[77] Dorothy Bryant recalled first hearing Knight Thompson on the radio. "There's a tough lady," she thought.[78] The lady in question would not have disagreed. "I have always had this intense feeling that I want things to be right," she told a friend in the last year of her life. "I want things to be beautiful, and will go to any lengths to keep things organized and keep things moving."[79] Knight Thompson did more than just keep things moving at KPFA, she reconceptualized its mission and pushed the station into the 1960s.

Elsa Knight was born in Bonner's Ferry, Idaho, in 1906, and grew up in Seattle. Her liberal father edited a magazine. One of her uncles had traveled to India with Theosophist Annie Besant. Like Eleanor McKinney, young Elsa read whatever was around the house, in this case William James, Havelock Ellis, and Freud. One afternoon her grandfather discovered the ten-year-old girl engrossed in an English translation of Richard von Kraft-Ebbing's *Psychopathis Sexualis.* He and her grandchild talked about the text almost as if they were both grownups.[80] When her mother discovered that her husband had a mistress, she divorced him and pleaded with her daughter to join her in Los Angeles. By the age of twelve, Elsa had become the classic example of an adult-child.

Although Knight reveled in the libertarian atmosphere of 1920s Los Angeles, she later speculated that it still might have been possible for her to wind up as a suburban housewife. "I could have returned to Seattle, I suppose," she mused, "gotten married, lived a conventional life, had cats, a kitchen, parakeets, and played golf."[81] But something happened that completely changed her sense of the possible. During a camping trip, a man she had thought of as a friend raped her. She then discovered she was pregnant and that he was married. Knight procured the services of a quack abortionist, who performed a procedure that almost killed her. She was rushed to the hospital, where a committee of doctors declared an abortion lawful on therapeutic grounds. For eight months the seventeen year old lay in a semi-conscious state, recovering from double pneumonia, her physicians waiting until she appeared strong enough to undergo the radical hysterectomy that would save her life.

Almost a year later, Knight left the hospital and gathered her strength in her mother's apartment. Devastated that she'd never be able to bear children, she struggled to make sense of the future, calling upon her grandfather for advice. "You know, Elsa, some women are deprived of motherhood and other women are relieved of it," she remembered him saying. "It's up to you." Knight saw these choices as valid. She determined, as she subsequently put it, "to live my life in a free and independent way, even as a man lived his life, to do what I thought right and let the devil take the hindmost."[82] How she'd achieve freedom and independence on her limited means was less obvious. But the problem appeared to have no solution, until the solution finally appeared. At some point in the late 1930s, Elsa Knight married into the British Empire.

It isn't clear when she began dating Francis Younghusband Thompson—"Tommy," as his family called him—but marry this Cambridge scholar she did. Knight also wound up supporting him because he couldn't find an academic job in the United States. This had not been the point of their getting married or his coming to America. Thus, the two returned to England to live with his family, the extended family of Sir Francis Edward Younghusband, knight commander of the Indian Empire and president of the Royal Geographic Society.[83] The Thompsons derived various forms of income from interests "overseas," as the British put it. Finally, in the late 1930s, Tommy got a job at the University of Rumania.[84]

Elsa Knight Thompson could not help noticing that all of Europe verged on chaos. "You could feel it under your feet," she later said. Franco was about to conquer Spain, and Hitler had invaded Austria. Like everyone else, Knight Thompson regarded war as inevitable. She came back to the United States for one last visit. By the time she returned to Europe, Nazi Germany had invaded Poland and the British government had assigned Tommy to Turkey. Her train pulled into London's Paddington Station on the eve of the Battle of Britain. Civil defense monitors declared a blackout just before she arrived.[85]

Despite the blitz, Knight Thompson refused to hide in air-raid shelters, instead taking long walks through the streets as German bombs crashed about in the darkness. As it had for Eleanor McKinney, the war created opportunities. Community leaders asked her to coordinate the evacuation of English children to the United States. One day, while holding a meeting at a cafe, someone asked her if her group intended to evacuate "illegitimate" children. "There is no such thing as an illegitimate child—there may be illegitimate parents," she briskly responded. "Yes we do."[86] Unknown to her, an editor for the British Broadcasting Company had been eavesdropping. He asked her if she'd like to produce commentaries on the war from an American perspective. She agreed and worked with the editor for several months. One afternoon Knight Thompson received a wire memorandum from the government informing her that she'd been assigned the position of staff journalist for the BBC. Thus began her career in radio, "strictly by accident," as she later put it.[87]

Knight Thompson's position on the BBC catapulted her into the center of British politics and culture. She wrote the first documented BBC report on the Nazi Holocaust.[88] She conducted interviews on international relations. During air raids, she talked all night at the BBC canteen with Dylan Thomas and George Orwell, who later proposed to her. She became friends with CBS correspondent Edward R. Murrow. Sometimes she could scarcely believe what was happening. "Here I was, an American woman, with my husband out of the country, in the middle of blitzes and things."[89]

Unfortunately, it didn't last long. After the surrender of Nazi Germany, Knight Thompson found it appalling that BBC editors refused to acknowledge that many of Britain's allies during the war had been communists. "The British needed the left, . . . and we used them on our broadcasts, used them ruthlessly." But afterward those BBC reporters who acknowledged the communist roots of resistance movements in Greece, Yugoslavia, and Italy were shunted to obscure staff positions. Her editors, however, were willing to be candid with her on another subject. "Elsa," she later remembered one telling her in 1946, "you've got the highest rating that any woman has held in the news division, but you'll never go up any higher because the next move up will put you over men and that they will not tolerate." By then she had divorced Tommy and was packing her bags for New York.[90]

It took about ten more years for Elsa Knight Thompson to get to KPFA. No matter how hard she looked between 1946 and the mid-1950s, she couldn't find a good position in radio. So she sold Singer sewing machines to Jewish refugees in New York City and worked as a clerk at Garfinkel's department store in Washington, D.C.[91] Finally, in desperation, she returned to Seattle. One day a British friend wrote to say that something very upsetting had happened the last time she visited California. Lady Margaret D'Arcy had dropped by a local radio station in Berkeley, probably to promote her then-popular *Book of Modern Prayers*. Her Ladyship had had a discussion with someone there, and to her annoyance they had recorded it without her permission.[92] Knight Thompson jotted down the station's call letters. Four days before Christmas 1958, the front page of the *Folio* listed her as a member of KPFA's regular staff.[93] She was fifty-two years old.

When Elsa Knight Thompson took over KPFA's public affairs department, she believed that the station desperately needed her help. "She was not a pacifist, but she was deeply committed to principles of world peace, world understanding, and high culture," her friend Chris Koch later reflected. "I think she always felt she was in some sense Lew's spiritual successor."[94] Knight Thompson put the matter less tentatively. "I had the feeling, rightly or wrongly," she said, "that in some ways I was the heir-apparent as far as Lewis Hill was concerned, because I was literally the only person whose political consciousness was acute."[95] She certainly projected this attitude shortly after her arrival. "Your leader is dead. I have come to be your leader," at least one KPFA staffer recalled her saying, hopefully in jest.[96]

Knight Thompson quickly concluded that the station had gone off track. It was top-heavy with programs about classical music, art, literature, and radio drama. Where, she wondered, was the politics? Alan Rich told anyone who cared to ask that he considered himself a "nonpolitical person."[97] The same could be said for Alan Watts and Pauline Kael. These people, Knight Thompson concluded, "did not have the background to really do what I thought Lew intended. I knew that telling the truth about what was going on in the world was one of his primary interests, and the most important thing the station could do."[98]

For Knight Thompson, telling the truth meant telling the truth about outsiders, telling Americans what she had seen at the BBC—that beyond the borders of the United States millions of people regarded communism as a potentially useful ideology; that many Americans saw racism, rather than the Kremlin, as the principal threat to their lives; that the culture of the Cold War had marginalized a generation of people who did not fit into its narrow parameters.

Chris Koch was right. Knight Thompson, like Harold Winkler, did not believe in pacifism. Nor did she appreciate or understand the concept of pacifist dialogue. Although she certainly approved of Pacifica's efforts to present "all points of view" on any social question, she valued this concept more as a professional journalist who sought independence than as a broadcaster concerned about creating lasting understanding. While she certainly believed that KPFA should give conservatism its share of impartial time, ultimately she saw the station as a place where the political ideas of the Bay Area left would openly be celebrated and receive the hearing they'd been denied elsewhere. Her recollection of an incident with station manager Trevor Thomas illustrated this perspective. In 1963, Knight Thompson and Thomas were listening to on-air comments from callers about Pacifica policy. All the callers expressed their support for the foundation. Thomas found this very disturbing. "Where are our enemies? Where are our enemies? Why doesn't anyone call in and object to what we're doing?" Knight Thompson found Thomas's reaction amusing. "I really don't know, Trevor," she said, "but it's just possible that you're in a situation now where you'll have to depend on your friends."[99] To Knight Thompson, Thomas's anxiety emanated from a liberal desire for fairness, rather than a pacifist desire for intercommunication. "He was absolutely desperate because no one was attacking the station. This was his idea, you see, of being objective," she said "You see," she later commented to several KPFA producers, "most liberals think that if you can find the middle of anything and you can squat there, that somehow or another virtue had been achieved."[100]

Elsa Knight Thompson had seen far too much in her life to worry about virtue. Liberals, she said, "are never prepared to admit that there is such a thing as right and such a thing as wrong and that if it's wrong, you say so and if it's right, you say so or at least you give the audience the opportunity to notice this."[101] As public affairs director, Knight Thompson confronted the same paradoxical question that had challenged Pacifica's first generation: how do you encourage free speech yet make certain that at the end of the day people freely come to your sense of truth? Knight Thompson's answer was simple: you tell them the truth yourself.

By the 1960s, many veteran KPFA staff members, such as Gertrude Chiarito and Vera Hopkins, intensely disliked Knight Thompson. Years later Chiarito accused her of deliberately provoking riots during the tumultuous days of the People's Park uprising, just to make news.[102] One can only wonder whether Hill would have encouraged Knight Thompson if he could have seen her sympathetically interviewing Black Panther Party leader Huey P. Newton, whom she put up at her house for three months after he left prison in 1969. "I hope everything is all right for Huey," she told a friend in the last year of her life. "I loved him very much."[103] In the late 1950s, however, she appealed to KPFA listeners and staff largely because of her professional skill and her experience with the BBC. The first generation of Pacificans admired Knight Thompson because she represented a continuation of KPFA's commitment to its own sense of high culture. The second generation loved her because she heralded "an openness toward the new," as Tom Hayden put it. In the end, she led KPFA from one broadcasting philosophy to another.

Knight Thompson's 1958 live studio interview with communist and civil rights activist Paul Robeson exemplified her duality of spirit. Dozens of awed KPFA volunteers pressed their noses against the glass of the station's main studio as she, Harold Winkler, and Phil Elwood spoke with the man who sang African American spirituals and Italian opera. The former Rutgers All-American chuckled as Knight Thompson began the program by suggesting they "kick off" the interview with a question about politics. KPFA represented one of the few radio stations where Robeson, who had just won his passport back from the government after years in court, could expect a sympathetic ear. "I always know I have a welcome here," he gratefully concluded. "so I want to thank you."[104]

Robeson represented for Knight Thompson the ideal mixture of radical politics and good taste—an "extraordinarily great human being," she later called him, and like so many of her broadcasting subjects, an outsider.[105] The roster of 1958 Knight Thompson interviews reflected her constant concern for the politically or socially dispossessed. She interviewed a priest on conditions at Alcatraz Island prison, conducted panels on the rights of the legally insane and the status of the artist in the Soviet Union, and talked to Vassar instructor Lloyd Barenblatt, whom the Supreme Court sent to prison for refusing to cooperate with the House Committee on Un-American Activities.[106] All of these interviews brought her praise. One made broadcasting history.

From her youth, Knight Thompson had always been concerned about the plight of homosexuals. Even as a child she sensed something disturbing about her maternal aunt's marriage. Only later did she learn that her uncle was homosexual and that the two had never made love. "But that's the way people were born and brought up in those days," Knight Thompson later explained. "So those of us who came into consciousness in the 1920s had a lot of pioneering work to do if we were going to break out of this."[107] In the autumn of 1958, she made good on this commitment by contacting Harold L. Call, who edited the *Mattachine Review.* The Mattachine Society—America's first gay rights organization—had been founded in Los Angeles eight years earlier by a close circle of ex-communists. By 1956, most of them had been driven from the group, thanks to a conservative bloc organized by Call himself.[108] A cautious movement, the Mattachines hoped they could soften America's hard stance toward homosexual men by forging alliances with mental health professionals.[109]

On November 24, 1958, Knight Thompson assembled Call, the mother of a homosexual man, and a small team of doctors, criminologists, and attorneys for a lengthy two-part program on the condition and rights of the "variant," as Mattachinists described themselves. Call understandably came to KPFA's studios with some trepidation. Within three minutes of the interview he had, without prompting, assured the other panelists that all 117 members of the Mattachine Society had celebrated their twenty-first birthday.[110] But he soon realized that he was among friends. All the participants concurred on the futility of laws against homosexuality and disputed the belief that it caused crime or constituted mental illness. "I do not look upon homosexuality as a neurotic problem, but more a basic personality pattern reaction," one psychiatrist said. "Just as some people prefer blondes and others prefer brunettes, I think that the fact that a given person may prefer the love of the same sex is their personal business." Two hours later, Knight Thompson heartily expressed her satisfaction with the broadcast. She offered no regret, as Lewis Hill had during his *Howl* panel discussion a year earlier, that no one who thought differently was at the table. Instead, she congratulated her guests. "Well, I think the panel has been in pretty complete agreement at many levels," she declared.[111]

Thus concluded what very likely constituted the first comprehensive gay rights radio documentary in U.S. broadcasting history. Gay people in San Francisco listened in stunned delight. Longtime KPFA supporter Bert Gerritz remembered getting together with his lover and some friends to listen. "The word 'homosexual' used to make me blush," he later recalled. "And here it was on the radio! Liberation! Fresh air! Free air! It was great."[112] A local gay publishing house had the discussion transcribed for a book. More significantly, no member of KPFA's sponsoring board resigned in opposition. As Red had once said that pot was no different from Coca-Cola, so someone now stated that preferring to sleep with someone of the same gender was no different from preferring to sleep with a blonde. The former, however, had been a stoned day laborer, the latter a psychiatrist. Wallace Hamilton and Elsa Knight Thompson shared the same broadcasting philosophy. But Knight Thompson knew better than to invite four working-class people into her studio to discuss the pleasures of gay sex. She knew how far from home one could venture and still return in one piece—a game Pacifica's president would soon be called upon to play as well.

One day in January 1960, Knight Thompson summoned William Mandel for a meeting. Mandel could tell that a difficult problem had come up, since she insisted that the two talk in her automobile. They drove to a street in West Berkeley, and she explained that a group of academics and journalists had complained about the presence of communists at the station. The consortium appeared to be led by a local writer named Paul Jacobs and included Eugene Burdick, author of the anticommunist bestseller *The Ugly American*. Seymour Martin Lipset, a Berkeley sociology professor and longtime KPFA programmer, had also spoken to Pacifica's staff. He too had become alarmed at the direction in which KPFA seemed headed. KPFA had transformed itself into "a fellow traveler station," Lipset insisted—thanks largely to the presence of Mandel. "He was a total apologist or supporter of the Soviet Union," the sociologist later declared. "His broadcasts painted everything in the Soviet Union as rosy as possible. He went along with shifts in the Communist Party line." Lipset wasn't happy with Knight Thompson either, whom he subsequently described as "very pro-Communist and fellow-travelish."[113]

Whether Lipset, Burdick, and Jacobs conspired together remains unclear. All knew each other, but it seems likely that they complained to the station individually. Shortly after the conversation with Knight Thompson, Winkler asked Mandel to cut his time at KPFA to a program every other week. The two compromised by eliminating the commentator's question-and-answer period at the end of each show.[114] Not surprisingly, this modification did little to satisfy Pacifica's critics.

During the first week of February, an article came out in *Counterattack: Facts to Combat Communism and Those Who Aid Its Cause* that surely must have horrified Winkler. The publication that virtually created the Hollywood blacklist now offered a scathing denunciation of Pacifica radio. Titled "Radio Station Promotes Communists," the article offered a breakdown of the communists, leftists, and liberals who had appeared on Pacifica stations over the years. Pacifica's president, the essay noted, had refused to sign a loyalty oath while teaching at the University of California. Perhaps sensing a shift in the political wind, the editors mixed their red-baiting with calls for academic responsibility. "We agree that Communism should be discussed intellectually and any other way that is possible. It should be taught in schools as well, and more important, the evils of its materialistic system should be pointed out and compared to our own system." Demands that the Pacifica Foundation replace its left-wing propaganda with right-wing propaganda could be easily dismissed. But the newsletter's concluding statement could not: "To open a channel of communication for propagandists without designating them as such, or without rebuttal, is economic and political suicide, and something the *Federal Communications Commission* should find important."[115]

Even coming from the anticommunist right, *Counterattack*'s final criticism offered Harold Winkler a chance to restore the Pacifica Foundation to its original mission: pacifist dialogue. He could have sat down with the managers of WBAI, KPFA, and KPFK and demanded that people of different political persuasions be required to talk to each other on the air, rather than receive separate spaces to opine. Granted, such a task would have required leadership and skill. Conservatives like Russell Kirk and William Rusher, editor of the *National Review*, offered commentary at WBAI only on the condition that "known Communists" not appear on the station. "We conservatives believe in free speech—," Rusher obstinately declared in a 1961 WBAI talk. "so much so, indeed, that we will not insult it by pretending that Communists are engaging in it when they talk to others."[116] But it is difficult to believe that in places like New York, Los Angeles, and San Francisco, suitable conservative replacements could not have been found. Ultra-right activist Gerald L. K. Smith had enthusiastically consented to an interview at KPFK in 1959.[117] A future Secretary of Defense had his own commentary show on KPFA around the same time. "Deathly dull," Phil Elwood characterized Republican state legislator Caspar Weinberger's KPFA commentary performance and thought he would have done better in a more interactive format.[118] Winkler could have insisted that Pacifica uphold its mission by inviting a wide range of individuals to address pacifist questions, face-to-face in the same place at the same time. But instead, he panicked.

On May 2, 1960, Winkler sent communist commentor Herbert Aptheker a letter explaining that he had been kicked off Pacifica's airwaves. "We have decided to give you a rest for a while and use your spot for other commentators on the left," the patronizing message concluded. Combined with the shortening of Mandel's show, this futile attempt at appeasing right-wing critics only served to enrage Pacifica's staff. Alan Rich, Knight Thompson, and three others dispatched a letter to Winkler. Why, they asked, had he given in so quickly?[119] What, inquired Pacifica's staff, is your policy? In the absence of an immediate reply, Knight Thompson looked for an opportunity to answer the question herself.

The End of the 1950s

Earlier in the year, the House Committee on Un-American Activities had announced plans to return to San Francisco to conduct more hearings on communist activities in the area. The last time HUAC had come to town was in 1957. That year a Stanford biochemist killed himself rather than appear before the committee. Two years later, HUAC considered a return engagement and canceled, but not before sending the names of one hundred allegedly subversive teachers to the state superintendent of public instruction.[120] By 1960, however, the political atmosphere in the Bay Area had changed, and to a greater extent than HUAC anticipated.

The San Francisco left had always been relatively nonsectarian, at least compared with the left on the East Coast. As Kenneth Rexroth had observed earlier, since wages in San Francisco were high, working-class intellectuals could afford to stay in the working class. Rather than emphasize theoretical differences, they usually preferred to get things done. "They didn't argue in coffee shops about 'contact with the masses,'" Rexroth wrote in 1957. "They didn't visit picket lines to write feature stories—they were on them because they worked at the job being struck."[121] In Los Angeles, the Communist Party came under the strong influence of a veteran organizer, Dorothy Ray Healey, who had grown up in the 1930s with the Young Communist League and the CIO. Vivacious and charismatic, she had chosen to remain with the party in the 1950s while it lost 75 percent of its members. In 1959, KPFK invited Healey to produce regular fifteen-minute talks for the station's public affairs department. "I jumped at the opportunity," she recalled. When not writing radio scripts, Healey spent the next two decades struggling to wean her party from its obeisance to Soviet authority.[122]

William Mandel sensed the power of the West Coast's politically fluid atmosphere. "I simply had a feeling that there would be a more civilized relationship between Communists and ex-Communists out here," he later said. "I was right."[123] Thus, when HUAC subpoenaed Mandel for a hearing on May 13, he felt certain that a statement of defiance would attract enthusiastic support. He was right about that too.

When Mandel arrived at City Hall in San Francisco for his hearing, hundreds of students were waiting to witness the proceedings. To the students' dismay, by 1:00 P.M. the police began admitting only those who had been invited to attend—members of conservative groups approved by William A. Wheeler, HUAC's veteran West Coast investigator.[124] Angry that they had been denied access to the proceedings, the anti-HUAC protesters staged a sitdown strike in front of the hearing room. The police quickly responded by turning water hoses on them. Some of the demonstrators answered by turning their backs, shielding their sisters and brothers. Enraged at this courage, the authorities charged the students, throwing them across the wet floor. Throughout, Fred Haines, a KPFA reporter, taped the events and recorded himself describing what he saw: officers dragging soaked and bloody protesters down a long wet stairway. "The police have grabbed a Negro by the ankle and are dragging him down the stairs on his—" Haines's voice betrayed his astonishment—"on his *back* by the ankle." Down a flight of some sixty steps, the students careened. "One policeman is presently dragging three girls all at once together," Haines reported.[125]

By then Knight Thompson had organized a relay race of KPFA reporters, who were rushing back and forth from City Hall with their taped material. Dale Minor, who took up where Haines left off, talked with witnesses who described an assault by a group of six police officers on one of the protesters. "The last I saw him he was lying up against a pillar," one observer said, "and these policemen were propping him up, and he, he looked—he looked—just, just completely beaten."[126] Somehow Minor managed to get past the carnage into the hearing room as William Mandel walked into the chambers. It was the third time Mandel had been subpoenaed to testify before an anticommunist committee.

Representative Edward E. Willis presided over the hearings. Willis had run HUAC hearings in the late 1950s designed to flush out communists from various labor unions.[127] HUAC attorney Richard Arens asked Mandel if he was represented by counsel. "I am," Mandel shot back, "to the degree that a counsel not able to speak for me can represent me." The ex-communist looked around and noticed a group of television reporters. "By the way," Mandel said, "if the television men want some news they can put their lights on. They can put them on if they want something to show their audiences." "You want the lights on?" Arens asked. "I want the lights *on*," Mandel shot back. "I want the fullest glare of publicity on this committee's activity."[128] The audience laughed nervously.

"Are you now or have you ever been a member of the Communist

Party?" Arens asked. Mandel gave a lengthy response to this famous question. He explained that since the Supreme Court had ruled invocation of the First Amendment an act of contempt before HUAC, and since he wanted to avoid the pain a jail sentence would cause his family, he would invoke his right under the Fifth Amendment not to reply.

As had Joe McCarthy in 1953, Arens offered Mandel the standard inqusitor's response. "Do you honestly apprehend, sir, that if you told this committee truthfully while you are under oath whether you are now this instant or ever have been a member of the Communist party you would be supplying information which might be used against you in a criminal proceeding?" At this point Mandel could have, as he had before McCarthy, answered with a reasoned explanation as to why this question was but a disguised version of the first. But that wasn't necessary now, and Mandel knew it. Joe McCarthy was dead. Jim Crow was dying. Richard Nixon, the destroyer of Alger Hiss, had lost a national election to a Catholic from Massachusetts. Hundreds of students had braved police violence to hear Mandel speak. They deserved a reward for their courage. "Honorable beaters of children and sadists, uniformed and in plain clothes," Mandel declared:

> Distinguished Dixiecrat wearing the clothing of a gentleman; eminent Republican who opposes an accommodation with the one country with which we must live at peace in order for us all and our children to survive; my boy of fifteen left this room a few minutes ago in sound health and not jailed solely because I asked him to be in here to learn something about the procedures of the United States government and one of its committees. Had he been outside where the son of a friend of mine had his head split by these goons operating under your orders, my boy today might have paid the penalty of permanent injury or a police record for desiring to come here and hear how this committee operates. If you think that I am going to cooperate with this collection of Judases, of men who sit there in violation of the United States constitution—if you think I will cooperate with you in any way, you are insane.

Arens attempted to ignore this speech. Doubtless he could tell what would happen if he did not proceed quickly. "Now, sir," he continued, "were you a lecturer . . ." But it was too late. Thunderous applause filled the room. Mandel spent the remainder of his testimony respectfully telling his inquisitors to go to hell. "My answer is 'no, sir,'" he concluded, "and no matter how many ways you ask that question it will remain the same."[129]

Minor rushed back to Berkeley, where he, Knight Thompson, and a production crew edited the footage into a documentary that they sent to WBAI and KPFK. They broadcast it, endlessly, on KPFA. Ecstatic listeners called in. They wanted to hear the Mandel speech. They wanted to hear the students. "Everything else just went by the boards," Rich recalled. "We just played those goddamn tapes over and over and over again until we made sure everybody in the Bay Area knew them by heart."[130] Mandel broadcast the recording on his own show. The Pacifica Foundation transcribed the documentary and published it in a book.[131] For a new, younger generation of KPFA supporters, the HUAC tapes literally represented the final hours of the 1950s. For them, the pacifist dilemma of communism had been overshadowed by the climate of fear, despair, and betrayal that red-baiting had wrought. The real issue was that anticommunism had left a vast "domestic void," as former UC-Berkeley student Todd Gitlin recalled. "Why take anticommunist moralism so seriously when the old moralists had so little to show for it?"[132] The broadcasts drew people to the station like a magnet. San Francisco Art Institute student Ernest Lowe listened to broadcasts in awe. He had been working at KPFA for about a month before the hearings. A "bursting open of the body politic," he called them. "The burden of McCarthyism was being pushed back. It was just an incredibly exciting time to be there."[133]

Elsa Knight Thompson had delivered her answer to *Counterattack* and Paul Jacobs. Watching this amazing drama unfold, Harold Winkler knew he had to provide his response, and soon.

Winkler's far more moderate statement appeared in the May-June issue of the journal of the National Association of Educational Broadcasters in an article entitled "Pacifica Radio—Room for Dissent: Why and How This Unconventional Operation Exists." The text began with a short nostalgic summary of the early style of the foundation. "Over one microphone and often face to face, men wrestled to make reasonable and human their disparate viewpoints," he wrote. "The listener in his turn found himself confronted by persons who talked without fanfare, and with obvious sincerity, as if they were friends in the present room." Although Winker used the past tense, he insisted this kind of programming remained a crucial part of the foundation's current fare. In addition, Winkler explained, Pacifica stations now aired what he called "intellectual shocks": the poetry of Ferlinghetti, the experimental music of Harry Partch, radicals of all varieties. "Alongside these extremes appear pacifists, opponents of capital punishment, and the critics who shade from rancor into expression of popular dissatisfactions. Who among these should be refused a hearing?"[134]

But "even at KPFA," Winkler said, "where seasoned subscribers appreciate being treated as mature individuals, who can think and select, we receive letters from listeners who ask why we did not present THE

OTHER SIDE within the hour." For the most part, Winkler said, Pacifica relied on volunteer pundits and lacked the resources to provide counterpoint on demand. Conservatives were becoming increasingly reluctant to appear on the station. In Winkler's opinion, such concerns reflected a simplistic view of public discourse:

> At its many levels of understanding, the demand for "balance" is destined to be disappointed, for it assumes that the subtle differences between viewpoints can be accurately assessed and their impact predicted, though listeners vary enormously in background and suggestibility. The solution of the large networks of equal time for major political views loses meaning when less institutionalized political views are under consideration. If a Russell Kirk cannot balance a Herbert Aptheker [whom Winkler had fired], neither can Pacifica's self-imposed obligation to present the full-range of political thought in its most competent expression be discharged when we have presented, as we did in California at KPFA and KPFK, the pre-primary conventions of the Republican and Democratic parties.[135]

Winkler's argument represented a clever evasion of the original Pacifica mission. The first Pacificans, as the institution's current president knew, had not been interested in "balance" but in encouraging "lasting understanding" or, as Winkler himself so eloquently put it, in making "reasonable and human" the "disparate viewpoints" in any conflict. The first Pacificans simply wanted people to know each other as human as much as they knew each other as others, this being their primary requisite for a pacific world.

But Winkler also knew that a new generation of staff and volunteers had run out of patience with this mission. They saw absurdity in the call for dialogue in a world ruled by HUAC. How could America engage in any kind of credible dialogue about communism when an entire generation literally dreaded to speak the word? When advocacy of civil rights, sexual freedom, civil liberties, or fluoridation of the water supply immediately tainted one as subversive? Such a world would first have to be exposed, rioted against, laughed at, and voted down until it had become a bad memory. William Mandel and Elsa Knight Thompson led the beginning of a flood of rage at those who had subpoenaed reality into silence and an outpouring of simple curiosity for silenced ideas. Winkler exemplified the leader trying to keep up with his followers, who themselves were not entirely certain where they were headed. "All of us in Pacifica Radio are in the midst of a serious rethinking of the role of Pacifica," he concluded. "It may be just coincidence, but this new decade appears to mark a general reappraisal in the United States." America now seems "more concerned with quality rather than quantity, with public rather than private possibilities."[136]

It did not surprise Elsa Knight Thompson that Winkler quit his job at Pacifica in September 1961, about a year after "Room for Dissent" was published. "After the first underground attack was squelched, I think Hal Winkler knew it was only a matter of time before an open attack was launched," she later said, "and he was not prepared to go through another one of those things."[137] Pacifica's directors elected longtime KPFA volunteer Trevor Thomas as acting president. Thomas quickly endorsed Winkler's views. "We do not attempt a one-for-one balancing of alternatives," he wrote in the January 1962 *Folio*. "We are committed to the presentation of minority views, views which may be challenging, unfamiliar, even obnoxious, but which are necessary to a full examination of The Establishment."[138] Perhaps mindful of this commitment, the foundation also hired a new executive vice president. One day Knight Thompson looked over his vitae. She glanced at the organizations he'd been associated with and the causes he'd backed in the past. Immediately, she understood who he was, where he'd been, and what was going to happen next.[139]

10) THE MAN AT THE DOOR

My chief concern has not been that Senator Eastland might find Pacifica subversive and a threat to the security of the nation but that he might find it otherwise.

—DENNY WILCHER,
Berkeley Daily Gazette, January 10, 1963

CHRIS KOCH was working in his office at WBAI in New York City when Richard Elman paid a visit. In a few years Elman would become a famous writer, publishing such acclaimed books as *The Poorhouse State* and *The 28th Day of Elul*. But at the time this deep-voiced Brooklyn native was the station's public affairs director.[1] Elman had someone with him he wanted to introduce. "I'd like you to meet Special Agent Jack Levine, Federal Bureau of Investigation," he told his friend. "Oh, God," thought Koch, "here it comes," referring to the police raid he expected sooner or later. But Levine, who spoke with a somewhat high-pitched voice, quickly corrected Elman: *former* special agent, he explained.[2] It was October 1962.

Alarmed at what he had seen during his training period, Levine had quit the bureau. Now he wanted to tell his story. Not surprisingly, hardly anybody wanted to publish it. People were terrified of the FBI and its director, J. Edgar Hoover. Since the days of his employ as a file clerk in Woodrow Wilson's Justice Department, Hoover had become lord of an empire of three-by-five cards and newspaper clippings detailing the personal histories of just about every prominent person in the country. In January 1962, Levine had gone to the Justice Department with his concerns. An official in the department asked him to write a report, for which he was thanked and the document ignored.[3] He then went to his representative in Congress, the aged Emanuel Cellar. "Are you crazy?" Cellar asked. "Don't you know that you're dealing with, if not the angriest man in America, the next angriest man?"[4] Finally, Levine approached *The Nation*. After printing a short article, Carey McWilliams, the publisher, suggested that Levine contact the staff at WBAI.[5]

In 1962, when Levine came to WBAI, Elman, Koch—and the station—had everything to gain by listening to the former agent. Having no advertising base, WBAI thrived on trouble. "Controversy had really led to the growth and empowerment of the stations," Koch later explained, ". . . if we then got attacked, that would bring out supporters and defenders and money."[6] Koch and Elman proceeded to take Levine to a studio, where they turned on a tape recorder. They interviewed their guest for almost four hours, then arranged for an edited version of the discussion to be broadcast on October 18, a Thursday.[7]

The result of their efforts, a documentary entitled "The Report of Former Agent Jack Levine," set in motion events that completed the shift in Pacifica philosophy that had been initiated in the mid-1950s with the marijuana show. Levine's report provoked a lengthy crisis that forced Pacifica to define itself publicly as a radio network dedicated to the promotion not of dialogue and intercommunication but of dissenting ideas. The organization would now place priority on giving voice to those who challenged what historian Daniel Yergin calls the national security state—that entity that since the emergence of the Cold War perceived itself threatened from every corner, justifying frequent military action abroad and repression at home.[8] These Pacificans would confront the warfare state not in the name of pacifist dialogue, as its founders had done, but as a self-conscious outsider. Forces within the foundation had struggled against this fate for almost a decade, but now the United States government would leave Pacifica no choice but to position itself as a dissent-oriented radio network.

Tempting Fate

Just before broadcasting the Levine interview, Koch and Elman sent out transcripts to journalists around New York. After receiving his copy, an Associated Press reporter met with the two producers at a bar. "Listen," Koch remembers the man saying. "I know you kids think you're doing a great thing here, but I want to tell you your life will be ruined if you go ahead with this broadcast." The station's program guide editor received a warning from the Washington headquarters of the AFL-CIO: stay out of WBAI's offices when the program airs, the building will be raided for sure. According to Koch, muckraking journalist I. F. Stone, who had earlier praised the document, suddenly called at the last moment. "Mr. Koch," he began, "I want to say that I've reread the transcript carefully and I want to publicly dissociate myself from it. I'm not going to devote any space in *I. F. Stone's Weekly* to it." Koch was stunned. "Izzie, we're in a private phone conversation. What do you mean you want to publicly dissociate yourself?" Koch protested. "That's just it," Stone replied, hanging up. This upsetting conversation concluded, Koch and Elman fled to a nearby bar.[9]

Fortunately, Jerome Shore, Pacifica's new executive vice president, had listened to the broadcast before its premiere. He also had it reviewed by an attorney. When WBAI began receiving threatening phone calls, he flew in from the West Coast to keep the staff calm. His reassurance, plus a few martinis, revived Koch and Elman's courage. They resolved to go ahead with their program.[10]

A professional union organizer, Shore had helped organize a walkout at a textile company's New York headquarters by the time he was eighteen. The strike brought Shore's leadership skills to the attention of the Congress of Industrial Organization (CIO), which had hired him to organize office workers in New England. Now forty-seven, Shore was a handsome man who could give an impressive speech. More important, he thought like an organizer. He knew his job was to clearly define objectives and make them easier to carry out. "I didn't want to intrude into broadcasting," he later said. "I wanted to make it possible for people to broadcast." For the most part, WBAI's staff saw the foundation's national leadership as well meaning but indecisive—with the exception of "Jerry." "He was always there when you needed him," Koch recalled.[11]

One can only speculate whether WBAI's listeners laughed or cried as they listened to "The Report of Special Agent Jack Levine." Levine's disclosures represented the agency as both a threat to democracy and a pathetic cult dedicated to supplicating the vanity of its eternal director. Levine told his interviewers that by the early 1960s the American Communist Party had become completely infiltrated with FBI informers—nearly one out of every six members, he estimated. Obsessed with the threat of communism, FBI officials told him that Adlai Stevenson had completely surrounded himself with communist advisers and that the NAACP functioned as a communist-front organization. Levine found appalling the use of ugly epithets by his colleagues to describe African Americans. Agents took delight in entertaining one another with anti-Semitic imitations and gestures. A student at a lecture on subversive organizations asked the instructor if he considered the American Nazi Party a subversive group. The teacher responded that he didn't see the group as subversive at all: "All they are is against Jews and I don't see anything subversive about that. Do you?"[12]

Levine described the bizarre cult of personality that surrounded Hoover. His class had received eight hours of preparation for their meeting with the director. After being arranged by height in descending order, supervisors advised agency hopefuls to have extra handkerchiefs available for the hand-shaking session and warned them against having an insufficiently dry grip. "It was explained that the director distrusts persons with moist palms," Levine explained, "as he considers this to be an indication of weak character."[13]

What Levine found most disturbing, however, was the extent to which the bureau engaged in what could only be described as criminal activity. One-third of the agency, Levine told WBAI, pursued "security" investigations without authority from any judge. In the event that agents didn't have a warrant for a wiretapping, they simply performed what functionaries called a "bag job," that is, an illegal search.[14] Anyone who displeased the FBI in any way frequently found themselves the subject of such practices.

This line of discussion provoked an obvious question. "Do you suppose that, if we broadcast this program," Elman asked, "that we'll be investigated?" Levine laughed nervously. "Well, that's—a very difficult question to answer. I really don't know. I think that—it's a thought that certainly should be considered, and I mean that seriously."[15]

Actually, the FBI had been investigating the Pacifica Foundation for some time. Beginning in 1958, it began sending agents to conduct what detectives cosmetically refer to as "pretext interviews" of Pacifica personnel, prompted by occasional letters of complaint to the bureau. Various operatives would show up claiming to be journalists or potential volunteers, grab some loose memo or foundation brochure, and file a report with their director. Until 1962, the bureau had cleared the foundation of subversive activity.[16] But a few days before the Levine broadcast, the FBI intercepted information through an inside contact that WBAI had a "QUOTE EX-FBI MAN UNQUOTE UNDER WRAPS AND WAS PREPARING PROGRAM TO QUOTE BLOW LID OFF FBI UNQUOTE." This news triggered an instant state of alert throughout the agency. Every operative knew that one ignored a public slight against J. Edgar Hoover at the risk of one's career. A flurry of teletypes shot between San Francisco, New York, Washington, and Los Angeles. Agents queried their informers and then rushed data to supervisors, who in turn submitted reports to regional assistant directors. Three days before WBAI's broadcast, the agency determined that the "ex-FBI man" was Jack Levine. In fact, none of the frantic espionage had been necessary. Shortly before the broadcast, Jerome Shore sent the FBI an advance copy of the Levine transcript. He also called a bureau official to offer the agency equal time on the air. "Lay off, sonny," came the surly response.[17]

Several days after the broadcast, Elsa Knight Thompson and KPFA's station manager, Trevor Thomas, conducted an interview with yet another FBI renegade. After serving the agency for more than ten years, William Turner had sent a series of letters to various members of Congress apprising them of what he saw as the self-serving nature of the bureau's decision-making process. The FBI fired him for his trouble. Turner's interview was hardly as colorful as Levine's, but he corroborated the roster of indignities Levine claimed the typical FBI operative endured, such as the need to regularly write letters of adulation to the director.[18]

By the end of October, the FBI was beside itself. Newspapers that had refused to print Levine's testimony now took it seriously. "If his assertions are false, the American people should be told so by a responsible source," read a *New York Times* editorial. "If they are true, in whole or in part, the American people should be told what is being done to correct matters."[19] Turner's disclosure on KPFA that he was writing a book about his former employer sent frantic operatives scurrying to their publishing sources. The agency obtained a manuscript of the text long before it was released eight years later.[20] In addition, a Los Angeles agent indignantly reported that KPFK commentator Dorothy Healey had recently given a talk in which she called Hoover a "fraud" as well as a "semi-literate buffoon." Finally, the bureau did not find it amusing that Trevor Thomas had dubbed a recent fundraising drive "KPFA's 1962 Anti-Red Crusade."[21] It was time to reconsider the bureau's assessment of Pacifica, and quickly.

The Levine and Turner interviews were soon overshadowed, however, by events of far greater magnitude. Four days after the Levine broadcast, President Kennedy threatened the Soviet Union with nuclear war. A U2 spy plane had identified a site near San Cristóbal, Cuba, where the Russians were storing nuclear missiles.[22] The Cubans had ample reason to accept military material—the United States had recently sponsored an attempt to overthrow their government. Although the United States enjoyed a 17:1 nuclear superiority ratio over the USSR, the Kennedy administration panicked when it discovered the weapons in Cuba.[23] On October 22, Kennedy went on television to announce a "strict quarantine on all offensive military equipment" being transported by naval vessel to the island. Furthermore, he warned, any hostility from Cuba would be met with a "full retaliatory response upon the Soviet Union."[24] U.S. forces went on full alert, and air force commanders broadcast their attack plans in unencrypted code so that Soviet intelligence monitors would hear them.[25]

In the midst of the crisis, Elsa Knight Thompson assembled a "Cuba panel" consisting of public opinion expert Richard Brody, student activist Saul Landau, and Stanford economist Paul Baran. The son of a Russian Menshevik, Baran had a reputation as an independent Marxist, critical both of U.S. imperialism and the home of his parents.[26] A trip to revolutionary Cuba in 1960, however, had restored Baran's hope for a Marxist future.[27] Knight Thompson's panel, obviously sympathetic to Castro's revolution, openly challenged the Kennedy administration's policy on Cuba.[28] If the second generation of Pacificans hoped to reach the attention of the powerful with such broadcasts, they succeeded magnificently.

On November 2, J. Edgar Hoover himself sent a memorandum to agents in New York, Los Angeles, and San Francisco stating that the bureau had just learned that the Senate Internal Security Subcommittee (SISS) planned to hold hearings on supposed communist infiltration of the Pacifica Foundation. The FBI intended to furnish the subcommittee with a thorough dossier on every person of consequence in the organization. "The officials, members of board of directors, office employees and announcers concerning PF and each station are to be determined," continued the memorandum. *"All subversive data on each individual is to be set out in each report, where applicable."* Be ready to furnish additional information when the list of subpoenaed Pacifica personnel is made known. The communiqué set a deadline for agent reports of November 23, 1962—*"without fail."* By the end of October, the SISS had already requested a copy of the "Cuba panel" from KPFA.[29] The FBI would now have its revenge.

McCarran, Eastland, and Dodd

Long after Senator McCarthy faded from the scene, the SISS cheerfully continued his work. Nevada senator Pat McCarran created his subcommittee in 1951, and, as intended, it quickly stole much of McCarthy's limelight. A staunch supporter of the Franco regime, McCarran investigated everything he could: trade unions, State Department officials, even the telegraph industry. He stacked the SISS with reactionaries like Senator Karl Mundt, friend of the insurance business and an ardent opponent of the New Deal.[30]

After McCarran's departure, the torch passed in 1955 to J. Edgar Hoover's close friend James Eastland of Mississippi. An unrepentant white supremacist given to violent outbursts, as late as 1965 Eastland continued to blame the civil rights movement on communists. To read the senator's remarks, I. F. Stone wisely observed, "is like reading the speech of Rusk and McNamara about South Vietnam before Diem was overthrown—in both cases the picture is of a happy land and a contented people torn apart by outside agitators." Eastland kept counsel with a second-rate Nevada politician named Jay G. Sourwine, who functioned as the SISS's attorney. In the winter of 1955, Eastland and Sourwine orchestrated a vengeance raid on the *New York Times*, which had irritated the senator with its sympathetic coverage of the 1954 *Brown* school segregation decision. Those editors who invoked the Fifth Amendment quickly received their walking papers.[31] Senator Thomas Dodd of Connecticut became chair of the SISS in 1960. In June of that year, Dodd subjected the chemist Linus Pauling to a detailed interrogation, referring to his "long record of services to Communist causes and objectives."[32]

The FBI quickly produced a small encyclopedia for the SISS containing synopses of the backgrounds of the 150 people associated with the foundation.[33] In addition, the document listed every communist who had recently appeared on a Pacifica program. Much of the study could be dismissed with relative ease. That communists spoke on Pacifica stations did not constitute a violation of any law or statute. But the bureau also produced the following statement about the foundation's newly hired executive vice president:

> SHORE, born December 19, 1915, in New York City as JEROME SCHWARTZ, changed his name legally to Jerome Shore, December 2, 1940, in Wayne County Probate Court, Detroit, Michigan. He resides at 695 Connecticut Street, San Francisco.
>
> [Three paragraphs blacked out.]
>
> The June 11, 1950 Michigan edition of "The Worker", page 10, column 2, identified SHORE as Secretary of the Michigan Labor Peace Committee (MPLC).
>
> The Michigan Labor Peace Committee was a communist initiated and controlled movement with a trade union front. [Sentence blacked out.]
>
> In 1952, SHORE was named as the State Chairman of the Michigan Progressive Party, whose programs, policies and activities are guided by and participated in by Michigan CP clubs and members. [Sentence blacked out.][34]

Shore's resume was the one Elsa Knight Thompson had reviewed just after his appointment. "He was from the outside, and as soon as I saw his vitae I knew he'd either been in the Party or very close to it," she later remarked.[35] Actually, the FBI exaggerated Shore's Party involvement. Although he'd joined the Young Communist League as a teenager, it was less clear how involved he was later on. And although Shore thought the CP was a "positive force for good" overall, as he put it, he didn't always support its policies and preferred to work in organizations that embraced both communist and noncommunist organizers.[36]

Nonetheless, the FBI knew it had hit pay dirt with Shore. It might be able to maneuver him into perjury before a congressional committee, or use him to weaken and discredit Pacifica's leadership—perhaps even deny the foundation FCC authorization. By late November, the bureau also knew that KPFA's FCC license had come up for renewal and that WBAI and KPFK still ran on construction permits. The FCC had some concerns about some supposedly obscene poetry and drama performed at all three stations. Further, an FBI agent had talked with a member of the commission and now claimed that commissioners had told him that in early 1960 the FBI had produced "data" for the FCC proving that WBAI existed for the transmission of "communist propaganda." This was nonsense. As late as 1960, the bureau had issued a report categorically clearing WBAI of any internal CP influence.[37]

The FBI's earlier assessment was now gone from sight. Suddenly, on the eve of the government's review, the bureau rewrote its earlier conclusions. It had always considered the Pacifica Foundation a hotbed of subversion, it said, and it had Jerry Shore, among others, to prove it.

On December 19, 1962, Peter Odegard, a member of the board of the Pacifica Foundation, received an alarming telegram. Before joining the foundation, Odegard, a political science professor, had been president of Reed College and active in the campaign to eliminate loyalty oaths.[38] The telegram informed Odegard that he could disregard the subpoena he had received from the SISS to appear in Washington. What subpoena? he wondered. He had never received one. Odegard called Trevor Thomas in Berkeley and told him about the telegram. Shortly afterward, a reporter for the *San Francisco Chronicle* called Thomas. "What do you know about those subpoenas?" he asked. Thomas claimed to have no knowledge of them. Thomas then telephoned Sourwine, the SISS's attorney, who explained that, despite the telegrams to the contrary, the SISS had every intention of inviting a group of Pacificans to Washington to talk about "possible Communist infiltration" at KPFA, KPFK, and WBAI. Sure enough, Thomas himself received a writ to appear before the Dodd Committee on January 10, 1963, a day before his thirty-eighth birthday.[39] Lewis Hill's Man at the Door had arrived. The entity that sought "to disturb in some measure the ability to see the self's image clearly and confidently" now confronted the Pacifica Foundation.[40] It demanded that the institution define its purpose to the government, to the public, and, most of all, to itself.

Invitation to an Inquisition

Trevor Thomas grew up in the Colorado Rockies in a mining camp called Breckenridge. A cave-in killed his father when Trevor was a boy, and his mother took him to a small town in the Sierra foothills. After moving to San Francisco as a young man, he became active with the American Friends Service Committee (AFSC)—in other words, Quakers. "I think I wasn't really a pacifist," he later reflected. "I guess I'm sort of a halfway pacifist." The AFSC hired Thomas, a patient, articulate man, as its civil rights lobbyist in Sacramento. There Thomas witnessed firsthand the power of anticommunist hysteria to wreck coalitions and put power into the hands of dangerously unstable men. A KPFA volunteer since the early 1950s, Thomas had a deep appreciation for the effort that had gone into creating the station.[41]

Now, as acting president of the foundation, he summoned all the organization's main players for a meeting one week before the SISS hearing. They gathered to consider a single issue: how to deal with the SISS.

To some, the answer seemed obvious: Pacifica would categorically refuse to cooperate with the government. Elsa Knight Thompson quickly took this position. "[The SISS] didn't call me, despite the fact that I was the one largely responsible for programming and the philosophy behind the programming," she explained. "They didn't call me because it was common knowledge that if they did I would refuse to answer on the grounds of the First Amendment, and say why, and go to prison if need be."[42] One of the last of the original Pacifica COs also took this stance. In 1959, Denny Wilcher had stood down an FBI man who had come to his home with questions. Wilcher "described himself as a present day 'anarchist-pacifist,' "the agent duly reported, "and one who does not believe in the numerous investigations being conducted in the United States."[43] In a letter to the *Berkeley Daily Gazette*, Wilcher made his current position clear: "My chief concern has not been that Senator Eastland might find Pacifica subversive and a threat to the security of the nation but that he might find it otherwise," Wilcher declared. He eloquently conceded that noncooperation might result in what he termed "a temporary loss of physical mobility for some individuals" as well as "the loss of three FM channels." It was time, however, for someone besides "our discredited Communists" to take a stand against McCarthyism. "There are other paths than acquiescence, as Socrates discovered a long time ago, to the corruption of the minds of the citizenry."[44]

Such calls to revolutionary suicide held little appeal to Pacifica's board of directors when it met on January 3, 1963, to decide its strategy. Russell Jorgensen, another member of the AFSC, also belonged to Pacifica's board and soon would replace Thomas as president of the foundation. Jorgensen had watched the foundation evolve over the years, repeatedly adjusting its language to satisfy the FCC and the Internal Revenue Service.[45] He knew that whatever concerns Hill might have had about upholding First Amendment rights had been tabled in recognition of a fundamental reality: the government would not authorize an FCC license if it didn't approve KPFA's application. Jorgensen and Thomas had years of experience working with hostile government bureaucracies. They knew that such entities could be managed, albeit with compromise. They also knew that ignoring them, whether out of principle or convenience, usually meant slow institutional death. Hence, they decided on a more complex course of action than noncooperation.

Seven days before the first hearing, the foundation issued a public statement: "We might question the propriety of this legislative hearing. However, we choose not to do so, not because we concede the right to compel testimony in these matters, but because Pacifica's policies and programs are open to everyone. No subpoena is necessary to secure this kind of information." Those who had been called to Washington would talk, but it was the right of those who had been subpoenaed "to respond to purely personal questions in the light of his own conscience and understanding of his constitutional rights."[46] In other words, if Jerry Shore and others wanted to, they could plead the Fifth Amendment before the subcommittee. Thomas had outlined a straightforward approach: it was better to discredit the SISS through cooperation than through confrontation. As William Mandel had pointed out at the recent San Francisco HUAC hearings, declaring one's First Amendment right not to cooperate with a government inquest simply invited a prison sentence. Such an assertion demonstrated not the power of the First Amendment but its impotence. Mandel himself thought that the foundation's leaders should not refuse to testify, since doing so would land them in the courts. "I had seen the subtle, exceedingly skillful, persistent destruction of the left, not only the

Communist Party, during the McCarthy years. . . . ." he later explained, "through an endless succession of trials which diverted these organizations from their real purpose, whatever the purpose was, to a bottomless appeal for money."[47]

Mindful of this reality, Thomas sought to generate support from the press, to prove "that the goddamn [SISS] committee [was] a fishing trip, and they were looking for somebody to hang."[48] He wanted his testimony to demonstrate the genuinely broad range of programming the Pacifica Foundation offered and make the case for its right to do so. Armed with strategy and plan, he headed for Washington.

But when Thomas got to the nation's capital, he discovered that the SISS had a plan as well: to badger him throughout his testimony. The members of the subcommittee cleverly played on the fact that, as they knew, Thomas did not like Soviet socialism, in theory or in practice. Early in his testimony, Thomas proudly described a typical week's programming at a Pacifica station, which might include commentaries by a "a Republican official, a Democratic writer, a labor leader, a communist official, a priest, a minister, or rabbi." What did Thomas think these individuals had in common? Sourwine asked "Each one of them is given a fifteen-minute period, either once a month or twice a month," responded Thomas. "I said aside from the fact they might all be on your station?" Sourwine exclaimed. "Well," Thomas replied, "they are people with opinions and ideas." The attorney saw his chance. "Don't you recognize that communism is not merely politics or opinions and ideas but is a conspiracy? That the Communist Party of the U.S.A. is not a true political party but a part of an international conspiracy?" he shot back. "Do I recognize this?" Thomas asked. "Yes, sir." Sourwine pressed. "Well," Thomas conceded. "I suppose it is."[49]

It went on like that for hours. Did Thomas know about Dorothy Healey's broadcasts? Did the foundation send tapes by communist commentators to other radio stations? Were there other communists on Pacifica stations that the committee did not know about? To scores of such questions, Thomas and subsequent witnesses could only tell the truth: they didn't really know much about these people. Mostly, they did fundraising and went to lots of meetings. Elsa Knight Thompson spoke of their performances with contempt. "The people who were asking these questions knew more about what we'd been broadcasting than these lovely board members knew," she told a friend.[50]

Not surprisingly, Thomas found his interrogation by Sourwine frustrating. "I would have gotten a great kick if I'd had the opportunity of punching him in the mouth," the half-pacifist later recalled.[51] But Thomas did manage to hold his ground, albeit just barely, on the fundamental issue: did communists have the right to speak on Pacifica stations? Senator Dodd put this question bluntly toward the end of his questioning. If Thomas knew that William Mandel had taken the Fifth on the question of whether he'd engaged in espionage against the United States, would he still allow the commentator on KPFA? "In the absence of any evidence that it was a fact that he had so engaged," Thomas replied, "the honest answer would have to be yes, I would allow him."[52] This response understandably pleased Mandel. "'Yes' is a wonderful answer," the commentator later said, praising Thomas's testimony. "It enables you to get on to the next order of business."[53] The next order of business, however, was Jerry Shore.

Accompanied by two attorneys, former FCC lawyer Harry Plotkin and ACLU attorney Lawrence Speiser, Shore went before the subcommittee on the day after Thomas. Had he personally known Earl Browder, former general secretary of the Party? they asked. Had he taught at the Communist Party training school in Chicago shortly after the war? Did he serve as state chairman of the Michigan Progressive Party?[54] Had he been connected with the Party in 1960? 1959? 1958? Finally, Shore broke in. "Can I, just to save time, can I make this statement? That have not had any connection with the Communist Party going back nine years from now?" Counsel Sourwine rewarded Shore by asking if his *wife* had been a member of the Party in 1960. Desperate to protect others from the subcommittee's scrutiny, Shore immediately took the Fifth on the question, then added that he had not *belonged* to the Communist Party for the last nine years.[55]

Several more witnesses testified, including a former KPFK fundraiser, Pauline Schindler, who did not recall who recruited her into the Party, exactly how long she stayed in it, or why she was kicked out. Was she still a communist? asked James Eastland. "Oh, dear, Senator, that is hard to say," Schindler replied, "because the word might be one thing to you and one thing to me and one thing to Jesus Christ."[56] A former KPFK station manager who'd been in the Party for several months during the war struggled to recall whether she'd gone to Asilomar one summer for a communist or a Quaker conference. The conversation eventually moved on to whether she remembered if KPFK announcers identified Dorothy Healey as a communist before her regular commentary. Healey herself had been subpoenaed to testify. Not having a radio network to lose, she refused to tell the senators anything more than her name. This must have disappointed the FBI greatly. Its Los Angeles bureau had transcribed nearly a dozen of her broadcasts for the SISS.[57]

When the hearings concluded at the end of January, the Pacificans who testified had achieved one significant victory: because they had told the truth, they could not be charged with perjury.[58] But other than that, the hearings caused the foundation nothing but trouble. Public sympathy for Pacifica deteriorated as the year progressed. The western edition of the *New York Times*, for example, issued a strong editorial in favor of Pacifica on January 14.[59] But on July 28, when the SISS finally released detailed transcripts of what had been said in its chambers, stories predicted the network's likely demise. "Probe Red Radio Ties, FCC Asked," declared the *Los Angeles Herald-Examiner*, whose reporter noted that CP members had sometimes been allowed to broadcast "without identification of their Red affiliations." "KPFA Faces a Doubtful Future," ran a July 29 headline in the *San Francisco News-Call Bulletin*. Most disturbing, veteran *New York Times* media reporter Jack Gould commented on the lack of interest that the National Association of Broadcasters (NAB) took in the controversy. "The coast-to-coast networks, which rush to the barricades over the slightest hint of Governmental intrusion," Gould wrote, "could not care less and the F.C.C. apparently wishes the Pacifica issue would just go away."[60]

If bad press and corporate indifference represented the greatest difficulty confronting Pacifica, its leaders might have considered themselves fortunate. The FCC might very well have wanted "the Pacifica issue" to "just go away," but its members feared the SISS far more than criticism from the liberal press. The FCC's new chairman, E. William Henry, a former Memphis attorney who had worked for John Kennedy in 1960, was embarrassed at how long the FCC had delayed in processing Pacifica's license renewal requests. They had been held up, in part, by the amount of work generated by the quiz show scandals of 1959. The license applications had for years been sitting in a box in the FCC's storage basement in Washington. Henry also knew that Senator Dodd took a particular interest in the matter. "I felt we were going to have difficulty with him . . . ," he explained. "Because [Pacifica] was a notorious case, we needed to get all the facts. I didn't want the agency to be in a situation in which we would be bombarded after the fact with questions we couldn't answer."[61]

To get the process going again, the FCC sent the foundation a series of complaints by listeners offended by Pacifica broadcasts. The letters represented a kind of mirror placed before the organization, reflecting a new generation of journalists eager to defy the Cold War's culture of containment. One complainant objected to a reading of Edward Albee's *Zoo Story*, which used "the vilest language I have ever heard. . . . They talked of sex perversion. They took the Lord's name in vain." A late-night discussion about homosexuality by an octet of gay men, entitled "Live and Let Live," also drew fire. Elsa Knight Thompson could have predicted the exception taken to this program, as articulated by FCC commissioner Robert E. Lee, formerly of the FBI: "When these subjects are discussed by physicians and sociologists, it is conceivable that the public could benefit. But a panel of eight homosexuals discussing their experiences and past history does not approach the treatment of a delicate subject one could expect by a responsible broadcaster."[62] In fact, the FCC could have monitored a Pacifica station on any day of the week and discovered that KPFA, KPFK, and WBAI were becoming magnets for those determined to exorcise the spirit of the 1950s from American political life.

Then, on October 7, 1963, the FCC sent the foundation a questionnaire to be completed by board members, general managers, and officers. It read as follows:

1. Are you now or have you ever been a member of the Communist Party? If the answer is yes, give dates of membership.
2. Are you now or have you ever been a member of any organization that advocates or teaches the overthrow of the Government of the United States, or of any political subdivision thereof, by force or violence? If the answer is yes, list the organization, or group and give dates of membership.[63]

Most members of Pacifica had anticipated receiving something like this and had spent months figuring out how to head it off. The process nearly tore the organization to bits. Shortly after the SISS hearings, Trevor Thomas attended a national board of directors meeting at which he discovered the existence of a right- as well as a left-wing contingent within the organization. On February 2, 1963, a group of directors offered a resolution affirming the foundation's "established policy" of refusing to hire anyone "who is a member of the Communist Party" or any other "totalitarian organization" that does not respect the Bill of Rights. This proposal, which in essence would have created an internal loyalty oath, appalled Jorgensen and Thomas. "I voted 'no' out of stubbornness that rebels against the preoccupation with Communism," declared Thomas, "and out of sorrow that Pacifica, after fourteen years, adopts a disclaimer when the political climate seems to be shifting away from such practices."[64] In addition, on January 28, Thomas, Jorgensen, and two other members of the foundation's executive committee fought off an attempt to force Jerry Shore out of the organization.[65]

Despite this vote of confidence, Shore resigned on March 1 anyway, acknowledging that his service as an officer had become "a source of embarrassment." Shore had taken on the job of executive vice president with the understanding that it would ultimately lead to the presidency.[66] But Trevor Thomas's left reacted to Shore's attempts to ease Pacifica's pains with a backlash. WBAI's staff strongly identified with Shore, certainly more than with the West Coast Quakers who dominated Pacifica in 1963. Chris Koch later struggled to convey Shore's popularity. "The other people who were involved—God bless their hearts in hindsight . . . "he reflected, "they were very sweet people, but they didn't have [Shore's] effectiveness."[67]

On March 12, WBAI staff and volunteers telegrammed the board to express their "shock" at Shore's resignation. "We are equally shocked by reports that the Board is considering action that will lead to a Pacifica loyalty oath," the message added. That day the board met to decide how to deal with the controversial vice president. At least one member felt his colleagues should appraise the situation honestly. Board member Alfred Heller recalled "a consensus that there was no significant future with Pacifica for Mr. Shore and he should be told." But a desire not to appease the FCC—at least not yet—won out. By eight to two, the board voted to appoint Shore manager of KPFK. Within the month, all three board members who had voted for the loyalty oath proposal handed in resignations. Theirs were accepted.[68]

The paradox at the heart of Pacifica had surfaced again: how to encourage free speech and yet at the end of the day make certain that everybody comes to certain conclusions—in this case agreeing that free speech was a desirable goal. One solution had been put on the table: certain kinds of people, specifically communists, would be free to speak on Pacifica radio, but banned from sharing in the network's governance. This proposal addressed itself less to Jerome Shore than the apprehension that communists saw freedom as a tool for political advantage. In the 1950s, an entire generation of idealistic Americans quit the Party largely because of this perception, particularly after Khrushchev's denunciation of Stalin in 1956.

But the proposed internal oath had an unacceptable contradiction: it coerced those who wished to be part of an institution that advocated free speech into taking a political position on communism. The true danger to freedom "comes not from a totalitarian political party which is without credit or size in this country," argued one member of the board of directors, "but from people who would deny to those *they* define as part of that totalitarian movement, the benefits of freedom."[69] Lewis Hill and the first Pacificans had not had to face this dilemma so starkly. Their Pacifica Foundation had placed its primary emphasis on intercommunication, rather than individual rights. As the purveyors of pacifist dialogue, Hill and McKinney took it as their mission to actively manage discourse on KPFA, to guarantee a place for all, but under strict limits and conditions. But now that the Pacifica Foundation spoke first and foremost in the name of "freedom," of individual rights, no barriers could be set, not even for those perceived as enemies of individual rights. The SISS had provoked a deep philosophical crisis. The October 7 questionnaire from the FCC would force the organization to resolve it.

By early October, Russell Jorgensen had become president of the foundation, replacing Trevor Thomas, who became general manger of KPFA. Jorgensen immediately sought the advice of former FCC attorney Harry Plotkin as to whether the foundation should answer the questionnaire. Jorgensen reported their conversation in a memorandum. "Plotkin says nonsigning is the end of licensing," he wrote. "He grants we may wish to fight on principle, but we cannot expect to win. The FCC probably considers tendering this 'test oath' to us as a generous act." The attorney estimated that it would cost the foundation $100,000 to fight the commission in the courts. He warned that in a previous federal case, *Borrow v. FCC*, a U.S. court of appeals had affirmed the right of the FCC to demand a declaration of loyalty from a broadcasting operation.[70]

To the second and for the most part younger generation of Pacificans, cooperating with the FCC by signing what amounted to a loyalty oath represented blasphemy. "The fact that 35 million Americans have signed such statements is, in our case, irrelevant to our own decision," wrote Chris Koch. "35 million Americans listen to television every night. Our subscribers subscribe because we offer something different; something based on a different concept of integrity and intellectual honesty."[71]

A tense standoff took place at a board meeting in Berkeley between those who demanded that the foundation "support Amendment One" and those who felt a compromise would have to be reached.[72] But in the debate now taking place throughout Pacifica, noncooperator rhetoric betrayed the suspicion that defiance might indeed undo the network. From New York City, WBAI's station manager reported that an October 14 staff meeting had resulted in absolute consensus. Sell WBAI to finance the court fight, he suggested, adding that he had an offer. Elsa Knight Thompson, who believed the foundation should take the loyalty matter to court, peppered her prose with unconvincing negatives: "I do not think signing would ensure survival, it would simply be one step on the road to certain defeat. I do not believe that refusing to sign would ensure our defeat. I am not convinced that such a refusal would necessarily mean the withdrawal of licenses."[73]

Such calls to the judicial roulette table did not inspire those still trying to sort out the problem. One board member, who declared it "utterly against [her] conscientious scruples to sign the oath," promised to sign it anyway. "Rightly or wrongly, I have signed the oath before," she wrote. "Maybe I should be 'converted' and sign the oath no more, but I think I would just as soon delay my conversion until I have sinned once more on behalf of Pacifica radio, if that is what is required to keep it on the air."[74]

Jerome Shore urged the board not to cooperate with the FCC. He could easily envision the foundation defying the commission, then taking its case to the public. But, unlike Shore, most members of the board had little organizing experience. They taught in colleges, ran other foundations, or practiced a profession. In the end, Pacifica's leadership decided that an organization created by a martyred pacifist to save the world would not go down on their watch. On November 14, Jorgensen and several board members went to Washington to talk to the FCC. They brought along copies of a compromise statement signed by all the members of the board of directors. It read as follows: "I, the undersigned, a member of the Board of Directors of the Pacifica Foundation, hereby assert my belief in and support of the Constitution of the United States, and my intention to uphold the spirit and obligations of the Constitution in the discharge of my duties as Director of the Foundation." Henry, the chair of the FCC, accepted Jorgensen's statement but said he'd still have to summon a few members of the board "for formal or legal questioning." To no one's surprise, the list he provided included Jerry Shore.[75]

At a December 12 meeting, Shore reminded his colleagues of their resolution to back up any Pacifican who refused to comply with a government interrogation. Could Shore still expect such solidarity? Ten days later, the board met again and made its position clear: if the FCC attempted to make political inquiries into the backgrounds of individual members of Pacifica, the foundation would most certainly support that member in his refusal to comply and try to convince the FCC to withdraw such questions, "or," the statement continued, "if it cannot so persuade the FCC, it will proceed as necessary to try to preserve its broadcasting licenses." Shore realized that he and his strategy of resistance had been abandoned, albeit with the politest of language. "We had all sorts of support," he later recalled. "But it would take a united fight. You couldn't make that kind of a broad-based fight with a board that didn't want to resist." Shore tendered his resignation. This time it was accepted.[76]

The announcement of Shore's departure outraged staff throughout the network. "I think the staff never really quite trusted management again for some time," Chris Koch commented.[77] Furious programmers at KPFK and WBAI threatened to shut down their respective stations, and Shore had to plead with them to stay on the air.[78] The conflict created the deepest of chasms between Trevor Thomas and Elsa Knight Thompson, who made no secret of her contempt for Pacifica's acting president. "The terrible part of it was that Trevor was really a very nice man," she later said, "with the best intentions in the world. But when the screws were on, he was dishonest."[79] Throughout the SISS/FCC conflict, Knight Thompson held frequent meetings with station producers. The subject, inevitably, was station management. "I can't recall her ever suggesting that we just sit down with the manager and talk over what was bothering us," a frequent participant recalled. "It was always 'we senior staff members' must find some way of preventing the manager from doing the stupid, weak, or evil thing which he intends."[80] As the new year progressed, tensions between Knight Thompson and Thomas headed for the breaking point.

Ironically, just beneath all this rancor lay a fundamental consensus on how Pacifica's stations should define their mission. Having looked for and found trouble, the staffs of KPFA, KPFK, and WBAI now struggled with the consequences—moral, practical, and philosophical. First, almost everyone in the organization agreed that the upholding of individual rights and free speech represented the primary function of the institution. Second, and just as important, almost everyone shared a fundamental distrust of communism. While they struggled against the national security state's invocation of a communist "conspiracy" to justify war and repression, they shuddered at Stalinism itself. They certainly admired the legacy of American communism: its contributions to the building of the CIO and its struggles on behalf of civil rights in the 1930s. But they often saw the individual communists they knew as obtuse and conventional in their thinking. "If the left-wingers of this country had had brains enough to figure out a left-wing position of their own as applied to this country," Knight Thompson once declared, "then things might have been different, but in point of fact too often the Communist Party was being influenced by foreign applications and didn't fit our needs."[81] Certainly none of the second generation of Pacificans, including William Mandel, cared to submit their intellectual life to the idiocies of democratic centralism. More often than not, they lavished their journalistic admiration on the *ex*-communists who visited Pacifica stations, such as Howard Fast, Al Richmond, and Knight Thompson's friend Jessica Mitford. Dorothy Healey thrived as a KPFK commentator in part because of her reputation as a Party renegade. When she finally did quit the Party in 1973, denouncing its "distorted version of democratic centralism to compel approval of decisions," she did so publicly, over KPFK's airwaves.[82]

The foundation's class of 1964 sought a broadcasting philosophy that upheld the right of communists to speak but enabled staff and subscribers to distance themselves from communism. They found such a stance in the words of the organization's next president.

The Politics of Balance

Hallock Hoffman, son of former Ford Foundation president Paul Hoffman, frequently offered commentaries on KPFK. He also served on Pacifica's board of directors. Hoffman worked for the Center for the Study of Democratic Institutions, whose roundtable discussions the Pacifica Foundation sometimes broadcast. A Quaker and participant in the anti–loyalty oath movement, Hoffman, an energetic man of fifty, was an ideal choice for the presidency of the network. When Thomas and then Russell Jorgensen successively quit in 1964, Hoffman accepted the job, without salary.[83] In addition to his politics and connections, the board no doubt saw value in Hoffman's leadership; in a single radio commentary, he fully developed the ideas that Wallace Hamilton, Harold Winkler, and Trevor Thomas had only partially outlined. Hoffman entitled his January 17, 1963, KPFK talk "The Problem of Balance."

The Pacifica Foundation confronts an old dilemma, he began: "the question of balance in programming." Hoffman outlined various schemes by which a station could apportion equal amounts of time to pundits from the far left to the far right. If a public affairs director tried to crowd them all into the same room, could he ever really locate all relevant positions on an issue? If such an editor spread the commentators out over the week even at the same time of day, how could the station make certain that listeners tuned in to hear all the perspectives? Perhaps a station "should rather try to achieve some proportion in respect to the spectrum of the whole broadcast media."[84]

"A strong argument can be made," argued Hoffman, "that the Pacifica stations should supply the program lacks resulting from the limitations of commercial radio." He cited general news coverage of the Cuban missile crisis, when those critical of President Kennedy's policies received hostile attention, if any at all. "To give a fair hearing to opposition views, within public affairs broadcasting as a whole, the Pacifica stations would become outlets for all the views not available on commercial stations—which would mean that the Pacifica public affairs programs would present a consistently high proportion of unpopular views."[85] Since Pacifica listeners tended to be more educated and critical than the general population, Hoffman suggested, they might expect Pacifica stations to devote most of their time to broadcasts on subjects most Americans found foreign and threatening. The speaker finished with a paragraph that perfectly captured the idea of what would soon be called alternative journalism:

> Pacifica should lean toward programs that present either opinions or information not available elsewhere. Just as I feel little obligation to spend time on my broadcasts saying what is wrong with communist governments, since everyone hears what is wrong with communist governments from every side, I think Pacifica serves the ideal of balance if it spends little time reinforcing popular beliefs. Just as I feel much obligation to point out what seems to me to be true about the claims of Communists or other unpopular people, because so little attention is paid to these matters elsewhere, so I feel Pacifica should be on the lookout for information that is hard for us to get from other sources.[86]

In the time it took Hoffman to articulate this position, one broadcasting philosophy died and another took its place. The ideas Hamilton and his followers expressed in 1954 were now Pacifica policy. Lewis Hill's hope that a Pacifica station would demonstrate the possibility of a pacific world through the encouragement of diverse exchange no longer held purchase with his heirs. KPFA, KPFK, and WBAI would now offer their services to the dissenter and his or her audience. The repressive atmosphere of the 1950s and the government's vicious assault on the foundation in 1963 had made wide-ranging dialogue appear pointless to Pacifica's second generation. They had barely been willing to talk to their persecutors, though the penalty surely would have been institutional suicide.

Hoffman's doctrine addressed a fundamental problem: in 1963, you still could not talk to a communist without becoming a communist yourself in the mind of the government. Hoffman's philosophy enabled the Pacifica programmer and subscriber to listen to the communist while maintaining a crucial political distance. The foundation broadcast voices of dissent not necessarily because it agreed with these voices, Hoffman explained, but because no one else gave them a fair hearing.

In reality, Hoffman's doctrine represented a kind of defensive ideological exterior. In coming years, KPFA, KPFK, and WBAI subscribers would not listen to Pacifica's voices of dissent out of some desire for balance but because they strongly sympathized with the dissenting views they heard, which more often than not had little if anything to do with communism. In 1966, Eleanor McKinney devoted her last year as an active member of the Pacifica Foundation to editing of *The Exacting Ear: The Story of Listener-Sponsored Radio, and an Anthology of Programs from KPFA, KPFK, and WBAI.* This collection revealed little concern with the idea of communism per se and far more for Native American lore, the philosophy of Gurdjieff, the Lamaze childbirth method, Pauline Kael's movie reviews, and interracial religious communities in Georgia. *The Exacting Ear* did address anticommunism and its impact on the Pacifica Foundation, however, making certain to publish KPFA's 1960 HUAC documentary and Hallock Hoffman's "Problem of Balance" essay.[87]

For generations of Pacifica listeners to come, the foundation's revised mission would open up the political space to explore the plethora of issues declared verboten in the 1950s: sexuality, race relations, drugs, nontraditional lifestyles, and critiques of the national security state, such as WBAI's Jack Levine interview. Such programming enabled the Pacifica listener to examine radical ideas without being accused of being a radical. "Pacifica is a patriotic organization," read a late January 1963 draft policy memorandum. "We are dedicated to the ideals of freedom and human dignity which underlie our American republic. These ideals are served by a continual search for truth."[88] The consumption of "un-American" ideas had been turned into an American idea, even a patriotic act. What Denny Wilcher suspected would happen *had* happened: the organization he had helped found had publicly reinscribed its mission in the language of American individualism and nationalism. The Cold War had compelled the foundation to reinvent itself, to complete its transition from a philosophy of dialogue to one of dissent.

"A Beautiful Sentiment"

"Morale, resulting from divisions among the staff, is at the lowest ebb since I have been at KPFA," Trevor Thomas, KPFA's station manager, wrote to Elsa Knight Thompson on January 13, 1964. "Consciously or not, you are at the hub of most of the situations which contribute to this situation." With that said, Thomas fired Knight Thompson, essentially for insubordination.[89]

For John Whiting, a member of KPFA's engineering staff, this represented the final outrage after the abandonment of Jerry Shore. "From then on," he later recalled, "we went about our business convinced that the government and our own directors, who had reached a highly publicized accommodation, together constituted 'the enemy.'" The production staff signed up with the National Association of Broadcast Engineers and Technicians (NABET) and went on strike, demanding Knight Thompson's restoration. Dissent radio now had its own resident dissenter. Some perceived a clear generational divide in the conflict. Dorothy Bryant remembered the walkout referred to as the "teenage takeover," although many of the picketers were hardly teenagers. After some months, the staff won a contract. Knight Thompson would soon get her job back plus a monetary settlement. Firing her was a "dumb mistake," Jorgensen later conceded.[90]

Interviewed on KPFA's sixteenth birthday program—on April 15, 1965—new station manager Al Partridge felt confident enough about the future to take issue with frequent references to KPFA as an "experiment." "After all, it's been a long experiment for sixteen years," he said. "I think we can take a little more assurance in the fact that we've experimented pretty well and things are still going along."[91]

The anniversary program began on a triumphant note. In early 1964, the FCC had renewed all three of the Pacifica Foundation's licenses. The show briefly aired Trevor Thomas reading from the January 22 ruling: "We recognize that such provocative programming as here involved may offend some listeners. But this does not mean that those offended have the right, through the Commission's licensing power, to rule such programming off the airwaves. Were this the case, only the wholly inoffensive, the bland, could gain access to the radio microphone or the television camera." The KPFA program did not mention that "on the basis of information obtained from Government sources," the FCC had cleared the foundation of any suspicion of Communist Party affiliation. The program's narrator simply stated that Pacifica's licenses had been renewed "over unwarranted charges of obscenity and subversiveness."[92]

Highlights from the year's best radio programs followed, including a satire on the accelerated U.S. military involvement in Vietnam. A later, more ethnically conscious generation of Pacificans would never have allowed this program to air, but in 1965 its particular brand of humor was still acceptable to the staff. The voice of a man attempting to reproduce a Vietnamese accent introduced himself as "Chin Yang" and told listeners that he wanted to introduce "da boys" in Vietnam to his good friend "Hanoi Hannah."

"Hallo, da boys!" exclaimed Hannah, "you surprised I speak your language? Hmmmm? This is Hanoi Hannah. Well, Chin Yang? Do you have the mail bag?" Someone fumbled with paper. "Yes I do, Hanoi Hannah," the man said. "Here is the firscht letter."

"I see," said Hannah. "This is a letter from Master Sergeant Marshall Efron.[93] 'Dear Hannah, I listen to you and it made me cry. It made me miss my momma.' Do you hear that Irving, Harold, Eddy, wherever you are?" she asked. "What are you doing in our rice paddies? Do you realize all the breakfast cereal we could puff from our guns instead of shooting at you if you would get out of our rice paddies?"

"That was very well put, Hanoi Hannah," said her assistant. "You know, Yank, you come to our country as guests of the most pleasurable and honorable people around. And now you cause devastation and trouble amongst the peasants and the quiet people who want to sit around and play their guitars. And Hanoi Hannah is my friend. And she's your friend too, and she tell you, 'Throw down your weapon! Hold you hand up in the air and say, 'I surrender Hannah'!"

"Hannah, what do you think of that?" Chin Yang asked.

"I think that's a beautiful sentiment. I couldn't have said it better mine self."[94]

Thus did listener-supported, nonsubversive radio celebrate its victory over McCarthyism. The Pacifica Foundation had talked to the Man at the Door and survived. The organization's leadership had constructed a formal self that it, society at large, and the national security state found acceptable. The FCC offered Pacifica its public blessing on April 7, 1964, when E. William Henry gave a remarkable speech before the annual convention of the National Association of Broadcasters. A year earlier, Henry had cleared the foundation of charges of subversion only after a private meeting with Senator Dodd, in which Henry outlined the commission's logic, step by step. "It was a courtesy," Henry later explained. "I think the chairman of any agency always feels that if he can avoid some after-the-fact political heat, it is better to do so if you can do so in a legitimate way."[95]

Now Henry told the convention delegates, in effect, that FCC had erred in delaying Pacifica's licenses, and the broadcasting industry shared the blame as well. "Which of you wrote me a letter urging the commission to dismiss these charges and to reaffirm the commission's time-honored adherence to the principles of free broadcasting?" Henry asked. "Where were your libertarian lawyers and their amicus briefs, your industry statesmen with their ringing speeches?" The chairman added that in holding Pacifica's licenses and demanding the organization sign an anticommunist oath, the FCC had operated outside its jurisdiction. Why didn't anyone in the industry protest? Henry demanded. "When you remain silent in the face of a threat which could shake the First Amendment's proud oak to its very roots," Henry concluded, "you tarnish the ideals enshrined in the Constitution and invite an attitude of suspicion."[96]

The Pacifica Foundation had won. The organization had won the liberal right to speak radical words. But this victory, like all victories, would have consequences.

Conclusion

Dialogue and Dissent

To define listener-sponsored radio is all but impossible, since there is no particular goal, other than an articulated addiction to the First Amendment.

— Steve Post,
Playing in the FM Band

The Cold War changed everything. The binary landscape created by Stalinism and the U.S. national security state forced postwar Americans to narrow their vision of the possible. William Mandel still remembers the day in 1947 that he gave a lecture at Palo Alto's public library, challenging the notion of Soviet expansionism. Outside, the police patrolled the building's parking lot, recording the license plate numbers of those attending the speech.[1] Thousands of miles away, the Soviet Union's minister of culture, A. A. Zhdanov, corroborated Mandel's analysis in the most horrible way. He organized a campaign against "cosmopolitanism" and "worship of things foreign," leading to the arrest of dozens of intellectuals and a wave of executions.[2] The Cold War created, in the words of one historian, "a time of extreme politicization of knowledge throughout the world."[3] The availability of ideas and information became contingent on the actions of the state. Moreover, the omnipresence of anticommunist sentiment imposed a difficult debate about freedom throughout America. This debate quickly established dominance over its reluctant subjects, forcing even radical Americans to forgo other concerns on behalf of a single agonizing dilemma: to what extent did they want to uphold the individual rights of people who aligned themselves with the American Communist Party—a movement that they felt did not respect individual rights? As an epidemic of loyalty oath laws, FBI shakedowns, state inquisitions, and subversion trials spread across the nation, a generation of postwar pacifists, socialists, and anarchists watched as cherished visions were abandoned, tabled by circumstances beyond their control. The Cold War forced a wide spectrum of radical ideas into a single shade of liberal thought.

Lewis Hill and his friends set out to create the Pacifica Foundation just before the onset of this stultifying condition. Released from years of rural exile during the Second World War, they emerged during a brief time and place of expansive optimism. Fascism had been crushed, and the United Nations had just been established. San Francisco's unique culture nourished a new generation of visionary poets. But this window of opportunity quickly closed. By the mid-1950s, the foundation's principals knew that their task would not be to encourage a pacific world in the present but to guide their network through the crossfire of McCarthyism. This painful passage forced its leaders to reconstruct their broadcasting mission, making a clean break from one mode of free speech to another. The first saw the encouragement of radical dialogue as its primary task. The second emphasized the right of the individual to speak, particularly the individual denied such a right. The first mode of free speech had its origins in American pacifism. The second had its roots in a liberal progressivism that sought to defend the free speech rights of communists while creating political distance between communism and itself. Ultimately, the latter mode blossomed into what we today call "alternative media." The former was largely forgotten, even by the institution its founders created.

It would be very simple to forget Lewis Hill and his friends yet again by burying them under a mound of nostalgic and superficial praise. In reality, the first Pacificans represent something of an embarrassment to the post–Cold War, multicultural present. Although the creators of KPFA spoke of dialogue and diversity, they were, for the most part, white Anglo-Saxon Protestant middle-class men. They claimed to want to reach out to the "average" person but often wound up broadcasting Bartok sonatas and "dithering discussions," in Pauline Kael's words, conducted by academic experts.[4] They stood for social justice yet refused to bear arms against Nazism, the most formidable evil of their time. Recognizing how politically unclassifiable or downright odd they appeared to others, the progenitors of modern public radio often obscured their true selves in the interest of fundraising.

Like the rest of us, Lewis Hill and his friends did not always exemplify their credo in practice. But they did create knowledge for the present. Their remarkable story offers crucial lessons for those who wish to encourage dialogue in our complex day.

THE IDEAS that formed the basis for the Pacifica Foundation emerged, as they so often do, from acknowledgment of failure. In 1942, Lewis Hill and his friend Roy Finch labored in a California CPS camp and pondered their fates. What had gone wrong? Why had the influential pacifist movement of the 1930s collapsed so easily? What should pacifists do now? As director of the National Committee of Conscientious Objectors in Washington, Hill spent much of the war tending to the legal needs of those COs who had chosen to resist the CPS system. From the perspective of his work at the nation's capital, Hill came to the conclusion that activists on the American left have repeatedly reached since the Russian Revolution of 1917. His movement had become isolated, caught up in little rebellions, unmindful of the larger picture. From the mid-1930s through the Second World War, pacifism had accomplished little with its fine statements and mimeographed newsletters besides assuring conscientious objectors and their allies of what they already believed to be true. Lewis Hill, Roy Finch, and others now struggled to find some way out of this self-defeating pattern.

Pacifists during the Second World War concluded that to wield greater influence, pacifism would have to create institutions that, by sheer existential will, positioned pacifist ideas in the center of American culture rather than at its margins. Organized pacifism would have to venture from its perch as a Cassandra-like outsider into American society. Adherents of nonviolence would have to create cultural institutions that placed pacifist beliefs at the core of an inclusive representation of the world—organized and managed by pacifists. "It was recognized that the confidence of a large audience must be gained first," an early Pacifica memorandum explained, "to make possible a more and more intensive cultivation of the interests of common people in resisting war, and to create a stable institutional basis for integrating this interest not only through radio programming but, as that work progressed, though supplementary activities of a revolutionary nature." These institutions and activities would draw to themselves people of all walks and political spectra, who would engage in conversation centered on pacifist questions. Such ventures would demonstrate the viability of pacifism and human cooperation rather than simply propagandize it. Ultimately, the founders of Pacifica radio anticipated an "eventual crisis," in which their network would be publicly sacrificed and the struggle for a free, warless society would escalate.[5]

These unique journalists did not see the final conflict, however, as one between proletarians and bourgeoisie. Influenced by the young Dwight Macdonald, they saw it as between the individual and the warfare-state systems that had arisen throughout the world. To them, the "individual" was not some romantic lone figure struggling against the powers that be, but groups defining their individuality through meaningful interaction with other individuals. For the first Pacificans, to be human meant to be engaged in creative and nonexploitative activity with other humans. This was what Eleanor McKinney meant when she referred to the Pacifica philosophy as one of "humanism."[6] The enemy of humanism functioned not as a class but as a system of armed nation-states, each with a rigid ideology that encouraged its subjects to view outsiders as inhuman and to support the maintenance of violence-wielding networks of "security."

Pacifists had to challenge this pervasive condition on two fronts. First, they had to expose it through protest and political action. But after his years as a CO, Hill believed that although such tactics sustained pacifism as a movement, they did not lead to a pacific world. True resistance to war would have to demonstrate that peace meant more than the absence of violence, that it meant aspiring to a rich connectedness among humans, even those who in the unjust course of events had become estranged from one another. This praxis came first, not a radio station.

The Pacifica Foundation's original 1946 mission statement outlined a variety of venues into which such an idea might fit, including a newspaper, a magazine, a school, and, at one point, even a chain of restaurants.[7] Hill and his associates arrived at the radio idea because they had experience with the medium and knew of the long-standing dissatisfaction many Americans had with commercial broadcasting.[8] As early Pacifica internal and public literature indicates, Hill wanted the Pacifica message to reach an ethnically and economically diverse audience. The first Pacificans intended to locate their pilot frequency in the working-class city of Richmond, California. Their first fundraising document called upon Pacifica's proposed station to reach out to the "average" person in "familiar and satisfying" ways, and warned against a broadcasting approach that appealed only to a pacifist inner circle.

In its early years, KPFA's staff drew to the station the San Francisco Bay Area's finest theatrical, literary, and performative talent. Sharing its resources with thousands of Bay Area residents, KPFA became a kind of matrix of human interaction. Its public affairs department sponsored numerous debates and discussions that encouraged ideologically diverse panels to grapple with anarcho-pacifist questions: Did atomic power threaten individual freedom? Did co-ops represent a better system than free-market capitalism? Programmers understood that they had everything to gain by inviting their political opponents to engage in a dialogue centered on pacifist/anarchist concerns. These former CO camp inmates had created a place where, on a local level, the rest of the world obeyed their rules and interacted on their terms.

The very nation-state that Pacifica's leaders sought to challenge, however, forced compromise on this bold vision. Denied a license for an AM radio signal in Richmond, Pacifica's organizers settled for an FM frequency in nearby Berkeley, where a relatively sizable segment of the population owned FM receivers. Suddenly, the class and ethnic backgrounds of KPFA's premiere audience shifted. It became more ethnically homogeneous, more affluent, and more formally educated. The pressing need to raise funds required Lewis Hill and his colleagues to constantly readjust the Pacifica Foundation's mission to appeal to various philanthropic sectors and, with the decline of organized pacifism in the early years of the Cold War, to tailor their fundraising message not to war resisters seeking a pacific world but to liberals in search of a fair and balanced world. The creators of KPFA sought an FM license during the formative years of what would later become the FCC's "Fairness Doctrine," a policy with a clear political objective: to ensure that liberal government would have the opportunity to respond to attacks on its policies by a broadcasting media controlled by conservatives. This priority compelled Lewis Hill to repeatedly deemphasize the foundation's goals of pacifist dialogue in favor of an emphasis on individual rights, particularly the individual's right to respond to the statements of others.

Most important, during the early 1950s—the worst years of McCarthyism—KPFA increasingly functioned as a culture of refuge. Besieged by loyalty oath laws, anticommunist inquisitions, and television, many Berkeleyans experienced KPFA not as a force for change but as a hideout from mainstream America. The station's subscribers often regarded themselves as exiles from a society whose citizens appeared incapable of making considered intelligent political and cultural choices. Journalist William Drummond recalled subscribing to KPFA for the first time in 1962. The first *Folio* he received featured an uncaptioned front-page photograph of "an owlish gentleman wearing horn-rim glasses." Drummond could not identify the man. Only years later did he discover it was poet William Butler Yeats. "In those days," Drummond wrote, "it was assumed that any KPFA subscriber would already know." Such a stance reflected an impulse to forgo inclusive pacifist dialogue in favor of an enclave-like broadcasting culture that, at its best, saw itself dispensing the values of "persons of education, mental ability, or cultural heritage" on the general populace, as Lewis Hill himself later put it.[9] Desperate for sources of institutional income, Hill encouraged such thinking in his later fundraising documents, particularly his final report to the Fund for Adult Education.

The leaders who inherited Pacifica after Hill's death—Harold Winkler, Trevor Thomas, and Hallock Hoffman—confronted a unique dilemma. Although the national security state ignored their sincere efforts to draw conservatives and even reactionaries into Pacifica radio's orbit, it took a keen interest in the handful of communists who regularly appeared on KPFA, KPFK, and WBAI. Furthermore, a new generation of programmers now emerged throughout Pacifica who saw anticommunism in monodimensional terms. To them, it meant Joseph McCarthy, HUAC, and the repressive culture of the 1950s. These Pacificans had only a vague sense of the pacifist anticommunism of Lewis Hill and Wallace Hamilton. Furthermore, they did not fear the anticommunist establishment. In some cases their boldness could be attributed to their youth. More important, many Pacifica staff members had been so marginalized by the Cold War that they did not fear to challenge McCarthyism on a public level. William Mandel and Elsa Knight Thompson represented the two most prominent exemplars of this new style. To this second, nonpacifist generation of Pacificans, the struggle for dialogue or even balance seemed pointless in a society that swiftly punished those Americans who spoke their minds. The foundation became increasingly committed to ever-more-daring journalistic exploits designed to confront state anticommunism.

When such exploits included publicly exposing the internal life of the most feared government agency in America, the national security state quickly retaliated. In 1963, no less than three sectors of the government investigated and imposed a loyalty oath/show-trial regimen on the Pacifica Foundation. The agonizing process by which the network resisted this attack forced its leaders to fundamentally redefine the organization's mission in the language of individualism and nationalism. The foundation emerged from this ordeal publicly reconstituted as "First Amendment Radio." It became America's "room for dissent"—the place where citizens could exercise their constitutional right to hear less popular viewpoints. The organization redefined its concept of balance. No longer would the network attempt to match individual political positions against one another on the same broadcast schedule; rather, it would offer dissent as a contrast to mainstream opinion heard elsewhere. Most important, the broadcast and consumption of dissent became defined as a form of "Americanism." The policies outlined by Winkler and Hoffman allowed Pacificans to broadcast and consider "un-American" ideas without risking public identification with them. One gave air time to the subversive not because one necessarily agreed with the subversive position but because it represented the "unpopular" point of view, which, in a free nation, was worthy at least of free consideration.

This doctrine became the Pacifica Foundation's raison d'être—its self-defined relationship with American society: "Sometimes a one-to-one balance is not even desirable (for example, an interview is different from a debate). An idea does not always demand an opposite," declared a 1965 Pacifica brochure. "We especially welcome those voices which are denied access to other media by those inside and outside of Government who confuse 'free speech' with 'safe speech,'" explained a Pacifica Foundation president five years later. "What established our reputation was being able to cover things, being willing to cover things in depth which weren't covered by other people, being able to furnish a kind of analysis and a kind of muckraking view of things that aren't provided elsewhere," argued a manager at WBAI in 1971. "Pacifica is high-risk radio," concluded a 1975 brochure, borrowing rhetoric from a crucial Supreme Court decision. "When the theater is burning, our microphones are available to shout fire."[10]

The courageous broadcasting fare that accompanied this doctrine would take an entire volume to celebrate. As early as 1963, Pacifica aired commentary by I. F. Stone and Bertrand Russell in opposition to U.S. involvement in Vietnam. Two years later, WBAI's Chris Koch became the first American to cover the war from Hanoi. In 1967, Pacifica broadcast a live interview with Marxist revolutionary Ernesto Ché Guevara, just months before his assassination in Bolivia. In 1969, Pacifica Radio provided an in-depth forum for Seymour Hersh's revelations on the My Lai massacre in Vietnam. In 1971, a WBAI manager spent time in prison for refusing to turn over to the police taped statements of men incarcerated in New York's notorious "Tombs" city jail. By that time, Pacifica Radio's reputation more than adequately preceded it. When the foundation opened KPFT in Houston, Texas, in 1970, the Ku Klux Klan bombed the station off the air twice in its first twelve months. It would take years of bureaucratic struggle before Pacifica would gain a license for its fifth frequency, WPFW, in Washington, D.C.[11]

In the 1960s, KPFA became identified with the remarkable events unfolding on the UC campus. In 1964, a coalition of Cal students mobilized against UC chancellor Clark Kerr's system of ordinances that restricted political activity on school grounds. On October 1, campus police moved in to arrest one of these activists. In response, hundreds of his peers surrounded the arrest scene for more than a day. The university dropped all charges, and the victorious students gave their insurgent cause an irresistible name: the Free Speech Movement (FSM).[12] From that moment on, whenever conflicts erupted between the university and the Berkeley left, KPFA subscribers could count on immediate updates from their station.

By the mid-1960s, the availability of portable, professional-quality tape recorders made on-the-spot coverage feasible. Even more important, the widespread distribution of FM stereo receivers turned a once obscure broadcasting medium into a fixture of everyday life. Listeners kept their dials tuned to KPFA through the remarkable convulsions that transformed a once-conservative town into the "People's Republic of Berkeley": the People's Park uprising and the occupation of the city by state troops.

For Neil MacGregor, the station became indispensable. Hospitalized during the free speech revolt for back surgery, he faithfully listened to KPFA's coverage of campus events throughout the day. "The important thing about KPFA was that whenever there was anything happening on the streets, you turned on KPFA because someone from KPFA was there," former commentator Dorothy Bryant remembered. Quickly recognizing the importance of the station to their cause, the leadership of the FSM invited William Mandel to sit on its executive committee.[13]

But as the forces of liberation broadcasting celebrated the dismantling of McCarthyism throughout the 1960s and early 1970s, a new philosophical crisis emerged. Now that the pioneers of dissent radio had all the freedom of speech they could possibly desire, what larger mission unified their network? What was the foundation's ultimate purpose? In the mid-1960s, Hallock Hoffman hired two people who, working on opposite coasts, struggled with this dilemma. So perplexing did they find the problem that each went so far as to publish a book on their experiences with Pacifica. What, they pondered, was the goal of listener-supported, First Amendment, free-speech radio above and beyond the celebration and consumption of free speech? Both writers arrived at the same conclusion: nothing.

Velvet Fog

Paul Dallas had been the host of *Thinking Allowed*, a fifteen-minute commentary on KPFK, for several years when, in 1966, Hallock Hoffman asked him to serve as general manager of the station. A convincing speaker and writer, Dallas had at least one published book to his credit, a science fiction novel entitled *The Lost Planet*. A year later, after departing from Pacifica, the bemused author added yet another work to his resume: *Dallas in Wonderland*, an act of revenge. Self-published, it outlined in painful detail the mishaps that led to the author's ousting from KPFK and why he was right and others were wrong about most of what happened during his employ. "I am enthralled by the concept of Free Radio," Dallas began. "I am in full accord with the ideals of the Pacifica Foundation which owns KPFK. But I find myself at hopeless odds with the handful of men who currently hold its power of free communication close to their vests."[14] Paul Dallas represented that greatest of threats to an institution's stability: someone who actually believed its propaganda.

Of the many problems Dallas described at the station, the most important centered on an annual fundraising event: the Renaissance Pleasure Faire. Bringing in about one-fifth of the station's annual income, this two-weekend neo-Elizabethan celebration had become central to KPFK's survival. Dallas took exception to a crucial aspect of the festival: KPFK did not control it. Entrepreneurs Ron and Phyllis Patterson ran and generated income from the Faire and shared a portion of their profit with KPFK. The majority of volunteers "labored under the belief that they were turning toil and dollars directly over to KPFK," Dallas complained. "Most people assumed that the Pattersons were among the most blessed of volunteers in this community effort."[15]

In 1967, Dallas decided that he wanted to exert more influence over the running of the Faire and managed to convince the Pattersons to relinquish their claim to total ownership of the event. Subsequently, a coalition of conservative activists, led by the wife of television actor Walter Brennan, filed an appeal with the Board of Supervisors of Ventura County and succeeded in canceling the Faire that spring.[16] Only one chore now remained: blame assignment. On May 13, 1967, a generous KPFK programmer named Elliot Mintz decided that he would donate his regular program to this task.

Mintz began his show, called *Looking In*, by asking a series of rhetorical questions about the debacle and then invited listeners to telephone with their comments. After a series of subscribers squared off on the question of the managerial competence of the Pattersons, Phyllis Patterson herself called to protest the discussion of such matters over KPFK. But after the show, Mintz got the couple to agree to participate in a live discussion on the failure of the Faire. They, their business manager, their secretary, Mintz, and a member of the KPFK board crowded into the station's broadcasting studio. The debate proved unsatisfactory to the Pattersons, who demanded additional air time. The station's public affairs department complied and granted them approximately two or three hours' worth. Finally, Dallas decided that he would add his views to the controversy and hosted a Wednesday-night talk show that also lasted almost three hours. In less than a week, KPFK had become a station dedicated to broadcasting news and views about its internal incompetence. It is unclear how long this would have continued had the head of the foundation not moved in to stop the bleeding.

On May 21, Lloyd M. Smith, who had replaced Hallock Hoffman as president of Pacifica, sent Dallas a script that Smith wanted read repeatedly on the air. Smith apologized to the Pattersons, condemned Mintz's broadcasts, and essentially told the staff to shut up about the Renaissance Faire controversy. Yes, Smith conceded, the Pacifica Foundation believed in freedom, but it also believed in "a limitation which is somewhat vaguely and inadequately described as 'responsibility.'" Everyone now knows what everyone thinks about this disaster, Smith said. "So I conclude with what may be an old Renaissance benediction — may peace be with us all."

Dallas found this communiqué infuriating. "It was an order!" he indignantly declared. After a series of meetings, he could not resist taking to the airwaves one more time for a lengthy talk about the Renaissance Faire that wasn't. Within two weeks he was fired.

Throughout *Dallas in Wonderland*, Dallas referred to something largely indefinable that he encountered at Pacifica. He confessed that often during conversations he would envision "little wisps of nonsense fog curl[ing] round [his] mind," usually when a person said one thing to him and clearly meant another. Dallas began to call this "the velvet fog."[17] Why, Dallas asked in his concluding chapter, did the foundation fire him if it agreed with Hallock Hoffman's recent statement on Pacifica policy: "We ought to remember that risk-taking means we will have some failures. . . . In ordinary circumstances, the first duty of the administrator is to sustain order. There needs to be order in Pacifica. . . . At the same time, the very act of creation involves change and disorder, and since we wish to be risk-taking and adventuresome, we are bound to have a sizable amount of disorder."[18] Dallas perceived none of the ambivalence in this statement, only the certainty. "The larger purpose of Pacifica is dissent," he wrote. "The innovators, the daring and nonconforming thinkers are the ones who created and supported Pacifica. And I cannot agree that this group needs a Big Brother to show it how it ought to nonconform." This proposition proved popular with a sizable percentage of KPFK's listenership, who held demonstrations against Dallas's firing and formed a group called Friends of the First Amendment: KPFK.[19] But the velvet fog really existed and would not be blown away. It consisted of Pacifica presidents, staff, and even a bookkeeper who could not escape the suspicion that freedom of speech surely meant something more than the absolute right to speak.

The Outsider

One afternoon in the summer of 1964, Hallock Hoffman received a phone call from a man in New York City looking for a job. At the age of twenty, Steve Post had flunked out of junior college, drifted from one low-paying clerical position to another, and finally found typing work with a Quaker peace group. This job, which involved the production of leaflets, provided only temporary satisfaction. "I finally grew disillusioned with the endless masses of words," Post later wrote. "Why, I wondered, were these people not out in the streets dressed in loincloths, leading the masses to nonviolent revolution?" Post decided that he'd "had it with Quakers" and became interested when a friend mentioned that WBAI was hiring staff. He called Hoffman—a Quaker—who asked him about his bookkeeping skills and willingness to work for a relatively low salary. These matters settled, Hoffman told Post to show up for work in two weeks. "I realized then that I had neither been asked to come by for a personal interview nor filled out an application, and that, finally, I didn't know what my job was to be," Post later recalled. "In retrospect, it seems, I should have recognized the handwriting, if not the wall."[20]

Within three years, Post had risen from auditor to the voice of a national movement called "free-form radio." Its most important practitioners—Post, Bob Fass, and Larry Josephson—became FM sensations throughout the greater New York area. No taboos inhibited their broadcasts on WBAI. Indeed, they sometimes pondered what limits could possibly exist, Josephson speculating, according to Post, that "if we presented several hours a week of nothing but farting, the program would soon have a large and dedicated following." They played black vinyl records simultaneously, or backwards, sometimes letting the needle repeat over damaged grooves while talking over the skips. They monologued about the most personal matters, or made fun of listeners, or fought with one another on the air. Unlike Pacifica's founders, they abhorred the center, positioning themselves instead as alienated men, looking in from the cold periphery. While the American people prepared to send Richard Nixon to the White House, they took dissent radio as far as it could go.[21]

Steve Post appropriately entitled his Saturday-night show *The Outside*, and delighted in turning the world on its head. He urged listeners to organize a "fat-in," celebrating the bodies of those deemed less than beautiful. Almost five hundred people responded ("in the flesh") with a Central Park gathering. For almost a year Post cultivated an on-air relationship with a caller known only as "The Enema Lady," who phoned in with poems and songs about her favorite bathroom pastime.[22]

Bob Fass's offering, *Radio Unnamable*, in Post's words, "proceeded from moment to moment, with Fass free-associating one record, tape, or thought to another, generally deciding upon the next record or tape only as the previous one ran out." Larry Josephson, a former computer programmer, dubbed his angry morning program *In the Beginning*. Josephson's stance toward BAI's listeners was obvious from the second one listened to him. "He hated them," Post recalled, and reveled in a "wretched hostile attitude" that implicitly satirized the false cheer of the drive-time morning deejay.[23]

Lewis Hill had detested the phony personality of the commercial radio announcer. He wanted broadcasters who could unceremoniously reveal their true selves. The heroes of free-form broadcasting detested conventional radio as well, but they enjoyed being its exiles far too much to engage in undramatic self-reflection. Dedicated to endless blasphemy, Post, Josephson, and Fass became the polar opposite of top 40 AM radio—its negative photograph. WBAI listeners adored them. College radio deejays launched careers by imitating them. Richard Avedon took their picture.[24]

Ten years after Post walked through WBAI's front door, a major publisher released *Playing in the FM Band: A Personal Account of Free Radio*. A remarkable book, it described a cultural movement verging on exhaustion, having gorged itself on post–McCarthy era freedom for a decade. Two years earlier, in 1972, after scores of factional struggles and personal conflicts, Post had written an essay entitled "Now I Know Why Lewis Hill Committed Suicide." Filled with oblique references, it appeared in WBAI's program guide and at the end of his book. Post wondered what he was still doing at the station. By then both Fass and Josephson had left (Fass temporarily). "I feel I have said it all—" Post quoted Josephson as saying, "and now need distance, quiet and most of all time—time to reflect, to replenish, to reorder, to grow."[25]

Actually, Josephson had departed obviously disturbed at the course dissent radio had taken: toward broadcasting feminist, gay, and ethnic dissenters, all understandably desiring their share of the free-form universe. "Radical lesbian ayatollahs," he later called them.[26] Josephson became increasingly interested in the ideological origins of the Pacifica Foundation, and in 1974 he assembled Joy Cole Hill, Eleanor McKinney, and Alan Rich for a retrospective program entitled "Pacifica Is 25," which the producer described as "getting back to our roots." Toward the end of the documentary, several participants expressed concern with what one described as the "breaking down" of American society. "What are we doing all this for anyway?" Joy Hill asked rhetorically. "We are doing it so that each of us achieves some kind of empathetic awareness of the other guy. So that we are not so isolated, so shut off, so separated from one another by our lack of experience." Her comments prompted another rhetorical question, this time from Josephson's interviewer: "But people tell me every day they're not interested in talking to the average listener or all the listeners," he said. "They're interested in talking to their own people. And we've had instances in the early days of feminism where a group of women on the radio would say: 'We're not going to take calls from men. In fact, we hope men won't listen . . .' What would Lew's reaction to that have been?"[27]

Doubtless Hill would have favored programs on feminism over programs on farting, but the pioneers of free radio now reconsidered their past. Post regarded the current situation "with particular personal despair," he confessed, "since I have supported, to a large extent, the current direction and management of the station, while ignoring, even ridiculing, the boy-who-cried-wolf-like warnings of my listener-sponsored contemporaries. . . . We have all become captives of the rhetoric of this deplorably fragmented culture, though as an institution of innovation we should, perhaps, have exercised greater restraint." It was all out of Steve Post's hands now. The process had progressed to the point where it could no longer even classify itself. "To define listener-sponsored radio is all but impossible, since there is no particular goal, other than an articulated addiction to the First Amendment," Post explained.[28] The purpose of freedom was to be free; no other purpose existed, at least none the host of *The Outside* could come up with at the moment.

The circle had been completed. While Lewis Hill and his associates saw freedom as a vehicle for peaceable dialogue, they distrusted freedom's power, its potential to run wild. Now the organization's leaders trusted freedom completely but could not define its larger task. What the scholar Richard S. Randall calls the "self divided" of liberal democracy had crossed from one side of its persona to the other. The democratic side yearned for definition, for community. The liberal side longed to transcend all definitions and boundaries, even those set by the democratic process.[29]

The second generation of Pacificans instinctively knew they had left something behind, but events now moved far too quickly to permit a comprehensive assessment of the past. Throughout Pacificana, stations began dividing into departments, subdepartments, and radio "collectives" devoted to wide-ranging interests, from women's rights to Latin American revolution to union struggles in the United States. All produced original, path-breaking programming, but the pervasive sense of fragmentation that permeated the network could not be denied. By 1983, KPFA station manager David Salniker consented to an interview with a scholar on radical media. How would he describe the station's institutional culture? the writer asked. "Bureaucratically managed individualism," Salniker tersely replied. "I have yet to have the experience of someone coming to me and urging that their program should be taken off the air. And rarely, of someone coming to me and saying they want to cede their time to give space to a key issue."[30] Indeed, as a totality KPFA more often resembled a single-room-occupancy hotel than a town hall meeting. Individual programmers fiercely guarded their programs, since the individually "owned" show now often represented the fundamental building block of the station's program schedule. This pattern was only exacerbated by FCC policies that made it difficult if not impossible to establish more than a few listener-supported radio stations in any urban region, creating, in effect, a planned scarcity of public-access airtime. Turf battles disguised themselves as ideological debates. A struggle raged within the station's Third World department on who represented an authentic Third World person. For some time the Third World department opposed the creation of a women's department, its representatives arguing that women's concerns already received more than adequate attention at the station.[31] A manager later reflected on the culture of KPFA during the 1970s: "We had conflicts within our dissenting groups all over the place. And not to mention conflicts between those groups as a whole and a whole other dominant group. And it was just an incredible task to even get these people to figure out what the commonality of what we were doing was."[32]

A labored lexicon, centered on what communications scholar Jeffrey Land aptly describes as "the claims of community," gradually emerged to justify this new but barely stable order of things. With the military withdrawal of the United States from Vietnam in 1973, WBAI in New York City quickly lost half its subscribers.[33] The problem became obvious: how would dissent radio attract listeners without an ongoing national security crisis? Gradually the foundation's spokepersons added a new ideological layer to Pacifica's mission: defining the network as "community" radio, tending to the concerns of diverse cultural constituencies. This nostalgic reformulation — created to give philosophical order to institutional chaos — obscured the fact that each Pacifica station broadcast over hundreds of square miles, covering huge regions that could hardly be defined as communities. KPFK in Los Angeles, for example, could be heard in San Diego, Santa Barbara, and as far east as Fontana. In 1976, network leadership attempted to reign in WBAI's particularly balkanized air sound, proposing a more coherent format that would have required the alteration or removal of many programs. In response, the station's volunteers locked themselves in WBAI's master control room for almost six weeks, ultimately winning union representation and autonomy over their airtime. Most of the protesters eventually recognized their victory as Pyrrhic, a triumph of individual agendas over collective needs. "We saved the station from the [Pacifica] board," one participant recalled years later, "but we couldn't save it from ourselves."[34]

In the larger sense, while Pacifica's diverse array of programmers each cultivated a radical stance toward the larger society, in their own institutional settings they operated within a framework of liberal individualism, inherited from the foundation's struggle with McCarthyism. The position of dissenter, disseminator of the "alternative" point of view, reified what Richard Hofstadter described as the "fiercely individualistic and capitalistic" nature of American culture.[35] Addicted, in Steve Post's words, to its constitutional right to speak, no matter what "community" values dissent radio claimed to uphold, as a fragmented and internally contested broadcasting schedule, it validated the dominant culture, one that functioned more as a legalistic system of individual rights than as a purveyor of dialogue. The ideology of dissent had proven indispensable in defending the Pacifica Foundation from McCarthyism, empowering the network to challenge the national security state throughout the 1950s and 1960s. Dissent ideology also aided feminist and ethnic programmers, who often encountered ugly hostility to their proposals for more diverse broadcasting at Pacifica stations. But as time progressed, the Pacifica Foundation's dissent culture overdispersed itself, inadequately substituting for what the network urgently needed: a general theory of noncommercial broadcasting that prioritized listening over talking, recognition over declaration, and mutual obligation over individual rights.

Yet the network carried on, sharing its resources with a constantly shifting array of constituents. From WBAI in New York, Margot Adler, granddaughter of the psychologist Alfred Adler, invited women in her audience to discuss the most intimate issues, such as their fear of having children. When letters poured in, she read them on the air. "Now, in the 1990s, several million people may listen to one of my reports on *All Things Considered*, and I might not even receive a single response," Adler wrote years later as a reporter for National Public Radio.[36] From KPFA, a small circle of Chicano activists inaugurated a Friday-night program called *La Onda Bajita*—two hypnotic hours of Low Rider music and commentary that reached from the barrios of San Jose to the cells of San Quentin prison. From KPFT in Houston came a bevy of programs—in no less than eleven languages—that served the Texas Gulf coast.[37] From WPFW in Washington, a deejay broke the news of the 1983 U.S. invasion of Grenada through live telephone interviews with musicians in Jamaica.[38] Apprenticeship and training programs sprang up across the network, drawing in radio producers from Crown Heights in Brooklyn, South Central Los Angeles, and East Oakland. Newcomers uneasily coexisted with long-established traditions, such as broadcasts of the music of Henry Cowell and rebroadcasts of Alan Watts's commentaries. Within the corridors and studios of Pacifica's five radio stations, the cultural elitist met the community activist, the feminist met the ethnic nationalist, and the spiritualist met the determined nonbeliever. Not always, but often, each came to acknowledge what Pacifica's founders wanted them to see: the complexity of life that cannot be explained by any one philosophical or political system of thought.

This narrative ends at the dawn of the multicultural era within an institution. Of late, our national debate about identity politics has left us with an implicitly Arcadian sense of the past—a portrait of 1940s and 1950s America free of today's sense of social fragmentation. This is a pretty but false picture. By the early 1950s, Lewis Hill already saw the price Cold War America would pay for its "vast suburbs," fear of omnipresent enemies, and mania for privacy.[39] What was lost during that time was not only the right of individuals to speak but a sense of free speech as something more than a right, of dialogue as a humanizing force and an essential requirement for the health of our society. What makes Pacifica radio, our nation's only independent nonprofit network, so important is that it offers the example of a series of efforts to resist that fragmentation on a very public level. That these efforts have met with mixed success should not surprise us. The Pacifica Foundation's remarkable history illustrates nothing less than the fate of public dialogue, the course it takes when allowed, even briefly, to function in a society as complex as ours. The Pacifica story also reveals what happens when dialogue comes under fire from forces that view its humanizing power as in conflict with their political interests.

In pursuit of an analysis of that story, this study has identified two broadcasting philosophies within Pacifica's past: one that emphasized humanist intercommunication, and another that championed the fundamental right of the individual to speak and to hear certain ideas. These dialogue and dissenting missions emerged out of specific social circumstances, and they addressed specific political situations and needs. Neither of these traditions has suited every circumstance; there were clearly times in Pacifica's history when it served the organization to emphasize one tradition more than the other. That is the central observation of this book. A wise historian once said that by revealing the socially constructed nature of the past, we free ourselves to think critically and creatively about the present. Things once perceived as inevitable are revealed to have a historical beginning, middle, and end—to have been made rather than simply inherited. Observing this, we can summon the creativity to reinvent what needs to be reinvented, to discover new ways to untangle old problems.[40] Those of us today who speak of dialogue and civic culture would do well to study the Pacifica Foundation's turbulent evolution. For by examining the choices made by its historical actors, we can more self-consciously and effectively make our own.

POSTSCRIPT

A Crisis of Containment

Radio B92 condemns in the strictest terms the repression and exertion of force against the staff of Radio KPFA and Radio WBAI and their listeners . . .

We wish you the strength to persevere in your struggle for the freedom of speech, truth, and the preservation of your authenticity.

Long live freedom of speech! And down with media repression which knows no ideological or national boundaries, in either Berkeley or in Belgrade.

— STATEMENT FROM BANNED RADIO STATION B92 IN SERBIA, JULY 28, 1999 (HTTP://HELPKPA.RTMARK.COM)

ON THE EVENING of Wednesday, March 31, 1999, I came home from work to discover five messages waiting on my telephone answering system. Rarely does anyone leave me that many messages unless something has happened at KPFA in Berkeley.

I pressed the *play* button on my machine.

" [BEEP] Matthew, they've fired Nicole. Please call me."

" [BEEP] Matt . . . are you there? . . . I can't believe they could be this stupid . . . did you hear about Sawaya?"

"[BEEP] Hi Matt. They've canned Nicole! Call out the troops!"

Having volunteered at KPFA for years, I know many people there and reached a few friends who told me that Lynn Chadwick, the executive director of the Pacifica Foundation, had that day terminated the employment of Nicole Sawaya, KPFA's general manager. Those I spoke to said that Pacifica, which owns KPFA's license, had given Sawaya no notice. The foundation had not consulted KPFA's local advisory board regarding Sawaya's job performance, nor did they explain their action to the KPFA community. Had they done so, they would have learned that Sawaya enjoyed the confidence of both listeners and KPFA staff.[1]

The dismissal came fourteen days before KPFA's fiftieth birthday—April 15—for which the community had planned a variety of festive events. KPFA is like a church to the Bay Area secular left, and Pacifica had, in effect, kicked out the minister two weeks before Christmas. When several KPFA reporters approached Chadwick about the matter, she warned the station not to broadcast a story about the dismissal on the 6:00 p.m. news. They did so anyway, of course, and also mentioned her warning. Estimates of KPFA's audience range from 140,000 to 200,000 listeners. "Jaws dropped all over Northern California," as one reporter put it.[2]

We all knew that Sawaya's termination meant trouble, but none of us thought it would to lead to the biggest crisis in the history of community radio, a social drama that would receive continual newspaper, Internet, radio, and television coverage throughout the United States, Europe, and Asia. Late that very night someone fired a gun into Pacifica's office next to the KPFA building. Over the next few months, Pacifica dismissed three beloved programmers who protested or talked about Sawaya's ousting over KPFA's airwaves, hired armed guards, then expelled the staff from the station.[3] In response, over 10,000 people gathered in a Berkeley park to demonstrate against Pacifica, demanding the resignation of its leaders.[4]

What larger factors precipitated these remarkable events?

Pacifica Radio Reborn

By the late 1960s, the Pacifica radio network had drawn to it a new generation whose perspective had been shaped by their conflicts with the Cold War university, largely over the Vietnam War and campus free speech issues. Remembered as the New Left, some of these activists took notice of a small groundswell of listener-sponsored frequencies. They included not only Pacifica's, but also the pioneering Lorenzo Milam's KRAB Nebulae, a "new non-institutional community [of] non-commercial free-form radio stations around the country," as he put it.[5]

The New Left saw in the community radio phenomenon something like what Lewis Hill had seen: a chance to demonstrate that the world could be run in a grassroots, decentralized fashion. Their perspective differed from Hill's in that, inspired by the civil rights movement, they spoke in the language of grassroots democracy and populism. An example of their spirit could be found in Meyer Gottesman of San Francisco, who in 1971 sought a radio station that would address the needs of the socially dispossessed. "Poor Peoples Radio. That's what it's for," Gottesman told anyone who would listen. To promote and exemplify his venture, Gottesman installed himself on street corners with a tin cup. "Give To Poor Peoples Radio," read a sign around his neck. Eventually his efforts led to San Francisco's KPOO.[6]

Situated next to Berkeley's Free Speech movement and the 1968 Columbia University uprising, the community radio spirit quickly touched the Pacifica network. At KPFA, its adherents worked uneasily with a genteel older generation of programmers who did not identify with the Black Panther Party and People's Park. Eventually, the desire to incorporate ethnic minorities, gays, and women into KPFA's schedule led to a lengthy strike in 1974, which received enthusiastic support from many quarters, including nine inmates at San Quentin prison. "You are a very important part of the people's struggle," they wrote to the rebels. "Only the common people are able to give the news."[7]

The 1974 conflict ended with a more democratic structure for KPFA and the beginnings of a Third World Department. The strikers won formal recognition of volunteers as "unpaid staff." Now programmers made decisions via huge meetings, sometimes eighty to a gathering. The Pacifica national governing board committed itself to the central assumption of community radio: that people ought to be able to represent themselves over the airwaves without the intervention of mediators. Paz Cohen, news director for WPFW in Washington, D.C., embraced this perspective in a 1977 directive to her staff. "[W]e are here to tell people what PARTICIPANTS (the perpetrators and those affected) are saying, doing, planning and thinking" she wrote. "NOT what WE THINK they stand for or really mean. Their actions speak louder than your adjectives."[8] In the coming decades, when Pacifica dissidents called for the network to return to its "democratic roots," most were thinking of the 1970s rather than the 1950s.

As the community radio movement grew, so did efforts to link its many participants. In 1975, representatives of fifteen community stations met in Washington, D.C., and formed the National Federation of Community Broadcasters (NFCB). The organization, declared its bylaws, was open to any non-profit radio station with "a stated and demonstrated commitment to the participation of women and Third World people in all aspects of its organization and operation." By 1990, the NFCB's membership roster had grown to 190 regular and associate members.[9]

A Dream Deferred

Pacifica, reinvented as community radio, brought fresh new voices to its airwaves. The organization's self-conscious decision to position itself at the ground floor of American life encouraged network staff to discover struggling writers, musicians, and performers like Alice Walker, Audre Lorde, Whoopi Goldberg, and Bobby McFerrin, long before they became enshrined in American culture. But at the very moment that a new generation of women and people of color claimed their places within Pacifica, the larger regulatory climate took a dramatic shift. With the election of Ronald Reagan in 1980, the government began to withdraw its support for locally based, public access broadcasting.[10]

The first blow came even before the Reagan presidency: the Federal Communication Commission (FCC) banned radio stations that operated with less than 100 watts of power. This was followed by the gradual centralization of National Public Radio (NPR). Initiated by William Siemering in 1970 to bring many disparate voices into a creative broadcasting schedule, NPR put increasing pressure on public radio stations to broadcast more of its fare and devote less time to local programming. The impact was felt at San Francisco's KQED, which dropped its unique drive-time classical music program in favor of more NPR-produced satellite materials.[11]

Then, in 1987, the FCC declared that it would no longer enforce the Fairness Doctrine. The now-defunct policy had obligated radio to provide airtime to the various parties concerned with any particular social issue, not just one side. The Fairness Doctrine ensured that local voices would be heard on the radio, albeit often at 3:00 a.m. Now it was gone. The FCC also extended the length of time that stations had to renew their licenses from three to seven years, a move that encouraged stations to take the commission's local access rules less seriously.[12]

The Corporation for Public Broadcasting (CPB) also played a role in this regulatory shift. Created in 1967 to facilitate public television, it gradually extended its operations to support radio as well. By the mid-1990s the Pacifica radio network received about a million dollars a year from the CPB. In 1995, the CPB began requiring many community radio stations to sustain even larger numbers of listeners in order to qualify for funding, its leaders questioning the very validity of local access programming. "With every Web-literate citizen [able to] craft their own local program service . . ." one CPB official asked, "what will be unique about public radio's broadcast-based definition of localism?" This rhetorical question ignored the fact that the vast majority of working class Americans still had no foreseeable access to Internet radio. As satellite technology became more available, community station managers began taking advantage of nationally distributed programming to boost their listener rates and cut costs. Again, local programming paid the price for this adjustment.[13]

But the *coup de grace* came in the form of the Telecommunications Act of 1996, which let buyers purchase up to eight radio stations in any regional market. Corporations now snapped up frequencies, inflating their price and creating ever higher debt for new buyers. This, in turn, made local programming less affordable. The impact of these policies on the San Francisco Bay Area quickly became obvious. The region lost one of its two classical music stations; its modern rock frequency replaced its local morning personality with Howard Stern; acclaimed shows like "Street Soldiers," a call-in program for poor youth, were dropped from Bay Area pop music formats.[14]

Worst of all, any station on the commercial section of the FM spectrum, such as KPFA's signal, suddenly became very valuable.

Inside the Hothouse

As a volunteer in KPFA's news department in the 1980s, I was vaguely aware of this gradual creation of a scarcity of local access airtime. At the same moment that hundreds of urgent new voices were making their presence known at KPFA in the 1970s, the potential or available space for community radio elsewhere began to close up. The station overflowed with hungry programmers not only from every conceivable identity group, but also from five successive generations of KPFA supporters. These people had few other places to go but KPFA; deluged with suitors, the institution struggled to maintain a focused mission rather than become an exercise in cultural power sharing.

What I did see at the time were the best community radio minds of my generation lose faith in any kind of inclusive governance for Pacifica and its radio stations. How would a decentralized system of decision making deal with ineffective programs and their hosts? Who would be authorized to ensure quality in a place where the rhetoric of free speech, identity politics, and worker's rights armored individual programmers with multiple layers of institutional autonomy? These vexing problems were potentially resolvable in an environment with an abundance of airtime, either at KPFA or elsewhere. Had there been many KPFAs on the Bay Area dial, a programmer ousted from one station might find a place elsewhere. But with so little local access airtime available in the Bay Area, quality control decisions became perilous—guaranteed to provoke trouble.

Gradually, station-paid staff began to distance themselves from KPFA's volunteers. As a reporter at KPFA's news department, I saw this in the late 1980s with the inauguration of staff "retreats" that did not include the unpaid staff. Indeed, when volunteers elected two representatives to attend one of these events, they were denied admission. Station department heads moved away from democratic decision making, an erosion that few of us at the time saw as rooted in external as well as internal factors.

Had network leadership offered nothing more than impatience for 1970s style governance, they would not have gotten very far. But they also brought a new enthusiasm for development and national programming. The success of some of their efforts highlights the rarely noted fact that Pacifica's rebellious constituents, when confronted by competence, are happy to go along with the program. Under the guidance of Pacifica's then Executive Director Pat Scott and Development Director Dick Bunce, the station moved from its shabby rented studios on Shattuck Avenue to a beautiful new adobe building near Berkeley City Hall in 1991. In 1996, Pacifica inaugurated a daily national public affairs show that, within a year, easily qualified as the most successful venture in the annals of alternative broadcasting. Hosted by the talented and hard-working Amy Goodman and Juan Gonzalez, *Democracy Now* won over the Pacifica network and its sixty-five affiliate stations with an urgent and clear coverage of world and national events.[15]

KPFA's staff also proved their mettle. The News Department's reporting on the Bay Area's 1989 Loma Prieta earthquake won them national awards, as had Pacifica correspondent Larry Bensky's coverage of the Iran-Contra hearings three years earlier. Listeners flocked to KPFA during the Bush administration's Persian Gulf War for an alternative to National Public Radio's uncritical coverage of the bombing of Iraq.[16]

But this flair for big projects came with an almost slap-happy enthusiasm for purging the network of its volunteers. In Houston, KPFT management wiped the station's slate clean of an entire generation of multi-language hosts and replaced them with a new schedule light on public affairs and heavy on popular music. "The Atheist program is gone," concluded the accounting of one despondent ex-volunteer. "The Viet Namese program is gone. The Chinese program is gone. The Pakistani program—gone."[17] Then, in August of 1995, KPFA management gave notice to eleven programs representing the input of about two dozen people. The volunteers had only a week to say goodbye to their listeners. In truth, I thought that some of these shows (for which I had occasionally done studio engineering) deserved their termination. Others did not. Some months earlier, William Mandel had a disagreement with station management; he raised the matter on KPFA's airwaves and lost his airtime for doing so. About fifty listeners picketed KPFA on Mandel's behalf, including poet Lawrence Ferlinghetti. "If things were working, we would have left them alone," KPFA's program director explained to the *San Francisco Examiner.* "If you have a mission and no one is listening, then you are not fulfilling your mission." People were listening, but the Pacifica network and the CPB now gradually raised the audience hurdle.[18]

Had these disparate programmers been exiled a decade earlier, they might have wandered off in various directions, nursing their separate wounds. But something new had just surfaced on the technological horizon. The Internet gave Pacifica's dissidents the power to unite in ways inconceivable to Wallace Hamilton or Roy Kepler. Elaborate Web sites and e-mail trees enabled angry programmers and listeners to convey the latest news—or rumor—across the country in minutes. A CPB auditor charged that Pacifica officials had begun limiting public information about and access to their official gatherings. But word of the whereabouts of governing board activities became common knowledge with breathtaking speed, and picketers greeted board members at their meetings. Equally important, ongoing "free Pacifica" discussion lists created a sense of unity among network fugitives, even if they had little in common besides their walking papers.[19]

By 1997, the network drew over 700,000 listeners a week to its stations and affiliates, but most of Pacifica's leaders were on their way out. The Pacifica national office in Berkeley began searching for new recruits. The organization undertook the difficult transition from an old guard that, while tired and disenchanted with community radio, understood its limits and their own to a new regime that would bring a fresh optimism and energy to their work.[20]

One could almost say they saw the possibilities as limitless.

Being Smart for People

To give Pacifica's leadership a sense of direction, the organization in 1997 drafted a Strategic Plan for its next four years of operation. The twenty-five-page document, largely produced during another series of staff retreats, often read like a fundraising brochure, which was probably intentional. "Three inter-related strategies are primary:" read a sidebar on page 17, "improving air sound quality; developing management, organizational structures, and support systems; and increasing Pacifica's financial resources."

The Strategic Plan's crucial prose, however, could be found not in its laundry list of institutional goals, but in an introductory essay subtitled "The Crisis of Democratic Communications." Noting the impact of mergers and conglomerates on the "public sphere" in general and in the public radio environment specifically, the prologue recognized the impact of the fall of the Fairness Doctrine. "By restricting the flow of information essential to political discourse and citizen participation, media trusts imperil democracy." But instead of exhorting the Pacifica network to take the lead in harnessing forces against this trend, it baldly suggested that the network take advantage of the situation. "The expansion of media trusts simultaneously illuminates the distinctiveness of Pacifica's programming and mission," read another sidebar. "By diminishing the supply of informational programming—Pacifica's and public radio's stock-in-trade—the commercial trusts have paradoxically increased audience demand for Pacifica and other public radio services." The strategy was clear—Pacifica would accept this containment, become more efficient, and build listener-sponsored socialism in one small radio network.[21]

Two new recruits would lead Pacifica in this reorganization. The position of chair of the governing board went, for the first time in Pacifica history, to an African-American woman and government official. Mary Frances Berry was born in 1938 in Nashville, Tennessee, to a family so poor she spent some of her childhood in an orphanage. The racism she experienced growing up only steeled her ambition. Her mother's advice became her motto: "Be overeducated," Berry later summarized it. "If somebody else has a master's degree, you get a Ph.D. If somebody has that, then you get a law degree too." She won renown as a talented and prolific historian, then took the job of university provost before occupying various slots in the Carter administration and the U.S. Commission on Civil Rights. In 1984, the Reagan administration fired her. Berry sued and was reinstated. "[T]he happiest day in my life was when Reagan fired me . . . "she later said. "I was fired because I did what I was supposed to do." She became head of the commission under the Clinton administration.[22]

The executive director's post went to Lynn Chadwick, long associated with the National Federation of Community Broadcasters (NFCB) as its executive director. Like Berry, Chadwick was a staunch supporter of diversity and affirmative action within the organizations she ran, dating back to her involvement with the Feminist Radio Network. She worked closely with the Corporation for Public Broadcasting and streamlined the NFCB, giving her staff tasks that had once been performed by the organization's board of directors, such as calling people to remind them about annual meetings. The limits of this approach became apparent to some when relatively few NFCB member station personnel attended Chadwick's last annual membership gathering in 1998. NFCB officials "expressed dismay at

[the] light turnout," one reporter noted, "particularly because [the] sensitive dues reform process was to be discussed." Dues collection had declined because of a significant drop in NFCB member stations over the last two years. To rekindle a "sense of connection" with federation stations, board members pledged to start calling them more often again themselves.[23]

Berry's own accounting of one of the more celebrated events in her life perfectly illustrated her perspective on political work. On Thanksgiving eve in 1984, Berry and two associates paid a visit to the South African embassy in Washington, D.C., with a list of demands, including freedom for Nelson Mandela. They refused to leave until the ambassador contacted Pretoria with their concerns. The action had been planned for a slow news day. Scores of reporters watched as police led Berry and company into a paddy wagon. "Here was not just another campus radical," reported *Ms.* magazine. "[H]ere was Dr. Mary Frances Berry, a member of the Commission on Civil Rights, a professor of history and law, a member of the bar, a scholar with published books to her credit, with more citations and honorary degrees than her wall could hold." Berry offered the lesson of the day: "If you're going to help people in their struggle, you should be smart for them. . . . If your demonstration doesn't get media coverage, you might as well not have it."[24]

Here were two people who, from a national vantage point, worked to further progressive politics in the Reagan era—that is, in the absence of a national progressive mass movement. As advocates for the people in the absence of the people, Berry and Chadwick functioned in a political culture that asked post-1960s questions: What was the point of having a demonstration without reporters? What was the use of keeping close to your constituents when you could get results by keeping close to the government? But the arts that they mastered in this context—the surprise media event, the bureaucratic *faits accomplis*, the carefully orchestrated staff/board meeting—would prove destabilizing in a part of the United States where an authentic grassroots left culture still existed. They would be experienced as provocative by a community of people who cherished loyalty, consensus building, and candid public discussion above all else.

Bridge Burning

Not long after Chadwick assumed the position of executive director, an article by the Pacifica leadership's harshest and most effective critic, syndicated columnist Alexander Cockburn, alerted network constituents to a proposal that would centralize Pacifica governance. The national board, Cockburn disclosed in late January of 1999, at its next meeting would decide whether to continue to accept members elected from each of the network's five Local Advisory Boards (LAB) among its body, which tended to veer from about twelve to sixteen members. Pacifica now claimed that this practice violated the Corporation for Public Broadcasting's conditions for funding. A "notice of by-law change" issued by Pacifica quoted a fragment of the CPB's guidelines stipulating that community advisory boards shall "in no case have any authority to exercise any control over the daily management or operation of the station."[25]

Reviewing the entire paragraph of CPB legal language regarding local boards cited by Pacifica, I could not figure out how the current board structure could be construed as a violation:

> The role of the board shall be solely advisory in nature, *except to the extent other responsibilities are delegated to the board by the governing body of the station*. In no case shall the board have any authority to exercise any control over the daily management or operation of the station. [italics added][26]

The language does not seem to deny the board's authority to allow individual LAB members to sit on the national board. In fact, the national board's minutes indicate that Pacifica had been electing local board members to the national since the late 1970s, possibly earlier, with no CPB objection noted. But now a letter from a CPB lawyer, solicited by Pacifica, insisted that this practice ignored "CPB's guideline that there be 'clear demarcation' between the two types of boards." Pacifica's solution, simply removing LAB members from the national board, left a dangerous political void. In the absence of any legal, clearly understood participation by the LABs at Pacifica, "Whose institution will it be?" Cockburn wondered. "Is this Governing Board likely to choose a structure of governance giving any other group within Pacifica, including its subscribers, any say in who gets to make the meaningful decisions at Pacifica?"[27]

By now the Pacifica network was crawling with dissidents—scores of people who had been purged from a station, each with a large coterie of sympathizers itching for a fight. Alerted to Pacifica's plans, they called their troops to the network's February 28, 1999, national board meeting. The meeting had been scheduled at a local Berkeley hotel—until its owner got wind of the impending fracas—and then was relocated to a UC Berkeley conference hall. Protestors gathered along a nearby off-campus road, "safe from the billy-clubs of the UC Police," wrote one amused journalist, "spreading news of the outrage to incoming shoppers from Orinda."[28]

I was now one of those protestors. The first edition of this book had just hit the stores. At my first bookstore reading, at Black Oak Books in Berkeley, people had asked me what I thought. In the recent past I had quietly endured Pacifica's various purges, all too aware of how fragmented the network had become. Cockburn acknowledged a similar dilemma. "I've held off for many months, years actually, from discussing Pacifica's affairs on the grounds that some house-cleaning was necessary at the various stations," the columnist confided in 1997. But it was clear that Pacifica was falling into the same trap that Lewis Hill had fallen into in 1953, discrediting itself by over-centralizing its authority—this time on a much larger scale. The formal presence of LAB members on the national board gave it representational legitimacy. Without them, how would Pacifica's governors justify their right to lead an already shaky radio network with a flagship show called *Democracy Now*, not to mention a Strategic Plan that called Pacifica "democratic communications"? Pacifica was surrounded by tens of thousands of people who fervently believed what they daily heard on its stations: that the world should be run more democratically, not less. I argued against the proposal on Nicole Sawaya's monthly on-air manager's report and spoke against it at the Berkeley board meeting.[29]

But none of the speeches given during the public comment section of the meeting seemed to matter to the board. At the last minute, an advisory letter from a CPB executive arrived with a troubling timeliness. The document threatened the loss of a huge chunk of CPB funding if Pacifica didn't cut LAB members loose from the national board. The CPB was notorious for issuing such warnings and then backing off after negotiations. But isolated from their constituents and faced with this news, the board's intimidated LAB members voted to enact the reform, then resigned from their respective local boards in order to remain on the national. "Tempers Rise as Pacifica Lets Board Select Itself," ran the headline in *Current*, public broadcasting's magazine. The writing on the wall was apparent to anyone who cared to look. "We want to centralize, as much as possible, administrative services," Mary Frances Berry declared before leaving the conference, "all of the managerial and administrative aspects of this place that can be centralized—in order to save money and in order to find ways to do things more effectively so that there will be more money to go into programming." I listened and shuddered, aware that to many, centralization would seem like a wise course for this unwieldy network. Dangerously out of sync with its own democratic rhetoric, Pacifica now had unlimited power to do only one thing: throw the organization into chaos.[30]

It was this context that the crisis at KPFA began with the dismissal of

Nicole Sawaya. Here was the first public manifestation of the new, streamlined Pacifica management style. To many of the station's supporters, this precipitous action, taken two weeks before the station's fiftieth birthday, seemed like a wretched decision—"moronic" as even Pacifica's loyal critic, Marc Cooper of KPFK, put it in *The Nation* magazine. A woman of Lebanese-American background, Sawaya had done well for KPFA; she had management experience with both National Public Radio and community station KZYX in Mendicino County ("Judy Bari country," as a host who interviewed me at that station proudly called it, invoking the memory of the radical environmentalist). A confident, hands-on manager, Sawaya had been cautiously reintegrating some of the people who had been ousted from KPFA in 1995.[31]

Sawaya's termination brought upon Pacifica the wrath of someone aptly described by *The New York Times* as KPFA's "signature voice." Larry Bensky, Pacifica's national correspondent, had spent the last four months wrangling with the organization over his future with the network. He had been dismissed and rehired once for his trouble. The fact that Bensky sometimes abruptly hung up on talk show callers irritated some of his fans, but his brilliance as a political analyst and radio personality easily overshadowed this foible. A former KPFA station manager, Bensky had taken Pacifica through endless international stories, from the Iran-Contra crisis to Nicaragua's crucial 1989 election. Now he became alarmed at the organization's direction, appearing at the February national board meeting with pie charts illustrating Pacifica's increasing power. As usual, he didn't mince words: "What is the justification for the proliferation of Pacifica's expensive, secretive, administrative bureaucracy? Aside from empire-building, there is none."[32]

The day after Sawaya's dismissal, Bensky appeared at an impromptu demonstration. "If, in the coming days, you should miss the voices you're used to hearing," he declared, "know that it's not voluntary." Several days later, he followed an interview about Yugoslavia with a live discussion about the situation at KPFA and Pacifica. By April 15 he had been fired again, this time for violating the "gag rule," Pacifica's dictum against discussing network internal matters over the airwaves.[33]

With both Sawaya and Bensky tanked, at least 750 of us demonstrated in front of the station on the anniversary, April 15, making our flatbed truck speeches. Why had the station's local board not been consulted before deciding about Sawaya, we asked, in accordance with Pacifica's own rules?[34] Why did our unanimity count for so little? Two starkly conflicting visions of politics would now play out: one that saw only the institutional ends and the other that cherished the democratic means. The struggle would be all the more bitter because it raged over social space that had been contained, made abnormally scarce by twenty years of government policy hostile to locally based public broadcasting.

War at KPFA

The evening after the fiftieth anniversary demonstration, I accepted Amy Goodman's invitation to appear the next morning on *Democracy Now* with Lynn Chadwick and public broadcasting scholar Ralph Engelman to discuss Pacifica's history and the current controversy. During the conversation, the obvious question came up. What do you think about the gag rule? Goodman asked us. Chadwick, ignoring the fact that we were all violating it at that moment, explained that Pacifica's airwaves were not open to the "personal issues" of its staff:

> This gag rule—so-called gag rule—has been in place for some thirty years, and I'm sure it came about after long discussions. . . . But it's important that at Pacifica we do not allow free speech. We don't allow anti-Semitic speech. We don't allow sexist speech. We don't allow racist speech. That's important to us. And those values we want to convey to our listeners. So, there's reasons behind that, and I think they are core to the value of what we're talking about, in terms of what Pacifica's goal is in presenting the progressive agenda to the country.[35]

Putting aside the questionable equating of personal matters or racist speech with discussion about the network's policies, Chadwick had clearly commenced what would become Pacifica's approach to this crisis: the rigid enforcement of rules and the disregard of traditions. Yes, I agreed, it was bad radio to spend lots of time on a station talking about internal politics. Through most of the organization's history, the practice had been discouraged. But there clearly had been turning points in Pacifica's development when the airwaves *had* been opened to the staff and listeners, such as the crises of 1954, 1963, and the community radio upheavals of the 1970s. Furthermore, Pacifica had over the last two months pushed KPFA so far to the edge and done such a bad job of explaining its purposes that its gag rule, and most other rules, had become irrelevant. Paul Rauber, influential reporter for the East Bay *Express*, had, until the firing of Sawaya, been skeptical of Pacifica's critics. Now he gasped at how little serious effort the foundation made to win over its constituents: "Their silence is far more disturbing because it suggests—especially to vocal, eloquent partisans—that there is no vision upstairs."[36]

Clearly, people were going to talk about this on the radio no matter whom objected; they would not be silenced by governors who had betrayed their trust. After all, was not KPFA the mother of free-speech, First Amendment broadcasting? By the time of Bensky's hiring, hardly anyone at the station honored the gag rule and the staff issued regular on-air statements about the crisis. Individual programmers offered less temperate comments about Pacifica. "I don't see that there's much of a point in protecting these sons of bitches anymore," declared David Gans, the host of *The Grateful Dead Hour.* Soon an organization called "Friends of Free Speech Radio" was formed to organize demonstrations in behalf of KPFA.[37]

Up to this point, Mary Frances Berry had said nothing. Thousands of people, myself included, wrote letters or e-mail urging her to come to KPFA, imagining that if only we could establish personal contact, she would see the light. "As soon as . . . Mary Frances Berry heard that the entire KPFA staff was willing to commit collective on-air civil disobedience to support its deposed manager," scolded Marc Cooper in *The Nation*, "she should have been on the first plane to Berkeley."[38]

On May 5, Pacifica's chairwoman offered an on-air report to the listeners. For those of us hoping for an epiphany, it was a painful audio experience. Chadwick attempted to supervise the event from KPFA's studio but did not remember to first identify herself to the listeners. All we heard from the executive director was "Wait 'til fadeout. OK, you're on." Then Berry, who presumably phoned in from Washington, D.C., launched into the party line, pointing to the larger purpose behind Pacifica's recent course: "Taken as a whole, our programmers, Local Advisory Board members, and listeners do not reflect the rich cultural and age diversity of our country, which our mission clearly requires us to do," Berry explained. "We must include more people of color as programmers and on Local Advisory Boards, and we must expand our listener base while keeping the listeners we have now, if we can, by attracting a younger and more diverse audience."[39]

Keep the current listeners, "if we can"? Whether Berry realized it or not, speaking of the listeners—her audience—in the third person implied that they were superfluous to the future of the station. Later, a group of Lynn Chadwick supporters who called themselves "the Diversity Coalition" issued a similar statement. The social composition of KPFA, they insisted, was the real issue:

> . . . the air sound usually reflects the Berkeley character and philosophy. As we move into the next decade we must ask ourselves the following questions: does

> Berkeley represent the local and regional description of diversity in *appearance* and philosophy? Does Berkeley represent the changing *face* of our national diversity? [italics added][40]

This racially coded rhetoric ignored the fact that 45 percent of Berkeley's residents were not white. As the situation deteriorated, statements that KPFA had too many "white males over 50" among its listeners, subscribers, and staff were continually repeated, ignoring the management decisions that contributed to the problem. In the 1980s, KPFA enjoyed a far more diverse staff than in previous decades and had won national recognition for its pioneering minority apprenticeship training program. Like many public radio outlets, however, it lacked the resources needed to reach out to a more diverse, working class audience. KPFA had been struggling with this issue since the days when Lewis Hill tried to base it in Richmond rather than in Berkeley. But the network's actions in the 1990s had significantly undercut Pacifica's credibility on the diversity question. The head of KPFA's Third World Department had recently been laid off. The KPFA and KPFT volunteer shakedowns of the mid-1990s, had, as even Pacifica insiders privately admitted to me, made these stations *less* diverse. Many of the purged had been people of color with late night or evening shows. Pacifica had encouraged these house-cleanings because of the perception that the network's air sound had become fragmented, broken down into too many disconnected programs. Now those people of color who had just been dropped from the network could hardly take seriously Pacifica's renewed calls for more people of color. Nor could those who had survived. "KPFA's African American programmers will not be complicit in any Pacifica-driven purge of KPFA staffers under the guise of 'diversity'," declared a statement by thirteen of the station's black programmers, from African studies scholar Walter Turner to hip-hop deejay David "Davy D" Cook. Here was stark evidence of the futility of trying to micro-manage so many people in so little space.[41]

The weeks after Berry's talk went by like a whirring machine spewing out trouble. On May 12, Pacifica began hiring security guards. Although no one had been hurt, the March 31 late night shooting into Pacifica's office next to KPFA had appalled just about everyone involved with the crisis. I would have sympathized with guards placed around Pacifica's doors. But instead, these uniformed men and women were stationed, weeks later, in front of the KPFA building. Then the foundation fired Robbie Osman, a seasoned organizer of benefits for political causes who had been hosting a music program at KPFA for many years. So influential was his show that the legendary folksinger Kate Wolf wrote a song for it, "Across the Great Divide," which became the program's title. To Chadwick's memo reminding the staff of the gag rule, Osman responded on-air : "You can come and get me now. I am conscience bound . . . By my sense of conscience, by my sense of morality, I understand the gag rule. I think it's illegitimate." Within days Osman's program was cancelled. The next Sunday KPFA broadcast silence during his scheduled time.[42]

By now rallies, sit-ins, and picket lines had become a daily event in front of Pacifica. I looked in vain for signs that the national board understood that they were creating martyrs, that the price of victory was unacceptably high. In the last week of June, Pacifica justified hiring a security agency whose armed operatives specialized in keeping order during corporate downsizings by claiming that thirty protestors had "stormed" into Chadwick's office at KPFA (she was now also functioning as station manager). Actually, it was about twelve people, according to the Catholic priest who accompanied the delegation, some of them quite elderly, including Berkeley's venerable vice-mayor, Maudelle Shirek. Meanwhile, the KPFA News Department, furious at Chadwick's efforts to control its editorial content, now watched Pacifica like a hawk. On June 24 they reported that Berry had called the U.S. Justice Department, which, in turn, had contacted the Berkeley police about how they were handling the crisis. Local newspapers picked up the story. "Wow," an astonished Berkeley Police Chief Dash Butler exclaimed to the *San Francisco Chronicle*, "What is this . . . why has this gotten to be such a big deal?"[43]

But what disturbed me most was the extent to which Pacifica appeared to view KPFA as did the mainstream — as alien. Pacifica's public relations officer, Elan Fabbri, constantly revealed this perception in her statements. The troubles, she told the *San Francisco Chronicle*, were the fault of the "life-time activists" who now refused to obey Pacifica's rules. When reporters sought justification for a tightly controlled Pacifica press conference to which some local alternative journalists were not invited, Fabbri responded: "It wasn't to exclude anyone," the *Berkeley Daily Planet* quoted her as saying. "It was to try to keep the protestors away." Did Pacifica, I asked myself, still see its constituents as human?[44]

Sell the Unit

Pacifica national board member Michael Palmer, who worked as a real estate broker in Houston, had for months advocated the sale of one of Pacifica's stations in order to capitalize the network. On July 13, Palmer assured himself a place in the history of broadcasting, inadvertently routing an e-mail message intended for Mary Frances Berry to San Francisco's Media Alliance, a progressive advocacy group now leading the fight against Pacifica. "I was under the impression there was support in the proper quarters, and a definite majority, for shutting down that unit and re-programming immediately," Palmer's message stated, referring to KPFA. "Has that changed?"

Palmer's memo, which Pacifica admitted to the *San Francisco Chronicle* was authentic, pitched the sale in enthusiastic terms: "This is the best radio market in history . . ." he declared. "The primary signal would lend itself to a quiet marketing scenario of discreet presentation to logical and qualified buyers." It could fetch about 65 to 75 million dollars. WBAI in New York, with its "similarly dysfunctional staff," might also be sold. "So, now I've exhaled more than I should, but you know where I'm at. Let's do something.—MDP."[45]

But Media Alliance did something first, holding a press conference that same day to publicize Palmer's memo. Thousands of people, including me, found the entire text in their e-mail in-boxes and the document instantly became famous. *The Texas Observer* printed it in full on its back page. Stunned and offended by what I had just read on my computer, I simply got up from my job in Berkeley and walked over to the nearby Hall of Justice. About forty activists had gathered there to alert reporters to the message and an impending lawsuit against Pacifica's governing board changes. We stood around watching each other talk to TV cameras about the future of the "unit," as Palmer called KPFA. Could it get any worse than this? I wondered.

As the evening approached, I took a bus over to Robbie Osman's house in Oakland, where a steering committee, representing KPFA's key constituencies, had begun meeting to work out the basis for negotiations with Pacifica. There I found KPFA morning show host Philip Maldari and several others standing out front, talking on cell phones. "They've shut it down, Matthew," Philip told me. "Pacifica has taken over the station." He looked angry but not surprised. We raced over to KPFA. By 6:00 p.m. police had surrounded the building. About 2,000 demonstrators pressed against hastily set up barricades. Staff inside refused to leave, frantically searching their desks for confidential source address lists, tossing possessions out windows to friends. The scene was all the more memorable because it was a beautiful Berkeley evening. I ran to a pay phone to call reporters and describe the riot squads rushing to the scene.

Querying people in the crowd, I gradually pieced together a picture of what had happened. At around 5:30 p.m., KPFA *Flashpoints* talk show host Dennis Bernstein began airing a discussion about the Pacifica crisis, including a taped commentary in support of KPFA by famed Philadelphia death-row inmate Mumia Abu-Jamal. This was followed by a rebroadcast of the press conference I had just witnessed. At 6:00 p.m., KPFA's Mark Mericle attempted to begin the evening news. He got past headlines and a taped health care story, and saw KPFA's latest acting manager, Garland Ganter, pursuing Bernstein with the help of several guards. Listeners heard the tape awkwardly break off, then ten seconds of silence followed by live, unscheduled action. "You're going to hurt me!" Bernstein was shouting. "I belong here!" Mericle, his voice trembling, spoke to the listeners. "We interrupt this story on HMO because Dennis Bernstein of *Flashpoints* has been put on administrative leave for his playing of a press conference on KPFA . . . they are trying to drag him out of the studio . . . ." In the background listeners could hear Bernstein angrily resisting. "Garland Ganter," Mericle continued, "who is the general manager of the Pacifica station in Houston, was brought in by Pacifica Executive Director—"[46]

Then silence. Pacifica had cut off the broadcast. After a few moments, listeners heard a prerecorded lecture on Marx's *Communist Manifesto*, followed by community radio tapes that had been gradually shipped in from the network's archives in Los Angeles. KPFA's entire staff was put on paid administrative leave; over fifty were arrested for trespassing. Within days the building was boarded up. The foundation issued a statement calling their actions a response to an "unauthorized takeover of the air by some members of KPFA's staff on Tuesday night, July 13th." About a week later, Pacifica rigged KPFA's transmitter to route programming from KPFT through KPFA's 94.1 FM frequency.[47]

"Administrative services" couldn't get any more centralized than this. At various times, Mary Frances Berry had drawn lessons from the civil rights era to justify her top-down governing style. One of her comments, referring to the 1955 Montgomery bus boycott, has become a popular aphorism: "If Rosa Parks had taken a poll before she sat down in the bus in Montgomery, she'd still be standing." But if Pacifica's chairwoman had more carefully considered her civil rights history, she might have thought twice about shutting KPFA down. In 1956, the Montgomery bus authority stupidly responded to the protest by canceling services in black neighborhoods. Neutrality became impossible—in Montgomery then or Berkeley now. [48]

From my vantage point in front of KPFA that evening I could see through the building's open windows. There sat KPFA staffers at their desks, spending their last moments telephoning their best contacts with the news. By placing everyone on administrative leave, Pacifica gave its opponents abundant free time to call in old debts from hundreds of organizers, world famous artists, musicians, politicians, and intellectuals. These people knew that KPFA represented their best source of exposure, indeed, sometimes the only source they had. They would now drop everything to rush to the station's defense.

The next day Alice Walker and peace activist Daniel Ellsberg spoke at a rally of 1,500 people in front of the station. "KPFA is my home," Walker told the crowd. "Pacifica has taken away my home." Days later Joan Baez performed to a capacity "Save KPFA" benefit at the Berkeley Community Theater, reviewed the next day by *San Francisco Examiner* columnist Phil Elwood—his own show on KPFA having been cancelled in 1995. On Saturday, July 31, over ten thousand protestors gathered at Berkeley's Martin Luther King Jr. Park. They called for the reopening of KPFA and the resignation of the Pacifica national board.[49]

Unionists dominated their ranks. They knew a plant closure when they saw one. It was the largest demonstration on behalf of a listener-supported radio station in the history of United States broadcasting.

IT IS DECEMBER 1999 and I am uncomfortably aware that by the time this update is published, the situation at Pacifica will have changed again. There are now at least half a dozen militant listener organizations within Pacifica attempting to reform a national board whose leaders appear equally determined to wield authority.

Three weeks after closing the station, faced with overwhelmingly negative public opinion, an impending state legislative hearing into the crisis, and demonstrations, hip-hop rallies, sit-ins, and teach-ins with no end in sight, Pacifica relented and gave KPFA back to its rightful occupants. On August 5, KPFA's exhausted staff returned to their building and went back on the air. The foundation still refused to rehire Larry Bensky or Nicole Sawaya, but Bensky resumed his program as a volunteer. Hundreds of people sent postcards and gifts. The staff collected them on a small table in the main hallway, which became a shrine. One card read as follows: "Imani = Faith. To believe with all our hearts in our people, our parents, our teachers, our leaders."[50]

For thousands of people in the San Francisco Bay Area and across the United States, the obvious question remained: Why did the network's leaders take such drastic steps against its first radio station? By the July 13 shutdown, many concluded that Pacifica had planned its actions well in advance, perhaps in preparation for putting KPFA up for sale. "The Pacifica Foundation is likely deciding on one of two options for KPFA, selling the frequency for tens of millions on the open market or drastically reformatting the station," speculated the *San Francisco Bay Guardian*. "Was the KPFA Lock-Out a Spontaneous Reaction or a Planned Management Coup?" wondered the East Bay's *Express*. The *Express* reported various signs that supported the latter theory: Pacifica's hiring of a management consultant who specialized in employee downsizing; the armed security guard agency, whose web site boasted that "during hostile terminations" its "protection specialists provide a virtual safety net" for a client; KPFA staff who told *Express* reporters that Pacifica's employees began shipping boxes of music and interview tapes to the station ten days before the lockdown. In addition, after the staff returned, KPFA engineers found a packing list left behind at the transmitter site in the Berkeley hills for an Integrated Services Digital Network (ISDN) device that can be used in transmitter reroutes. The item had been ordered on June 29, just days after the last national board meeting, and more than two weeks before the shutdown of KPFA. It listed "Garland G" as the shipping recipient for the package waiting at a Federal Express station in Oakland.[51]

Michael Palmer's recommendation of a sale must also be factored into the equation, along with his stated impression that a majority on the board favored "shutting down that unit [KPFA] and re-programming immediately." A dissident member of the national board corroborated the existence of this sentiment. On July 28, national board member Pete Bramson held a press conference in Berkeley, charging that Pacifica was considering a proposal to sell KPFA as he spoke, this time outlined by its vice-chairperson, David Acosta of Texas. "[Acosta] proposed taking out a five million dollar loan against the value of the KPFA license," Bramson told reporters. "That could happen quickly. He proposed selling the KPFA frequency, which has an estimated value of 65 to 75 million dollars. That would take longer to accomplish. With a small portion of the proceeds of the sale of KPFA, Acosta proposed that Pacifica set up another Northern California station—perhaps in Palo Alto, which Mary Frances Berry said might be a friendlier city than Berkeley." To many, it certainly appeared that Pacifica had been spending cash like it knew where it was coming from. Shortly after KPFA reopened, faced with subpoenas from the state legislature, Chadwick disclosed that the foundation had dropped an amazing amount of money: $390,000 on security guards, $58,317 for a public relations firm, $9,000 more on transmitter equipment, and $10,000 to board up KPFA's windows. "What did they use," asked a dumbfounded Brenda Payton, columnist for the *Oakland Tribune*, "bronze nails?"[52]

But as a historian, I know that such evidence, precisely because it seems so compelling in the moment, can often obscure other scenarios. Sometimes years, even decades, must pass until things calm down and scholars with critical distance can learn what the key players really intended during an institutional crisis like this. It is also possible that Pacifica's actions were taken without a larger agenda—out of anger, panic, pride, or the simple conviction that hierarchies should be honored and orders must be obeyed. "We have to stop the rudeness, the bullying, the you-can't-tell-me-what-to-do attitude," Chadwick declared at the February national board meeting. As of this writing, the network's leaders publicly insist that they do not want to sell KPFA and never did. Michael Palmer's proposal attracted little support on the board, they claim. "I'm just sorry that a wrong keystroke on my part has created such an uproar," a July 19 Pacifica press release quoted him as saying. "I still think we should look at selling one of our frequencies, but it's evident that the board and national organization don't agree with me." The release concluded with a statement from Berry herself. "KPFA and all of Pacifica's other frequencies are not for sale, and the board is not considering selling any of them," she declared. In late October, the national board met in Houston and passed a resolution stating that Pacifica would not put any of its licenses or stations up for sale. "The purpose of the resolution is to end rumors that the board was intending to sell one of the stations," declared a subsequent Pacifica press release.[53]

Time will tell if they were just rumors. But even if we take Pacifica at its word, the events described here serve as a cautionary tale for anyone interested in "furthering the public sphere," to borrow the Strategic Plan's phrase. What happened in Berkeley during the summer of 1999 is the story of leaders who, after two frustrating decades, lost faith in their cause. Caught between an exploding cultural movement and government policies that blocked it at every turn, Pacifica's embittered administrators slowly turned away from their own constituents. In the end, they literally came to see them as the enemy. "The left gets pissed off about anything that works," former Pacifica executive director Pat Scott told the *LA Weekly* during the crisis. "It's a whole culture of losers." Stymied and discouraged, the network's national board and top staff gradually retreated into their own internal culture—built on the assumption that Pacifica's credo of democratic communication could only be furthered by secrecy and fiat.[54]

Now it is up to the rest of us. The task is more formidable than seeking a legitimate structure for our nation's first listener-supported radio network. For even if that is accomplished, and it should be, Pacifica will remain a tiny space on a spectrum dominated by corporations. As a revolution in Internet broadcasting continues, it is up to us to ensure that the aspirations of people to represent themselves over the airwaves are not pushed to the margins, as they have been for decades. We must act now so that the next generation of radio visionaries does not waste years fighting over resources deliberately made scarce. Whether we are cultural avant gardeists, or populists, or advocates of diversity, we must revive the task begun by the radio critics of the 1930s, continued by Lewis Hill, and transformed by the community radio movement. We must create the broad noncommercial domain that we so clearly need—or we would not have worked and fought so hard for so long.

NOTES

Preface to the First Edition

1. Robert D. Putnam, "Bowling Alone: America's Declining Social Capital," *Journal of Democracy* 6 (January 1995): 65–78, remains the flagship text that addresses this concern.

2. Jim Sleeper, *In Defense of Civic Culture* (Washington, D.C.: Progressive Foundation, 1993).

3. Glenn C. Loury, *One by One from the Inside Out* (New York: Free Press, 1995), 143; Nathan Glazer, *We Are All Multiculturalists Now* (Cambridge: Harvard University Press, 1997), 122.

4. *Encouraging Public Dialogue* (Washington, D.C.: National Academy of Public Administration Foundation, 1994); http://www.clearlake.ibm.com/Alliance/clusters/rd/citfewc0.html.

5. Allen J. Matusow, *The Unraveling of America: A History of Liberalism in the 1960s* (New York: Harper & Row, 1984).

6. Arthur Schlesinger, Jr., *The Disuniting of America: Reflections on a Multicultural Society* (New York: Norton, 1991), 119, 138; Glazer, *We Are All Multiculturalists*, 159.

7. Todd Gitlin, *The Twilight of Common Dreams: Why America Is Wracked by Culture Wars* (New York: Holt, 1995), 1.

8. Lewis Hill, "The Private Room," *Beacon: The Bulletin of the Mental Health Society of Northern California* (Fall 1952): 1.

9. Ibid., 2

10. Ibid., 6.

11. Louis J. Halle, *The Cold War as History* (New York: HarperPerennial, 1967), xvi.

12. Daniel Yergin, *Shattered Peace: The Origins of the Cold War and the National Security State* (Boston: Houghton-Mifflin, 1977).

13. Richard S. Randall, *Freedom and Taboo: Pornography and the Politics of a Self Divided* (Berkeley: University of California Press, 1989), 255–56, 266–67.

14. Vera Hopkins, interview with author, November 13, 1995; Vera Hopkins, "Public Opinion in the 1934 'EPIC' Campaign," typescript, Claremont Colleges; Vera Hopkins, "Tolerance: A Critique Prepared by Mrs. John Selden Hopkins in Dr. Russell M. Story's Seminar in Public Opinion," typescript, Claremont Colleges, 1.

15. Vera Hopkins, "Growing Pains, with Special Reference to KPFA," typescript, 1987, Pacifica National Office Papers, Berkeley (hereafter PNOP); Vera Hopkins, ed., "Sampler from Pacifica Foundation: KPFA KPFB KPFK KPFT WBAI WPFW: Various Papers Preserved or Written to Show the Founding, Development and Problems of Listener-Sponsored Radio, 1946–1984" (hereafter "Pacifica Sampler"), Pacifica Foundation documents, Bancroft Library, University of California, Berkeley.

Chapter 1

1. Quoted in Jo Ann Robinson, "A. J. Muste and Ways to Peace," in Charles Chatfield, ed., *Peace Movements in America* (New York: Schocken Books, 1973), 91.

2. Jeanette Foster, "KPFA: Storm Clouds Gathering in the Air," *San Francisco Bay Guardian*, March 14–27, 1974, 9.

3. Vera Hopkins, "Summary of Conversation with Bill Triest," March 21, 1974, "Pacifica Sampler," 1.

4. "Pacifica Is 25: A Documentary by Larry Josephson," WBAI radio program, 1974.

5. Letter, Stewart Albert, Ace Investigations, to Peter Franck, president, Pacifica Foundation, May 14, 1980, PNOP, Box 3, Folder 1.

6. James Weinstein, *Ambiguous Legacy: The Left in American Politics* (New York: New Viewpoints, 1974), 93–96.

7. Carolyn Goodman, *Pacifica: Non-Commercial Listener-Sponsored Radio* (Berkeley: Pacifica Foundation, n.d.).

8. Henry Roy Finch, Jr., interview with author, September 21, 1994, 4–5.

9. David Caute, *The Great Fear: The Anti-Communist Purge under Truman and Eisenhower* (New York: Simon and Schuster, 1978), 38–39.

10. Upton Sinclair, *Reminiscences about Some of His Novels and about His Political Career* (Claremont, Calif.: Claremont Graduate School, 1963), 1.

11. Henry Roy Finch, Jr., *Wittgenstein—The Early Philosophy; An Exposition of the "Tractatus"* (New York: Humanities Press, 1971).

12. Finch, interview, 6.

13. Kerwin Whitnah, interview with author, March 16, 1995, 1–2; Richard Moore, interview with author, January 20, 1995, 2.

14. *National Geographic Atlas of the World*, rev. 6th ed. (Washington, D.C.: National Geographic Society, 1992), 21.

15. Cynthia Eller, *Conscientious Objectors and the Second World War: Moral and Religious Arguments in Support of Pacifism* (New York: Praeger, 1991), 30.

16. Letter, Finch to author, March 28, 1995, 2.

17. Finch, interview, 1, 5.

18. U.S. Senate, *Pacifica Foundation: Hearings before the Subcommittee to Investigate the Administration of the Internal Security Act and Other Internal Security Laws of the Committee on the Judiciary* (Washington: U.S. Government Printing Office, 1963), 74.

19. Letter, Hill to Gene R. Stebbins, July 12 and July 16, 1968, cited in Gene R. Stebbins, "Listener-Sponsored Radio: The Pacifica Stations" (Ph.D. diss., Ohio State

University, 1969), 33; Joy Cole Hill, quoted in John Whiting, "The Lengthening Shadow: Lewis Hill and the Origins of Listener-Sponsored Broadcasting in America," *The Dolphin* 23 (1992): 183; Joy Cole Hill, quoted on "Pacifica Is 25."

20. Robert Hill, interview with author, March 26, 1995, 2–3; Michael Wallis, *Oil Man: The Story of Frank Phillips and the Birth of Phillips Petroleum* (New York: Doubleday, 1988), xxi, chaps. 2, 8, and 21; Whitnah, interview, 6; letter, Lewis Hill to Finch, January 15, 1944, PNOP, Box 11, Folder 1.

21. Kenneth L. Tracy, "Henry Simpson Johnston, Governor of Oklahoma, 1927–1929," in Leroy H. Fischer, ed., *Oklahoma's Governors, 1907–1929: Turbulent Politics* (Oklahoma City: Oklahoma Historical Society, 1981), 177–91.

22. Letter, Hill to Finch, January 15, 1944, PNOP, Box 11, Folder 1; Hill interview, 3.

23. Hill, interview, 3.

24. Joy Cole Hill, quoted on "Pacifica Is 25."

25. Finch, interview with author, September 21, 1994, 1; Joy Cole Hill, letter to author, November 21, 1994; Hill, interview, 2–3.

26. Lewis Hill, "Commentary, October, 1949," in Eleanor McKinney, ed., *The Exacting Ear: The Story of Listener-Sponsored Radio, and an Anthology of Programs from KPFA, KPFK, and WBAI* (New York: Random House, 1966), 250.

27. Letter, Hill to Finch, July 9, 1948, PNOP, Box 11, Folder 1.

28. Søren Kierkegaard, *Fear and Trembling* and *The Sickness unto Death*, Walter Lowrie, trans. (Princeton: Princeton University Press, [1941] 1954), 27, 30.

29. Diogenes Allen, *Three Outsiders: Pascal, Kierkegaard, Simone Weil* (Cambridge: Cowley Publications, 1983), 87–95; Dion Scott-Kakures et al., *History of Philosophy* (New York: HarperCollins, 1983), 338–44; Kierkegaard, *Fear and Trembling*, 64–91.

30. Letter, Hill to Finch, July 9, 1948, PNOP, Box 11, Folder 2.

31. Letter, Hill to Finch, April 26, 1948, PNOP, Box 11, Folder 2.

32. Finch, interview with author, April 24, 1995, 2.

33. Letter, Hill to Finch, September 11, 1949, PNOP, Box 11, Folder 2.

34. Lewis Hill, "The Private Room," *Beacon* (Fall 1952): 5.

35. Richard Moore, interview with author, January 20, 1995, 3.

36. Ibid; Finch, interview with author, September 21, 1994, 1.

37. William Allan White, quoted in Lawrence Wittner, *Rebels against War: The American Peace Movement, 1941–1983* (Philadelphia: Temple University Press, 1984), 3.

38. Ibid., 2–3; Allen F. Davis, *American Heroine: The Life and Legend of Jane Addams* (London: Oxford University Press, 1974), 266–67.

39. James Russell Tracy, "Forging Dissent in an Age of Consensus: Radical Pacifism in America, 1940 to 1970" (Ph.D. diss., Stanford University, 1993), 49.

40. Wittner, *Rebels against War*, 24–25.

41. Weinstein, *Ambiguous Legacy*, 45–47.

42. Wittner, *Rebels against War*, 7.

43. William Mandel, interview with author, February 6, 1995, 2.

44. Moore, interview.

45. Cited in Jo Ann Ooiman Robinson, *Abraham Went Out: A Biography of A. J. Muste* (Philadelphia: Temple University Press, 1981), xiii.

46. Finch, interview with author, September 21, 1994, 7.

47. Robinson, *Abraham Went Out*, 3; Tracy, "Forging Dissent," 31–32; A. J. Muste, quoted in Nat Hentoff, ed., *The Essays of A. J. Muste* (Indianapolis: Bobbs-Merrill, 1967), 75.

48. Wittner, *Rebels against War*, 31.

49. Richard B. Gregg, *Gandhiism versus Socialism* (New York: John Day, 1932), 7–8, 10–11

50. Ibid., 28.

51. *The Mind of Mahatma Gandhi*, R. K. Prabhu and U. R. Rao, eds. (Ahmedabad-14: Navajivan Publishing House [1945] 1967), 45.

52. Tracy, "Forging Dissent," 37.

53. Americo Chiarito, interview with author, April 6, 1996, 2.

54. Muste, "The World Task of Pacifism," in *Essays of Muste*, 224–25.

55. Finch, interview with author, September 21, 1994, 3.

56. Letter, Hill to Finch, August 14, 1945.

57. Finch, interview with author, September 21, 1994.

58. Wittner, *Rebels against War*, 24.

59. Geoffrey Perrett, *Days of Sadness, Years of Triumph: The American People, 1939–1945* (Madison: University of Wisconsin Press, 1985), 31–32; Eller, *Conscientious Objectors*, 12.

60. Finch, interview with author, September 21, 1994.

61. A. J. Muste, "Where Are We Going?" in *Essays of Muste*, 236–37, 239.

62. Finch, interview with author, September 21, 1994, 3.

63. Muste, "Where Are We Going?" 245.

64. Reinhold Niebuhr, quoted in Wittner, *Rebels against War*, 15.

65. Letter, Hill to Finch, April 26, 1948, PNOP, Box 11, Folder 2.

66. Muste, "Where Are We Going?" 243.

67. Finch, interview with author, September 21, 1994, 2, 10.

68. Letter, Joy Cole Hill to author, November 21, 1994; letter to George Reeves, author unknown (probably Finch), November 11, 1943, PNOP, Box 11, Folder 1.

69. Whitnah, interview with author, 4.

70. Letter, Hill to Finch, December 26, 1943, PNOP, Box 11, Folder 2.

71. National Service Board for Religious Objectors, *Directory of Civilian Public Service: May 1941 to March, 1947* (Washington, D.C., 1947), xviii–xix, quoted in Tracy, "Forging Dissent," 71, 111; Wittner, *Rebels against War*, 84.

72. Lillian Schlissel, ed., *Conscience in America: A Documentary History of Conscientious Objectors in America, 1957–1967* (New York: Dutton, 1968), 216.

73. Letter, Hill to Finch, March 14, 1943, 2, PNOP, Box 11, Folder 1.

74. Letter, Hill to Finch, January 15, 1944, PNOP, Box 11, Folder 1.

75. Wittner, *Rebels against War*, 11.

76. Letter, Hill to Finch, January 15, 1944, PNOP, Box 11, Folder 1.

77. Whiting, "Lengthening Shadow," 185.

78. Joy Hill, "Death Sentence of GI Objector Commuted to 5 Years," *Conscientious Objector,* May 1945, n.p.; letter, Hill to Finch, February 12, 1945, PNOP, Box 11, Folder 1.

79. "Notes for Initial Exploratory Letter," n.d., PNOP, Box 11, Folder 1.

80. "Remembering Denny," *Alaska Conservation Foundation Annual Report 1993,* 8.

81. Trevor Thomas and Denny Wilcher, "The Subscriber Talks Back," radio program, Pacifica Radio Archives, Los Angeles, 1963.

82. Denny Wilcher, "Shall the C.P.S. Camps Continue?" *Christian Century,* December 16, 1942, 1557, 1559.

83. Denny Wilcher, "Conscientious Objectors in Prison," *Christian Century,* March 8, 1944, 302.

84. Wallace Hamilton, "The Aquarian Conspiracy: An Inquiry into the Effects That Aquarian Values May Have on Urban Development in the United States," typescript, 1, 11–13, 4, Wallace Hamilton Papers, Box 9, Bancroft Library.

85. Henry David Thoreau, "Essay on Civil Disobedience," in *Thoreau's Vision: The Major Essays* (Englewood Cliffs, N.J.: Prentice-Hall, 1973), 199.

86. Robinson, *Abraham Went Out,* 95.

87. "Proceedings of the Chicago Conference on Social Action for Men in Civilian Public Service and Others Who Have Filed Form 47, or Have Refused to Register," April 19–25, 1943, 13.

88. "The CPS Strikes," *Politics,* July 1946, 178; "Supreme Court Denies Appeal of Germfask Seven," *Germfask Newsletter,* CPS Camp 148, Minersville, Calif., n.d., 1, Kepler papers, Santa Cruz Peace Center.

89. "CPS Strikes," 178.

90. "12 Men Arrested; Blanket Charge Brought," *Germfask Newsletter,* February 1946, 1, Kepler papers; "E. John Lewis, 78, Network Founder, Dies," *New York Times,* October 17, 1994, B11.

91. Ira Sandperl, interview with author, January 25, 1995.

92. Wilcher, "Conscientious Objectors in Prison," 303.

93. Roy Kepler et al., memorandum to "All members of the CPSU," July 15, 1945, Kepler papers.

94. "CPS Strikes," 179.

95. Lewis Hill and E. John Lewis, "An Open Letter to Glendora," n.d., PNOP, Box 11, Folder 1.

96. Letter, Lewis Hill to Mrs. J. Sargeant Cram, July 3, 1945, PNOP, Box 11, Folder 1.

97. Lewis Hill, "On Missing the Boat," 1945, PNOP, Box 11, Folder 1.

98. Finch, interview with author, September 21, 1994, 10.

99. Hill, "On Missing the Boat," 2.

100. Letter, Hill to Kepler, March 6, 1948, Kepler papers.

101. Letter, E. John Lewis to Hill, March 18, 1945, PNOP, Box 11, Folder 1.

102. Kepler, "Comments at a Chicago Pacifist Conference," 1945 or 1946, Kepler papers.

103. Stephen J. Whitfield, *A Critical American: The Politics of Dwight Macdonald* (New York: Archer Books, 1984), 6–17, 20–22, 52.

104. Ibid., 43, 45.

105. Simone Weil, "The Iliad, or, the Poem of Force," Mary McCarthy, trans., *Politics*, November 1945, 322–31; Michael Wreszin, *A Rebel in Defense of Tradition: The Life and Politics of Dwight Macdonald* (New York: Basic Books, 1994), 165–66.

106. "CPS Strikes," 177–78, 180.

107. Dwight Macdonald, "The Root Is Man, Pt. II," *Politics*, July 1946, 208.

108. Letter, Hill to Jay Tuck, March 15, 1945, PNOP, Box 11, Folder 1, and Dwight Macdonald, "Notes from Dwight Macdonald," 1949, and Roy Kepler, letter to Macdonald, August 22, 1949, Kepler papers.

109. Macdonald, quoted in *Germfask Newsletter*, February 1946, 1, Kepler papers.

110. Macdonald, "The Root Is Man, Pt. II," 207.

111. Macdonald, "The Root Is Man, Pt. I," *Politics*, April 1946, 112, 114.

112. Macdonald, "The Root Is Man, Pt. II," 213.

113. Macdonald, "The Root Is Man, Pt. II," 210.

114. Letter, Hill to Tuck, March 15, 1945, PNOP, Box 11, Folder 1.

115. Letter, Hill to Finch, August 17, 1944, PNOP, Box 11, Folder 1.

116. Robert Hill, interview with author, 3.

117. Moore, interview with author, 11.

118. Hill, "Private Room," 3.

119. Roger Daniels, *Concentration Camps, North America: Japanese in the United States and Canada during World War II* (Malbar, Fla.: Krieger, 1989), 110, 116.

120. Letter, Hill to Finch, May 30, 1945(?), PNOP, Box 11, Folder 2.

121. Joy Cole Hill, interview with author, 2.

122. Letter, Hill to Finch, November 3,1944, PNOP, Box 11, Folder 1.

123. Joy Hill, "Death Sentence of GI Objector Commuted."

124. Letter, Hill to Finch, February 18, 1951, PNOP, Box 11, Folder 2.

Chapter 2

1. *The Promise of Radio* (San Francisco: Pacifica Foundation, 1947), 19.

2. Letter, Hill to Finch, May 6, 1946, PNOP, Box 11, Folder 2.

3. Quoted in Sean Wilentz, *Chants Democratic: New York City and the Rise of the American Working Class, 1788–1850* (New York: Oxford University Press, 1984), 389.

4. Michael Kazin, *Barons of Labor: The San Francisco Building Trades and Union Power in the Progressive Era* (Urbana: University of Illinois Press, 1987), 82, 93.

5. Quoted in John Bernard McGloin, *San Francisco: The Story of a City* (San Rafael, Calif.: Presidio Press, 1978), 292.

6. Quoted in Herb Caen, *One Man's San Francisco* (Garden City, N.Y.: Doubleday, 1976), 1.

7. Mike Quin, *The Big Strike* (New York: International Publishers, 1949), 111–18; McGloin, *San Francisco*, 316–19.

8. Matthew Lasar, "Organized Labor at the Crossroads," *San Francisco Bay*

Guardian, April 24–May 1, 1985; photograph on page 19 shows ILWU's motto painted across a banner.

9. Quoted in McGloin, *San Francisco*, 329.

10. Philip Elwood, interview with author, February 17, 1995.

11. Quin, *The Big Strike*, 212.

12. Lincoln Bergman, "The Book of Elsa: An Oral History of Elsa Knight Thompson," typescript, 1985, 14.

13. Quoted in "Exploring the Human Condition," *San Francisco Examiner*, July 6, 1995, A-8.

14. Robert V. Hine, *California's Utopian Colonies* (New York: Norton, 1973), 33–42.

15. Thomas B. Harrison, "Anchorage Artist Is Remembered as 'a Little Bit of Light,'" *Anchorage Daily News*, November 4, 1990, G3; letter, Wilcher to Finch, July 31, 1946(?), PNOP, Box 11, Folder 2.

16. Lewis Hill et al., "Exploratory Letter (Initial)," April 21, 1945; letter, Hill to Geiger, February 24, 1945, and Geiger to Hill, December 17, 1945, PNOP, Box 11, Folder 2; Finch, interview with author, April 24, 1995, 4.

17. "MANAS," *MANAS*, January 7, 1948, 4; Roy Finch says that *MANAS* was "almost entirely written" by Geiger. Finch, interview, 4.

18. *MANAS*, August 3, 1949, 4.

19. Alexander Meiklejohn, "The First Amendment: The Core of Our Constitution," in Eleanor McKinney, ed., *The Exacting Ear: The Story of Listener-Sponsored Radio, and an Anthology of Programs from KPFA, KPFK, and WBAI* (New York: Random House, 1966), 129–37.

20. Meiklejohn, letter to Hill, December 3, 1952, PNOP, Box 2b, Folder 14.

21. Cynthia Stokes Brown, "Alexander Meiklejohn: Teacher of Freedom," in Cynthia Stokes Brown, ed., *Alexander Meiklejohn: Teacher of Freedom* (Berkeley: Meiklejohn Institute, 1981), 1, 15.

22. Alexander Meiklejohn, "Education for a Free Society: Selected Papers," 2 vols., mimeo, Fund for Adult Education, 1957, 22, 195–96.

23. Stokes Brown, *Alexander Meiklejohn*, 37.

24. Ibid., 38; John Powell, *Education for Maturity* (New York: Hermitage House, 1949), 80.

25. Lewis Hill et al., "Forum: What Should We Do about Unemployment?" *Direct Action* (Autumn 1945): 1, 25, 30.

26. Quoted in Gene R. Stebbins, "Listener-Sponsored Radio: The Pacifica Stations" (Ph.D. diss., Ohio State University, 1969), 42.

27. Robert Neptune, *California's Uncommon Markets: The Story of the Consumers Cooperative, 1935–1976* (Richmond, Va.: Associated Cooperatives, 1977), 8–9, 14–17.

28. Lawrence Ferlinghetti and Nancy J. Peters, *Literary San Francisco: A Pictoral History from Its Beginnings to the Present Day* (San Francisco: City Lights Books and Harper and Row), 168.

29. Louis Hill, "Imperative to a Pragmatist," *Illiterati* 3 (Summer 1944): 13; Roy

Finch, "The Invaders" and "Proloegomenon," *Illiterati* 3 (Summer 1944), 11. Lewis Hill sometimes spelled his first name "Louis."

30. Ferlinghetti and Peters, *Literary San Francisco,* 169.
31. Ibid., 148.
32. *Illiterati* 3 (Summer 1944): 1.
33. Quoted in Michael Davidson, *The San Francisco Renaissance: Poetics and Community at Mid-Century* (Cambridge: Cambridge University Press, 1991), 6.
34. Richard Moore, interview with author, January 20, 1995, 9.
35. Kenneth Rexroth, "San Francisco's Mature Bohemians," *The Nation* 184 (1957): 159.
36. Richard O. Moore, "Berkeley/San Francisco Poetry Communities in the Early 1940s," *Talisman* 10 (Spring 1993): 110.
37. Linda Hamalian, A *Life of Kenneth Rexroth* (New York: Norton, 1991), 3–4; John D'Emilio and Estelle B. Freedman, *Intimate Matters: A History of Sexuality in America* (New York: Harper & Row, 1988), 69.
38. Hamalian, *Rexroth,* 14–15, 20–21, 87.
39. Quoted in Hamalian, *Rexroth,* 103.
40. Ibid., 107.
41. Jack Kerouac, *The Dharma Bums* (New York: Penguin Books, 1958), 194.
42. Quoted in Richard Candida Smith, *Utopia and Dissent: Art, Poetry, and Politics in California* (Berkeley: University of California Press, 1995), 36.
43. Moore, interview, 7.
44. Alan Rich, interview with author, November 21, 1994, 2.
45. Quoted in Hamalian, *Rexroth,* 156.
46. Kenneth Rexroth and James Laughlin, *Selected Letters* (New York: Norton, 1991), 210.
47. Quoted in John Whiting, "The Lengthening Shadow: Lewis Hill and the Origins of Listener-Sponsored Broadcasting in America," *The Dolphin* 23 (1992): 183.
48. Moore, interview, 7.
49. Moore, interview with Veronica Selver, no date.
50. Moore, interview with author, 7.
51. Ibid.
52. Eleanor McKinney Sowande, "Resume," possession of author.
53. Letter, Hill to Finch, May 9, 1947, PNOP, Box 11, Folder 2.
54. Sidney Roger, interview with Veronica Selver, July 7, 1992, 1.
55. Minutes, October 7, 1946, 1, PNOP.

Chapter 3

1. Eleanor McKinney, interview with author, July 8, 1995, 5–6.
2. Ibid., 1.
3. *Eleanor McKinney v. John R. McKinney, Jr.,* San Francisco Superior Court, Civil Index, 1945–1949, Roll #XC1655–4, Suit #345936, October 29, 1945.

4. McKinney, interview, 2.

5. Letter, Finch to author, November 19, 1994.

6. Letter, Hill to Rupert Pray, June 12, 1947, PNOP, Box 1, Folder 4.

7. "Pacifica Foundation Radio Prospectus," July 1946, note prior to table of contents, PNOP, Box 1a, Folder 2.

8. Letter, Hill to Virginia Brownscombe, November 10, 1946, PNOP, Box 1, Folder 4.

9. "Prospectus," iii–vi.

10. Letter, Hill to Finch, April 16, 1951.

11. "Prospectus," vii.

12. Richard Moore, interview with author, 5.

13. McKinney, interview, 4.

14. Moore, interview, 5.

15. James N. Gregory, *American Exodus: The Dust Bowl Migration and Okie Culture in California* (New York: Oxford University Press, 1989), 175–76.

16. "Prospectus," 17, 28–29.

17. Ibid., 18–19.

18. Ibid., vii.

19. Ibid., 25.

20. Ibid., 26.

21. Ed (with Ethel) Meece, interview with Veronica Selver, April 24, 1994, 22–23.

22. Letter, Hill to Finch, April 16, 1951, PNOP, Box 11, Folder 2.

23. Fred W. Friendly, *The Good Guys, the Bad Guys and the First Amendment: Free Speech vs. Fairness in Broadcasting* (New York: Random House, 1976), 23; Erik Barnouw, *The Golden Web: A History of Broadcasting in the United States,* vol. 2, *1933 to 1953* (New York: Oxford University Press, 1968), 52.

24. Quoted in Friendly, *The Good Guys,* 20–21.

25. "Prospectus," 15; "Pacifica Foundation Radio Prospectus," November 1946, 13, PNOP, Box 1a, Folder 2.

26. Letter, Hill to Finch, November 23, 1946; Lawrence Wittner, *Rebels against War: The American Peace Movement, 1933–1983* (Philadelphia: Temple University Press, 1984), 194.

27. Letter, Jerome H. Spingarn to Hill, January 21, 1947, PNOP, Box 1, Folder 4; see Jerome Spingarn, *Radio Is Yours* (New York: Public Affairs Committee, 1946).

28. "Pacifica Foundation Radio Prospectus," January 1947, 13–14, PNOP, Box 1, Folder 2.

29. Ibid.

30. *The Promise of Radio* (San Francisco: Pacifica Foundation, 1947), 2.

31. Ibid., 19–20.

32. Letter, Hill to Carl Gamer, May 20, 1947, PNOP, Box 1, Folder 4.

33. Letter, Hill to Senator Glen Taylor, December 6, 1946, PNOP, Box 1, Folder 4.

34. Bruce Bliven, "How Radio Is Remaking Our World," *Century Magazine,* June 1924, 149; quoted in Susan J. Douglas, *Inventing American Broadcasting: 1899–1922* (Baltimore: Johns Hopkins University Press, 1987), 310.

35. Quoted in Robert McChesney, *Telecommunications, Mass Media, and Democ-*

racy: The Battle for the Control of U.S. Broadcasting, 1928–1935 (New York: Oxford University Press, 1993), 88.

36. James Rorty, *Order on the Air!* (New York: John Day, 1934), 24–25.

37. Ibid., 9.

38. McChesney, *Telecommunications,* 196–210, 228, 261.

39. Barnouw, *The Golden Web,* 165–66, 227–30.

40. Ibid., 179, 229, 266.

41. *Public Service Responsibility of Broadcast Licensees,* March 7, 1946, quoted in Friendly, *The Good Guys,* 22.

42. Cited in Vera Hopkins, "Excerpts from Minutes of Pacifica Foundation," 2–3.

43. *The Promise of Radio,* 5, 7–8.

44. Lewis Hill (?), memorandum, 10–12, I343-I341, I43-I38, PNOP, Box 3, Folder 2.

45. "KPFA: A Prospectus of the Pacifica Station," May 1948, vi, National Public Broadcasting Archives, Box 8, Folder 4.

46. Letter, Hill to Pray, March 2, 1947, PNOP, Box 1.

Chapter 4

1. Finch, interview with author, September 21, 1994, 1.

2. "KPFA: A Prospectus of the Pacifica Station" May 1948, vi, and "Pacifica Foundation Radio Prospectus," November 1946, 38, PNOP, Box 1, Folder 2.

3. Letter, Hill to Rupert Pray, June 12, 1947, PNOP, Box 1, Folder 4.

4. Eleanor McKinney, interview with author, July 8, 1995, 9.

5. Minutes, Pacifica Foundation, August 8, 1946, in Vera Hopkins, "Excerpts from Minutes of the Pacifica Foundation," 1, PNOP; Kenneth Rexroth and James Laughlin, *Selected Letters* (New York: Norton, 1991), 210.

6. Letter, Hill to Francis Heisler, May 7, 1947; also see letter, Hill to Carl Gamer, May 20, 1947, PNOP, Box 1, Folder 4.

7. Gene Stebbins, "Listener-Sponsored Radio: The Pacifica Stations" (Ph.D. diss., Ohio State University, 1969), 50; minutes, Radio Committee of the Pacifica Foundation, June 16, 1947, in Hopkins, "Excerpts of Minutes," 7.

8. Letter, Hill to Pray.

9. Stebbins, "Listener-Sponsored Radio," 51.

10. Minutes, Radio Committee, June 30, 1947, in Hopkins, "Excerpts of Minutes," 7.

11. "KPFA: A Prospectus," vi; letter, Hill to Pray.

12. Don V. Erickson, *Armstrong's Fight for FM Broadcasting: One Man vs Big Business and Bureaucracy* (University of Alabama Press, 1973), 51; Tom Lewis, *Empire of the Air: The Men Who Made Radio* (New York: HarperCollins, 1993), 266–67.

13. Lawrence P. Lessing, *Man of High Fidelity: Edwin Howard Armstrong: A Biography* (Philadelphia: Bantam, 1956), 170.

14. Erickson, *Armstrong's Fight,* 50.

15. Lessing, *Man of High Fidelity,* 160–61.

16. Lewis, *Empire of the Air,* 267.

17. Ibid, 169.
18. Erickson, *Armstrong's Fight*, 52.
19. Ibid., 59–60; Lewis, *Empire of the Air*, 268.
20. Erickson, *Armstrong's Fight*, 90–91.
21. Lewis, *Empire of the Air*, 300–307.
22. Ibid.; Erickson, *Armstrong's Fight*, 96.
23. Letter, Hill to Pray.
24. Charles A. Siepmann, *Radio's Second Chance* (Boston: Little, Brown, 1946), 240, 241, 250–51.
25. Letter, Hill to Siepmann, January 8, 1947, PNOP, Box 1, Folder 4.
26. Letter, Hill to Pray, October 2, 1947, PNOP, Box 1, Folder 4.
27. "Escrow Agreements, Pacifica," November 1947–July 1948, PNOP.
28. Memorandum, Hill to Wilcher, June 4, 1947, in Hopkins, "Excerpts from Minutes," 7, PNOP; minutes, Radio Committee meeting, March 5, 1948, in Hopkins, "Excerpts from Minutes," 11; minutes, executive membership meeting, September 16, 1947, in Hopkins, "Excerpts from Minutes," 10.
29. Memorandum, Hill to Wilcher; minutes, Radio Committee meeting, 11; minutes, executive membership meeting, 10.
30. "KPFA: A Prospectus," 8.
31. W. J. Rorabaugh, *Berkeley at War: The 1960s* (New York: Oxford University Press, 1989), 6–7, 52, 57.
32. Neil Macgregor, interview with author, June 22, 1995, 5.
33. "KPFA: A Prospectus," 15.
34. Ibid.
35. Ibid., 5.
36. Memorandum, Hill (?), I341, 12, PNOP, Box 3, Folder 2.
37. Memorandum, April 30, 1947, in Hopkins, "Excerpts from Minutes," 5; "Pacifica Foundation, Radio Prospectus," November 1946, 16, PNOP, Box 1, Folder 3.
38. Eleanor McKinney, interview with author, July 7, 1995, 4.
39. Letter, Hill to Norman Jorgenson, June 9, 1948, PNOP, Box 1.
40. Lewis Hill, "Report to the Executive Committee of the KPFA Sponsoring Group on KPFA's Financial History and Situation," PNOP, Box 1.
41. Eleanor McKinney, "KPFA History," January 1960, PNOP, Box 4, Folder 18.
42. Moore, interview with author, January 20, 1995, 10.
43. "Executive Committee," January 11, 1948, "Special Meeting of the Executive Membership," January 10, 1949, and "Director's Meeting," January 17, 1948, in Hopkins, "Excerpts from Minutes," 11, 14.
44. Pacifica Foundation "Progress Report," January 24, 1949, 1, PNOP, Box 11, Folder 2.
45. Ed and Ethel Meece, interview with Veronica Selver, April 24, 1994, 12.
46. McKinney, "KPFA History," 3; Ed and Ethel Meece, interview; "Report to the Executive and Advisory Members of the Pacifica Foundation on the Experience of Radio Station KPFA in Its First Five Months," October 1949, 12–13, PNOP, Box 1, Folder 9.
47. Ibid., 13.

48. Quoted on "Pacifica Is 25: A Documentary by Larry Josephson," WBAI radio program, 1974.

49. Gertrude Chiarito, interview with Veronica Selver, June 1993, 3.

50. Moore, interview, 11.

51. Chiarito, interview, 3.

52. "Pacifica Is 25."

53. McKinney, "KPFA History," 4.

54. Phil Elwood, interview with author, February 17, 1995, 2.

55. George Voigt, "KPFA Seeks Answer to Commercial Programming," *San Francisco Chronicle*, April 15, 1949, 4H.

56. Meece, on "Pacifica Is 25." Vera Hopkins, "Growing Pains, with Special Reference to KPFA," PNOP, 1987, 1.

57. "Report to the Executive Committee of the KPFA Sponsoring Group," March 1, 1950, PNOP, 1.

58. "A Report to the Listeners," radio program, July 5, 1950, Pacifica Radio Archives.

59. "On the Virtues of Mimeographing," *KPFA Interim Folio*, December 18–31, 1950, 8.

60. Dolly L. Lewis, interview with Rita Lasar, February 15, 1995.

61. McKinney, "KPFA History," 7.

62. Minutes, executive membership special meeting, August 4, 1950, and Committee of Directors, August 16, 1950, in Hopkins, "Excerpts from Minutes," 19–20.

63. Minutes, executive membership special meeting, 20.

64. McKinney, "KPFA History," 7.

65. Minutes, executive membership meeting, October 30, 1950, in Hopkins, "Excerpts from Minutes," 20.

66. Minutes, special membership meeting, November 20, 1950, in Hopkins, "Excerpts from Minutes," 20; "Local People Subscribe to Keep Station on the Air," *Palo Alto Times*, November 2, 1950; "KPFA WILL RETURN TO THE AIR," leaflet, n.d., PNOP, Box 11, Folder 2.

67. McKinney, "KPFA History," 8.

68. Letter, Hill to Finch, June 4, 1950, PNOP, Box 11, Folder 2.

69. Dwight Macdonald, *The Ford Foundation: The Men and Millions* (New York: Reynal & Company, 1956), 130–31.

70. Ibid., 3–4, 132–33.

71. Frank K. Kelley, *Court of Reason: Robert Hutchins and the Fund for the Republic* (New York: Free Press, 1981), 30.

72. Macdonald, *Ford Foundation*, 139, 142.

73. Kelly, *Court of Reason*, 14.

74. "'Ping' Ferry," *The Nation*, October 23, 1995, 452.

75. Macdonald, *Ford Foundation*, 79; Kelly, *Court of Reason*, 37.

76. Macdonald, *Ford Foundation*, 79.

77. "KPFA Campaign Bulletin," September 30, 1950, PNOP, Box 11, Folder 2.

78. Finch, interview with author, September 21, 1994, 12.

79. Macdonald, *Ford Foundation*, 56–57.

80. Letter, Hill to Finch, April 16, 1951, PNOP, Box 11, Folder 2.

81. Macdonald, *The Ford Foundation*, 57; "Invitation to Thinking," *KPFA Program Folio*, August 28–September 10, 1949, 1.

82. Macdonald, *The Ford Foundation*, 57.

83. Kelly, *Court of Reason*, 7.

84. Hopkins, "Growing Pains," 3.

85. Lewis Hill, "The Theory of Listener-Sponsored Radio," *Quarterly of Film, Radio and Television* 7 (1952): 169.

86. Lewis Hill, *Voluntary Listener-Sponsorship: A Report to Educational Broadcasters on the Experiment at KPFA, Berkeley, California* (Berkeley: Pacifica Foundation, 1958), 10, 12.

87. Ibid., 10.

88. Otto Nathan and Heinz Norden, eds., *Einstein on Peace* (New York: Schocken Books, 1960), 117.

89. Hill, *Voluntary Listener-Sponsorship*, 13–14.

90. Ibid., 6.

91. Moore, interview with author, January 20, 1995, 14.

92. Martin Quigley, "Philanthropic Stew," quoted in Macdonald, *Ford Foundation*, 144.

93. William Triest, on "Pacifica Is 25."

94. Minutes, Fred S. Martin, Acting Deputy Director, IRS, March 24, 1947, PNOP; minutes, August 25, 1948, 2; Norman Jorgenson, statement to the IRS, September 13, 1948, 3, PNOP; minutes, Lewis Hill, letter to Norman Jorgenson, May 10, 1949, PNOP.

95. Letter, Hill to Norman E. Jorgenson, August 11, 1949, PNOP, Box 1, Folder 5; Committee of Directors, Pacifica Foundation, "Special Announcement," December 7, 1949, PNOP, Box 1, Folder 7.

96. "KPFA: A Prospectus," 12, PNOP.

Chapter 5

1. "KPFA: A Prospectus of the Pacifica Station," May 1948, PNOP, Box 1, Folder 3.

2. A. J. Muste, "Communism and Civil Liberties," in Nat Hentoff, ed., *The Essays of A. J. Muste* (Indianapolis: Bobbs-Merrill, 1967), 323.

3. Kerwin Whitnah, interview with author, June 11, 1995, 2; Vladimir Vyacheslavovich Tchernavin, *I Speak for the Silent Prisoners of the Soviets*, Nicholas M. Oushalkoff, trans. (Boston: Hale, Cushman & Flint, 1935).

4. Eleanor McKinney, interview with author, July 8, 1995, 5.

5. Letter, Hill to Roy Finch, April 26, 1948, PNOP, Box 11, Folder 2.

6. Erick Barnouw, *The Golden Web: A History of Broadcasting in the United States*, vol. 2, *1933 to 1953* (New York: Oxford University Press, 1968), 257–58, 295, 307–8.

7. Jack Gould, "TV Transforming U.S. Social Scene; Challenges Films," *New York Times*, June 24, 1951, 1, 36.

8. George Voigt, "Is TV Being Used as a Club to Beat Down Show Prices?" *San Francisco Chronicle*, June 2, 1949, 2.

9. Leo Bogart, *The Age of Television: A Study of Viewing Habits and the Impact of Television on American Life* (New York: Frederick Ungar, 1956–58), 15.

10. Peter Fornatale and Joshua E. Mills, *Radio in the Television Age* (Woodstock, N.Y.: Overlook Press, 1980), 4, 6.

11. Merlin H. Aylesworth, "Radio Is Doomed," *Look*, April 26, 1949, 66, 69–77.

12. Christopher Koch, "Pacifica," *KPFA Folio*, February 1972, 13.

13. Walter Goodman, *The Committee: The Extraordinary Career of the House Committee on Un-American Activities* (New York: Farrar, Straus, 1968), 223.

14. Richard H. Rovere, *Senator Joe McCarthy* (New York: Meridian Books, 1960), 55, 124, 130.

15. Callum A. Macdonald, *Korea: The War before Vietnam* (New York: Free Press, 1986), xiii; Burton I Kaufman, *The Korean War: Challenges in Crisis, Credibility, and Command* (Philadelphia: Temple University Press, 1986), 303.

16. "Bridges Hearing: Jury Closes Books—No More Indictments," *San Francisco Chronicle*, June 9, 1949, 1; David Caute, *The Great Fear: The Anti-Communist Purge under Truman and Eisenhower* (New York: Simon and Schuster, 1978), 200–1, 238.

17. Edward L. Barrett, Jr., *The Tenney Committee: Legislative Investigation of Subversive Activities in California* (Ithaca: Cornell University Press, 1951), 310.

18. "U.C. Loyalty Oath: Faculty Opposition Led by Conservative Senior Professors," *San Francisco Chronicle*, June 15, 1949, 5.

19. Hallock Hoffman, *Loyalty by Oath: An Essay on the Extortion of Love* (Wallingford, Pa.: Pendle Hill, 1957), 24; Hallock Hoffman, interview with author, October 28, 1996, 2.

20. Koch, "Pacifica," 13.

21. "A Debut on Channel 7: KGO Premiere on Television Tonight," *San Francisco Chronicle*, May 5, 1949, 17.

22. J. Fred Macdonald, *Television and the Red Menace: The Video Road to Vietnam* (New York: Praeger Special Studies, 1985), 9; Tom Lewis, *Empire of the Air: The Men Who Made Radio* (New York: HarperCollins, 1993), 297.

23. Macdonald, *Television*, 38–40.

24. Ibid., 24, 66–71.

25. Quoted in Laurence Wittner, *Rebels against War: The American Peace Movement, 1933–1983* (Philadelphia: Temple University Press, 1984), 154.

26. "Call for February Conference," quoted in Neil H. Katz, "Radical Pacifism and the Contemporary American Peace Movement: The Committee for Nonviolent Action, 1957–1967" (Ph.D. diss, University of Maryland, 1947), 10–11, quoted in James Tracy, "Forging Dissent in an Age of Consensus: Radical Pacifism in America, 1940 to 1970" (Ph.D. diss., Stanford University, 1993), 177–78.

27. "A Discussion of Problems in Non-Violent Revolution," February 1945, Swarthmore College Peace Collection, CNVR folder, quoted in Tracy, "Forging Dissent," 179.

28. Wittner, *Rebels against War*, 155.

29. Letter, Hill to Roy Finch, April 15, 1947, 1, PNOP, Box 11, Folder 2.

30. Lewis Hill, "Hill Recapitulates February Conference and Makes Recommendation," *Bulletin* (Committee for Non-Violent Revolution), May 10, 1946, 4, Kepler Papers.

31. Quoted in Wittner, *Rebels against War,* 157.

32. Ibid., 156–57.

33. "Minutes of Peacemakers Executive Committee," February 22, 1952, Swarthmore College Peace Collection, War Resisters League manuscripts, Series B, Box 10, quoted in Tracy, "Forging Dissent," 205–6.

34. Wittner, *Rebels against War,* 188.

35. Roy Kepler, letter to Dwight Macdonald, August 22, 1949, Kepler paper; Macdonald, quoted in Michael Wreszin, *A Rebel in Defense of Tradition: The Life and Politics of Dwight Macdonald* (New York: Basic Books, 1994), 237.

36. Letter, Hill to Finch, April 26, 1948, 1, PNOP, Box 11, Folder 2.

37. Letter, Hill, letter to Muste, July 23, 1950, 1–2, PNOP, Box 2b, Folder 12–14.

38. Roy Kepler, "Report on Country-Wide Trip" (1949), War Resisters League manuscripts, Box 11, quoted in Wittner, *Rebels against War,* 211.

39. Time, July 10, 1939, 37, cited in Jo Ann Robinson, "A. J. Muste and Ways to Peace," in Charles Chatfield, ed., *Peace Movements in America* (New York: Schocken Books, 1973), 81.

40. Amy Swerdlow, "Ladies' Day at the Capitol: Women Strike for Peace versus HUAC," in Vicki L. Ruiz and Ellen Carol DuBois, eds., *Unequal Sisters: A Multicultural Reader in U.S. Women's History* (New York: Routledge, 1994), 479–96.

41. KPFA sponsoring group form letter, n.d., PNOP, Box 11, Folder 2.

42. "Minutes of Peacemakers Executive Committee," quoted in Tracy, "Forging Dissent," 204, 206.

Chapter 6

1. Adam David Miller, interview with author, July 1, 1995, 1.

2. Richard Moore, interview with author, January 20, 1995, 1.

3. "Highbrow's Delight," *Time,* February 24, 1958, 63; Thomas Whiteside, "Radio's 'Egghead' Organization," *Coronet,* January 1961, 44–48.

4. "Report on KPFA Listeners Survey, 1956," 9, PNOP, Box 2a, Folder 7; "Report to the Executive Membership of the Pacifica Foundation," December 9, 1956, PNOP, Box 2B.

5. "Report on KPFA Listeners Survey"; *Census of Population: 1950,* vol. 2, *Characteristics of the Population, Pt. 5: California* (Washington, D.C.: U.S. Government Printing Office, 1952).

6. Neil MacGregor, interview with author, January 22, 1995, 1.

7. Ibid., 1–2.

8. Ibid., 1.

9. Marilyn MacGregor, interview with author, June 12, 1995, 2.

10. Neil MacGregor, interview, 3, 7.

11. Dorothy Bryant, interview with author, December 21, 1995, 1–2.

12. Ibid., 7; Louis Wasserman, *Modern Political Philosophies and What They Mean* (Garden City, N.Y.: Halcyon House, 1944).

13. Bryant, interview, 3.

14. Ibid., 2

15. Alan Klinger, interview with author, April 18, 1995, 1.

16. Ibid., 2–4.

17. Ibid, 6.

18. MacGregor, interview, 3.

19. Vera Hopkins, "Growing Pains, with Special Reference to KPFA," typescript, 1987, PNOP, 2.

20. William Triest, quoted on "Pacifica Is 25."

21. Gertrude Chiarito, interview with Veronica Selver, June 1993, 7.

22. "Radio for Adults Only?" *KPFA Interim Program Folio,* July 31–August 13, 1949, 8.

23. Richard Moore, interview with author, January 20, 1995, 15.

24. *Census of Population, 1950,* vol. 2, 5–73.

25. *Census of Population: 1960,* vol 1, *Characteristics of the Population, Pt. 6: Calinia* (Washington, D.C.: U.S. Government Printing Office, 1963), 6–51, 6–80.

26. "Report on KPFA Listeners Survey," 6, 10.

27. McKinney, interview with author, July 8, 1995, 8.

28. Letter, Kerwin Whitnah to Roy Finch, October 21, 1947, PNOP, Box 11, Folder 2.

29. McKinney, interview, 9.

30. Ibid.

31. Lawrence Ferlinghetti and Nancy J. Peters, *Literary San Francisco: A Pictorial History from the Beginnings to the Present Day* (San Francisco: City Lights Books, 1980), 160; Bob Callaghan, "The World of Jaime de Angulo [an interview with Robert Duncan]," *Netzahualcoyotl News* 1 (Summer 1979): 1.

32. Ibid.

33. Moore, interview, 15; Bob Callahan, "World of Jaime de Angulo," 1.

34. Klinger, interview, 9.

35. Moore, interview, 15.

36. Callahan, "World of Jaime de Angulo," 1.

37. Watson Alberts, interview with author, August 17, 1995, 3.

38. Jaime de Angulo, "An Indian Tale," in Eleanor McKinney, ed., *The Exacting Ear: The Story of Listener-Sponsored Radio, and an Anthology of Programs from KPFA, KPFK, and WBAI* (New York: Random House, 1966), 309–16.

39. "Report to the Executive and Advisory Members of the Pacifica Foundation on the Experience of Radio Station KPFA in Its First Five Months," October 1949, 50, PNOP, Box 1, Folder 9.

40. Flora Arnstein, "Flora Arnstein Ongoing: Poetry, Teaching, Family in San Francisco, 1885–1985: An Interview Conducted by Suzanne B. Riess," typescript, Regents of the University of California, 1985, 13, 38.

41. Ibid., 53.

42. "Report on the Experience of KPFA," 50.

43. Arnstein, "Arnstein Ongoing," 63.

44. "Report on the Experience of KPFA," 50.

45. Moore, interview, 13; *KPFA Program Folio,* September 9–September 22, 1951, Monday, September 10, 5:00 P.M.

46. Flora Arnstein, *No End to Morning* (n.p., n.d.), Bancroft Library, University of California, Berkeley, ii.

47. "Report on the Experience of KPFA," 51; Amber Eustus, "The Art of Good Stories, [interview with Josephine Gardner]" *San Francisco Chronicle*, October 3, 1948, 9S.

48. McKinney, interview, 8.

49. Josephine Gardner, "The Ship That Went as Well on Land as on Sea" and "Dumbling," phonograph record, side 2 (Berkeley: Thomas Tenny Records [probably the 1950s]).

50. "Report on the Experience of KPFA," 51.

51. McKinney, interview, 8.

52. Moore, interview, 13.

53. "Radio for Adults Only?" *KPFA Interim Folio*, July 31–August 13, 1949, 1.

54. "RICH, Alan, 1924–," in Contemporary Authors, vol. 9–12 (Detroit: Gale Research Co., 1974), 754.

55. Alan Rich, interview with author, November 21, 1994, 1.

56. Americo Chiarito, interview with author, April 6, 1996, 3.

57. Rich, interview, 2–3.

58. Ibid., 3.

59. Bryant, interview, 4.

60. Alan Rich, *Music, Mirror of the Arts* (New York: Ridge Press, 1969), 11.

61. *KPFA Program Folio*, August 9–August 22, 1953, 2–3.

62. "Report on the Experience of KPFA," 33.

63. Jon Rice, interview with author, February 14, 1996, 1.

64. "What Is a Folk Song?" *KPFA Interim*, July 31–August 13, 1949, 8; see Matthew Lasar, "Hybrid-Highbrow: KPFA's Reconstruction of Elite Culture," *Journal of Radio Studies* 5 (Winter 1988): 46–67.

65. Letter, Americo Chiarito to David Brubeck, September 28, 1949, 1, PNOP, Box 1, Folder 5.

66. Phil Elwood, interview with author, February 17, 1995, 2.

67. Ibid.

68. "Report on KPFA Listeners Survey," 4.

69. Gertrude Chiarito, interview with Veronica Selver, June 1993, 5.

70. Elwood, interview, 7.

71. "KPFA 1960 Questionnaire Results," vii, PNOP, Box 4, Folder 14.

72. Elwood, interview, 7; Craig Marine, "Familiar Voices Disappearing from KPFA," *San Francisco Examiner*, August 1, 1995, B-1.

73. Gertrude Chiarito, interview, 15; Elwood, interview, 4.

74. William Mandel, interview with author, February 6, 1995, 15.

75. Gertrude Chiarito, interview, 16.

76. Sandy Troy, *Captain Trips: A Biography of Jerry Garcia* (New York: Thunders Mouth Press, 1994), 1–3, 30.

77. Ibid., 36–37.

78. Darius Milhaud, *Notes without Music: An Autobiography* (New York: Knopf, 1953), 311.

79. Ibid., 3.

80. Ibid., 284.

81. Andrea Olmstead, *Roger Sessions and His Music* (Ann Arbor: UMI Research Press, 1985), 7.

82. Ibid., 12; John Vintor, ed., *Dictionary of Contemporary Music* (New York: Dutton, 1971), 675.

83. Olmstead, *Sessions*, 97.

84. Ibid., 16, 97; Vintor, *Dictionary of Contemporary Music*, 675.

85. "Report on the Experience of KPFA," 25; Olmstead, *Sessions*, 97.

86. Miller, interview, 2.

87. Advertisement, *San Francisco Chronicle*, June 11, 1949, 12.

88. Rich, interview, 1.

89. Alberts, interview, 2.

90. Bill Blackbeard, "Anthony Boucher (William Anthony Parker White)," *Dictionary of Literary Biography*, vol. 8, *Twentieth Century American Science Fiction Writers*, Pt. 1: A–L (Detroit: Gale Research Company, 1981), 53.

91. "Autobiographies," in Annette McComas, ed., *The Eureka Years: Boucher and McComas's* The Magazine of Fantasy and Science Fiction, *1949–54* (Toronto: Bantam Books, 1982), 1.

92. Anthony Boucher, *The Case of the Baker Street Irregulars* (New York: Simon and Schuster, 1940).

93. Anthony Boucher, "The Model of a Science Fiction Editor," *Eureka Years*, 26.

94. Ibid., n.p.

95. Don Herron, *The Literary World of San Francisco and Its Environs* (San Francisco: City Lights Books, 1985), 189.

96. Marilyn MacGregor, interview with author, June 12, 1995, 3–4.

97. Ibid., 4.

98. Anthony Boucher, "The Other Inauguration," in *Eureka Years*, 178–81.

99. Ibid., 184.

100. Ibid., 186.

101. Moore, interview, 7.

102. Letter, Hill to Harry Givertz, July 28, 1949, 1, PNOP, Box 1, Folder 5.

103. Lewis Hill, "Commentary," in *The Exacting Ear*, 243.

104. Miller, interview, 1.

105. "Report on Experience of KPFA," 37, 39.

106. Letter, E. John Lewis to Jack Tenney, May 23, 1949, 1, PNOP, Box 1, Folder 5.

107. Unnamed San Francisco listener, quoted in letter, McKinney to Roberta Dobbins, October 20, 1949, 6, PNOP, Box 1, Folder 5.

108. Lewis Hill et al., "Is Free Speech Still Free," radio program, 1952, Pacifica National Archives, Los Angeles; "Report on the Experience of KFPA," 37.

109. "Report on Listeners Survey," 10.

110. Alberts, interview, 3.

111. "The Gospel according to Saint Luke," *Holy Bible*, Red Letter ed., King James version (Boston: Books, Inc.), 1:11–22, 48–49.

112. McKinney, interview, 6–7.

113. Rich, on "Pacifica Is Twenty-Five."
114. Miller, interview with Veronica Selver, January 26, 1996, 2.
115. Ibid.
116. Miller, interview with author, 2.
117. Herron, *The Literary World of San Francisco*, 136–37.
118. Richard Candida Smith, *Utopia and Dissent: Art, Poetry, and Politics in California* (Berkeley: University of California Press, 1995), 62–63.

Chapter 7

1. Elaine Tyler May, *Homeward Bound: American Families in the Cold War Era* (New York: HarperCollins, 1988), 11.
2. Ibid.
3. Monica Furlong, *Zen Effects: The Life of Alan Watts* (Boston: Houghton-Mifflin, 1986), 96.
4. Ibid., 110–18.
5. Quoted in ibid., 122–23.
6. Quoted in ibid., 124.
7. Moore, interview, 16.
8. Alan Watts, *This Is It, and Other Essays on Zen and Spritual Experience* (New York: Pantheon Books, 1958, 1960), 35–36.
9. Ibid., 103–4.
10. Ibid., 92.
11. Ibid., 18.
12. Ibid., 120.
13. Ibid.
14. Alan Watts, "The Problem of Death," in "Sample of KPFA Commentaries, *1953–1971*," Pacifica Radio Archives, Los Angeles, 5–6, 8.
15. Felix Greene, *A Curtain of Ignorance: How the Public Has Been Misinformed About China* (Garden City: Doubleday, 1964), xi.
16. Vera Hopkins, note written on page C2 of Felix Greene, "This and That: Series of Six Commentaries Delivered on KPFA, Berkeley, California, Spring, 1959," *Sample KPFA Commentaries, 1953–1971*, Pacifica Radio Archives.
17. Greene, *Curtain of Ignorance*, xi.
18. Greene, "This and That, Number 1," 4.
19. Felix Greene, "The American Woman," KPFA broadcast, April 13, 1953, *Commentaries (KPFA) and Special Reports, 1953–1971*, Pacifica Radio Archives, 2–3.
20. Greene, "This and That, Number 2," 3.
21. "GREENE, Felix, 1909–," in *Contemporary Authors*, New Revision Series 6 (Detroit: Gale Research Company, 1982), 200.
22. Greene, "This and That, Number 5," 1.
23. Greene, *Curtain of Ignorance*, 331.
24. Ibid., xiv; emphasis added.
25. Greene, "This and That, Number 5," 1.
26. Felix Greene, *The New Human Being in the People's Republic of China* (*Far East Reporter*, n.d.), 10.

27. Felix Greene, *The Enemy: What Every American Should Know about Imperialism* (New York, Random House, 1970).

28. Kenneth Rexroth, "Letters from Aix—Broadcast 20 November 1958," Pacifica Radio Archives.

29. Quoted in Linda Hamalian, *A Life of Kenneth Rexroth* (New York: Norton, 1991), 221.

30. Philip Levine, *The Bread of Time: Toward an Autobiography* (New York: Knopf, 1994), 205.

31. "KPFA Program Participants: Kenneth Rexroth," *KPFA Program Folio,* May 25–June 7, 1958, 1, quoted in Hamalian, *Rexroth,* 220.

32. Kenneth Rexroth, *New World Writing #11,* quoted in *World outside the Window: The Selected Essays of Kenneth Rexroth* (New York: New Directions, 1987), 54–56.

33. Ibid.

34. "Colin Wilson Interviews Kenneth Rexroth," radio program, Pacifica Radio Archives, 1962.

35. Kenneth Rexroth, *An Autobiographical Novel* (New York: New Directions, 1964), 337–38.

36. Watts, *In My Own Way,* 84.

37. Rexroth, *Autobiographical Novel,* 116.

38. Quoted in Morgan Gibson, *Revolutionary Rexroth: Poet of East-West Wisdom* (Hamden: Archon Books, 1986), 23.

39. "KPFA Program Participants," 1.

40. Quoted in Hamalian, *Life of Rexroth,* 316.

41. "Letters from Aix—Broadcast 12 March 1959," Pacifica Radio Archives.

42. "Letters from Aix—Broadcast 1 January 1959," radio program, Pacifica Radio Archives.

43. Ibid.

44. Quoted in Hamalian, *Life of Rexroth,* 370.

45. "Pauline Kael's Last Broadcasts—December 8, 1962–January 5, 1963," Pacifica Radio Archives.

46. Ibid.

47. Moore, interview with author, 16; Leah Brummer, "Pauline Kael's Berkeley Days," *Berkeley Insider,* July/August 1995, 15.

48. James Broughton, quoted in ibid.

49. "Orpheus in Sausalito, Drama by Pauline Kael," broadcast Sunday, October 7, 1962, Pacifica National Archives, Los Angeles.

50. Pauline Kael, *I Lost It at the Movies* (Boston: Little, Brown, 1954), 26, 141–49, 176–79, 203–9.

51. Quoted in Brummer, "Kael's Berkeley Days," 15.

52. Pauline Kael, *For Keeps* (New York: Dutton, 1994), 15.

53. Pauline Kael, "What's Happened to Film Criticism," broadcast March 12, 1963, Pacifica Radio Archives, Los Angeles.

54. Ibid.

55. Pauline Kael, "The Movie Lover," *New Yorker,* March 21, 1994, 133.

56. Kael, *I Lost It at the Movies,* 141–42.
57. Tyler May, *Homeward Bound,* 117.
58. Ibid., 228–31, 234.
59. Pauline Kael on "KPFK through the Years," radio program, Pacifica Radio Archives, 1969.
60. Philip Elwood, interview with author, February 17, 1995, 6.
61. Kael, "Kael's Last Broadcasts."
62. Lewis Hill, "The Private Room," *Beacon: The Bulletin of the Mental Health Society of Northern California* (Fall 1952): 1.
63. Ibid., 5.
64. Ibid., 6.

Chapter 8

1. Raymond Pierce, "Radio Praise of Marijuana Use Probed," *San Francisco Call-Bulletin,* April 24, 1954, 1.
2. "Marijuana," radio program, 1954, Pacifica Radio Archives, Los Angeles.
3. Pierce, "Radio Praise of Marijuana," 12.
4. "Brown Orders Release of KPFA Dope Record," *San Francisco Chronicle,* April 25, 1954, 1.
5. Ibid.
6. "Report to the Federal Communication's Commission from Pacifica Foundation," June 7, 1954, 2–3, PNOP, Box 2b, Folder 15.
7. Philip Elwood, interview with author, February 17, 1995, 8.
8. "KPFA Statement, April 24, 1954," Kepler Papers, 1–3.
9. John Bell Condliffe, *Agenda for a Postwar World* (New York: Norton, 1942); "Madi Bacon: Musician, Educator, Mountaineer: Oral History Transcript," interview by Janet G. Harris, Bancroft Library, Berkeley, University of California, 1989; letter, E. John Lewis to Daniel E. Koshland, April 9, 1948, in "Escrow Agreements, Pacifica," November 1947–July, 1948, *PNOP.*
10. "23 Sponsors End Radio Station Aid," *San Francisco Call-Bulletin,* May 3, 1954; "24 Resign from KPFA over Policy," *Berkeley Gazette,* May 3, 1954.
11. "HAMILTON, Wallace, 1919–1983," *Contemporary Authors,* new rev. series (Detroit: Gale Research Company, 1981–), 15:184; Wallace Hamilton, "The Invasions of Pre-Christian Ireland," typescript, Hamilton Papers, Bancroft Library, Box 8.
12. Wallace Hamilton, "M.CCC.XXI—Combustio Leprosorum," typescript, Hamilton Papers, Box 8.
13. "Hamilton," *Contemporary Authors,* 15:184; Wallace Hamilton, Clash by Night (Wallingford, Pa.: Pendle Hill, 1945), 3.
14. Wallace Hamilton, "The Aquarian Conspiracy," typescript, Hamilton Papers, Box 8.
15. Wallace Hamilton, "Hospital Notes 2," typescript, Hamilton Papers, Box 8.
16. Wallace Hamilton, typescript and "employment record," Hamilton Papers, Box 8.

17. Letter, Hill to Finch, December 16, 1951, PNOP, Box 11, Folder 2.

18. Letters, Hill to Finch, January 8, 1952; Hill to Finch, January 23, 1952, PNOP, Box 11, Folder 2.

19. Wallace Hamilton, *Christopher and Gay: A Partisan's View of the Greenwich Village Homosexual Scene* (New York: Saturday Review Press, 1973), 205.

20. Elwood, interview, 5.

21. "Pacifica Says Goodbye to First Amendment Radio," Take Back KPFA leaflet, quoted in "Flyer Distributed at NFCB Meeting," February 23, 1996, freekpfa@coco.ca.rop.edu.

22. Alexander Meiklejohn, "The First Amendment: The Core of Our Constitution," in Eleanor McKinney, ed., *The Exacting Ear: The Story of Listener-Sponsored Radio, and an Anthology of Programs from KPFA, KPFK, and WBAI* (New York: Random House, 1966), 133.

23. Philip S. Boone, "The San Francisco Symphony: 1940–1972, an Interview Conducted by Harriet Nathan in 1973–1974," typescript, Regents of the University of California, 1978, 52–54, 56.

24. Alan Rich, interview with the author, November 21, 1994, 2.

25. Letter, Hill to Finch, August 11, 1953, 2, PNOP, Box 11, Folder 2.

26. Letter, Hill to Finch, minutes, Americo Chiarito, "To: Present and Past Executive Members of the Pacifica Foundation," November 10, 1953, PNOP.

27. Minutes, executive membership, Pacifica Foundation, May 14, 1953, 2–3, PNOP.

28. Allen Ginsberg, *Howl and Other Poems* (San Francisco: City Lights Books, 1956, 1959), 13, 21–22.

29. Edward de Graze, *Girls Lean Back Everywhere: The Law on Obscenity and the Assault on Genius* (New York: Random House, 1992), 333–34.

30. Ginsberg, *Howl,* 10, 14, 22; "Allen Ginsberg's 'Howl': A Pacifica Discussion," radio program, 1957, Pacifica Radio Archives.

31. "Ginsberg's 'Howl.'"

32. Lewis Hill, "Voluntary Listener Sponsorship: A Report to Educational Broadcasters on the Experiment at KPFA, Berkeley, California," Pacifica Foundation, Berkeley, 1958, 7.

33. Moore, interview, 16.

34. Minutes, executive membership, October 9, 1952, PNOP.

35. Ibid.

36. Roy C. Kepler, "The Terror during the KPFA Revolution: A Chronicle of Division and Dissent," typescript, n.d., Kepler Papers.

37. Minutes, executive membership, October 9, 1952, PNOP.

38. Moore, interview, 18.

39. Minutes, December 5, 1946, PNOP.

40. Minutes, executive membership, October 9, 1952, PNOP.

41. Minutes, October 10, 1952, PNOP.

42. Kepler, "The Terror," 1.

43. Minutes, special meeting, October 14, 1952, PNOP.

44. Letter, Rose Triest to a friend, November 10, 1952.

45. Jürgen Habermas, "What Does a Crisis Mean Today?" in Steven Seidman, ed., *Jürgen Habermas on Society and Politics* (Boston: Beacon Press, 1989), 275, 266, 283.

46. Moore, interview, 18.

47. Ibid.

48. Vera Hopkins, "Proposed Air Plug," PNOP.

49. Eleanor McKinney, interview with author, July 8, 1995, 5.

50. Kepler, "The Terror," 5.

51. Norman Jorgensen, quoted in "Pacifica Is 25: A Documentary by Larry Josephson," WBAI radio program, 1974.

52. Minutes, "Statement by Robert Schutz," November 20, 1952, 2, PNOP.

53. Minutes, "Synopsis of an Executive Membership Meeting Held at KPFA," August 5, 1953, PNOP.

54. Minutes, Committee of Directors, October 13, 1952, PNOP.

55. Minutes, Special Meeting, executive membership, October 14, 1952, PNOP.

56. Letter, Alan Klinger to the executive membership, October 14, 1952, PNOP.

57. Minutes, Lewis Hill, "To the Pacifica Foundation Members and KPFA Staff," November 19, 1952; letter, Robert Schutz to staff, November 20, 1952; minutes, special meeting of the executive membership of Pacifica Foundation, December 9, 1952, PNOP.

58. Minutes, Richard Moore, "Memorandum to Members of the Pacifica Foundation," January 1, 1953, PNOP, 2–4.

59. Minutes, letter, Hill to Norman Jorgenson, July 3, 1953, PNOP.

60. Minutes, letter, Hill to Betty Ford-Aquino, July 3, 1953, PNOP.

61. Minutes, special meeting, Committee of Directors, July 6, 1953, PNOP.

62. Minutes, William Triest statement, July 7, 1953; Wallace Hamilton statement, July 8, 1953; Watson Alberts statement, July 8, 1953, PNOP.

63. Minutes, special meeting, Committee of Directors, July 8, 1953, PNOP.

64. Moore, interview, 20.

65. Ibid., 19.

66. Minutes, special meeting, executive membership, July 9, 1953; Moore statement, July 9, 1953, PNOP.

67. Moore, interview, 20.

68. Minutes, Wallace Hamilton, statement to the Committee of Directors, July 12, 1953, PNOP.

69. Minutes, special meeting, Committee of Directors, July 10, 1953, PNOP.

70. Eleanor McKinney, interview with author, July 7, 1995, 6.

71. Minutes, special meeting, Committee of Directors, July 10, 1953, PNOP.

72. Minutes, "To Whom It May Concern," July 22, 1953, PNOP.

73. Minutes, letter, Robert Schutz to G. H. Griffiths, October 16, 1953, PNOP.

74. Wallace Hamilton, "False Gandhianism," Fellowship, February 1957, 21.

75. Kepler, "The Terror," 10.

76. Moore, interview, 20.

77. Letter, Hill to Finch, August 11, 1953, PNOP, Box 11, Folder 2.

78. Minutes, Lewis Hill, "Notice to the Executive Members of Pacifica Foundation and the Staff Members of KPFA," July 12, 1953, PNOP.

79. Ibid.

80. Minutes, memo, Moore, July 10, 1953, PNOP.

81. Minutes, Eleanor McKinney, "To the Executive Members of the Pacifica Foundation," July 12, 1953, PNOP.

82. Minutes, Vera Hopkins, notes to press statement by Lewis Hill, July 15, 1953, PNOP.

83. Minutes, Vera Hopkins, "Typed Version of Notes by Vera Hopkins at 'Save KPFA' Meeting," July 27, 1953, 3, PNOP.

84. Minutes, letter, Alan Watts to Hill, July 28, 1953, 1–4, PNOP.

85. Minutes, letter, Hill to Watts, July 31, 1953, PNOP.

86. Letter, Rose Triest to a friend, November 10, 1952, in possession of author.

87. Minutes, letter, Elton M. Davies to Gertrude Chiarito, July 31, 1953; Committee of Directors, August 4, 1953, PNOP.

88. Minutes, "Resolution by the Committee of Directors of the Pacifica Foundation," August 3, 1953, PNOP.

89. Minutes, letter, Ida Mae Zapf to Hill, August 1953, PNOP.

90. Minutes, letter, Robert Schutz to Hill, August 24, 1953, PNOP.

91. Minutes, letter, Hill to the Committee of Directors, August 10, 1953; letter, Hill to G. H. Griffiths, FAE, August 11, 1953, PNOP; minutes, National Association of Education Broadcasters, special delivery to Pacifica Foundation, August 21, 1953, PNOP; letter, Kepler to Mrs. Charles A. Eldon, June 24, 1954, 1, Kepler Papers.

92. Minutes, Wallace Hamilton, "Memorandum," November 10, 1953, PNOP.

93. Gregory Bateson, "Conventions of Communication," in Jurgen Ruesch and Gregory Bateson, *Communication: The Social Matrix of Psychiatry* (New York: Norton, 1951), 222.

94. Watson Alberts, interview with author, August 17, 1995, 5.

95. Minutes, "Memorandum, From the Structure Committee," February 10, 1954, 1, PNOP.

96. Minutes, "To: Pacifica Foundation, From: Structure Committee," February 10, 1953, PNOP.

97. Minutes, Committee of Directors, February 13, 1954, PNOP.

98. Minutes, "Memorandum," Committee of Directors, February 13, 1954, PNOP.

99. Minutes, "Promotion Report," November, 2, 1953, 1, PNOP.

100. Minutes, letter, Schutz to Ed Howden, September 16, 1953, 5, PNOP.

101. McKinney, interview, 6.

102. Rich, interview, 3.

103. Minutes, letter, Ernest Besig to the Pacifica Foundation, April 20, 1954, PNOP.

104. Eleanor McKinney, letter to the editor, San Francisco Chronicle, May 13, 1954.

105. Minutes, Eleanor Moore, Robert Schutz, Ida Mae Zapf, Allen Klinger, Lori Campbell, untitled statement, April 25, 1954, PNOP.

106. "A Rational Community," *KPFA Program Folio*, May 14, 1954, Kepler Papers.

107. Letter, Frank E. Freeman, Mrs. Kenneth A. Hayes, and Kenneth A. Hayes to the FCC, June 11, 1954, PNOP, Box 2b, Folder 15.

108. Minutes, Wallace Hamilton, "Accountability," May 7, 1954, 1–2, PNOP.

109. Minutes, Alan Watts, "Statement," May 3, 1954, PNOP.

110. Minutes, Anthony Boucher, "Preliminary to Golden Voices," May 9, 1954, PNOP.

111. Letter, Mrs. P. H. Pratt to KPFA, May 14, 1954, Kepler Papers; letter, Kepler to Mrs. William A. Brownell, May 19, 1954, Kepler Papers.

112. Anthony Boucher, "'Vague Talk' and KPFA," letter to the *San Francisco Chronicle,* May 19, 1954.

113. Minutes, "Resolution #1 (Creating Position)," "Resolution #2 (Offering the Position)," August 4, 1954; "Copy, Minutes and Papers related to Actions of EM and CD period, August 3–20, 1954," 1–5, PNOP.

114. Minutes, Watson Alberts, Wallace Hamilton, Bruce Harris, Roy Kepler, and William Triest, "To the Committee of Directors, Pacifica Foundation," August 5, 1954, PNOP.

115. Minutes, Bruce Harris, "Executive Membership, Pacifica Foundation," August 11, 1954, PNOP.

116. Minutes, "KPFA, Report to the Listener," August 29, 1954; PNOP.

117. Rich, interview, 1994, 1; Charles Shere, *Thinking Sound Music: The Life and Work of Robert Erickson* (Berkeley: Fallen Leaf Press, 1995), 37.

118. Minutes, Lewis Hill, "Report to the Listener," October 30, 1954, PNOP, 1–3.

119. Letter, L. A. Dunlap, postmaster, to Kepler, September 7, 1954, Kepler Papers.

120. Roy Kepler, letter to the editor, *San Francisco Chronicle,* typescript, August 25, 1957, Kepler Papers.

121. Roy Kepler, "The Vulgarian Revolution," typescript, October 25, 1953, 3, Kepler Papers.

Chapter 9

1. Lewis Hill, "KPFA's 8th Birthday: Pt. 2 of the Brash Experiment," 1957, Pacifica Radio Archives.

2. Ibid.

3. Floyd S. Daft, "Wonder Drugs," *Hearings before the Subcommittee on Patents, Trademarks and Copyrights of the Committee on the Judiciary, U.S. Senate,* 84th Congress, 2d sess. (Washington, D.C., U.S. Government Printing Office, 1957), 8.

4. Ibid.; Sidney M. Wolfe, M.D., et al., *Worst Pills/Best Pills: The Older Adult's Guide to Avoiding Drug-Induced Death or Illness* (Washington, D.C.: Public Citizens' Health Group, 1993), 18, 21, 24; "Cortisone," *The New Encyclopedia Britanica,* 3, Micropaedia (Chicago: Encyclopedia Britanica, 1995), 655.

5. Joy Hill, quoted in John Whiting, "The Lengthening Shadow: Lewis Hill and the Origins of Listener-Sponsored Broadcasting in America," *The Dolphin* 23, (1992): 206.

6. Vera Hopkins, "Growing Pains, with Special Reference to KPFA," typescript, 1987, PNOP, 16.

7. Gertrude Chiarito, interview with Veronica Selver, June 1993, 12.

8. Lincoln Bergman, "The Book of Elsa: An Oral History of Elsa Knight Thompson." typescript, 1985, 162.

9. Sidney Roger, interview with Veronica Selver, July 16, 1992, 1.

10. Letters to G. H. Griffiths, June 15, July 2, and August 27, 1956, quoted in Gene R. Stebbins, "Listener-Sponsored Radio: The Pacifica Stations" (Ph.D. diss., Ohio State University, 1969), 193.

11. Letter, Denny Wilcher to Roy Finch, August 12, 1957, 1, PNOP, Box 11, Folder 2.

12. Letter, Lewis Hill to Roy Kepler, March 6, 1948, Kepler Papers; Joy Cole Hill, interview with author, April 16, 1995, and August 17, 1996, 2.

13. Alan Rich, interview with author, November 21, 1994, 4.

14. Felix Greene et al., "Report to the Executive Membership of the Pacifica Foundation," December 9, 1956, Berkeley, Pt. II, 6, Kepler Papers; Felix Greene, "An Open Letter to Members of the Pacifica Foundation," January 7, 1957, 4, and note attached to copy, Kepler papers.

15. "Minutes of Interview with Mr. Lewis Hill," July 19, 1957, 1, 3, Kepler Papers.

16. Hopkins, "Growing Pains," 15.

17. Letter, Wilcher to Finch, 1.

18. Letter, Wilcher to Finch, August 4, 1957, PNOP, Box 11, Folder 2.

19. "Lewis Hill Dead; Founder of KPFA," *San Francisco Chronicle*, August 2, 1957, 20.

20. Rich, interview, 9.

21. R. Gordon Agnew, statement, *KPFA Program Folio*, August 18–August 31, 1957, 8.

22. Bergman, "Book of Elsa," 165.

23. Hopkins, "Growing Pains," 19.

24. "Lewis Hill Dead," 20.

25. Russell Jorgensen, interview with Veronica Selver, April 1993, 38.

26. Finch, interview with author, September 21, 1994, 13; Eleanor McKinney, interview with Veronica Selver, December 14, 1994, 13; Moore, interview with Selver, 4.

27. Steve Post, *Playing in the FM Band: A Personal Account of Free Radio* (New York: Viking Press, 1974), 226.

28. Lorenzo Milam, *Sex and Broadcasting: A Handbook on Starting Community Radio Stations* (Saratoga, N.Y.: Dildo Press, 1972), 73. Gertrude Chiarito, interview with Veronica Selver, June 1993, 11–12.

29. Harold Winkler, "The Way Is Freedom," (Ph.D. diss., Harvard University, 1942); "Vitae and Biographies of Group Members—Harold Winkler, Ph.D." Papers of the Group for Academic Freedom, Bancroft Library, Box 1.

30. Letter, Wilcher to Finch, November 5, 1957, PNOP, Box 11, Folder 2; ellipses in original.

31. "UC Oath Feud Flares in Naming of Non-Signers," *Fresno Bee*, August 23, 1950, A1, 23A; "25 U. of C. Professors Named as Oath Rebels," *North Hollywood Valley Times*, August 23, 1950, 1; "25 Names Made Public," *San Francisco Call-Bulletin*, August 23, 1950, 1.

32. "UC Profs Order Probe of the FBI," *San Francisco Chronicle,* November 28, 1953.

33. David P. Gardner, *The California Oath Controversy* (Berkeley: University of California Press, 1967), 183.

34. "Contributions, 1951," Papers of the Group for Academic Freedom, Bancroft Library, Box 1.

35. Harold Winkler, "Pacifica Radio—Room for Dissent," *National Association for Educational Broadcasters Journal,* May-June 1960, 95; Gabrielle Morris, "Oral History Interview with David Brainin—Revenue Estimator, California Department of Finance, 1950–1985," April 19 and June 9, 1988, California State Archives, Bancroft Library, 52–53.

36. Hopkins, "Growing Pains," 17–18.

37. Kerwin Whitnah, interview with author, June 11, 1995, 2.

38. Henry Geiger et al., "To the Supporters of Listener-Sponsored Radio in Southern California," PNOP, Box 3, Folder 2.

39. Bergman, "Book of Elsa," 166.

40. Chris Koch, "The Pacifica Papers," *KPFA Folio,* February 1972, 14.

41. "Statement of Resignation of William Webb," PNOP, Box 3, Folder 2.

42. Hopkins, "Growing Pains," 18.

43. McKinney, interview with author, 10; Alan Rich, interview with author, November 21, 1994, 5.

44. Post, *Playing in the FM Band,* 13–14; Koch, "Pacifica Papers," 13.

45. William Mandel, interview with author, February 6, 1995, 1, 5.

46. William Mandel, "Joe, HUAC and Me," Pacifica Radio Archives; William Mandel, *The Soviet Far East and Central Asia* (New York: Institute of Pacific Relations, 1944); Mandel, interview, 4.

47. David Caute, *The Great Fear: The Anti-Communist Purge under Truman and Eisenhower* (New York: Simon and Schuster, 1978), 317–21.

48. William Mandel, "William Mandel's First Broadcast on KPFA, 1950," Pacifica Radio Archives.

49. Mandel, interview, 2–3.

50. Mandel, "Mandel's First Broadcast."

51. Ibid.

52. Robert Rudolph Schutz, "Transfer Payments and Income Inequality" (Ph.D. diss., UC Berkeley, 1952).

53. Adam David Miller, interview with author, July 1, 1995, 4.

54. Mandel, "Mandel's First Broadcast."

55. Mandel, "Joe, HUAC and Me."

56. Mandel, "Mandel's First Broadcast."

57. William Mandel, *Man Bites Dog: Report of an Unusual Hearing before the McCarran Committee* (New York: National Guardian, 1952).

58. Mandel, "Joe, HUAC and Me."

59. Mandel, interview, 8.

60. William Mandel and Laurie Garrett, "The Guy Who Got Senator Joe: The 1953 Testimony of William Mandel before Joe McCarthy," Pacifica Radio Archives, 1979.

61. C. P. Turssell, "Browder, McCarthy Clash at Hearing," *New York Times*, March 25, 1953, 1.

62. Mandel, "Joe, HUAC and Me."

63. Mandel, interview, 7–11, 16.

64. Craig Marine, "Familiar Voices Disappearing from KPFA," *San Francisco Examiner*, August 1, 1995, B-1.

65. Sidney Roger, interview with Veronica Selver, July 16, 1992, 2.

66. William Mandel, Dorothy Healey, and Suzi Weissman, "Communists Viewpoint: A Debate," broadcast April 1, 1982, Pacifica Radio Archives.

67. William Mandel, *Soviet But Not Russian: The "Other" Peoples of the Soviet Union* (Palo Alto: University of Alberta Press and Ramparts Press, 1985).

68. William Mandel, "Soviet Press and Periodicals: Transcription of Ad-Lib Responses," July 25, 1960, Mandel personal papers.

69. Lawrence Ferlinghetti, interview with Veronica Selver, n.d., 9.

70. Neil MacGregor, interview with author, January 22, 1995, 4; Marilyn MacGregor, interview with author, June 12, 1995, 3. "The KPFA Annual Questionnaire, 1959," tabulations of question 6, PNOP, Box 2a, Folder 7.

71. "The KPFA Annual Questionnaire, 1959," tabulations of question 6, PNOP, Box 2a, Folder 7.

72. Stephen J. Whitfield, *The Culture of the Cold War* (Baltimore: John Hopkins University Press, 1991), 124.

73. Phil Elwood, interview with author, February 17, 1995, 10.

74. Bergman, "Book of Elsa," 162.

75. Ibid., appendix.

76. Elwood, interview, 10.

77. Rich, interview, 7.

78. Dorothy Bryant, interview with author, December 21, 1995, 5.

79. Bergman, "Book of Elsa," 30.

80. Ibid., 14, 17–18.

81. Ibid., 41.

82. Ibid., 35–41.

83. Ibid. 49; "Younghusband, Sir Francis Edward," *Encyclopedia Britannica* 23 (Chicago: Encyclopedia Britannica. 1966), 905; Patrick French, *Younghusband: The Last Great Imperial Adventurer* (London : HarperCollins, 1994).

84. Bergman, "Book of Elsa," 49–51.

85. Ibid., 63, 64–73, 74.

86. Ibid., 91.

87. Ibid., 92.

88. Ibid., 121.

89. Ibid., 113, 137–38.

90. Ibid., 141.

91. Ibid., 155.

92. Ibid., 161.

93. *KPFA Program Folio*, December 21–January 3, 1958, 1.

94. Koch, quoted in Moira Rankin and Gary Covino, "Elsa Knight Thompson: A Remembrance," Pacifica Radio Archive, 1983.

95. Bergman, "Book of Elsa," 166.

96. Chiarito, interview with Veronica Selver, 13.

97. Rich, interview, 6.

98. Bergman, "Book of Elsa," 166.

99. Ibid., 173.

100. Ibid.; Elsa Knight Thompson, quoted in Rankin and Covino, "Elsa Knight Thompson."

101. Rankin and Covino, "Elsa Knight Thompson."

102. Chiarito, interview, 25–26.

103. Bergman, "Book of Elsa," 243.

104. Ibid., 167; Caute, *The Great Fear,* 247–48.

105. Ibid.

106. "Chaplain at Alcatraz: Reverend McCormack, Interviewed by Elsa Knight Thompson," 1959, Pacifica Radio Archives; "Art in the Soviet Union, Moderated by Elsa Knight Thompson," 1959, Pacifica Radio Archives; "Legal Insanity, Moderated by Elsa Knight Thompson," 1959, Pacifica Radio Archives; "Freedom in Education and Investigating Committees, Moderated by Elsa Knight Thompson," 1959, Pacifica Radio Archives; Caute, *The Great Fear,* 572, 579.

107. Bergman, "Book of Elsa," 14.

108. Stuart Timmons, *The Trouble with Harry Hay* (Boston: Alyson Publications, 1990), 177–79.

109. John D'Emilio, "Gay Politics and Community in San Francisco since World War II," in Martin Duberman et al., eds., *Hidden from History: Reclaiming the Gay and Lesbian Past* (New York: New American Library, 1989), 460.

110. *The Homosexual in Our Society: Transcript of a Radio Program in Two Parts* (San Francisco: Pan Graphic Press, 1959), 5.

111. Ibid., 6.

112. Bert Gerritz, interview with Julia Hutton, July 27, 1995.

113. Seymour Martin Lipset, interview with author, April 17, 1996, 1, 3.

114. Mandel, interview, 16; Vera Hopkins, "Pressures on Pacifica-KPFA around 1960," 2, in "Pacifica Sampler."

115. "Radio Station Promotes Communists," *Counterattack,* February 5, 1960, 15–18, 19.

116. William Rusher, "Commentary," in Eleanor McKinney, ed., *The Exacting Ear: The Story of Listener-Sponsored Radio, and an Anthology of Programs from KPFA, KPFK, and WBAI* (New York: Random House, 1966), 159; Harold Winkler, "Pacifica Radio: Room for Dissent," *NAEB Journal* 19 (May–June 1960): 99.

117. "Crusader, Traitor, or Neither: Gerald Smith, Interviewed by Terry Drinkwater," 1959, Pacifica National Archives; Gene Marine, interview with author, April 22, 1996, 5–7.

118. Ronald Brownstein and Nina Easton, *Reagan's Ruling Class: Portraits of the President's Top One Hundred Officials* (New York: Pantheon Books, 1982), 434–35; Elwood, interview, 3.

119. Hopkins, "Pressures on Pacifica," 2.

120. Caute, *Great Fear*, 102.

121. Kenneth Rexroth, "San Francisco's Mature Bohemians," *The Nation*, February 23, 1957, 159.

122. Vicki L. Ruiz, *Cannery Women, Cannery Lives: Mexican Women, Unionization, and the California Food Processing Industry, 1930–1950* (Albuquerque: University of New Mexico Press, 1987), 74; Dorothy Healey and Maurice Isserman, *Dorothy Healey Remembers: A Life in the American Communist Party* (New York: Oxford University Press, 1990), 169.

123. Mandel, interview, 13.

124. Caute, *Great Fear*, 570–71.

125. "The House Un-American Activities Committee," in *The Exacting Ear*, 78–79.

126. Ibid, 82.

127. Caute, *Great Fear*, 361.

128. Mandel and Freedberg, "Joe, HUAC and Me."

129. Ibid.

130. Rich, interview, 6.

131. "The House Un-American Activities Committee," 62–95.

132. Todd Gitlin, *The Sixties: Years of Hope, Days of Rage* (New York: Bantam, 1987), 121.

133. Ernest Lowe, interview with author, October 16, 1995, 2.

134. Harold Winkler, "Pacifica Radio: Room for Dissent," *NAEB Journal* 19 (May–June 1960): 98.

135. Ibid., 99; NAEB's typesetter inadvertently omitted the words "loses meaning when the less institutional political views are" from its publication of Winkler's essay. A Pacifica reprint of the piece includes the line typed in on the margin of the column. See PNOP, Box 4, Folder 8.

136. Winkler, "Room for Dissent," 103.

137. Bergman, "The Book of Elsa," 171.

138. Trevor Thomas, "Some Thoughts on Operating a Radio Station, II," *KPFA Folio*, January 28–February 11, 1962.

139. Bergman, "Book of Elsa," 171.

Chapter 10

1. "Elman, Richard (Martin) 1934–," in James M. Ethridge et al., eds., *Contemporary Authors: A Bibliographical Guide to Current Authors and Their Works* (Detroit: Gale Research, 1968), 19–20.

2. Chris Koch, interview with John Whiting, October 4, 1994, 1.

3. Ibid.

4. Jerome Shore, interview with author, June 9, 1996, 5.

5. Jack Levine, "Hoover and the Red Scare," *The Nation*, October 20, 1962, 232–35.

6. Koch, interview, 4.

7. "The Report of Special Agent Jack Levine: A Documentary Broadcast by WBAI," transcript, 1962, 1, PNOP, Box 3, Folder 7; Koch, interview, 2.

8. Daniel Yergin, *Shattered Peace: The Origins of the Cold War and the National Security State* (Boston: Houghton Mifflin, 1977), 196.

9. Koch, interview, 1–3.

10. Ibid., 2, 4.

11. Ibid., 2, 4.

12. "Report of Jack Levine," 18, 21, 30.

13. Ibid., 33.

14. Ibid., 29.

15. Ibid., 6.

16. "Office Memorandum, U.S. Government to Director, FBI," June 9, 1958, PNOP, Box 3, Folder 2.

17. "Teletype, URGENT—to Director, FBI," October 15, 1962, and "Domestic Intelligence Division, Informative Note," October 15, 1962, PNOP, Box 3, Folder 2; Shore, interview, 6; Athan Theoharris, *J. Edgar Hoover, Sex, and Crime: An Historical Antidote* (Chicago: Ivan R. Dee, 1995), 34–35.

18. "Report of Former Agent Turner," transcript, October 26, 1962, 1, 17, PNOP, Box 3, Folder 7.

19. *New York Times,* October 23, 1962, quoted in William Turner, *Hoover's FBI* (New York: Thunder's Mouth Press, 1993), 142.

20. Curt Gentry, *J. Edgar Hoover—The Man and the Secrets* (New York: Norton, 1991), 387–88.

21. "U.S. Government Memorandum, To: Mr. W. C. Sullivan; Re: Jack Levine," October 22, 1962, 3, and "KPFA's 1962 Anti-Red Crusade," enclosed in letter to J. Edgar Hoover, November 5, 1962, author's name blacked out, PNOP, Box 3, Folder 2.

22. Martin Walker, *The Cold War: A History* (New York: Holt, 1994), 171.

23. Ibid., 172.

24. President Kennedy, quoted in Walter LaFeber, *America, Russia, and the Cold War, 1945–1975* (New York: Wiley, 1972), 228.

25. Walker, *The Cold War,* 176–77; LaFeber, *America, Russia and the Cold War,* 228–29.

26. Paul M. Sweezy, "Paul Alexander Baran: A Personal Memoir," in *Paul A. Baran (1910–1964): A Collective Portrait* (New York: Monthly Review Press, 1965), 30–40, 58.

27. Ibid, 47; Paul Baran, "Commentary," typescript, April 1961, in "Commentaries (KPFA) and Special Reports: 1953–1971," Pacifica Archives, 3, 7–8.

28. "Panel Discussion on Cuba/Moderated by Elsa Knight Thompson," 1962, Pacifica Archives.

29. "COMMUNIST INFILTRATION OF PACIFICA FOUNDATION INTERNAL SECURITY; From: Director, FBI," November 2, 1962, 1–3, PNOP, Box 3, Folder 2; Vera Hopkins, "Growing Pains, with Special Reference to KPFA," typescript, 20, PNOP.

30. David Caute, *The Great Fear: The Anti-Communist Purge under Truman and Eisenhower* (New York: Simon and Schuster, 1978), 91, 104–5.

31. Ibid., 451–52; I. F. Stone, "If We Acted in Selma as We Act in Saigon," in Neil Middleton, ed., *I. F. Stone's Weekly Reader* (New York: Vintage Books, 1974), 135.

32. Caute, *Great Fear*, 472–73.

33. "Communist Infiltration of the Pacifica Foundation," FBI report, November 21, 1962, 1C-1J, PNOP, Box 3, Folder 2.

34. Ibid., 63–64.

35. Bergman, "The Book of Elsa: An Oral History of Elsa Knight Thompson," typescript, 1985, 171.

36. Shore, interview, 3–4.

37. "Communist Infiltration of Pacifica," 3; letter, [name blacked out] to J. Edgar Hoover, February 2, 1960; "U.S. Memorandum to Director, FBI," May 31, 1960, PNOP, Box 3, Folder 2.

38. *Pacifica Foundation: Hearings before the Subcommittee to Investigate the Administration of the Internal Security Act and Other Internal Security Laws of the Committee on the Judiciary* (Washington, D.C.: U.S. Government Printing Office, 1963), 71.

39. Robert Schutz, "The Investigation of Pacifica," 1, in Vera Hopkins, ed., "Pacifica Sampler."

40. Lewis Hill, "The Private Room," *Beacon* (Fall 1952): 2.

41. Trevor Thomas, Interview with the author, January 22, 1995, 3.

42. Bergman, "Book of Elsa," 171.

43. "Communist Infiltration of Pacifica," 66.

44. Denny Wilcher, quoted in Schutz, "Investigation of Pacifica," 4.

45. Russell Jorgensen, interview with Veronica Selver, April 1993, 2–3.

46. Schutz, "Investigation of Pacifica," 18.

47. William Mandel, interview with author, February 6, 1995, 19.

48. Thomas, interview, 3.

49. *Pacifica Foundation*, 83.

50. Bergman, "Book of Elsa," 172.

51. Thomas, interview, 2.

52. *Pacifica Foundation*, 114.

53. Mandel, interview, 19.

54. *Pacifica Foundation*, 174–91.

55. Ibid., 197–98.

56. Schutz, "Investigation of Pacifica," 12.

57. Ibid., 6; *Pacifica Foundation*, 240, 253; "Communist Infiltration of Pacifica," cover page, C, PNOP, Box 3, Folder 2.

58. Vera Hopkins, "FBI File on Pacifica Foundation, Summary," II, 4, PNOP, Box 3.

59. The *New York Times* and *San Francisco Examiner*, quoted in Schutz, "Investigation of Pacifica," 15–16.

60. Jack Gould, *New York Times*, August 3, 1963, quoted in Schutz, "Investigation of Pacifica," 21.

61. E. William Henry, interview with author, July 19, 1997, 1–3, 7.

62. Listener, Lawrence Ferlinghetti, and Robert E. Lee, quoted in Schutz, "Investigation of Pacifica," 30–33; Henry, interview, 5.

63. Schutz, "Investigation of Pacifica," 37–38.

64. Minutes, special meeting, Pacifica Foundation National Board, February 2, 1963, 2–3, PNOP.

65. Minutes, Executive Committee, Board of Directors, Pacifica Foundation, January 28, 1963, PNOP.

66. Shore, interview, 4.

67. Koch, interview, 5.

68. Minutes, Board of Directors, March 12, 1963, 1–2, PNOP; Schutz, "Investigation of Pacifica," 25.

69. Minutes, Dr. Gordon Agnew, statement to the National Board, March 12, 1963, 2, PNOP.

70. Schutz, "Investigation of Pacifica," 38–39.

71. Ibid., 41.

72. Thomas, interview, 4.

73. Schutz, "Investigation of Pacifica," 42.

74. Ibid., 43.

75. Minutes, Executive Committee, Board of Directors, December 4, 1963, PNOP.

76. Shore, interview, 11; minutes, Executive Committee, Board of Directors, December 4, 1963, 2; Gordon Agnew, "Re: Special Board Meeting in Los Angeles, December 14th," December 5, 1963; Board of Directors, December 14, 1963, 2.

77. Koch, interview, 5.

78. Shore, interview, 10.

79. Bergman, "Book of Elsa," 173.

80. Ernest Lowe, "Continuation of Statement," November 25, 1964, 2, PNOP, Box 4, Folder 17.

81. Elsa Knight Thompson, interview with Melinda Rorick, in Bergman, "Book of Elsa," 228.

82. Dorothy Healey and Maurice Isserman, *Dorothy Healey Remembers: A Life in the American Communist Party* (New York: Oxford University Press, 1990), 243.

83. Frank Kelley, *Court of Reason: Robert Hutchins and the Fund for the Republic* (New York: Free Press, 1981), 37; Paul V. Dallas, *Dallas in Wonderland* (Los Angeles: Paul V. Dallas, 1967), 1; Shore, interview, 2; minutes, Board of Directors, October 10, 1964, PNOP; Hallock Hoffman, *Loyalty by Oath: An Essay on the Extortion of Love* (Wallingford, Pa.: Pendle Hill, 1957), 2.

84. Hoffman, Hallock, "The Problem of Balance," typescript, January 17, 1963, 2, in possession of author.

85. Ibid.

86. Ibid., 5.

87. Eleanor McKinney, ed., *The Exacting Ear: The Story of Listener-Sponsored Radio, and an Anthology of Programs from KPFA, KPFK, and WBAI* (New York: Random House, 1966), 27, 43, 62, 116, 146, 212, 217, 309.

88. Minutes, "Draft II, Policy Memorandum—Pacifica Foundation Board of Directors," Executive Committee, Board of Directors, January 28, 1963, PNOP.

89. Letter, Trevor Thomas to Elsa Knight Thompson, January 13, 1964, PNOP, Box 4, Folder 17.

90. Vera Hopkins, "Chronology of Tribulations," 1–2, PNOP, Box 4, Folder 17;

John Whiting, "William Mandel's 1964 Post-Strike Broadcast: A Response" (100707.731@compuserve.com, April 14, 1996), 1; Whiting, "The SISS/FCC/EKT/NABET NEXUS" (100707.731@compuserve.com, April 15, 1996), 2; Dorothy Bryant, interview with author, December 21, 1995, 8; Thomas, interview, 6; Jorgensen, interview, 30.

91. "1965 KPFA Birthday Party," April 15, 1965, Pacifica Radio Archives.

92. Ibid.; "The Federal Communications Commission Decision," in McKinney, *Exacting Ear*, 322.

93. Marshall Efron is a New York City-based comedian who has long been associated with WBAI; see Post, *Playing in the FM Band: A Personal Account of Free Radio* (New York: Viking Press, 1974), vii.

94. "1965 KPFA Birthday Party."

95. Henry, interview, 8.

96. James Deakin, "New FCC Chairman Emerges as Tough Regulator, Sharing Minow's Concerns about Radio and TV," *St. Louis Post Dispatch*, April 18, 1964, quoted in Hopkins, "Pacifica Sampler."

Conclusion

1. William Mandel, interview with author, February 6, 1995, 4.

2. Roy A. Medvedev, *Let History Judge: The Origins and Consequences of Stalinism* (New York: Knopf, 1972), 483.

3. Lawrence Goodwyn, *The Populist Moment: A Short History of Agrarian Revolt in America* (Oxford: Oxford University Press, 1978), xxiii.

4. Pauline Kael, "Pauline Kael's Last Broadcasts—December 8, 1962–January 5, 1963," Pacifica Radio Archives.

5. Lewis Hill(?) memorandum, I343, PNOP, Box 3, Folder 2.

6. Eleanor McKinney, conversation with author, July 9, 1995.

7. Letter, Hill to Finch, August 11, 1953, 2, PNOP, Box 11, Folder 2.

8. Hill (?), memorandum.

9. William Drummond, "The Sell-Out of Public Radio," *San Francisco Chronicle*, April 25, 1996, A23; Lewis Hill, "Voluntary Listener-Sponsorship: A Report to Educational Broadcasters on the Experiment at KPFA, Berkeley, California," Pacifica Foundation, 1958, 13–14.

10. Pacifica Foundation president Rudy Hurwich, WBAI manager Ed Goodman, and Pacifica brochures, quoted in "Pacifica Radio: Purposes and Goals, 1946–September 1977," 8–10, in Vera Hopkins, ed., "Pacifica Sampler."

11. Sharon Maeda, "Pacifica: Radio with Vision," Pacifica Foundation, 1996, 14–16, 20.

12. W. J. Rorabaugh, *Berkeley at War* (New York: Oxford University Press, 1980), 11–21. 20.

13. Dorothy Bryant, interview with author, December 21, 1995, 8; Neil Macgregor, interview with author, January 22, 1995, 5; Mandel, interview, 19.

14. Paul V. Dallas, *The Lost Planet* (Philadelphia, J. C. Winston, 1956); Paul V. Dallas, *Dallas in Wonderland* (Los Angeles: Paul V. Dallas, 1967), first page in unnumbered preface.

15. Ibid., 18–19.

16. For a recounting of the "Pleasure Faire" incident, see chap. 9 in Dallas's *Dallas in Wonderland,* especially 169–73 and 177–85.

17. Ibid., 136, 212.

18. Hallock Hoffman, quoted in ibid., 203–4.

19. Ibid., 207, appendix, xxxvi.

20. Steve Post, *Playing in the FM Band: A Personal Account of Free Radio* (New York: Viking Press, 1974), 28–29.

21. Ibid., 36.

22. Ibid., 84–86, 105–7.

23. Ibid., 71, 80–81.

24. Ibid., Avedon, photograph in unnumbered page; some of this description comes from the recollections of the author, a faithful WBAI listener and occasional phone volunteer from the late 1960s through the mid-1970s.

25. Ibid., 226.

26. Quoted in Jeffrey Richard Land, "Active Radio: Pacifica's 'Brash Experiment'" (Ph.D. diss., University of Oregon, 1994), 364.

27. Joy Cole Hill, on "Pacifica Is 25: A Documentary by Larry Josephson," WBAI radio program, 1974.

28. Post, *Playing in the FM Band,* xxii, 226.

29. Richard S. Randall, *Freedom and Taboo: Pornography and the Politics of a Self Divided* (Berkeley: University of California Press, 1989), 266.

30. John Downing, *Radical Media* (Boston: South End Press, 1983), 82–83.

31. Ibid., 88, 90–91.

32. Larry Bensky, interview with Veronica Selver, April 1993, 18.

33. Land, "Active Radio," 334, 335.

34. Ibid. 380.

35. Richard Hoftstadter, *The American Political Tradition and the Men Who Made It* (New York: Random House, [1948], 1976), xxxix.

36. Margot Adler, *Heretic's Heart: A Journal through Spirit and Revolution* (Boston: Beacon Press, 1977), 27–29, 293.

37. Maeda, "Pacifica," 19.

38. Ibid., 20; Jon Arquette Degraff, "Radio, Money, and Politics: The Struggle to Establish WPFW-FM" (Ph.D. diss., University of Maryland, 1995).

39. Lewis Hill, "The Private Room," *Beacon* (Fall 1952): 2.

40. Herbert Gutman, interview with Mike Merrill, in Mid-Atlantic Radical Historians Association, ed., *Visions of History* (New York: Pantheon, 1983), 203.

Postscript

1. Paul Rauber, "War at KPFA," *Express* (May 7, 1999), 1, 9; Sherry Gendelman, Chair, KPFA Local Advisory Board, interview with author (September 10, 1999).

2. Rauber, "War at KPFA," 9.

3. Marc Albert, "No Sign of End to KPFA Stalemate," *Berkeley Voice* (May 20, 1999), A1, A11.

4. Marc Albert, "KPFA Rally Packs Punch, Fills the Streets," *Berkeley Voice* (August 5, 1999), A1.

5. Lorenzo Milam, *The Radio Papers: From KRAB to KCHU,* (San Diego: MHO and MHO Works, 1986), 103.

6. Ibid., 102.

7. James Andrew Lumpp, "The Pacifica Experience—1946–1975: Alternative Radio in Four United States Metropolitan Areas," (Ph.D. dissertation, University of Missouri, Columbia: 1977); 278

8. Ibid., 275–84; Paz Cohen, "To All News Department Volunteers, 1977," cited in Jon Arquette Degraff, "Radio, Money, and Politics: The Struggle to Establish WPFW-FM, The Pacifica Foundation's Black-Oriented Washington Station," (Ph.D. dissertation, University of Maryland, College Park: 1995), 113.

9. Peter M. Lewis and Jerry Booth, *The Invisible Medium: Public, Commercial and Community Radio* (Washington, D.C., Howard University Press, 1990), 120–21.

10. Mimi Anderson, "Audre Lorde–Series: Talk with a Bedford Whaler ; no. 4 , Poet reads selections of her own works" (Pacifica Radio Archives, Los Angeles: Broadcast: WBAI, September 1972); Dennis Bernstein, "Alice Walker Reads Her Poetry," (Pacifica Radio Archives, Los Angeles, recorded on October 11, 1978); McFerrin, and Goldberg's interactions with Pacifica radio are based on my own recollections.

11. Peter Franck, "The Fight for Micro Radio Enters the Home Stretch: Paradise or Paradise Lost?" (San Francisco: Website of the National Lawyers Guild Committee on Democratic Communications, www.nlgcdc.org/articles/paradise_lost.html, no date); Ralph Engelman, *Public Radio and Television in America: A Political History* (Thousand Oaks: Sage Publications, 1996), 91–106; KQED shifts are the recollections of the author, a frustrated classical music fan. After a long campaign the FCC will relegalize micro-radio. See Stephen Lebaton, "F.C.C. to Approve Low-Power Radio, Seeking Diversity," *The New York Times*, (January 20, 2000).

12. Susan Douglas, *Listening In: Radio and the American Imagination* (New York: Times Books, 1999), 296–99.

13. Corporation for Public Broadcasting, "Corporation for Public Broadcasting Adopts New Performance Standards for Public Radio Grantees," (Press release, January 22, 1996), cited in Jesse Walker, "With Friends Like These: Why Community Radio Does Not Need the Corporation for Public Broadcasting," Cato Institute Policy Analysis No. 277, (Cato Institute: Washington, D.C., June 24, 1997), www.cato.org/pubs/pas/pa-277.html; Jacqueline Conciatore, "CPB asks whether community radio is achieving intended purposes," *Current* (April 5, 1999), 5; Andrea Adelson, "A Wider Public for Noncommercial Radio," *The New York Times* (February 10, 1997), C8; Douglas, *Listening In*, 295.

14. Douglas, *Listening In,* 297; Joshua Kosman, "Roll Over Beethoven; Classical Radio Stations Vanishing, Changing Formats," *San Francisco Chronicle* (December 29, 1998), D1; Sam Whiting, "KMEL Axes Call-in Show for Youth," *San Francisco Chronicle* (July 21, 1999), B1.

15. "Highlights of Pacifica Radio's 50 Year History of Radio Broadcasting," (Pacifica Foundation Web site, no date) www.pacifica.org/about/history/high.html.

16. Ibid.

17. Jacquelyn Battise, "Radio Lost," *Houston Peace News* (August 1999), 6–7.

18. Craig Marine, "Familiar Voices Disappearing from KPFA," *San Francisco Examiner* (August 1, 1995), B-1, B-5; Belinda Griswold, "Battle for KPFA's Soul," *San Francisco Bay Guardian*, (December 25, 1996), www.radio4all.org/fp/baygl296.htm; Ryan Tate, "Radio Legend Off the Air Waves," *The Daily Californian* (Friday, May 12, 1995), 3.

19. Armando J. Arvizu, "Compliance Audit of Pacifica Foundation," (Washington, D.C.: Corporation for Public Broadcasting, April 9, 1997), 1–2; see www.savepacifica.net and www.radio4all.org/freepacifica/index.html, the two most prominent Pacifica reform web sites.

20. Pacifica Foundation, *A Vision for Pacifica Radio: Creating a Network for the 21st Century* (Berkeley: Pacifica Foundation, 1997), 12.

21. Dick Bunce, "The Crisis of Democratic Communications," in *A Vision for Pacifica Radio*, 4–5, see also 7–8, 17.

22. "Mary Frances Berry," *Contemporary Black Biography*, Volume 7, (Gale Research Inc., 1994), 11–15.

23. "Chadwick Praised as NFCB Enters New Era," *Public Broadcasting Report* (March 27, 1998), 7–8. The article states that over two years NFCB member stations dropped to 87 from 99, and associate stations to 94 from 127; Diversity Coalition Press Release, "RE: The situation at KPFA," (June 26, 1999).

24. "Mary Frances Berry, *Contemporary Black Biography*.

25. "Notice of By-Law Change," in *Pacifica Foundation National Governing Board Meeting Booklet* (Berkeley: Pacifica Foundation, 1999), ii.

26. United States Code, Title 47 – Telegraphs, Telephones, and Radiotelegraphs, Section 396(k)(8)(C).

27. Paul Rauber, "Bad Blood," *Express*, (March 5, 1999), 5; "Pacifica National Board Meeting, September 14–15, 1979, Berkeley, California," (College Park, MD: *National Public Broadcasting Archives*, 1999), 7; Alexander Cockburn, "The Neutering of Pacifica," *Counterpunch* (January 15, 1999), http://www.counterpunch.org/pacifica.html.

28. Rauber, "Bad Blood," 5.

29. Alexander Cockburn, "National Notes," *Anderson Valley Advertiser*, (April 16, 1997).

30. Rauber, "Bad Blood," 5; Jacqueline Conciatore, "Tempers Rise as Pacifica Lets Board Select Itself," *Current* (March 8, 1999), www.current.org/rad/rad906p.html#board; Heidi Belton, reporter's transcript, "Pacifica Board of Directors Meeting, Berkeley, CA," (February 28, 1999), www.radio4all.org/fp/tran9906.html; Jacqueline Conciatore, "The Amazing Shrinking 'Dis List'," *Current* (March 16, 1998), www.current.org/cpb/cpb805d.html.

31. Marc Cooper, "Exchange: The News from Pacifica," *The Nation* (May 31, 1999), www.thenation.com/issue/990531/0531exchange.shtml.

32. Ellen Nieves, "Power Struggle Disrupts Oldest Public Radio Station," *The New York Times* (June 30, 1999), 5; Rauber, "War at KPFA," 10–11; Larry Bensky, "Dear Everyone," December 11, 1998.

33. Ibid., 10.

34. "Pacifica National Board of Directors, Minutes, October 6–7, 1990," (College Park, MD: *National Public Broadcasting Archives*, 1999), 24: "Motion: That the language contained in Section 10—Firing of General Managers be approved as amended. Part C to read: Prior to the end of contract term, the Manager shall undergo a formal review by the station board and the Executive Director. Following such a review, the Executive Committee may vote not to renew the contract of the Manager. A vote by the Executive Committee not to renew or extend the contract shall terminate the employment contract. M/S/P Unanimous."

35. Lynn Chadwick quoted on *Democracy Now* (April 16, 1999), transcribed by John Sommers, www.radio4all.org/fp/04–16dem_now-transcript.htm.

36. Rauber, "War at KPFA," 13.

37. Ibid., 11.

38. Marc Cooper, "Whose Pacifica?" *The Nation* (May 10, 1999), www.thenation.com/issue/990510/0510cooper.shtml.

39. Transcript, "KPFA On-Appearance of Mary Frances Berry and Lynn Chadwick," (May 5, 1999), www.radio4all.org/fp/mfb-callin.htm.

40. John Gregg Sr., Jim Yee, Frank Blythe, Peggy Berryhill, Karolyn vanPutten, "Open Letter from the Diversity Coalition in Public Broadcasting to the Pacifica Board of Directors, the Staff and Volunteers of KPFA, and the General Public," (June 26, 1999).

41. "Open Letter to Dr. Mary Frances Berry, From: The African-American Programmers at KPFA," (May 21 1999); Evelyn Nieves, "The Battle for the Berkeley Airwaves Rages On," *The New York Times* (July 23, 1999), A10; 1990 Census U.S. Data for City of Berkeley, www.pacunion.com/demographics/berkeley.htm, percentage calculated by author.

42. Marc Albert, "No Sign of End to KPFA Stalemate," *Berkeley Voice* (May 20, 1999), A1; "Transcript—Robbie Osman Statement On-Air, 6/13/99," www.savepacifica.net/0613AGD.html.

43. Charles Burress, "125 Protesters Rally at KPFA, Demand Ouster of Director," *The San Francisco Chronicle* (July 23, 1999), A16; Father Bill O'Donnell, parish priest, St. Joseph the Worker, Berkeley, interview with author (September 11, 1999); Charles Burress, "14 arrested in protests outside KPFA," *San Francisco Chronicle* (June 22, 1999), A15; KPFA Evening News, (June 24, 1999), real audio at www.radio4all.org/freepacifica/hear.htm; Robert Selna, "Furor Over Firings Comes from Struggle Between Local Station and Network," *San Francisco Examiner* (June 25, 1999), A2; Paul Rauber, "Pacifica's Big Guns," *Express* (July 2, 1999), 5.

44. Charles Burress, "125 Protesters Rally at KPFA;" Rob Cunningham, "KPFA Showdown," *Berkeley Daily Planet* (July 13, 1999), 1.

45. Michael Palmer to Mary Frances Berry, e-mail message, July 13, 1999, reprinted in *The Texas Observer*, (August 6, 1999), back page; Henry K. Lee, "KPFA Broadcaster Dragged Away from Studio," *San Francisco Chronicle* (July 14, 1999), A11.

46. Paul Rauber, ""Radio ImagiNation," *Express*, (August 27, 1999), 5; Dennis Bernstein and Mark Mericle, "Last 30 Minutes of Live Programming on KPFA," (July 14, 1999), www.savepacifica.net/990813_cooper_response.html.

47. Pacifica Press Release, "Programming at KPFA," July 19, 1999, www.pacifica.org/board/docs/pr990719c.html.

48. Mary Frances Berry, quoted in *Heartmath*, www.heartmath.com/Library/Quotes/Women.html; Jo Ann Gibson Robinson, *The Mongomery Bus Boycott and the Women Who Started It* (Knoxville: University of Tennessee Press, 1987), 84.

49. William Brand, et al., "1,500 Rally at KPFA's Doorstep," *The Oakland Tribune* (July 15, 1999), 9; Venise Wagner, "Huge Berkeley Rally Calls for Local Autonomy at KPFA," *San Francisco Examiner* (August 1, 1999), D1, D8; Philip Elwood, "Baez Blasts from Past for KPFA," *San Francisco Examiner* (July 21, 1999), C1.

50. Paul Rauber, "Stay, Mary, Stay!" *Express*, (September 10, 1999), 5.

51. A. Clay Thompson, "Pacifica's Endgame?" *San Francisco Bay Guardian* (July 21, 1999), 15; Chris Thompson, "Was the KPFA Lock-out a Spontaneous Reaction or a Planned Management Coup?" *Express* (July 23, 1999), 3; IPSA International's hostile termination services outlined at www.ipsaintl.com; Packing List, Telos Systems, "Zephyr-9200, ISDN SU, Ship to: Pacifica, Federal Express, 1221 Broadway, PO# Garland G," Order date 6/29/99, Ship date, 6/29/99; Jim Bennett, KPFA's acting station manager, interview with author (September 9, 1999).

52. Pete Bramson, "Pacifica National Board member Pete Bramson's statement," www.radio4all.org/freepacifica/bramson.htm; Debra Levi Holtz, "Nearly $500,000 Spent During KPFA Lockout," *San Francisco Chronicle* (Wednesday, September 8, 1999), A21; Brenda Payton, "Pacifica Runs Up $428,315 Tab," *Oakland Tribune* (September 14, 1999).

53. Lynn Chadwick, "My First Hundred Days, Pacifica Foundation Executive Director Report, Board of Directors Meeting, Berkeley, CA, February 1999," 1; Pacifica Press release, "KPFA is not for sale," (July 19, 1999), www.pacifica.org/board/docs/pr990719e.html; Charles Burress, "KPFA Back On Air After Battle Over Local Control," *San Francisco Chronicle* (August 7, 1999), A15; "Pacifica Board Concludes Successful Meeting," Pacifica Foundation press release (no date), www.pacifica.org/board/docs/pr110299.html.

54. Kate Coleman, "Tuned In, Turned On and Locked Out," *The LA Weekly* (July 30-August 5, 1999), www.laweekly.com/ink.99/36/news-coleman.shtml.

INDEX